EMLYN

An early autobiography
1927-1935

A SEQUEL TO

GEORGE
1905–1927

Emlyn Williams

THE BODLEY HEAD
LONDON   SYDNEY
TORONTO

THANK YOU: Angela Baddeley, Josephine Bott, Edward Bowen, Richard Clowes, Robert Crawley, Ida Franklin, John Frost, Dorothy Heseltine, Dolores Gallego, Margalo Gillmore, Nellie Jones, Leueen MacGrath, Raymond Mander, Joe Mitchenson, William Perrone, Ann Plugge, John Roberts, Glen Byam Shaw, Joan Tracey, Casey Walters, Stephen Watts, Margaret Webster, Cyril Wheeler, Alan Williams, Brook Williams, Job Williams, Thomas Williams

© Emlyn Williams 1973
ISBN 0 370 10483 8
Printed and bound in Great Britain for
The Bodley Head Ltd
9 Bow Street, London WC2E 7AL
by William Clowes & Sons Ltd, Beccles
Set in Linotype Caledonia
First published 1973

To Molly, Alan and Brook

Contents

vii

CONTENTS

PART THREE

Into the Clear

1934–1935

PART ONE

Available
1927–1930

CHAPTER ONE

ENTER AN APPRENTICE

'I don't think I'll read this—it says it's a sequel and I didn't read the first one so I'd feel out of it from the first page . . .'

And even if you did read 'the first one', your mind needs refreshing. It is up to me to ensure that the reader need know nothing of *George* by supplying rapid salient information about my life up to April 1927.

Before I do so, one thing: at the moment when I embarked on the 'first one' I decided I would travel no further than the age of twenty-one, feeling that while a writer's first two decades might be of interest, the third must present a formidable task. Can he be as honest about it?

I knew that without honesty the story would deteriorate into a parade of professional ventures interspersed with cautious anecdotes. The alternative must be a marriage between Candour and Taste, with the continuous likelihood of one partner pushing the other out of bed; even then, it would have to be a different book.

It took years of persuasion, by my wife and others, to start me working through diaries and letters. *Emlyn* does include ventures, and anecdotes; and it is indeed a different book, for as the narrator matures and toughens the narrative must toughen too. If once or twice Taste has been elbowed to the floor by the lustier partner, I have tried to keep the peace.

The information: son of Richard and Mary Williams, both of Welsh peasant stock (Flintshire, North Wales, near Chester) as far back as can be traced. *George*: 'My family tree is the shortest in the wood: the Japanese variety, healthy but stunted.'

They had met in Liverpool, both about twenty. She, 'small, fair, frailly pretty', had left her village at fourteen to become a housemaid; he was a stoker on a transatlantic liner; 'thick-set dark hair close-cropped, deep-set blue eyes, moustache trimmed over lips liberally curved . . .'.

They were opposites: he improvident and sanguine, she an incorruptible home-saver—thank God—and a defeatist. Later Dad was to tell me of an excursion, during my childhood, to the seaside resort of Rhyl; it was war-time and the *Lusitania* had been sunk.

Standing next to Mam watching us paddling, the ex-sailor commented on the smoothness of the water. 'Yes,' she said, 'but think of the dead bodies underneath.'

His love of company shadowed the marriage with a drinking problem which led to poverty. They returned to Flintshire, where they would remain for life; he became in turn coal-miner, greengrocer, publican and steelworker. 'There were dark days but with time they lightened.'

Their eldest child George Emlyn was born in 1905 over a greengrocery shop in the village of Rhewl Fawr and spent his first nine years in the White Lion Inn, Glanrafon, an even smaller community. From there, aged four, he attended Talacre Convent and Picton Council School, speaking Welsh as his first language and learning English gradually in class.

From Trelogan Council School, at ten, he won a scholarship of three pounds a year to 'Holywell County', a small mixed dayschool, the equivalent of a modest grammar school.

At the end of his first year the family moved from the Welsh countryside to Connah's Quay, an industrial township on the Dee estuary between Holywell and Chester. With his father working at Summers' Steelworks as fireman, the family is still living here at the opening of this book.

At Holywell, at the age of eleven he came to the notice of the Senior Mistress: Miss Sarah Grace Cooke, aged thirty-five, a Yorkshirewoman.

A born teacher, vibrant and outspoken—'here was that rarest of anomalies, a full-blooded spinster'—she catapulted him into French, Latin, Greek and Italian; when he was fifteen she paid for him to attend a village school in Haute Savoie and when he was seventeen she entered him for an Open French Scholarship to Christ Church, Oxford, which he won.

During three years at Oxford he neglected studies for amateur acting (for the ouds) and playwriting, and began to be 'Emlyn' rather than 'George'. In his last term, 1926, a month before final exams, he suffered a nervous breakdown precipitated by an emotional friendship with another undergraduate.

During the months at home he wrote his first full-length play, *Full Moon*, presented—for a repertory week at the Oxford Playhouse—by J. B. Fagan. A month later he made one of those sudden decisions which direct a life: with his royalties—four pounds something—he left home for London, where he had the luck to replace an actor in a tiny part in Fagan's comedy about Pepys, *And So To Bed*.

And on April the 18th, 1927, aged twenty-one, Easter Monday matinée at the Savoy Theatre, he 'went on the stage'.

On that date—when *George* closed and *Emlyn* opens—Miss Cooke (44) was still teaching in Holywell: father 57, mother 58, brothers: Job 19, Tom 16.

'... My bit opened the play: curtain up on street scene, enter an Apprentice carrying hare, knock at front door opened by Blackamoor maid. "Is Mistress Pepys within?"... In the wings, I felt my hands tremble as I pulled on my wig... The music came to a spirited close; applause, silence; above me a voice muttered, "House out." I was gripped with fright... A rustle and a sweep, like a calm wind. The curtain was up.'

Then the words THE END. On second thoughts, on from there.

* * *

The curtain was up.

I heard it settle far above, and in the silence which whispered 'Over to you' a thought spluttered in my head like a firework: my two muttered rehearsals with Mr Storie, the stage-manager, had been *behind* that curtain; I was a beginner who had not begun. I had not once spoken my six lines facing the auditorium, never mind the stage lighting. Suppose it dazzled me and I fell over?

I felt panic, then stamped it out—was I not well prepared? Having been given the minimum of instructions—'cross, stand, knock, speak'—I had written out my own: 'stop, look uncertainly at house, trace of swagger, cheeky, casually scratch thigh...'.

I looked back at Mr Storie in the shadowed prompt-corner; he nodded, I moved. And made my 'first appearance on any professional stage'. Sauntering.

As I scented the whiff of heat from blinding footlights and from the invisible crowd beyond—each individual looking at me, there was nobody else to look at—I felt too the flash of an inner eye, which by remote control watched from the back of the pit.

[5]

It saw a round-faced boy, not tall but sturdy without—I hoped
—being squat, in kneebreeches tight across trim jock-strap and
cotton stockings over calves adequately curved; under the matted
wig, good blue eyes, a full mouth and a strong nose. But, that
done, I was so rattled by the light and the abyss beyond that I
obeyed none of my own instructions, and before I knew where I
was, the lady stood at the door.

'Yes?' 'Is Mistress Peeps within?' In my room I had said it over
and over again, aiming at lackadaisical standard English. I now
heard myself shouting each syllable, and separating them as if
Mistress Blackamoor were deaf. 'Is Mistress ... Peeps ... Within?'

In answer, the startled ebony of her eyes told me that while
for months she had thought Pelling's 'Prentice had been born
near Bow Bells she was now discovering that he hailed from
further away. Not even Oxford. North Wales. A West End
audience was being treated to a comic stage Welshman: 'Iss Miss-
tress Peepss within, whateffer?'

Whatever happened to that Oxford undergraduate, whateffer?
And as I held out the hare I thought it odd that a cheeky errand-
boy should have such shaky hands. Before I knew what was
what, I was stumbling back into the dark of the wings; blinded,
I gave Mr Storie's silhouette a sheepish look. He nodded briskly
and pressed a switch: the cue for the footpads to rush on. I had
got through.

From the stage I heard voices, realized the play was continu-
ing without me, and dawdled upstairs, wig in hand. I was as
tired as if I had just played King Lear.

✽ ✽ ✽

The empty dressing-room—the six others were on stage, foot-
padding—smelt of powder and perspiration.

I could do better, I could; I longed to plunge downstairs, play
the scene again and play it right. But instead I opened a new tin,
took off my make-up with sticky white cold cream, changed,
picked up my books and was quickly downstairs and out into the
sun, which was a shock—had I really just stood on a stage facing
a darkened audience?

I bounded up the steps to the forecourt of the Savoy Hotel,
where great post-luncheon limousines bore away the rich and

important middle-aged. The cars were a gratifying sight on the threshold of my theatre, but their owners' richness and importance were cancelled out by their advancing years; I thought with pride of the sweaty dressing-room and of my dim bed-sitter in Bloomsbury. At the same time, though, I saw my sagging bed and the one chair with the burst seat. I turned back and descended to the sun: to the little riverside park below the hotel.

People were strolling or sitting, young and old, looking around with vague holiday smiles. I sat on a bench and extracted from my trouser pocket a pound and a couple of shillings: just enough to last me till my first salary on Friday.

A man passed whistling 'Bye, Bye, Blackbird'; popular music stirred me, and always would. I felt a rush of well-being, for this was the beginning of life.

Not only in the theatre but in this city. Looking round at the strangers, I was a Londoner too; if one of them inquired what I did I had my answer: 'I'm an actor, just had a matinée.'

I sat back and asked myself casually, 'Is Mistress Peeps within?' I must remember that when the English say 'is' they buzz: 'izzz'. 'Izzz Mistress Peeps within?' It sounded better.

Though I had no doubts about my future—no crystal ball was ever less clouded— I looked down at the money in my palm with the concentrated look I remembered on my mother's face . . .

*   *   *

But I couldn't dwell on them now; hadn't I my own problems?

And yet I did think of 314a High Street, Connah's Quay: of the little kitchen clean as a pin, though not a new pin; nothing new about that tired four-roomed house facing the scrubby waste of weeds and the backs of other houses, its own backyard —with the one tap and the outside lav and the rickety shed— in the shadow of the railway embankment.

I saw my two brothers sitting at the table neatly newspapered to save the cloth: Job, three years younger than me and already a bread-winner at the steelworks, while even Tom, at fourteen, earned a few shillings delivering papers; Mam standing cutting bread-and-butter, Dad in his armchair near the fire, in his shirt-sleeves. She smaller than ever, white-haired and timid: he square, expansive, geniality twinkling behind the metal-rimmed spectacles, one of his delicate hands weaving a pencil stub over the betting page of the *Liverpool Echo* like a scholar's over a manuscript.

Not that he was genial the day I walked out. He hardly ever got angry; but when he did, he towered. From Oxford the least he had expected was a Double First and 'my son Professor Williams' and on that day he erupted. 'You get up and do as your mother tells you, *now!*'

Then, after he and Mam had exchanged rapid Welsh—'Be haru'r bachgen, what's the matter with the boy?'—which since we had come to anglicized Connah's Quay they only did when excited or upset, he had turned on me, eyes blazing with unspoken words. 'Wantin' to go gallivantin' in front o' strangers, you think about earnin' an honest penny, my lad, like Job here . . .'

No, I wouldn't write, I would just keep in touch with young Tom so they would know I was making a living, if a dishonest one. I opened my notebook headed MORPHOLOGIE FRANÇAISE, wrote PLAN FOR EXPENSES SUMMER 1927 and held a committee meeting of one.

Salary £3 per wk. Mr Fagan's insistence that I sit for the Oxford Finals which I had ducked last summer—my 'Schools'—meant that I would leave the play on June the 18th, so Total Earnings £27, out of which I must save for the blank weeks before New York. New York! Mr Fagan had said I would go with the play but I mustn't think about that yet . . .

Room, ten-and-six a week; food—for breakfast cornflakes, buy spoon and plate from Woolworth's; other meals at ABC's, Lyons and coffee-stalls. Transport nil, I would walk everywhere; laundry nil, I would wash shirts and socks.

Ironing: no need, I would lay shirts under the mattress with trousers. Baths: public, once a week, in between lashings of water in bowl and basin; hadn't Mam told me that 'anybody can keep theirself clean if they put their mind to it'? No drinks and I did not smoke; no films, not even *Ben Hur* down the Strand at the Tivoli.

Having regulated my life I turned to my Old French notes; as the only actor in London swotting for an Oxford degree, I felt special. 'In Gallo-Roman period, Langue d'Oc was spoken in S. France, Langue d'Oil in N., then after 850 A.D. . . .'

I looked up as a pleasant young man along the bench sat

back with a yawn, closed his eyes and slid his body forward, at a loose holiday end. I was surrounded on all sides by hundreds of houses and streets, by thousands of people ... I bent again over my Ocs and my Oils. It was going to be hard to swot.

The light was thinning; the wrist-watch Miss Cooke had sent me for my twenty-first birthday said five o'clock. I hurried back— just in time, the audience was pouring out of the theatre— streaked up the steps, into the foyer and down into the stalls. After a dive under a seat I was out again past a puzzled commissionaire, clutching a crumpled programme.

Had the management—a ten-to-one chance—bothered to replace my predecessor's name with mine? Outside the reverberating hotel I rustled past the advertisements till I found the all-important Cast of Characters. My eye raced down. Samuel Pepys EDMUND GWENN Mistress Pepys YVONNE ARNAUD Pelling's 'Prentice EMLYN WILLIAMS—all in the same bold type. I felt disproportionate pleasure. One copy went to Miss Cooke and one to Tom to hand to Dad, as proof of status.

❖   ❖   ❖

'Dear Miss Cooke ... Re Schools in June, it's doubtful if I can do well as having one's living to earn makes demands on one's time ... Yours very affectionately, George.'

I had exaggerated: six lines of dialogue add up to one minute a day, two on matinée days. Eight minutes' work a week, but my existence did revolve round that wage-earning minute: nightly 8.35–8.36 p.m.; Wed., Sat. 2.35–2.36. The Apprentice no longer had the shakes, neither shouted nor mumbled and reasonably disguised his origins.

Every night I hoped for a manager in front searching for a new face—'That boy's different, he's a personality ...' I once ran into Mr Fagan on the stairs; he smiled kindly. 'How's the work getting on?'

I was about to answer, 'Thank you, sir, I think I'm settling down in the part', when I realized he meant my book-work.

And for that I had my routine. Daily I attended the British Museum Reading Room, free. Under the dome, with the vast imprisoned air echoing with silence and musty from the million million entombed words, I sat surrounded by a bowed, gnomish regiment of readers. There were solemn young Indians, wild-eyed old ladies with magnifying glasses and tumbling stockings, and stubby-bearded old sages clutching great tomes to their palsied bosoms.

After a life of set meals it was a joy to eat when I was hungry and to choose what I liked: poached eggs or veal-and-ham pie, plus ice-cream or a twopenny bar of chocolate; then I would stay on, studying.

In the evenings after my scene, a call at various cafés for a cup of tea and a swot, after I had overcome the temptation to loiter backstage. Fagan's company was attractive; his regal wife Mary Grey wore the crown with charm while Yvonne Arnaud was gay, funny and adored: she knew, to the last rolled r and misplaced stress, how to make the French tongue irresistible.

Asked if she attended the Berlitz School to keep up her French accent, 'Of course,' she said, 'it eez my bread and my bitter!' 'There goes a born one,' Bill Bragg the stage-doorkeeper murmured once. 'She'd make a bishop piss 'is gaiters.'

One evening I did stay behind, having asked Archie Storie if I could perch high in the flies and watch the play through the ropes and the wires.

I was a privileged audience as I peered down at the players' heads below, swimming in light. I became even more privileged, after the curtain had fallen on the bowing principals—in 1927 calls were still being taken at the end of each act—to watch a small army of stage-hands scurry into the Pepys house and strip it bare with the expertise of trained burglars expecting interruption.

I saw them scamper around, to a sprightly minuet from the orchestra, laden with carpets, furniture, hangings and even great swaying panelled walls. Then, by the same sleight of hand and foot, Mistress Knight's withdrawing-room came into miraculous being under the eyes of a fascinated child.

I never ventured near the star rooms. But one evening, after my minute's work, loneliness descended on me. I hung around and was asked in for tea by Mr Pepys' two ladies-of-the-town during their second-act wait.

They were high-spirited, racy and cultivated—all I thought actresses should be—and for me it was a tonic to sit with two bouncing women in their late thirties, tightly laced and bosomed, extravagantly made up with beauty patches, wigs off and their own hair pulled behind their ears like an Eton crop, smoking cigarettes. The shabby, scented dressing-room, with streams of telegrams along the wall and frivolous mascots among the powder and paint, could have been the brothel of one's dreams.

Miss Cooke's first London letter arrived. 'Dear Ɇ, I nearly wrote Emlyn, Dear George, Yr news to hand, ah well I dunno ...'

It was strewn with the usual headlong abbreviations. 'H'ever, gang yr own gait & if I'd been a man I shld ha' done the same. Being a woman, it struck me that "fitting in" was my only way. A propos de nowt, this m'ning an urchin of 12 translated "Cette femme fait honneur à la patrie" as "This woman does honour to pastry". Ho hum, good luck to him, Yrs very affectionately S.G.C.'

* * *

The actor-student, though, had another side.

Under the heading 'Sex', my committee of one had passed a law forbidding me to become emotionally involved with anybody. But I was healthy. Waking on a hot night from a restless dream, like a thousand other young men in the packed square miles around, I longed for someone to be sharing my bed.

But the dream had not been of a beautiful youth: the Oxford episode had been a precariously romantic structure and for that reason it had foundered.

No, this was physical. My desire was to pull on my clothes, walk round the corner and take them off again, in the little brothel—in the Rue des Cordeliers, Rouen—into which I had strolled three years ago, arm in arm with a matelot.

I had not been to bed with a woman since and had not forgotten the mounting pleasure, through friendly fondling and cooing, of bodily rightness. Filles de joie ... Now, awake in the dark, it was those noises I remembered. But the thought of one of the harpies who hovered off Piccadilly muttering blandishments, and of then slinking up to a dim eyrie to be rooked for a ten-bob note—no, London was not Rouen.

One morning in the vacuum of the Museum, hunched among hunchers, I sensed a murmur in my ear. I had not seen Angus Rae since Oxford: he was the heavy-faced Scottish laddie who had sorrowfully adored, from afar, a dim aesthetic high-necked-jumper boy in Oxford bags from St Edmund Hall.

He informed me, *sotto voce*, that he was working in a book-shop off Charing Cross Road—'and I'm liberrated!'

In the West End, apparently, the undergraduate yearnings had boldly blossomed. 'I do *everything* shorrt of wearing a red tie! Remember how you used to call me John Knox? Weel, John Knox has flung his tartan bonnet over Eros and turrned into Mad Meg Merrilees!'

The gesture had certainly made him better company. 'And what about you?'

I told him of my resolution.

'But, my dear, ye can have fun without friendship, this is London!'

The conversation, from being whispered in that vast cradle of learning, had an added flavour. 'D'ye mean tu say ye've never hearrd of the Long Bar at the Troc, or the Chalice or the Tea Kettle, *verra* amusing, lend me your pencil . . .'

Back to work, but in between, attacks of curiosity. One afternoon I walked to 7 Wardour Street and boldly up some stairs into the Tea Kettle.

Instead of alcoves masking doubtful shapes, I found a cheerful fake-Tudor establishment with Dainty Teas being prepared by a waitress. There were two customers, elegantly thin young men chattering like harmless birds, one balancing a teapot. 'Before we dish the dirt, shall I be mother?'

He giggled and poured. I left.

The tiny Chalice Bar, corner of Lyons' Corner House, Coventry Street, was a bit wickeder but not much; I strolled to the counter and ordered a lemonade. An older man in glasses was sitting with lips pursed over a gin-and-it.

I settled near him; he nodded and smiled, I smiled back, we chatted. I told him I was in *And So To Bed* and asked what he did. He hinted that he was secretary to Mr Horace Collins at the Society of West End Managers.

If this wouldn't make for a stage career, what would? He insisted on buying me a gin-and-it, then had to go; a new customer entered and sat down.

I walked to the bar and was regretfully about to order a second lemonade when the barman said, 'I must ask you to leave.'

I was puzzled. 'Are you closing?'

'Near enough.' Then he went up to the new arrival. 'What can I get you, sir?'

I was in Leicester Square before it dawned on me what it was all about, and I looked thoughtfully at the book I was holding. Was I the first Londoner to have a copy of *French Syntax* under his arm at the moment of being turned out of a West End bar for soliciting?

I wondered why I was not feeling dashed. On the contrary, I felt dashing.

The following Wednesday afternoon, after my minute's work, I was strolling up the Avenue when I saw SOCIETY OF WEST END MANAGERS. Why not a social call on my new friend?

I ran up the stairs and into the outer office; there he was. 'Hello,' I said, 'I was just passing...'

As I spoke I realized that he was less a secretary than an elderly office-boy: he was emptying a waste-basket. I also noticed he had gone pale.

'Not here,' he hissed, and pushed an inner door shut. Two seconds later I was out in the street. It was the end of a short friendship. I was never, under any circumstances, to land a job by pulling a string at the Society of West End Managers.

No, the 'amusing' resorts were not for me, and I continued to have my acute summer bouts: wanderlust. Hyde Park is extensive, Hampstead Heath immense and the grass warm enough to lie on; looking up from my studies to find a stranger near me, I did not always return to my book.

Vague monosyllables eased into an interlude filled with lazy silences and empty of names or addresses, a drift towards the casual fraternization when stealth had to set in and newspapers were flung negligently across. In my fleeting Edens I felt none of the pangs of Adam and Eve, even if my forbidden provender was less idyllic than theirs. The unknown drew me: drew the mind as well as the body.

And if ever shame had shadowed my day I would have recognized it. Last summer, in the parlour of 314a after the nightmare of Oxford failure, it had nuzzled up to me as I sat alone and stripped of self-respect: the self-appointed victim of a blameless passion.

Shame? I picked myself up, took my books, brushed grass off me, said so-long and moved on, mollified. I had learnt my lesson and forged my armour. Not a chink in it; I was free.

One verbal exchange: I had just mentioned that good cheap digs were hard to come by. My companion turned and looked me in the eye. 'Rent?'

'Ten-and-six a week but no bathroom.'

He looked puzzled. 'I meant d'you want money?'

'Good God, no,' I said. 'Do *you*?'

I tried to feel insulted and again felt dashing. Perhaps there was something wrong with me.

CHAPTER TWO

DOMICILE, LONDON

'Dear Miss Cooke, I'm writing in the sun on the Thames excursion, this exciting city offers something for everyone. Passing the Tower, I just committed to memory the arresting news that the nominative French pronoun had, by the 17th cent., become atonic . . . Miss Arnaud's favourite poet is Ronsard . . .' I wanted to make the theatre sound intelligent and respectable to the other world I knew.

It was indeed another world. ' . . . See here, George, it's always struck me as nonsense to put education in diff. pigeon-holes, I dunno. A Belgian boy trekked here today for advice, poor nipper. then a widow from Llanerchymor wrote to ask how her 15-yr-old lad could get German tuition & I've arranged for the Blg. boy to teach him at 2/- per hr. & hope for the best . . .'

I sometimes took advantage of free seats for matinées at other theatres, learning something from each—from the bad ones as much as from the good—about writing and acting. Alan Napier, who had been in *Full Moon* at Oxford and was now in *And So To Bed*, noted that for an aspiring dramatist my visits were unadventurous. I shirked the Old Vic, knowing it was brave but pedestrian.

'What about G.B.S.?' I said I had a blind spot about Shaw—'he sounds like a schoolmaster being funny.'

'What about that play next Sunday from the Finnish, with new techniques and masks—symbolism, expressionism, don't they fascinate you?'

My mind balked at them as a stomach rejects food; as for new techniques, I was too intent on mastering the old ones. I did try *The Dybbuk*, translated from the Hebrew and hailed by the critics as a masterpiece; all I saw was a crowd of ugly people milling about in the dark, wailing and muttering complaints in stilted English. Looking round at the empty seats, I was depressed.

'The trouble with you,' Alan said, 'is that you're stage-struck. And yet wasn't *Full Moon* symbolic?'

Was it? I hadn't meant it to be . . .

All I wanted, passionately, was to sit in the middle of an audience which was being completely held by a play which was holding me too, one moment emotionally, the next through laughter. At the same time, I longed to be *in* the play, or to have written it. Or both.

I even paid, every Monday afternoon, for a cheap seat at the Coliseum, which offered twice-daily Variety highlighted by legitimate stars in sketches; I loved the heady, blaring music and again every item taught me something, from Nazimova (In Person ! ! !) to the Houston Sisters (The Irresistibles).

Some evenings after my minute onstage I would moon past theatres and look at the photographs; once I stopped behind the Hippodrome, in the half-light of Little Newport Street. Through the scene-dock door I could just hear the faint throbbing beat of many voices: Jack Buchanan and the chorus of *Sunny*—'Who-o-o Stole My Heart Away . . .'

Yes, I was stage-struck.

* * *

The city with something for everyone even offered murder. On Friday May the 6th, outside Charing Cross Station down the road from the Savoy Theatre, a porter, watching the stream of cars wheeling into the Strand, saw a hand appear at a taxi window and toss out a bit of paper: a cloakroom ticket.

Who would deposit luggage and discard the means of reclaiming it? He handed in the ticket; the trunk contained four parcels containing the dismembered body of a woman.

That evening the front pages were shrill, and as the curtain rose I pushed away the thought that in the street an hour ago I could have walked past a monster; that at this very minute he could be sitting in the front row.

A few minutes after his victim had been recognized by a friend in Sydney Street, Chelsea, he had picked her up, taken her back to his office in Rochester Row, quarrelled with her and killed her. The case was as stereotyped as his name, Robinson.

But I walked down Sydney Street, imagined myself overhearing the fatal 'Hello' which was to lead him to the scaffold, then proceeded to Rochester Row to look up at the office window. My first contact with murder had aroused an interest to be permanently tangled with my professional life.

I had hinted to Tom that I would welcome 'a word from home' and it was good to see Dad's meticulous writing on the ruled sheet, after his hand had hovered while he pondered 'what to put'.

'My dear Son George, We are relieved, this Mr Fagan sounds a proper gentleman to be on at you to get your Degree so you can later go in for the schoolmastering line. Now from your Mother.'

In the familiar, timid scrawl, 'Dear Goerge'—she was still unable to spell it, or to write 'have'—'we of worrid about your health while in that play with them giving short weight in them London shops i am not a good scolor with spelling hoping you will Xuse it.' Then Dad: 'from your loving Dad Mam and Bros. Job and Thomas.'

'That play.' For an actor with disapproving parents, its title was not a happy one; *And So To Bed* implied not only lechers, but lazy lechers.

Anyway, we had made it up and from then on, as with Miss Cooke, I was to exchange a weekly letter with them.

'Dear Miss Cooke, I am moving to stay with an old Oxford friend, Comte Pierre de Rilly.' The sentence contained four untruths: Pierre was not an old friend, Pierre had been a visitor and not an undergraduate, Pierre was not a Count and Pierre's name was not Pierre.

I had met him the night before, when I had broken my rule, for a rendezvous with Angus. The Criterion Restaurant was staid enough—luncheons, thé-dansants, banquets—until ten p.m. By then the great ornate hall, reached by a staircase descending from Lower Regent Street, had been emptied of respectable clientèle and refilled with well-behaved male trash.

'I must war-rn you,' Angus had said, 'that it's known alter-r-nately as the Witches' Cauldron and the Bargain Basement.'

I was not prepared for the staircase, which caused every chatty head to crane and give any new arrival the once-over. Luckily the orchestra, liable accidentally to greet the same arrival with a

familiar serenade, was tuning up. Angus had once had the doubtful luck to descend to the strains of 'Five Foot Two, Eyes of Blue'.

From a far corner a wave from him, and I threaded through,
trying to look carefree and yet clean-cut: not easy. Angus presented me to Pierre, then to a morose merchant seaman who had
clearly not warmed to the titled friend.

'Says 'e's a count,' he muttered to me, 'what's 'e put an O in it
for?'

Pierre was thirty, with a long body pliant as a reed, topped—
under a small pork-pie hat—with little pretty features put together with grey paste and adorned with a monocle which
screwed the cheek up to give the effect of buck teeth.

But his voice was his distinction: a shrill hotch-potch of
Middle-Western American grinding into British drawl grinding
into vaudeville French. It was whispered that he had been born
in Pittsburg, not Pierre de Rilly but shanty-Irish Peter O'Reilly.

He commiserated busily with me. 'But mon pauvre cher, your
chambre is hell, come and stay dans mon pied-à-terre!'

It was actually à ciel, a large attic in Wentworth Studios,
Manresa Road, Chelsea. It meant Bohemia and I moved in next
morning.

Without being asked, Pierre informed me that I was not his
type: 'All those goddam classics under your arm an' in the
theatre, non merci honey chile!' It simplified life; when I got
back that night it was good to find him there and to hear him
prattle in the dark from his bed to mine.

He was amazed by my innocence, and soon so was I. 'Honey,
you have the nerve to tell me you don't know what "t.b.h." means,
but, chéri, what did you all do up at that university, it means "to
be had", naturellement ...'

The secret jargon babbled on, fluent as thieves' slang. 'Then
there's my antique dealer friend, likes chickens and since anything
under age is dangereux I warned him to prendre garde à Lily
Law. He told me he's made a map of all the cottages in London
including les environs so I christened him Miss Footsore. He
calls them Comfort Stations of the Cross, c'est drôle!'

It was as good as the Coliseum, but just as I was congratulating
myself on my broadmindedness and dropping off, I was yanked
back. 'Bugger's such an ugly word, don't you agree? Sodomite has
so much more panache!'

The only time I had ever heard 'bugger'—except as a term of affectionate abuse—had been at Oxford, walking along the High with an OUDS friend.

'See that man,' he whispered quickly, 'walking this way?'

The 'man' was a nineteen-year-old undergraduate like us, with a dull face and plus-fours: the student in the street. I asked who he was.

'I was at school with him. He's a bugger.'

'A bugger?' He looked at me. 'You must know, he buggers other chaps.'

In mixed Holywell County I had led a sheltered life. The boy walked past us, whistling. A whistling leper.

Pierre, clacking on in the other bed, asked the leading question and I answered it indignantly.

'Mon cher,' he said, 'you've *never* been? But you haven't lived, c'est bliss. And doesn't have to mean you're un peu Marjorie, I know a guardsman who's just crazy 'bout it an' growls into the pillow "I wish my missus was under me now, *blimey*"'. I was too bemused to laugh.

We got up late and sat around in dressing-gowns drinking more coffee. Two Chelsea friends came in, ex-Cambridge replicas of Pierre without his preposterous verve; listless and palely loitering, they had 'just enough money to live on, my dears'. One was writing a novel and painting a picture, the other was painting a picture and writing a sonata.

It had been the first morning since my stage début when I hadn't opened a book, and two days later I was back in North London: 13 Handel Street, King's Cross, a top-room replica of my old one. I felt refreshed from my brief wallow in la boue, but with no nostalgie.

At the back of my mind, sharing space with sex, was my next play: it kept pushing to the fore, such as on the evening when, before the show, I sat in the sun outside a Soho café opposite the Lyric stage door, checking my letter to Miss Cooke.

'Petrarch's passion for Laura is somewhat too cerebral for my taste ... Tallulah B. opens tonight in *The Garden of Eden* ...'

Looking up, I saw that the queue ran right past the stage door, where it parted every five minutes for flowers to go through. I reflected that she was less than three years older than me.

Excitement ran subdued in the little street, and I shared in it. The rumour was that the play was trash but it had Tallulah, plus a climax when the star tore off her wedding-dress and stood hands on hips in her undies; the excitement was undiminished by the photographs, in which the undies figured as a stout camisole longer than a Scotsman's kilt.

'About my next play. Very different from *Full Moon*, nothing "Chekhovianly poetic". You once told me, in Fr. Lit., that the drama was a more difficult art for Racine than for Shakespeare: that Shakespeare, being a Romantic, could hop at will from blasted heath to throne room and back again, *and* from January to December, while poor old Racine had to stick to the classic Unities of Time and Place.

'To me, too, the technical difficulty of the one-set play, as well as of keeping an audience interested in the minimum of dramatis personae is an artistic temptation.'

A financial one too, it having crossed the tyro's mind that a manager tends to be put off by a script in which 'the scene moves to a crowded beach on the Côte d'Azur'.

'I'm afraid I'm going to make it more difficult for myself than for Racine. The Time will be the actual date and time of the performance, and the Place the stage of whatever theatre the piece is being played in . . .

'Yesterday I sent home my first contribution to the family coffers, a ten-shilling note. Back to Petrarch, "hac est humanarum varietas actionum . . ."'

But not immediately: I took out a new notebook and wrote, 'A MURDER HAS BEEN ARRANGED, by Emlyn Williams'. A bit long, but 'Six Characters in Search of an Author' was longer.

'A Ghost Story in Three Acts.' I started hazy notes.

Somebody decides to give a party on the stage of a haunted theatre. Well, more of a family gathering, one which a London manager can count on his fingers. Not a trick, a real ghost . . . I looked up at the queue waiting to see Tallulah in A MURDER HAS BEEN . . . I put away my notes, studied for five minutes and left for my theatre: 'Is Mistress Peeps within?'

CHAPTER THREE

APPRENTICE TO SORCERY

June the 20th, Oxford.

I had forgotten how mean and ugly the railway station was, and how brazenly ordinary the street leading to Carfax; I wheeled right and there was Christ Church as I had first seen it four years ago; in my fist I held the same suitcase.

Tom Tower looked down at me, pontifical and changeless; I stared back, with respect and even gratitude. But without affection. Undergraduates scurried indifferently past, trousers flapping and mile-long scarves flung arrogantly over a shoulder; like Tom Tower, they had not changed.

But I had; out in the world now, I was as indifferent as they.

In Tom Gate I went up to the same porter who, four years ago, had pointed at that same notice board where a paper had fluttered to tell me of the scholarship which was to give me the key to life. He did not remember me. For tomorrow, I arranged to 'borrow' cap, gown and white tie, in exchange for a tip.

I crossed vast hushed Tom Quad for the first time since I had left for home, defeated. I smelt the old desolation, then righted myself.

My borrowed cell was as stark as my room had been that last term; there was nobody I had to visit, neither Dean, Censor nor tutor, I was an exile. Walking past staircases, I was surprised to see familiar names: Rosse, Auden, Lennox-Boyd—could they still be up, was it only a year and a bit?

I unpacked, hung up my good suit, dark enough to be the 'subfusc' required for the morning, hurried out again, strolled down Meadow Walk to the deserted barges on the Isis, sat with my back to my college and opened a book for eleventh-hour cramming: the Gypsy's last impersonation of the Scholar.

In bed early, I forced myself not to listen to my college bell Great Tom, sounding the night dirges which had once prostrated me. I swotted for two hours, then slept till woken at 7.30 by a poker-faced scout: I would have to tip him as well, in a non-earning week ...

I padded down for a bath and cold shower and hurried out of Canterbury Gate over to the High, there to join the stream of white ties and mortar-boards. Unshining morning faces creeping like snails unwillingly to Schools—to the grim three-hour prison known as just that, Examination Schools.

With the sun spotting ruled paper and fountain-pen at the ready, there was no sound but the flick of the question-paper on each desk.

'The development of the Tonic Closed E from the 8th Century to 1835. Discuss briefly.' Since I knew the Tonic Closed E by name only, what else could I be but brief?

But I was off, at a jog-trot. That night I sat up stuffing my head full of shrewd quotations, to insert like raisins into a series of insipid puddings. 'The incident puts one in mind of Napoleon's other wise saw *"Du sublime au ridicule il n'y a qu'un pas ...".*' A mean occupation.

On Thursday at 12.30 my voluble pen fell silent; it was over. At Tom Gate, with my mind straining forward to *A Murder Has Been Arranged*, I found a scribbled note from Archie Storie: could I come to all-day dress-rehearsal Strand Monday, *Spook Sonata*, walk-on for 8 perfs, £3?

Fagan, with characteristic courage, was presenting Strindberg's play for one special week at the Strand Theatre, with *The Desert Song*, Drury Lane, on one side, and on the other *Lido Lady*, Gaiety.

I stepped from the sunlight bustle of Tavistock Street into the stage-door and down steps. Opening a door, I found myself in a dream: facing me, a spectral square in a crazy toppling town nowhere on this planet.

Peasants sprawled, eyes closed, against houses which also sprawled; on a bier, a corpse, swathed and ghastly. Standing next to it, motionless, a beautiful wild student stared straight before him, pale to the lips, which moved in a rhythm without speech. The only sound was from the sky: the endless tolling of church bells, first loud, then fading, then loud again. Lights rose and fell; distant organ music; over all, the chill of a nightmare.

The corpse was carried first across the back, then across the front; nobody stirred, time had stopped. Up in the London street, the honk of a car could have been the croak of a vulture.

From the black auditorium, a gentle Irish voice. 'Set that, will you?' Mr Fagan was testing the bells and lighting the funeral. Walkers-on were lying about to rest their feet; the student—Glen Byam Shaw, who at Oxford had played the boy in *Full Moon*— told me later that while waiting he had been mouthing new cuts.

The play was never to give me another moment as good; it was too obscurely symbolic. One character thought she was a bird, locked herself in a cupboard and made parrot noises. When Saturday night came I was not sorry. I had my own spook sonata.

*　*　*

There was nearly a week before my Viva—short for *Viva Voce*, the dreaded oral post-mortem on defunct written efforts—and I would spend the interim immolated outside Oxford; at Paddington I studied the stations: Woodstock, Culham, Radley ...

Radley would do, and in a scattered village I picked a small house in a row facing the station, Number 3 Council Houses, knocked and asked the aproned lady if she knew of a room; she had once let the front bedroom to a farm hand.

Half an hour later it was mine; socks and shirts put away, the typewriter Miss Cooke had given me at Oxford lay open on the small table at the window, next to pencils and quarto sheets. After veal-and-ham pie on a tray, another exam.

Subject, Dramaturgy. 'A man is murdered in a theatre and his ghost appears. Construct on this theme a convincing three-act play, creating the illusion that the action takes place "here, at this precise moment", typing on one side of the paper only.'

After my week of gruelling spade-work I could have sat down to my new task very jaded; but I was back in my scholarship mood, crisp-fresh, quietly in love with what I had to do and no longer feeling guilty about not working. The play *was* my work, just as playing would be. I was committed for life to the Sorcerer: to the business of make-believe.

From my hurried notes I had an outline, peppered with Question and Answer.

Q: Host gives party in theatre. Why? A: Birthday, theatre haunted, his hobby the supernatural, and hopes to see ghost.

Q: Murdered? Why? A: Millionaire, pathologically jealous of young wife, made will that if he dies before eleven p.m. (hour of birth) on 40th birthday, fortune will go to only distant relative, Maurice Mullins; this *is* 40th birthday. Mullins turns up host's death by eleven . . .

Feeling buoyant and lucky I poised my four typing fingertips to test the letters and one after the other they clicked to attention, QWERTYUIOP. An Indian chieftain?

To work; I typed my first heading and looked at it with pride, for it was not ACT ONE, not even PROLOGUE, and not followed by 'The drawing-room of a house in Mayfair, the butler is arranging flowers'. The heading was BEFORE THE PLAY.

I gazed at a bicycle as it passed from shadow into sun. 'Entering the Exe Theatre, you find nothing out of the ordinary. The auditorium is lit and the curtain is down. At 8.30 you expect something to happen. It does.'

Nothing could stall the typewriter now; it turned into a hungry woodpecker.

A woman is standing near the orchestra rail. As she is in a neat black-and-white dress, you thought she was a programme-seller. MISS GROZE *climbs over the footlights, leans behind the curtain, brings round a telephone and lifts the receiver.*

MISS GROZE: Gerrard 6728 please . . . the Exe Theatre speaking, *everything's ready* . . . There's somebody coming, goodbye . . .

'Somebody' is the orchestra, trooping out from under the stage. Well, not exactly trooping, it's a *small* orchestra: four . . .

Then dialogue—keep it brisk and natural—establishing (a) that the men have been hired for the party and will now rehearse for it and (b) that Miss Groze and a maid will then switch off the house lights, take the curtain up and switch on the stage lights.

The orchestra rehearse: joyous current tunes. Overture over, they disappear under the stage; curtain up in darkness, three characters stumble on, thinking they are in a dressing-room.

An echo of Pirandello? Ah, but this is *real life* . . . The stage is a blaze of light. 'The set is left over from the last play at this theatre.'

I typed until Mrs Tindall called up that my supper was in the kitchen, then I rolled in a blank page, left my three people

suspended like marionettes on my lighted stage and sat absent-
mindedly to my meal while Mrs Tindall patched a pair of men's
drawers.

ᵗᵒ ᵇᵉᵈˢ ᵘlike being at home. 'Excuse me, would you be a bank-
clerk? . . . But that machine . . . ?'

'I'm typing a play.'

She looked polite: 'An' what play would that be, " 'Amlet"?'

'No, I'm making it up.'

She stared: 'Out of your own 'ead?'

After cold ham and tinned pears I went walking in the evening
light, pad and pencil in hand. For party, host has arranged fancy
dress, guests dressed as Ghosts of History: Mary Q. of Scots, etc.,
. . . My mind was too busy to enjoy its own peace, and when I
halted to look unseeingly at the sleepy ruffle of water, at serene
woods melting into night, I was reminded of the childhood times
when I had first tasted the honey of reading stories in English—
when, on my country meanders, I could think of nothing but the
open book waiting on a window-sill. Except that now I was not
the reader but the teller. Tomorrow morning, on the blank page,
the hero would appear.

Or rather the non-hero. Having broken one rule—'in a thriller
the supernatural is taboo'—I planned to make Maurice Mullins,
under his surface charm, a cold-blooded killer; at a time when
drama was tailored for golden-haired Owen Nares or noble
Matheson Lang, it was new.

Then I would break a third rule: 'the identity of the murderer
must be a secret till the last scene'. Mine would even commit the
crime in front of the audience. More than new, this was an
eccentricity.

I made more notes, though by now it was hard to see: host has
beautiful young wife, loved by young journalist. Well, you can't
be a pioneer all the time . . .

Dreamless sleep, awake at eight, tea and cornflakes in the sun
at my window work-table, the typewriter open by nine. In between abstracted looks at the shadows changing on the country
road, I tapped steadily; the marionettes were twitching, turning
into flesh and blood. On my evening walk, I concentrated on an
important problem: how to make the murder water-tight.

Alibi? No, fake-suicide. Suicide note left. Forged? No, must be
in host's own writing. Hypnosis? No, Mullins has posed as serial

writer, must get instalment to Fleet Street tonight, pretends to have cut hand, asks host to take dictation.

Heroine of serial is explaining her conduct to her sister; host finishes page. As he starts new one, M. dictates, 'My dear, I've done this because what you've done is the unkindest thing that has ever happened to me . . .'

Then another knotty obstacle: I may have that last climax up my sleeve, but how to bring the actual curtain down on a tableau and still maintain the illusion of 'real life'?

Next morning at nine, Mullins' bravura speech, alone with his accomplice:

MISS GROZE: What sort of man are you?
MULLINS: I'll tell you. (*Rising, and advancing to the foot-lights.*) There's something about a theatre that always makes me want to make a speech. (*Addressing the empty auditorium.*) I've studied myself for years, and I've always been interested in my subject.

The woodpecker pecked on. 'Some men are born good, they grow up to be saints, or preachers, or ideal husbands. I, Maurice Mullins, however, was born bad. Very bad indeed. I like to be well dressed, to feel comfortable in a big car . . . I like to drink champagne. Not because I like the stuff, but because it's so gloriously expensive. I don't take furtive sniffs at the cup of vice: I drain it to the dregs, with a gesture. I am the complete criminal.'

Yes, this will hold . . . On Saturday, an unwelcome break: my Viva.

After my five-mile walk to Oxford, looking blindly up at Magdalen Tower I talked to myself: that damned last curtain, how to make it believable?

Must be arranged beforehand by the distraught wife: 'You will bring it down when such-and-such happens . . .' Ah, that will be when the murderer is unmasked, to prevent his escape via the auditorium! . . . No go, the audience knows too well that the curtain parts in the middle. An easy get-away . . .

As I approached the High the dreaming spires meant no more than suburban Cowley—I had it, the *safety* curtain! It will come grinding down, believable and startling as well. That was settled.

In Schools I was ushered into the presence of three examiners with rubbed-out faces, colourless and ageless. Forty? Fifty? A hundred and ten?

I sat opposite mine as he scurried through notes.

'You affirm here that it is important to remember the date of the Battle of Agincourt.'

'Indeed it is, sir.'

'But you don't give it. What was it?'

'The Hundred Years' War.' I smiled weakly, he did not.

And so it went on: 'I fear that your analysis of *Le Contrat Social* leaves much to be desired.' Then he tested my 'Conversational Power' by launching into a polite chat in French. His own Power also left something to be desired. An academic handshake and I was out. I walked to Radley like a trained dog, to ham, tomatoes and typewriter: back to the reality of make-believe.

Eighth day, last lap: the ending which I had worked out before starting the play. Out of sight behind the curtained alcove, sprawled in a chair, is the host's dead body.

JIMMY: Listen to me all of you. We're up against something I never knew existed. And we're locked up with it, between the four walls of this theatre. It may kill us . . .

In the darkness beyond the archway, a faint light. It fades slowly . . . away. Out of the darkness appears the shape of a man. It is the ghost of Charles Jasper . . .

Enter Mullins; he stares at the ghost, decides the poison did not do its work, and in his rage boasts of his plot. The ghost rises, walks and melts into the curtains; Mullins tears them open, to reveal the dead body sprawled as before. From above a clanging noise, and the safety curtain begins its descent.

MULLINS: It's a wall . . . A prison wall! . . . (*Falling to his knees, in a crescendo of madness*). Shutting me in! Shutting me in . . .

The curtain will not rise again. A murder has been arranged; a murder has taken place; and the murderer has been brought to book. The evening's adventure in a haunted theatre is over.

I typed 'The End' and sat back. 'Dear Miss Cooke, Eight days' work, twelve hours a day, 120 pages of a printed book, 36,000 words. If I don't sell it I'll eat every one of them.'

I said goodbye to Mrs Tindall—she gave the typewriter a wary look, as if it might bite—and sat back in the London train, exhausted but as exhilarated as if I had spent a week sun-bathing by the sea.

Back in Wentworth Studios, the distractions in Pierre's attic could no longer woo me; while he dispensed coffee and scandal to droppers-in, I sat in a corner and cut and polished.

In between, on a midnight impulse I would be drawn to the alleys of Chelsea for a quick dip in the murky briny, to emerge invigorated for revision till dawn. A typist would be an extravagance and I typed the final copies myself, even underlining the stage directions in red ink. It was donkey-work, but not really.

* * *

In mid-July, rehearsals for a special two-week Fagan season at the Oxford Playhouse. He had fitted me in while waiting for New York.

Having as an undergraduate sat on my creaky subscription chair watching play after play, longing to be one of the company and to be walking afterwards not back to college but to digs, here I was.

I had one line as a workman in *Uncle Vanya*—'If you please, Michael Lvovitch, they have sent for you'—and no lines as a footman in *The Circle*, but I was to be the Burglar in *Heartbreak House* and—my plum—Aguecheek in *Twelfth Night*.

Every morning I walked across Central London, from Chelsea to a room in Great Russell Street. It was my first experience of professional rehearsals, and while the others murmured and felt their way round the marked floor, I felt impelled to impress the director. (In 1927, in the English theatre the director of a production was known as the 'producer', and it was not until the nineteen-fifties that the American term 'director' came into general use; to avoid confusion, however, it will be used throughout.)

Book still in hand, I leered and stood about—'I am not such an ass but I can keep my head dry'—with toes pointed inwards and finger to corner of mouth. Nobody seemed amused.

From Miss Cooke: 'No pay for rehearsals! Hang it all, r'sls seem to me the hard part & shd be remunerated handsomely. Encl. 30 pound-notes to tide you over.'

I asked Alan Webb how I was getting on; if I had known how direct he could be, I would have hesitated. Playing in *Full Moon*, at our first meeting he had expressed surprise that 'our author's nothing but one of those callow Varsity boys...'. Seven months younger than me, with an imperious sweep of nostril backed by talent and experience, he now took his revenge.

'Trouble is, dear boy, you're giving your all much too early. Anyway Sir Andrew Aguecheek may be a fool but he's not the village idiot.'

I winced but got the point: 'You mean not enough of the Sir and too much of the Ague?'

'Exactly.'

He might have added that there was too much of the Cheek too, the impertinence of an Oxford amateur tackling a famous part professionally. I did more than tackle: I wrestled, bent on extracting, in twelve scurried rehearsals, every speck of gold.

I found none. Conscious that I ought to be skinny and aristocratic, I was moreover unable to warm to jokes like, 'What is "Pourquoi", do or not do?' or 'Your horse now would make him an ass!' It was only when I listened to the opening scene—'If music be the food of love, play on ...' ... 'My brother he is in Elysium'—that I scented something I could love.

But to play Viola I would have to be a boy actor three hundred years ago. And smaller. For Orsino, taller. The Welsh pony, faced with romantic thoroughbreds, lowered his mane and jogged to a corner of the paddock.

Shaw's Burglar was different: one very funny scene half-way through. But he was a Cockney burglar. I worked at it. A lodger downstairs had a ripe twang, but worked in an office and fancied himself as a grammar school type: 'Righty-ho!' So I could hardly say, 'Would you mind reading this out in your inimitable Cockney?'

I had an idea: I confided in him that the only way I could learn lines was to hear them spoken by a kind friend. 'Could you say that just once more?'

'Righty-ho!'

For several days, I had taken to running across the road to the library for a free scan of *The Times*: any day it would contain the results of Schools.

They came: 'Modern Languages Class List, Oxford.' Four wodges of names, Classes I to IV. A First indicated outstanding achievement, a Second solid achievement, a Third routine achievement, a Fourth no achievement at all.

'... W. G. Moore, Magdalen; G.E. Williams, Ch. Ch.; Sybil Asprey, Lady Margaret Hall ...' I was among the Seconds.

All along, surreptitiously, I had nursed the idea of a First—Against-Odds-Genius-Did-It, but I had prepared Miss Cooke; also she would appreciate the asterisk after my name, 'signifying distinction in colloquial French'. Whatever I might be in the evenings—workman, footman, idiot, thief—by day I could soon dub myself, for life, 'M.A., Oxon.'

The Company migrated to Oxford for two intensive weeks' work on all four plays. It was the Long Vac, and in digs off Walton Street I might have been in any provincial city; I did not once set eyes on the High or Christ Church.

'Playhouse, Aug. 2. Dear Miss Cooke, I'm writing (on my feet) at 2.20 in the afternoon in the middle of a dress rehearsal—*The Circle*, opening tonight. We rehearsed yesterday from 10 a.m. till 9 p.m. It's been like that for a fortnight and we are getting very tired. But I'm very happy.'

At six p.m. I was flying on a borrowed bicycle to the station to collect my footman's uniform from Clarkson's, and two hours later I was in rep, at Oxford.

Opening a programme, I found a list of all the Fagan seasons: Wilde, Ibsen, Sheridan, Congreve, Goldsmith, Pirandello, Maugham, Barrie, Molière, Shaw, Emlyn Williams, Strindberg.

I scrounged two more for Miss Cooke and Dad, to show his mates at the Works; that time when I had shown him the same list for the term which included *Full Moon* his comment had been 'I notice here, George, that while they only give the surnames of the other buffers they give your Christian name as well, now that's a honour, isn't it?'

During four plays in eleven days every bit of time off was snatched for typing my own play, until with mounting excitement I approached the climax. *'Out of the darkness appears the shape of a man. The ghost of Charles Jasper ...'*

Twelfth Night went well enough, considering the stolid out-of-term audience; I worked hard at not appearing to work hard, and garnered a few sniggers. At the second performance I felt free enough to try a less knowing reading of such lines as 'I was adored once too'.

When I heard an appreciative murmur, I sensed a truth which I had been too inexperienced to know before: that the secret of even the most complicated acting is simplicity. I should have started by standing still and speaking shyly from Andrew's hero-worshipping heart—'Many do call me fool'—and built from there. On the third and last night the chuckles turned into laughs and I wanted the rehearsals to start again.

During the last night of *Uncle Vanya*, after my bit I stayed to watch the last scene. It was a wet night, the house was thin and apathetic, but the play glowed softly with its own steady lustre. 'We shall see all our sufferings dissolve in mercy that will fill the whole world . . . Poor Uncle Vanya, you are crying. We shall rest. We shall rest . . .'

I walked to my digs in the rain; it should have been a dismal journey but I walked partly by the light from the play, partly by the knowledge that tonight, if I sat up late, I would be typing the last definitive page of *A Murder Has Been Arranged*: six copies, one to be retained. I sat up late.

*   *   *

'Dear Miss Cooke, I've sent off my five galleons and quite soon every morning I shall be climbing my tower to watch the sea. One of these days, will one of them show the tip of its mast over the skyline, coming home with the glint of gold-sacks on its decks and flags at the prow? If so, I'll send you a telegram . . .'

August the 12th, *Heartbreak House*. Shaw having unhappily described the Burglar as 'an old and villainous-looking man', Alan Napier helped me to make up. After a long nervous wait I was dragged on, cringing and old before my time, into the usual Shavian debating society where I gave vent to some very funny Shavian lines which were received in silence; I shuffled off.

Would a Cockney genius—say Dan Leno—have captivated that audience? But it seemed not to have done me active harm; I had got off lightly.

On Sunday, to London for the four-week tour of *And So To Bed* prior to New York; Glen Byam Shaw (*Full Moon, The Spook Sonata*) was to play a Frenchified fop while the King would be

Gyles Isham, the romantic OUDS Hamlet who had so deeply impressed me and who now both disappointed and charmed by having become the embryo of a cheerful cultivated country squire.

I graduated from *An Apprentice* to *Pepys's Boy*, assistant stage-manager, Glen's understudy, and to four pounds a week instead of three.

As the Boy, I was on and off during Acts One and Three, and had one conspiratorial half-minute scene with Miss Arnaud: in answer to her quick-fire instructions, I said, 'Yes Mistress', six times, then ran off.

But it made me feel marvellous. And several times I was to rat-tat on a door-knocker screwed into the lid of a large empty box, then a smart bang of the lid to simulate a front door closing hard, and once I had to stand against the back wall and clatter coconuts against it to simulate horses' hooves. I was impatient for it all.

These rehearsals were for me unique. If a beginner has the luck to land a tiny part in a star company, the first weeks of rehearsal can prove disillusioning: under a muggy working light, people who to him have been exotic humming-birds sit huddled over an unfamiliar part looking as doleful as the nonentities he has just left in the Underground.

Then the stumbling after text and interpretation, the trials and the errors: by the first night, it can be hard for him to look upon a star as anything but a jumpy human being. My first experience happened in reverse. Not only had I never seen *And So To Bed* rehearsed, I had never (after my first presentation in her dressing-room) seen Miss Arnaud except from the wings, a few feet away but before an audience, teasingly unapproachable in billowing costume, a Restoration *poupée* bathed in light.

In this bare room, perched on a kitchen chair under a skylight, holding a grubby coffee-cup making do as a goblet, was a sonsy little woman in cloche hat, pullover and pleated skirt to the knee. Mistress Pepys had legs!

But the shock was salutary, for I was able to watch a first-class player at work on a part which she knew, and which I knew too. Scrabbling through routine scenes, she made jokes and invited them with the stifled laughter of an irresponsible child; but when she reached the intricate comedy duologue with the new King, it was serious business.

'Gyles, my dear, here you will speak very quick, then stop and I will turn my head so, it makes the laugh you know?'

I was seeing a watch being taken apart and put together again. When I was not dragging benches or filling the cups with water to make do as wine, I was learning.

❀   ❀   ❀

'Dear Miss Cooke, A Murder H.B.A.: no laden galleons yet. Managers are evasive; "original idea but can't see a real ghost on the stage". Patience ...'

On the Sunday train-call at Euston, four compartments drew puzzled looks; they had AND SO TO BED on the windows. I had never—except for trips from North Wales to Liverpool, Oxford and London—travelled in the British Isles, and here I was, fares paid.

On the journey I half-learnt to play poker, on a suitcase, with Glen, Gyles and a dapper little fair-haired schoolboy of a man who turned out to be Mr Fagan's business manager, Harold Gosling. At Chester I gave a thought, affectionate but swift, to 314a, eight miles away; in the old days, I would just about be leaving for Sunday School, Welsh Wesleyan Chapel.

I finished the glass of beer which had lasted through the hours of camaraderie, felt emancipated, then gave Glen the daily ten minutes' French lesson.

'What's this?' Harold said. 'The understudy coaching his principal in the part? What's the theatre coming to?'

'Very simple,' Glen said. 'This understudy's had an education. I went to a public school.'

I would write that to Miss Cooke, she'd be pleased ...

The new Apprentice sat in a corner engrossed in a tattered volume in brown-paper; he told me it was published in Brussels and promised to lend it overnight. I had never handled a dirty book; it would be a perfect end to an exciting day.

Glasgow was exciting too, booming, glowering, foreign: the digs were along a stone alley and up many stone steps, and when the landlady said, 'Wull Ah be infusin' yerr tea?' you felt like reaching for a phrase-book.

From the window I looked down across a livid landscape of stone walls and roofs, hazily outlined against a blood-red sky raddled with smoke.

'It's a fire,' she said, 'over in the Gorrbals.' She made it sound like Hell. I sat in bed with my forbidden book and in my nose the acrid fumes of a savage city.

Sunday meant Yorkshire, the Prince's, Bradford, and I took a bus to Armley, outside nearby Leeds, where Miss Cooke was spending the holidays with her sister. I was to stay the week.

Although it was little more than six months since I had seen her—just before I had 'run away to go on the stage'—for me they had been so uprooting that I half expected her, at the age of forty-four, to have aged.

Or would she still be the fearless realist who had repeatedly cut me down to size? I recalled her in 314a, just after my Oxford breakdown, when she first met my parents at close quarters, then looked me straight in the wandering eye and said, 'You'd feel better if you got your hair cut.'

She was the same striding clear-voiced power-house, and the walls of the tiny suburban villa seemed to strain outwards; at any moment an ornament would be swept to the floor. I was surprised to find her sister a mild English housewife. From my suitcase I unpacked *La Cousine Bette*, which I was re-reading; I had returned the brown-papered book published in Brussels.

Miss Cooke sat on the small sofa and folded her arms. 'This play you've been at, give me a précis of the action.'

Back at my desk in Holywell County, I got good enough marks. 'Well, I reckon a Second isn't to be sneezed at considering, dash it all you were working under a handicap, well you seem in pretty good shape, I expected you to look quite theatrical.'

I did not ask what she had in mind. Plucked eyebrows? *Papier poudré*?

Next, as of old, matters of which I knew nothing. Since I went to Oxford she had always broached politics as if I were in the House of Commons, with access to secret documents; moreover, she always referred to Parliamentary figures, from the Prime Minister down, as if they were fifth-form schoolboys. See here, George, if the coal issue doesn't make Ramsay Mac pull his socks up they'll all be in the soup, what's your opinion?'

I could only nod; we should have had with us the young lady

I had fleetingly tutored in North Wales, in Italian, between Oxford and *And So To Bed*: 'Gentilissima Miss Megan'.

Except that Miss Cooke had no use for her or her father. 'All very well for you Welsh to maintain that Lloyd George won the war through vision, the man just had the gift of the gab, fair play to him for that . . .'

I remembered Dad's verdict on her, 'She's got the bark, George, but God bless her, no bite.'

She came to the play next night: 'I enjoyed Miss Arnaud thoroughly, my word what *élan* and it's a good play, a feeling for words.'

It was a seesaw of a week, by day schoolboy with teacher, by night itinerant mummer; on Sunday morning early, before the train-call for Portsmouth, a farewell handshake; 'I'll drop a line to your father to say you seem well and flourishing, good luck for New York.'

In the meantime Dad was picking up the stage lingo and flavouring his own with it. 'I see by the Liv. Post that you lot are signed on the dotted line to have a whack at the Great White Way . . .'

I had been so busy that now, for the first time, it was borne in on me that I was bound for the New World, and I saw a million faces raked by searchlights. At the back of my new little wardrobe trunk—second-hand, Railway Lost Property—a bomb ticked steadily prior to exploding into success: A MURDER HAS BEEN ARRANGED.

Behind Broadway and the million faces, the great beyond: Hollywood. Had not Chaplin sailed the same route, and only two years ago, Greta Garbo? I was on the edge of adventure.

CHAPTER FOUR

FIRST WHACK AT THE GREAT
WHITE WAY

On October the 1st, boarding the boat-train at Waterloo, I joined Miss Arnaud, Glen, Gyles, Harold the manager and a new arrival, Beryl Freeman; the Fagans were crossing on a bigger liner, and we all felt it was fun not travelling with the Head.

None of us had been to the States, though there existed many beautiful Americans whom we knew, intimately, from the Pictures: stars whom we would no more have thought of calling Silent than of referring to a four-legged horse. What else could a film star be but speechless?

We knew them from spit-curl to crooked finger, from straw hat to co-respondent shoes; we had looked on smiles melting over white teeth which would quickly bite the bee-stung lip as the tear coursed down the cheek, then a dissolve to the clean-cut manly stare.

But while we watched them chatter, they never uttered. It would not be easy to adjust to a city crammed with talking Americans.

On the train, the news that the American Legion was to be on our boat evoked the gleam of Roman helmets as the togas swung along the deck. In Southampton I recognized from the outline of the *Carmania* that she was a sister to the *Lucania*, hanging on our parlour wall, in whose bowels my father had once worked; peering down at the black-faced stokers straining at coal, I saw Dad among them.

I joined Glen and Gyles in a walk round the main deck.

It was awash, not with water, with people, all with a single voice. Rumbling in endless monotone when it was not barking in argument, it was the sound of the American Legion: ex-soldiers returning from their annual jaunt to the Western Front.

There were twelve hundred of them but they offered not only

one voice but one face and one body, the last encased in a dark waistcoated suit and with a wide Stetson hat pushed back from the furrowed brow of an ageing schoolboy with leather lips, to which a bottle or a cigar would be fed at intervals. They whinnied and cackled and spat and bickered in flat snarled monosyllables which seemed to originate as far back as the nape of the neck: shucks saps bum cripes nuts son-of-a-bitch where's-de-janes fuck-dat-crap.

'I never thought,' Glen said reflectively, 'of an American saying "fuck". Nice to have something in common.'

After the Legion's glazed stares at our flannel trousers, we took care not to let them hear our prim accents and joined Yvonne and Beryl, the only females on board, huddled in a corner of the lounge.

After three marooned days we were tired of books and of the ship's newspaper, a typed foolscap sheet which wriggled its way in under the door like a flattened white insect and sounded like a kindergarten magazine.

Glen said, 'Why can't Emlyn read us his play?'

*　　*　　*

I said, 'Oh, no . . . ,' then thought: I couldn't have a better audience, alert to every subtlety and as I go along I can gauge exactly which joke out of five may misfire . . .

What about Beryl Freeman?

She was to play one of the roguish doxies but off the stage, in tweeds and flat shoes to match a face handsomely severe, she was not so much roguish as broguish. She clipped her words off like coins to be carefully dispensed, being the genuine ones.

And genuine they were. 'That hat, dear, is a bit young for you . . .' 'Emma-line' (she was the first, and not the last, to find difficulty with a name which seemed to me straightforward, being a perfect rhyme for 'Kremlin' and whoever heard of the Kremma-line?). 'Emma-line, what are those specks on your shoulder?'

I stumbled down to the cabin and had a lurching shampoo. Later I said to Glen, 'You know the way in Wales we call people Jones the Milk and so forth? This one's Beryl the Frank.'

At the reading, I would risk Beryl the Frank.

[37]

At teatime, the six of us gathered in Yvonne's spacious cabin and lights were turned out—'I *adore* ghosty stories.'

I settled, tense, under the one lamp and blurted out, 'A Murder Has Been Arranged': a murmur of approval.

'Entering the Exe Theatre, you find nothing out of the ordinary ... A clock shows the exact time, for the action takes place in this theatre, here and now.'

'But Emma-line,' murmured Beryl, 'this is very original.'

The mysterious telephone call went well, then the quick scene with the conductor. I was discovering the play for the first time.

The third character appeared, which meant that the plot was now spiced with comedy. 'Enter Mammy, an old retainer; she is a fat jolly negress.'

'What,' Beryl said sharply, 'did you say her name was?'

'Mammy,' I repeated, 'it's her nickname.'

Spiced? With comedy? I had had the rash idea of this character in order to build up a superstitious fear of the haunted theatre. It now struck me that while I knew nothing about white Americans I knew less about black ones.

I thought too, God I've got to *speak* her lines ... And the rot set in.

The secretary explains to her that because of the strong lights people will put on make-up. '"De good Lawd chile, paint on ya face, ya all mebbe try be play-actors next, an' go to de Debble good an' strawng!"'

A chuckle from the corner. The joke didn't deserve it, but thank you, Glen. Then the conductor had his moment: '"Well, Mammy, *you* won't need any paint anyway!"' Silence.

I made a rush at Mammy's rejoinder—'"Keep yo' mind on dat ole baton, Massa."'

I was afraid Beryl would weigh in with 'What did you say, *Massa*?' but she didn't; at the same moment I heard myself, in desperation, falling back on dat ole Welsh accent.

Enter wife's mother, a shrew, and her husband, a comic Frenchman; I was now to adopt a French accent in front of Yvonne Arnaud.

'"I 'ave spoused Angleesh lady. Our 'ost 'ave une femme charmante, he 'ave a nice woman!"' Short loyal laughs, from a captive audience which had two alternatives: the American Legion or the sea-bed.

Prolonged back-chat, an endless quarrel scene, then at last Mullins and his accomplice were alone for his bravura monologue. ' "There's something about a theatre that always makes me want to make a speech . . . I've studied myself for years, and I've always been interested in my subject." '

Good. I went on.

And on. ' "That's the basis of my nature, and you may say it's a little sordid." ' Too long.

' "I've been fulfilling my destiny ever since I extracted chocolates from slot-machines with incredible ingenuity." ' Better.

' "When I compare my reactions with my own short stories in particular . . ." ' *Too long.*

By the time I got to ' "I am the Complete Criminal" ' I had dissipated my effect. We were at page 30 and the last was 140. What had given me the idea I had cut enough? . . .

Enter host and young wife, chat, chat, banter, banter.

MRS NORTH: I'd hate to be a chorus-girl and have to climb all those stairs.
MADAME: They've got legs, haven't they?
ACHILLE: Ah oui!
MADAME: Taisez-vous.

'Emma-line, dear,' said Beryl, 'you're reading too quickly.'

I came to more squabbles, to provide the motive for the pseudo-suicide; then to the scene which was to strike the note of foreboding. Mullins notices a large black vase, centre stage.

BEATRICE: If you break it open, it's supposed to help you in a supernatural way. Isn't it quaint?
MULLINS: Very.

Contrived too. Very.

Act Two: talk talk, with my mind lacerated by every line. Watch out, here's dat ole Mammy again, five pages of her. She doesn't fancy Mullins: ' "What an heathen, Lawdie shoo him into de Furnace!" ' Lawdie shoo her into de Wings . . .

The murder scene came at last and the ingenuity of the suicide note could not fail to interest; but after this discovery of the body, arguments about how to trap the murderer. Pages of them.

That rare week in Radley, had I been drained of self-criticism? Re-enter characters dressed as Ghosts of History, Mammy

dressed as Topsy ... Finally, finally they are told of the murdered host behind the drapes. His widow points to the vase.

'"If that is broken, his ghost will walk here ..." She flings it to
the ground: it smashes open and out rolls a human skull.'

As I said it, I realized that here was a device powerless to
convince a child that a goblin might flit across the stage, never
mind an audience which was too exhausted to be scared, in mid-
Atlantic, by an iceberg. I stopped abruptly; 'I'm sorry, I haven't
corrected any further.'

They were very tactful: 'Oh, yes, wants cutting, but most
promising.'

I thanked them for their patience, went to my cabin and sat
staring at the corpulent script. I thought of Sophie Tucker: nobody loves a fat play, but, oh, how a fat play can long to be
loved.

It had been a bitter lesson; I opened my trunk and stuffed the
script behind shirts. A murder had been arranged and would not
take place, ever.

*　　*　　*

After dinner, sitting with Glen and Gyles in a corner of the
smoking-room, I took mildly to drink. They could tell I wanted
no mention of the reading; the nearest Glen got was 'I'm convinced the way to get a first play on is to write it for a star.'

In the middle of an argument about Chekhov—The marvellous
thing about *Three Sisters* is ...'—we heard a growl behind us:
the sound of a mastiff baring its teeth. 'Goddam British pansies!'

The word was new but it froze us; the open window framed
seven identical grey middle-aged masks, mouths twisted, pig-
eyes glaring derision.

Gyles murmured into his glass, 'Take no notice, unless anybody
feels like a swim.' He was right: from behind, a concerted shriek
—'Mawvellous three sistahs, mawvellous!'—then guffaws dying
away.

Next morning we went walking with Yvonne and Beryl; several
approached. We waited.

It came, like hissing steam. 'Cheese, here's de bunch!' Then
blind rage lassoed even the females. 'Goddam Bri'ish pansies, *all*
of 'em!'

'Philistines!' clipped Beryl. 'Outsiders!'

Yvonne had the last word, eyes wide. 'Pansies?'—she was a gardener—'And what piece do they think we will play in their countree, "And So To Flowerbed"?'

*   *   *

At seven a.m., Boston, Mass. Glen was up and dressed: 'This is America, I must set foot on it!'

An hour later he arrived back, hair ruffled by land breeze, eyes shining from New World sun. 'I walked across the Common. Do you realize they've got *horses*, exactly the same as the ones in Hyde Park?' I knew what he meant: we had seen hundreds in cowboy pictures, but this was real.

Some hours later Gyles said, 'As the jokers put it, she's a big girl but kinda impressive.'

I looked at her and was unexpectedly moved. I had seen photographs of the Statue of Liberty—had even watched Pearl White, clinging, in close shot, to one of the spikes round the head—but the real thing, like the horses, was different. Face to face with the great figure against the skyline of a new continent, I understood a little how thousands of desperate immigrants must have felt when confronted with the superb gesture of the torch held aloft.

Glen showed me a small bottle of whisky before he slipped it into a pair of pyjamas: 'The steward reminded me it's Prohibition. By the way I'm told we tip him.' That hurt.

In a solemn silence the ship glided majestically to a halt, then the crash of a brass band—welcome home the Legion—sparked off the deafening Gershwin symphony of New York. A breezy young man—'I'm from the Shubert office'—doled out dollar bills and strange change.

I broke away to grab my trunk and pull it on to the moving staircase, so that my first dime should not fall into the hands of a porter. We bundled into taxis and our guide's warm husky voice explained the sights. 'That's the Woolworth Building, the highest...' Yvonne murmured, 'Not like the Legion is he?' Nobody was, but everything was peculiar. I saw a shoe-shine booth.

We descended at the Bristol Hotel, West 48th Street, and were whirled up in a lift that felt like a balloon. Abruptly I found myself sitting in a luxurious little room, looking at my trunk.

It was getting dark. I walked to the window, and recoiled. I was on the edge of a luminous cliff, among cliffs. After ten days of sliding sea, it was too soon to be in the sky; I felt dizzy, and sat down again.

At dinner I read words like chowder and clams and lima beans and Yankee Pot Roast, then there was the iced water and the recurrent reminder, from the waiter, of how welcome we were.

After the meal Glen whipped out his dram of whisky, we each gulped one illegal mouthful, became drunk immediately, emerged from the hotel—next door the Playhouse, JANE COWL IN THE ROAD TO ROME—and went for a stroll round Times Square, hugging the alien sidewalk like two tipsy cats negotiating stepping-stones over a turbulent current.

My first sight of Piccadilly Circus had been a revelation, but that was a country fair compared with this. Sky and street were alive with lights, catherine wheels spat slogans of every colour in letters a mile high, electric bulbs chased one another in a race never to end: millions of frantic phosphorescent mice of the Great White Way.

It was a genial hell drunk with self-expression: THE CIGARETTE THAT KNOWS HOW TO BE ITSELF KATHARINE CORNELL IN THE LETTER EDDIE CANTOR ZIEGFELD FOLLIES NOT A COUGH IN A CARLOAD GAIETY DE MILLE'S KING OF KINGS.

'It's not real,' Glen called, 'but we're welcome, they tell us so!'

'You're welcome,' I shouted nasally, 'you're *welcome*!' I was glad the Legion was not at our elbow.

I was woken by traffic a mile below on earth. Committee Meeting of One: my salary—sixty dollars a week—meant a princely jump from four pounds to twelve, but I would not be paid for this week's rehearsals and had just enough till my first week's pay.

So it was a shock, at the desk, to find that my night in the clouds had cost me four dollars: sixteen shillings. I would have to live as frugally as before; I soared back to my room, packed, lugged my trunk down to the baggage room, checked out, and walked in the sun to the Shubert Theatre.

We had five days' rehearsal, for the newcomers to the cast. Beryl's companion doxy was to be Mary Robson, English but the antithesis of Beryl: big, voluptuously handsome, highspirited. The new King, for whom Gyles had deputized, turned out to be Charles Bryant, a suave Hollywood personality.

He was also the brother of Mary Grey—Mrs Fagan—and the spectacle of his Majesty reclining on a couch nuzzling his mistress (Miss Grey) became strange. From the wings, Yvonne stared: 'But my dear this eez incesticism. God knows what weel 'appen when de Spring comes!'

In the later afternoon I bought the *New York Times*, turned to 'Furnished Rooms West Side', found one at fifty cents a night —'Nice, Clean, nr Bath'—returned to the Bristol and dragged out my trunk.

At the revolving door I met Yvonne. 'Bravo,' she said, 'go find a nice leedle Snuggery Nook!'

I bumped the trunk over to Ninth, staggered on to an uptown tram, got off at 72nd Street and came to a block of small houses, brownstone pitted with eczema.

A slattern pointed to a black inside room, with no window and neither Nice nor Clean and with Bath nowhere to be seen. Except for a folding bed there was nothing but a wan fly-pitted bulb and a sly smell. I heaved the trunk up, it had grown twice as heavy. On the stairs a sad Negro said hello.

I hurried out and walked back to the bright lights to meet Glen; he had seats for a Maxwell Anderson play, *Saturday's Children*. When I walked back, the street was dark, the house a tomb and my room closer and more squalid than before.

I dozed off, and woke up itching. The smell was by now acrid; when I turned on the light the sheet, grey and web-thin, looked somehow busy. Bugs.

I had never seen one before. I beat the sheet against the wall as if it were on fire, dressed and lay along the edge of the bed, feeling sick and thinking, this is an item which will be missing from my letter this week. Then I tried to cheer up by evoking Count Pierre and muttering, 'Yvonne, this is no snuggery, it's a buggery.'

The hours passed in black silence, scratched at by little scuttling noises, and by the first glimmer of daylight I was on the doorstep clutching my newspaper.

The Negro gave a lifeless shrug: 'Try downtown.' I fled. For one night I had brushed shoulders with despair.

*   *   *

Way down on Eighth I called at a drugstore for a five-cent cup of coffee, sat on a tall swivel-seat like on the pictures, and had a chat with the proprietor, in Italian; he was so pleased with me that he refilled my cup, and that would go into my letter. I made a ring round three addresses in 23rd Street and set off.

The first two were little better, but I plodded on, to 246 East. It looked the same, a poor four-storey house in a block: but when 'the woman' opened the door, I knew I was in harbour. She looked like a Welsh housewife, with grey hair drawn back to a bun from a scrubbed country face: a Swede. I followed her up naked stairs which smelt of soap; on the top floor she opened a door on to a room the size of a ship's cabin, but the sunlight from a good window was further brightened by white paint.

Everything—single bed, small table, deal chair—was clean; tap outside, lav and bath downstairs, but I did not even look. Compared with the Bristol at four dollars a night, this was four dollars a week.

After fetching my trunk across town from my buggery, I opened it against my wall and it made my wardrobe. From my bed I could see across the wide street to the roof of the last-century building opposite, with 'School of Music' chiselled in the stone and on each side a head blowing a stone trumpet up to the sky.

It was a snuggery. I unpacked, leaving one item out of the way. That fat script.

After four days' rehearsal, a dress rehearsal—three p.m. to three a.m.—in a 'dark' (unoccupied) theatre where, as ASM, I raced up and down stairs with shirts, shoes and stockings or laden with immense dresses to be cleaned, pressed, lengthened, shortened.

In the New World the species Call-boy was already extinct, and it seemed agreed that I assume the part for the run, doubling it with errand boy; ravenous for work, I was delighted.

Between my racing, I realized again that the New World was a friendly one: if Miss Grey had called for help at a London rehearsal the wardrobe mistress would have answered, 'Comin', madam,' but our Mrs Shepherd carolled cheerfully, 'I'll be with you, honey!'

Passing a group during a break, I stopped for a quick story Mary Robson was telling, about 'this girl who runs into the chemist's—"I want some Kotex...thank God!"' They all laughed. I was unsophisticated enough to have no idea why.

There were long breaks, and I spent many five-minute sittings under the stage with Mrs Shepherd while she sewed and told me about shows she had been with: a needle's eye view.

'Fancy not knowing about the *Shuberts*, you must be kiddin', them two brothers just about *own* Broadway...Odette Myrtil in *Countess Maritza* now *there* was a star, her ball-gown as good at the end o' the run as on opening night, never lost a sequin, what an artist! An' Fannie Brice in the *Follies*, now I figure that was her best ever, a dilly, sakes alive them quick changes! An' Texas Guinan in *Padlocks of 1927* on a *live horse*!'

We would be on the road for three weeks, Stamford one night, New Haven two, Washington three, Toronto a week, Montreal a week. My landlady told me she could let my room in the interim and that I could return to it.

I asked Mrs Shepherd if Lee Shubert, the brother who was presenting us, would be coming to Stamford; she stared. '*Mr Lee?* Oh, Mr Lee *never* goes to a show on the road. Why, it'd be same as God turning up at a memorial service. No, he just sends one of his people.' Let my people go. On a cloud?

'Emil, I hear tell you wrote a show, you oughta run it over to Mr Lee's play-reader.' She made it sound as if Mr Lee was illiterate.

'A thriller? That's swell, why next to musicals that's right up Mr Lee's alley!...There's a what in it? A *ghost*? Oh, I don't think Mr Lee'd care for it to get around that one of his theatres was haunted...'

Arriving in Montreal on the Sunday evening I asked a porter —en français—if he knew of somewhere to stay. He scratched his head, and named a street.

I got off the tram at the corner, walked down a quiet side road and knocked at a pleasant little house. A lady answered the door, soberly dressed, motherly. 'Mais entrez donc!'

I planted my trunk and followed her into a bright sitting-room, where she left me. I heard a rustle and turned. Five people had entered and were facing me in a row. Five girls, smiling and naked to the waist. My French had not been up to Canadian standard.

I explained, they chirruped and all kissed me bonne nuit, and

Madame directed me to a little pension where I was very comfortable. But the next night, after the performance, before returning to it I walked round the corner, where they all greeted me as an old friend. I shook hands with four girls and kissed the fifth, the plump one. 'Alors,' she said, 'on monte?'

With racing pulse I followed her upstairs; I was back in Rouen, three years and four months ago, a long time. She undressed me, chattering gaily about the weather. I told her about the play—'c'est du temps de Molière'—but she hadn't heard of Molière. 'Alors on fait l'amour?'

It was like Rouen, refreshing and natural. We lay back, she smoked a cigarette, we had a short anatomical chat, then I asked her about herself.

'Tiens!' she said, 'it is nice that you talk. Most men go flic-flac and where is my hat. C'est gentil!' It was like listening to the prattle of a little girl, precocious and overweight.

'Dear Miss Cooke . . . A porter directed me to a nice pension and I have a chance to practise my French . . .'

On the Friday night, sitting next to our electrician—a giant fatty who, while being sure, was so slow he was nicknamed Speedy—I told him about my visit. He said there was a whole red-light district; after the show he and a coupla buddies were going on the town for a piece o' tail, wanna tag along?

Immensely flattered, at the end of the show I tore upstairs, peeled off breeches and stockings, and in three minutes was at the stage-door.

I waited. Half an hour. They had decided I would be a responsibility. Walking dispiritedly to the front of the theatre, I looked up at the electric sign. AND SO TO BED. It went out. I obeyed.

We opened in New York on November the 9th at the Shubert. If the play was a success I would buy, for my room, a spray of artificial daffodils from Woolworth's.

After calling the half-hour, I gave Glen a special three-minute refresher in his French and my wig a special oiling. It was a gala first night with names being whispered in the wings: Alexander Woollcott, Ina Claire, Clifton Webb, Guthrie McClintic, Dorothy Parker. . .

'Say,' Mrs Shepherd said after a peer through the curtain, 'lotta soup an' fish out there.'

Everybody went afterwards to parties, Glen and Beryl joining the famous playwright, S. N. Behrman. If I had been asked anywhere like that I would not have had the strength of mind to refuse, but I knew instinctively that the shallows were more my present measure than a venture into the swim. Walgreen's drugstore in Times Square, then a walk home.

Next morning in the little Soda-Luncheonette two doors down, as I sat sipping my breakfast—one black coffee, five cents— Louie the barman, a laconic friendly young Bronx Italian, lent me his paper, *The World*. Woollcott: 'A bright, spirited and engaging comedy'.

I showed it to Louie. 'I figure you gotta hit, bud. Once in a while Broadway kinda takes a shine to them costume-party shows, like Barrymore in that *Hamlet*. I gotta hunch you'll be here on your ass for months.'

I went to Woolworth's and bought the artificial daffodils.

＊　　＊　　＊

During those months each morning would start like that, with coffee and last night's opening in Louie's paper, and for the rest of the day my money-saving pattern was set.

My night walk to work was as timetabled as my morning tramp to school when I was ten. At 7.25 p.m. I stepped out of 246 East 23rd and walked west under the trains of the El, then at Madison Square, where the clock high on the Metropolitan Building tower showed 7.30, I joined Broadway where it wove its diagonal path across the chess-board of Streets and Avenues.

Way ahead I could see approaching the gigantic ball-headed Paramount Building; below it, the burst of light which meant Times Square at 44th and the Shubert Theatre. Drawing nearer, I could make out the electric sign across the Capitol and negotiated the last blocks to the rhythm of one long word streaming out of blackness and in again, a different word each week— GARBOTRIUMPHSINTHEDIVINEWOMAN . . .

Mats Wed Sat 2.30. On Sat I set out at 1.25, but on Wed I was earlier: 1.10, to allow for a call at the Greenwich Savings Bank on 36th Street (interest 2 %) with, in my wallet, the sixty dollars I had been paid the Friday before: I deposited forty, had them stamped in my book and walked apace to the theatre. 'Half an hour, please!'

Between matinée and evening shows, I would walk home for the couple of hours and then back, for the exercise; the discipline was a stimulant.

Meals fitted in when they happened, on high stools at drug-store counters. For days the only people I talked to were counter-men: they were like Louie, friendly, wise and with a quizzical respect for the British. 'You're from *Wales*. Is that so?'

One morning Louie said, 'Ain't that what he's Prince of? Gee, must be kinda nice to be looked after by a Prince, I'd like that...' A truck-driver looked up from his salami sandwich. 'My name's Earl, do I qualify?'

On special mornings I would set out at 9.25 and by 10.5— cheap early prices—find myself the only sprawler in an enchanted Times Square Sahara called the Paramount Cinema, while Jesse Crawford's Mighty Wurlitzer Organ thundered up from below. As alone as Ludwig, and as little in touch with reality, I watched anything from Pola Negri in *The Secret Hour* to Colleen Moore in *Her Wild Oat*.

In between such lotus-meals I had to find occupation. I looked at my typewriter, a large toad asleep under the table. After that *Carmania* reading it had a right to sleep....

A novel? From *Full Moon*: the Mediterranean retreat, quiet descriptions of pure love awakening... I succumbed to the bad habit of pre-writing reviews: 'a new talent, sensitive, evoca-tive...'.

Chapter One: 'The waves that curl round a magic island have many voices...' Were the words forming into single file too obediently? I went no further.

Dancing lessons? I was nimble without being graceful, and as for singing, much as I loved the effect of music in any play I must be the only Welshman born tone-deaf.

If the Actors' Studio had existed, would I have applied?

At the prospect of exposing a tentative performance to a narrow-eyed group contradicting one another ('No, it's the emotional imbalance, see what I mean? Try the voice higher in the head, a rounder texture') I would have recoiled, convinced that a player's interior—his way of making his effects, half instinct, half preparation—is more private to him than his body.

I would have been as unwilling to ask Yvonne Arnaud about the 'soul' of her acting—as opposed to the technique, which I could watch for myself, with profit—as to question her about her inside.

I decided to study German. My six lessons at the Berlitz in Liverpool, paid for by Miss Cooke, made a good enough grounding and I took a grammar out of the little Carnegie Free Library next door. For the length of the second act I was required to sit in the prompt corner, but prompting was a sinecure and throughout the run I was to spend the time studying.

During that second act the play only intruded once, but at each performance: when Mistress Knight spoke to Pepys of Italy. 'Music, marble, the night of stars! St Peter's, where the boys' voices climbed and climbed till they seemed to break upon the dome in sparkles of sound. A sea of music beating at the gates of heaven . . .'

I looked up for that, every time. And was proud to be to do with the play.

I was glad of letters. 'Your brother Job off to work, must peel potatoes . . .'

Miss Cooke: 'I am treating myself to a daily help, who said just now, "Oh no, Auntie'll be cremated where her sister was so the two ashes can be together in the Moslem." Mausoleum??? Fair play to her, correcting speech seems harder every yr., the Bank Manager phoning today finished up with "Bye, bye." I consider "Moslem" correct by comparison.'

'Dear Mr Williams, I came to your matinée and was delighted to see your name, you may remember I wrote to you in London about my thesis on Welsh drama. Would you care to come to Philadelphia for a weekend? Sincerely, Olive Ely Hart.'

A professor's intense wife perhaps, and the fare . . . I hesitated, then risked it. By return came my round trip—not the money but the ticket itself—and that disarmed me. After the Saturday show I ran down Eighth to Penn Station, just caught the train and arrived at Philadelphia at one a.m.

Miss Olive and Miss Ada were middle-aged sisters, schoolteachers: Ada gaunt, downright and jolly; Olive the dramatologist, with a round, serene bespectacled face, a pigeon-plump, furswathed figure and a pigeon-cooing voice. She looked like the mother of five girls.

In spite of the hour, they were as fresh as a fine morning; a car was outside, Olive drove. 1720 Thomas Avenue was in a pleasant tree-lined suburb, a wooden house with garden straight on to the road and on to other gardens, which I found utterly friendly.

As for the inside, I was still unfamiliar with good living so what was—I imagine—a comfortably unpretentious house seemed to me a blur of luxury: wall-to-wall carpets, a fire ... There was a tray of food for me, next to a whisky-and-soda. That, in the Prohibition era, was hospitality.

Olive taught English and had always been obsessed by 'theatre'. On her last day trip to New York, alone, she had seen four shows: *Hedda Gabler* at Eva le Gallienne's Civic Repertory Theatre in the morning, *And So To Bed* in the afternoon, the film *Sunrise* at six, and the Reinhardt *Jedermann* at 8.30 ... She talked intelligently about each. The sisters even subscribed to the fastest-talking trade paper in the world, *Variety*: 'We see Helen Hayes in *Coquette* is doing boffo business!'

Olive also spoke of her school class, particularly of two coloured girls: 'Oh, they are so dear, and things are never easy; one said to me, "Why, Mizz Hart, I feel in your class there's nuthin' to worry 'bout in life, 'cept to learn"—isn't that nice?'

She made all life sound reasonable, as if there was a solution to everything if you looked it in the face. Before bed I had a bath, and met the sisters emerging briskly from another door, in dressing-gowns and rubber caps: I adjusted to the idea of two middle-aged spinsters taking a shower.

Breakfast was brought to me in bed by a Negro maid who had been with them for years; later they drove me along the Schuyl-kill River. I noticed that in spite of Ada's no-nonsense high spirits she concurred with the gentle sister-voice in the back. The play *The Cradle-Snatchers* was mentioned.

'Let me think,' Olive purred. 'I don't remember much about it ...'

'Oh, I do,' Ada said firmly. 'You didn't like it, did we?'

In the evening they took me to visit friends, and I toasted two schoolmarms holding martinis and wearing hats which Miss Cooke would have described as saucy; then the dress-rehearsal of some one-act plays, college amateurs, sort of Little Theatre.

'Mr Williams is playing on Broadway and writes plays.' People were impressed, and so was I.

Every three weeks or so the ticket would arrive and I would leave clanging Manhattan and repeat the weekend. If I were seeing them every day, would the soothing become the soporific, would I hanker after a pinch of salt? Maybe, but they were my first encounter with prosperous academic America, gentle and liberal, and cheerful benevolence was enough.

To Miss Cooke I described Olive as a writer. I shirked the thought that I might spend my adult life as Teacher's Pet.

*   *   *

In the half-light of the back of my mind, I once more perceived something stir and peer out.

One evening the doorman had a message for Miss Robson and would I leave it on her table. I ran up and opened the door: Mary was standing alone, about to pull a petticoat over what I imagined were called cami-knickers. She was naked to below the navel.

Something must have irritated her, for this warm-as-toast woman planted her hands on her hips while her eyes glared unrecognizably at me. 'For God's sake, will you learn to bloody well knock?'

I backed out—'I'm terribly sorry'—shut the door, slipped the note under it and stumbled downstairs. A clumsy urchin had been clouted.

When I called the half she was making up, in her dressing-gown: 'Sorry I turned on you, dear.'

I felt better, but that night in bed I reverted to the beautiful angry creature stripped to the waist, the tips of her generous breasts blazing at me like another pair of outraged eyes.

I had seen, for the first time and by accident, the body of a woman who was not a prostitute. Here was a seductive creature and yet I had never thought of her sexually. Nor of any other female I knew.

I tried to work out why. It was because I had a fear of entanglement, not only of emotional trouble but of day-to-day responsibility—why didn't you phone; you're not even listening to me; will you never understand how complicated a woman is? . . .

More than anything I felt distaste for the preliminaries: for the stroking of hands, then the bolder move—oh darling, I have to know you much better before anything like *that*; what was I saying about Stanislavsky? . . .

I thought of the actor—an American—who dressed next to me, a great womanizer, who one night had a couple of drinks and started talking. 'Listen, sport, why don't you get yourself a girl?'

When I explained, he looked thoughtful. 'I'll tell you something. I'm crazy about all that feminine carrying-on. I guess the billin' an' cooin' kinda teases me up. Then when we get in the hay an' I know she wants it an' the kissin's gotta stop an' no holds barred, the squawkin' kinda offends me an' I feel the old pecker foldin' up on me.

'Now you sound the dead opposite, strange thing . . . I reckon what starts *you* tickin' is a dame with a woman's body which she knows how to move around but who out o' bed acts like a man. Kid, you're not easy to please.'

Lying in bed, I lived a dream with Mary Robson.

I knock at her door. 'Come in'. She stands stripped to the waist. 'I like going to bed but darling I can't stand involvement, would you like to kiss them?'

A couple of evenings later I arrived at the theatre just as a man was seeing Mary out of his car and embracing her in a way which indicated considerable involvement. He was large and handsome, and it was a large handsome car.

* * *

November the 26th, my twenty-second birthday. One night the following week Glen developed appendicitis and at 7.45 the next evening, in his blue velvet costume, I sat on his stool and took up his wig. As Pepys's servant, mine was a page-boy bob and not unbecoming to a page-boy physique; since Glen was tall, slim and elegant, his wig suited him too. I planted it on my head and looked in the mirror.

My face fell. And since I had just tried to give it a foppish air with red cheeks and cherry lips—and also framed it in sausage curls cascading over a lace collar—it could ill afford to fall.

A head appeared round the door: Harold Gosling. There being no understudy for me, he had shed his managerial suit for my clobber as the Boy. He stared at me in the glass.

'It's Mary Pickford,' he said, 'as Little Lord Fauntleroy, strewth!'—and was gone.

Startled, I looked back at myself. It was.

I sprang up and stood before the long mirror. All I needed was the sash; I was a short lord with a high fever. I hurried back, wiped off the fever and returned to the mirror. I was still the short lord, only peaky.

I looked at my legs. What good is aristocratic French, spoken above the calves of a farm-hand?

'There's one thing settled,' I murmured into the mirror, 'you'll never play a gentleman, but it's experience.'

I stood in the wings, weighed down by Glen's wig, while Harold stood next to me, in mine; I was too nervous to look at him. He had not rehearsed, the theory being that my part was so bitty he could pick it up as he went along.

Waiting, I did remember that not only had Harold never trod the boards, one of his charms was what might be termed a jumping stutter; instead of getting stuck in a syllabic ditch he chose to vault it, and when excited could suggest a palate not entirely uncleft.

The moment came for him to walk on and announce me and my companion; I signalled to him, he gave a convulsive shake and shot on to the stage. Listening for him to give me my cue—'Master Pelham Humphrey and Master Caesar'—I heard him say, in a voice so low as to be conspiratorial—the audience *must not hear*—'Melham Pumph a Mass Teaser!'

I strode on. 'Ah, Monsieur Pepys, votre serviteur!'

But Monsieur Pepys was staring at his Boy. I stared too.

Harold was slight, a man of thirty who looked seventeen; below my wig, he had made himself a present of a pink-and-white face which made him look twelve. On top of which—rouge-drunk amateur that he was—he had enlarged his already wide mouth with lipstick so that it looked as if you could post a script in it. I may have resembled Mary Pickford but he looked like a ventriloquist's doll whose master, in the wings, had just picked him off his knee and hurtled him on to the stage.

It was for me to battle on, with a song thrown in, in French, self-accompanied on a mimed guitar. Experience.

Just before the last-act dinner-party, Beryl the Frank said behind her hand, 'You're doing well, Emma-line, but keep your shoulders back.' As she turned away I gave her a cold look.

But I kept my shoulders back, when I was not keeping my corkscrew curls out of Mistress Pepys's soup.

Straight shoulders, however, never got anybody the part: another actor was engaged, so back to short wig and prompt-corner Deutsch, while Harold put away for ever his lightning sketch of a thunder-struck choir-boy.

I studied in my room too. And when I woke on a sunny morning and saw the two stone heads across the street with above them the crisp New York sky, I imagined the trumpets blowing unheard music, for me. I liked my life.

But there were the Sundays to face.

Sunday afternoon could be tolerable, and I would force myself to tramp in Central Park, past the boulders and the coaxed greenery and the incongruous statues of Burns and Byron: then along a cinder-path skirting the reservoir sealed off behind wire like a concentration-lake. Once or twice I wandered way downtown as far as the Battery, a walk into echoing tunnels of streets and along sunlit Wall Street, deserted as if its moneyed minions had run for their lives.

The evenings were different. The Sunday after my first escape to Philadelphia, I sat on my bed. 7.25 came, the week-day moment when I set out for work. No movie tempted me; I would start Schiller's *William Tell* . . .

7.45. On the black oblong of uncurtained window I saw the gleam of rain, and the feeling of being alone darkened into loneliness.

Since 7.25, my room had changed: the white of the walls was ribbed with shadows, my good suit drooped from its hanger. The house felt empty. Against the rumble of the El and the patter of rain I saw the dark plains stretching west to the Pacific, and to the east the Atlantic wastes separating me for ever from everything I had known. I must get out.

Then I remembered something in New York which Pierre my French count had boasted of: 'London, mon cher, is *nothing* compared to it . . .'

I swung my feet off the bed, pulled on my raincoat and hurtled down into the drizzle over to Madison Square and up Broadway. At 28th I turned left, into the Everard Turkish Baths.

* * *

Up some stairs, at a desk, an ashen bored man in shirtsleeves produced a ledger crammed with illegible scrawls. I added mine, paid my dollar, was handed key, towel and robe, hung the key on my wrist and mounted to a large floor as big as a warehouse and as high: intersecting rows of 'private rooms', each a windowless cell dark except from a glimmer from above, through wire-netting shredded with dust and containing a narrow workhouse bed.

I took off my clothes, hung them up, pulled on the robe—threadbare cotton, with a scrap of cotton to tie round the waist—and strolled down my passage to a large frosted window glowing faintly from the street-lamp below. By its eerie light I saw that passages not only led crossways but girded the area in a never-ending circle; along these padded noiselessly a slow perpetual two-way procession of white-faced, white-draped ghosts, the white so washed out that it was grey.

They could have been in skimpy Roman togas, and gave the effect of a sedate orgy. Was my bed-sitter only a few blocks away?

On and on they trudged, the nameless and the faceless, past one cell door after another, each behaving as if alone and with eyes anywhere but on another walker: on and on, inhaling from cigarettes which made a stealthy zig-zag of fireflies.

The air was heavy with decorum. No ghost spoke, each isolated in a personal trance on a timeless treadmill of solitude; it would have looked right if one of them had glided past carrying his head in one hand, with between the drained lips a glowing cigarette. Now and again a phantom stopped outside a locked door and with no more shame than a man on a beach with a sea-shell, put his ear to the plywood and listened intently.

Another would stop at a door which was ajar, give it a gentle push and peer inside; he might then either slide noiselessly in and click the door shut, or move on. When the latter happened, it was impossible to tell whether he was rejecting or had been rejected, for each slid back into the treadmill with the same empty eyes focused past the walkers approaching him.

Occasionally a ghost would sway or totter or hiccup. Very faintly, from the canteen downstairs, there wafted a crooning mother voice: 'When the moon comes over the Mountain...'. Kate Smith, on the radio. Then Al Jolson, stridently on the brink of tears: 'Climb up on my knee, Sonny Boy...'

I returned to my cubicle, left my door ajar, and lay down.

In a tawdry temple of the body, in which I was as conscious of my own as of everybody else's, I felt at the same time disembodied—as if hovering just below the wire-netting over my head, looking down at my silhouette and at the half-open door, listening.

The ghosts flitted soundlessly by. Then I would catch the glimmer of a firefly as it stopped, hesitated, then moved on; I was in the discreetest dormitory that ever lacked a matron.

But as I listened, the silence became interwoven with sounds from the surrounding metropolitan haven of the randy male, of the drunken, the frustrated, the lonely. Undertones like shapes waving in muddy water: the scrape of a match, the bold click of a bolt, a cough, the rustle of cotton falling,

There would come a casual whisper, a sigh lighter than thistledown, a smothered moan. Then appeasement: the snap of a lighter as two strangers sat back for a smoke and polite murmured small-talk, such as they might exchange in a gym after a work-out which has done something for them both.

In between, the rude clump of unsteady feet, the slam of a door, the squeak of rusty springs as a body flopped heavily down and a shoe thudded to the bare boards. From another direction the same defiant slam, this time from a departing customer, followed by a purposeful stride along the passage, to a nonchalant whistle.

He was easy to envisage: Roman apparition transformed into business-man—hat, overcoat with velvet collar, spats, brief-case— to be seen on weekday evenings in his hundreds on the sidewalks, hailing a taxi to take him to Grand Central and home to his wife in Westchester County.

Once, from the next cubicle, a choking cry as if somebody were being strangled. I felt a twinge of alarm, it was not an impossibility ...

But the horrific is two-faced, and you never know the minute when it will spin round and flash the comic grin. Across the noise, a hoarse 'ouch'.

The strangling stopped, then turned into a genteel voice, putting a question which might be asked of a dentist by a courteous patient, or of a victim by a solicitous suburban Dracula.

'Pardon me, are my teeth botherin' you?'

✻   ✻   ✻

Next morning I was awakened by the sun streaming in past the stone trumpets, tackled the compounds of a new verb and changed my library book. I spent the following weekend with Aunt Olive and Aunt Ada.

From Miss Cooke. 'I'm sending you a box of Flintshire earth & moss with some snowdrops in it. Don't forget to tell me what a speakeasy is...'

I wrote back: 'They're all on the table in front of me.'

They were, except for the snowdrops, which had arrived—predictably—as dead as the nails in the box. But the earth and the moss became every day more part of the room.

Long before any news percolates to the cast of any running show, the wardrobe mistress and the scene-shifters know its future. 'Mr Lee,' Mrs Shepherd announced, 'plans to close you folks in May.'

I pulled up my typewriter. 'Dear Mr Shubert, I assume you have many plans for New York and the road. It occurs to me that...' I checked the letter through and it was lucky I did: 'I assume you have many plans for Jew York.' I retyped.

Sealing, I wondered if this might lead to three years on the road in *The Student Prince,* hoisting a beer-mug and being extolled by Mrs Shepherd for polishing my buttons Nightly and on both Mats.

My second thought was that there was as little chance of the letter reaching Mr Lee as if I had mailed it down a drain. The second was the right one. I never heard.

'Dear Miss Cooke, Enclosed a cheque from the richest man in America, for £30 15s. 1d., a strange sum the equivalent of $150. Since I owed you £30, the 15 shillings can be counted as interest. I'm tackling *Wilhelm Meister.*'

One Philadelphia Sunday a friend of Olive's told me her cousin was a movie executive. I thought no more of it until I received a note, with at the top PARAMOUNT PICTURES, asking me to come up for an interview next day.

'Up' was right, for his office was on the thirty-somethingth floor of the Paramount Building, my celluloid palace on Times Square.

Walking up Broadway with my eyes fixed on the palace, in my good suit and with hair redolent of shampoo, I day-dreamed. Name the film star who was not spotted by a talent-scout with initiative . . .

When spotted, what image would I project?

At that time a young male film star had to have sex-appeal—a phrase not yet in current use—but it disguised itself as spirituality: straight nose, dimpled chin, melting eyes. John Barrymore. The idea that a young man could become a star through 'ugly' parts—gangsters, drunks, heartless opportunists—was untenable; such freaks hovered, out of focus behind the romantic profile, threatening it with a series of silent snarls.

No, I will break the mould as a new sort of star, male and muscular like Nijinsky, yet with a brooding sensitivity in eyes and mouth. With a face sad and yet funny; all over the world I am loved as much as Chaplin: a faun-poet. At the studio too I am adored—a real guy, gee!—though I live in lone simplicity in a vast mansion with high walls, patio and swimming pool.

Sex? Not on the screen, for there the subject is as yet only hinted at by brisk overcrowded orgies where, before you can tell the men from the girls, you are whisked to a sub-title: where extras flirt with grapes, laughing mutely and immoderately or twitching to show their navels while contriving to look over-dressed.

No, we mean sex in the Star's private life. The fan magazines give away nothing, and sitting by his pool he is impenetrable. A heart-breaker . . .

By this time I was in the Paramount Building, shooting up in one of the dozen elevators, but not conscious of rising since I was doing my own levitation.

A lady ushered me into an office as palatial as downstairs. From behind his desk, Mr van Steur Junior was friendly and asked appropriate questions: 'How's dear old London Town?'

The phone rang, and into it he asked appropriate questions, about ratings and circuits and blockbusters. He was an important executive in the distribution department of the Paramount empire. For anyone bent on Hollywood, an interview with him was like hoping to get into Heaven via a chatty three minutes with St Peter's barber. We shook cordial hands, I stepped into an elevator and zoomed to earth. In every sense.

But I had enjoyed lounging by my swimming pool in the sun, famous, loved and totally unspoilt. And there was a nice smell of shampoo.

*　　*　　*

Walking up Broadway for the Easter Monday matinée, April the 9th—I had been on the stage a year—I sniffed the spring, and in the sun the sky-signs looked frowsty. As I turned into the baking alley beside the theatre, I felt a prickle of homesickness, and slaking my thirst at the water-cooler I decided to seek no more jobs in America: I had felt at home but it could never become my home.

On my last Saturday morning I went to my bank and drew out my savings: nine hundred and fifty dollars—a hundred and ninety pounds plus two per cent interest.

Our last performance—the 205th—was enlivened by our two doxies. When I announced them onstage they were still in their dressing-rooms packing, and I had no choice but to improvise to my master that his visitors were hanging their cloaks and would be with him immediately.

Pleased with myself I strode on: 'Sir, the ladies will be with you betimes, they are removing their clothes.'

There was a flurried movement on the other side of the stage as two dishevelled Restoration beauties sailed into the Pepys drawing-room, one after the other, skirts billowing, from inside the huge fireplace.

'This,' said the host with a bow, 'is an unexpected pleasure.' Nobody laughed. The audience must have hazily thought, we love these quaint old British customs but *down the chimney*?

At the end, the farewells which are the occupational fleeting heartaches of the theatre. 'Waal,' drawled Speedy the electrician —and he really did say 'Waal' as he put out a drowsy paw— 'Waal, I guess after eight months i' the States ya'll find 'em kinda *slow*, huh?'

And next morning I said goodbye to my room; literally, for I turned at the door and looked round it. I had spent longer alone here than anywhere in my life.

The giant *Aquitania* meant five days of nothing; watching the ship forge towards my future, I began to chart it. A play. Not a thriller, and about real people ...

In the Southampton boat-train I counted that I had been in the New World for eight months. I may have been a hundred per cent Welsh, but this was home too: from the train window, tiny green fields, tiny trees, tiny winding roads.

The ticket collector seemed over-polite and pernicketty— 'Thenk yew . . .'—and waited while each passenger searched leisurely for his ticket. Speedy had been right. Life *was* slower.

CHAPTER FIVE

PERFECTLY WILLING TO TOUR

As when I had walked out of 314a last year, I arrived rootless in London and once more the family of my Oxford friend Campbell Hackforth-Jones were putters-up in need: his stockbroker brother Oliver and his wife had offered me their spare room for a week.

Emerging from the Tube for Belsize Avenue I watched a red bus shoot past. I was home.

They took me to the new Coward revue *This Year of Grace*, which was 'sweeping the town'—it certainly swept me—then on to 'a spot of grub' at the Kit Kat, still the smartest night club. The band played 'Dance Little Lady'. 'More bubbly?'

While Oliver and Trixie danced I sat alone and let the champagne and the music throb to my head, enjoying myself and yet not: the only reason for my being here should be my success and my hosts' pride in the discreet glances at their table.

The solution would be my new play, sweeping the town. Watching the couples revolve with mechanical abandon, I made my lips form words they might be saying: true, funny, moving, you *must* go . . .

I looked down at my hand holding the glass, and moved my other hand to it. As if performing a rite I gripped the skin below the knuckles, between finger and thumb, and squeezed with all my strength. It felt like a red-hot skewer as I said aloud, 'It will be written.' Next morning, I puzzled over a small blue bruise.

The days were more practical. I bought *Dalton's Weekly* (*And Boarding House Guide*), went in search of a Room Vacant Unfurnished, and at the end of a fourth day's tramping found what I was after, an address which, at the head of a letter, would do wonders for a jobless actor: 34 Vincent Square, Westminster, S.W.1.

A beautiful Square it was too, though it defied geometry by

presenting four unequal sides: they see-sawed between grandeur
and near-slum.

Number 34 had been a handsome little house, but it had fallen
on times bad without being evil; the lobby and stairs were dark
from age-old distemper and the 'bathroom' was an outhouse
including among its lumber a zinc bath blotched with every shade
of rust, some of it bitten in deep enough to skin the occupant.
There was also a bad-tempered-looking geyser with unpredicta-
bility written all over it, in stains.

My room, top-floor-back, fifteen shillings a week, overlooked a
mason's yard with, beyond, the murmur of traffic in Vauxhall
Bridge Road. My first essential was a telephone, for which I
would have to wait three weeks. I decided not to look for work
until I had writing paper with the vital number on it, and to spend
the time settling in.

The first day I walked to Pimlico, studied second-hand furniture out on pavements and bought a single divan with its legs in
the air, a table and a sagging armchair. From Woolworth's I got
cups and saucers, curtain rings and two yards of cotton bright
with cherries to be made up by Campbell's sister.

By Monday evening I had unpacked the artificial daffodils and
was installed in my first London home; at six I heard Big Ben
half a mile away and wondered if Dad was sitting at his crystal
set with his earphones on, listening too. I missed my family.

I had forgotten bedclothes, but it was nearly June and I had
my overcoat. The feeble gas threw a jumpy quarter-light on to
the naked window: I must buy an Aladdin oil-lamp.

It was a chilly night and my home looked hideous. I scissored
up under the overcoat and felt like a pioneer.

❄   ❄   ❄

From Miss Cooke: 'You've saved £190, hurrah. Now here's my
idea. For you to open an acct at my Midland Bank here in Holywell & arrange to cash small cheques on it thru a bank in yr
vicinity.' I guessed that after my Oxford lapse into extravagance
she wanted to see it didn't happen again. I agreed.

I was to be on nodding terms with the Irish couple on the first
floor, and less than that with elderly Mrs Mellowfield, ground-
floor-back, described by the landlord as 'a refined lady'. To me she

was a ghost on the landing, with grey dank hair and a grey dank face who looked through me as if I were calling on somebody.

It was different with my neighbour in the top-front room. Mr Higley—I never dropped the Mr—was a large bald widower, fifty, florid and overflowing, who had been a singer of small solid repute and now gave private lessons. In his shirt-sleeves and big hobnailed boots he looked like a country publican, though he boomed in the effortless accents of what he called 'a decayed gentleman'.

'Suffice it to say that though my voice was never my fortune it has given me unalloyed pleasure which I am willing to share with any stranger, fifteen bob per hour. You see before you, my dear Williams, a whore with a bass voice.'

An austere whore; my room was fanciful compared with his, which had neither curtain-ring, rug nor book. His quarters were as spotless as any old salt's, at least what was visible: in the middle of the floor were two battered chairs, a battered upright, a concertinaed camp-bed and a primus stove, all in a huddle as if banded together for a losing battle against the enemy closing in. A cohort of canvases. There was a sharp invigorating smell which I could not place.

'I collect pictures,' Mr Higley informed me with the modest pride of a Duveen. 'I've done it for donkey's years.'

I was impressed. 'Where do you track them down, Christie's?'

He guffawed as if Christie was a pawnbroker. 'Good lord, no, the Caledonian Market!' I had never heard of it. 'Tuesdays and Fridays, I'll take you.'

His unframed treasures were stacked against the walls like paving stones; I knelt and turned some over.

There were landscapes, seascapes, fruit, fish, cherubim cloud-borne, satyrs earth-bound, haloed saints and bewigged burgo-masters. All had in common cracks, holes and dirt; several were so smoky that I could not tell whether I was faced with a Madonna and Child or a brace of dead pheasants.

'I clean 'em myself as I go along.' The table was laden with rags and bottles; the nice smell was turpentine.

'Just finished this chappie.' The chappie was a disembowelled ox. 'Ripping detail, what? Look at that entrail . . .'

His prize was on an easel, obscuring fireplace and mantelpiece: a huge hip-length painting of a gleefully naked ringleted youth brandishing an enormous gory head with rolling eyes. 'David and Goliath,' he said reverently, 'a Tintoretto if not a Rubens, look at that matted hair. I'm having it looked at next week.'

Had I pitched my tent on the threshold of a gold-mine?

Every day I acquired something new. First the Aladdin lamp, and its rosy evening light was a vast improvement. One morning my score of books arrived from 314a; from the shelf I had nailed up, the spines of my school prizes looked down like familiar faces.

Another day, from Miss Cooke, an etching of Rheims Cathedral, 'a man called at the school selling art'. When I told Mr Higley I would have it framed he looked taken aback, as if I had suggested the same treatment for a bath-mat.

Next day I unpacked an enormous biscuit tin, again from Miss Cooke, with a hasty scrawl KEEP YOU GOING FOR A BIT. She was not confining herself to my spiritual needs; it was full to the brim with Welsh honey.

On Tuesdays and Fridays I took the Tube to North London with Mr Higley: the Caledonian Market. Radiating from a clock tower, a vast area of lanes offered stalls selling everything: suites of furniture, books, pictures, ornaments, kitchen stuff, food—for the bargain hunter it was a Cockney paradise.

From each visit, for shillings or even for pence, I brought home a haul: towels, blue tasselled cover for the divan, oblong mirror, red paisley square for the wall, two candlesticks, a pile of shabby little leather-bound volumes of Corneille, 1744, a shilling; 'Come back, son, ye can 'ave the lot for a tanner . . .'

We would stagger down into the Tube, laden to the eyes. Then, exhausted over mugs of tea—he had no cups—we shared bread and honey while he cleaned a corner of today's canvas. 'By Jove, what have we here, a female bum? An Etty d'you suppose?' At such moments he was much younger than me.

* * *

Sitting with Oliver and Trixie, I told them that as soon as I was settled I would be writing to managers for appointments.

'Good egg,' Oliver said, 'what'll you wear?'

'That best suit you gave me last year, it's as good as new.' I did know one axiom which applied in those days: that for an actor to get work, he had to look as if he was *in* work.

'You might consider a couple of touches to smarten you up. With your suit, what'd be wrong with gloves and an umbrella rolled good and tight and a bowler?'

I looked at him as if he had suggested a bishop's mitre. 'I've never worn a hat in my life!'

'Start now.'

I did, and when I put on my good suit and the bowler and swung my brolly for Mr Higley he was impressed. 'Ye gods and little fishes, Williams, you've turned into a swell!'

He did agree, though, that I looked like the office boy dressed as the boss. I was ready for action.

In the meantime I worked hard to improve my room. I had my ups and downs: scrupulous in menial tasks such as washing-up and scrubbing the floor, at anything demanding skill I was inept.

Having varnished my peeling door a brown which looked like running treacle, I turned to the walls; I dragged the divan into the middle of the room, covered it with newspaper and borrowed a ladder from the landlord.

He seemed gratified to have acquired a model tenant; ''Ow's that rubbish of 'is in the front?'

I bought a brush and yellow distemper. As well as the walls, I must do the ceiling; climbing the ladder I heard the voice of Mr Higley's regular pupil, a powerful contralto whom he was accompanying in their favourite class piece, from 'Samson et Dalila'. I hummed with her, 'Softly Awakes . . . My Heart . . .' I did not hum long.

Walls are tiring to paint, but ceilings, as Michelangelo could have told me, are hell.

After five minutes I had a crick in the neck, I was dizzy, my hair was sprinkled with brown and my face filthy with a mixture of dust and sweat.

Worse, the distemper was not behaving. Instead of what they showed in the ads—one long stroke merging gracefully into the next—all I could achieve was a series of dabs and jabs which looked as if a flying dog had dipped his tail in the bucket, soared to the ceiling and swished the tail; by comparison the sallow walls looked immaculate. I had ruined my first home.

I climbed down, lay on the newspapers on the divan and heard Mr Higley's creak. 'Spot of painting? Mmm? Clever the stippled effect.' And he was gone.

It was not the moment for sarcasm. I looked up at the ceiling, and blinked. From this distance primrose yellow, superimposed irregularly on sober brown and merging into it, made for a deliberately haphazard effect. It looked . . . clever.

I stumbled up the ladder, sloshed away and finished as the light went. When the distemper had dried, the effect was even better; the room looked joyously vernal. The stippler's work was done.

I was less fortunate with my cooking. Able to make a pot of tea and boil an egg, I decided that given a gas-ring and a box of Quaker Oats with printed instructions, I could hardly go wrong.

I could. Even Mr Higley could not persuade himself that a mass of grey glue, speckled with dots and tasting of ashes, was an ingenious Welsh dish.

'Your talents, my dear Williams, appear to reside elsewhere.' I would stick to cornflakes.

Another failure was window-dressing. In the Square I had spotted geraniums on the ledge of a top floor. Next Market day I invested in four pots, bought wire netting, nailed it round my ledge and arranged them within the barricades. For a whole day, they brightened my window.

But in my spotting, I had missed one detail: the pots had been skewered down. Next morning, out of the blue, a high wind.

I was not in time to get to my geraniums before they were seized by an invisible hand and hurtled down into the basement, next to old Mrs Mellowfield. I settled for artificial daffodils. Indoors.

*   *   *

One June morning two secret agents materialized at last and installed the telephone, an operation to me as weird as table-turning; they stood it on my desk, receiver on hook, just as I had seen it on the stage.

I looked round my room. Though it was rough and ready it was mine, and colourful: all I wanted now was work.

'What beats me, Williams,' Mr Higley said, 'is how you actor chaps set about landing engagements.' It sounded like deep-sea fishing.

I looked at VICTORIA 9924 on my writing paper and started to type. 'Dear Mr Basil Dean, I have just returned from Broadway where I have been playing in *And So To Bed* and am now available.'

I did not mention *Full Moon* in case it made me sound like a playwright dabbling in acting. As well as to Mr Dean, the letter went to dear Mr Nettlefold, dear Mr Prinsep, dear Mr Clift, dear Mr Limpus, dear Mr Rea . . .

An alternative series represented the second string to my twanging bow: addressed to touring managers, they offered me— strictly for a leading part—to dear Mr Barry O'Brien, dear Mr Fortescue, dear Mr Brinkerman.

The first paragraph—'I have just returned . . .'—stayed the same; then 'though I would prefer to stay in town' (did I not have a town house, in Vincent Square, Westminster?) 'I would consent'—no, too grand—'I would be perfectly willing to tour in *Young Woodley*, in the Robert Haslam part in *Thunder in the Air*, in the Henry Kendall part in *The Silent House* . . .'

Fifteen letters, posted before six.

Next morning was a Market one, but I told Mr Higley I had to stay home for a couple of calls. By ten, offices were open and by a quarter past I was shaved, bathed and combed: behind the door, the bowler hat was dangling at the ready. I got into my old trousers and did my weekly clean-out, with an occasional glance at the telephone, perched like a blackbird with its beak inquiringly in the air.

Eleven. Twelve. Twelve-thirty. I made my first telephone call: to Inquiries, was my line out of order? Thirty seconds later I received my first call. A cold voice assured me that my phone was working perfectly.

Mid-afternoon, my second call. A wrong number.

After that, five days of perfect peace. I stared at the phone, and with its large single black eye the phone stared at me: a maimed bird with a single ebony wing. And dumb.

Miss Cooke was a weekly tonic. 'Just been listening to Julian Huxley whose flat voice makes me shudder, the voice of an offspring of a crocodile and a porcupine. Talk talk talk, sometimes when I hear a lot of bunkum I want to go into the garden and *dig* . . .

'But Pax . . . There's talk of starting a hostel in H'well for pupils living 5 miles off & over, I've advised no, my hat fancy *you* in a hostel aged 11! Any poor home, I say (not any *bad* h.) is better than a gd hostel . . .'

July. I was glad of Mr Higley—more than twice my age—an impoverished outsize cricket. I was grateful for the hobnailed boots on the landing, even for the moments when 'Pale Hands I Loved' battered at the frail walls as if to get out of the booming little room and into the open.

Then his voice would resound at my door: 'Williams, may I shout the praises of my prize contralto, Miss Edgeley?' He put me in mind of Miss Cooke.

Once, 'Silly old rhyme's been running through my head all day . . .' Then a clarion call, in a pious curate's voice: 'Uncle John and Auntie Mabel, Fainted at the breakfast table, And that—my children—is a warning, *Not* to do it in the morning!' I had heard the poem at Oxford, at one of my less intellectual conversaziones, but it cheered me up.

I took up German again, Thomas Mann's *Tonio Kröger*; it was tough going and I welcomed it. 'I would be perfectly willing to tour in the Jack Hobbs part in *The Fourth Wall* . . .'

With August, I lowered my sights by proffering my services not direct to managers, but to agents: Vincent Erne, Akerman May, Denton and Warner.

One or two gave me a quick interview; even when I was possible for a leading part I had 'no touring experience', and also there was always the actor who had toured in parts created by the London actor of the part in question. And to go on a long tour in a small part and understudy was a backward step I refused to contemplate.

Not yet. The bowler began to look jaded; I brushed the dust off and laid it away with the gloves and the umbrella. Perhaps they would all come in useful for a wet funeral.

At last, something.

* * *

'Come and see me 12 noon Wed; Miriam Warner Agency.'

She did mostly tours, but so long as it was a leading part . . . At eleven I emerged in my bowler, with brolly and gloves carelessly carried and in a pocket, a shoe-rag. It was a hot day and as I sauntered up Whitehall, a possible Foreign Office type, the bowler was a vice across my brows.

In Gerrard Street I bent down, gave my shoes a flick with the rag and entered a shabby outer office, impersonal despite the yellowing photographs of actors and actresses beaming their

thanks at Miss Warner for having over the years accepted ten
per cent of their salaries: 'to Miriam without whom . . .'

The room bulged with the presence of four young men sitting
as if at the dentist's; all were tall, all handsome. One wore plus-
fours and a cap and smoked a pipe; the others were in dark
suits, with on their knees bowlers and between their knees
brollies. All were reading: two a morning paper, two the *Stage*.

They made four casual nods at me. I sat. I should have brought
reading matter. Thomas Mann would have drawn a couple of
looks; 'Oh, it's in German, actually . . .' Removing my bowler to
wipe my brow, I saw in the mirror a scarlet weal, like an Indian
caste-mark.

The inner door opened; Miss Warner was large, swarthy and
forbidding. The first dummy followed her in. They all in turn got
three minutes and in turn left, then I was absently beckoned.

She was holding my letter and—I felt—my future. She looked
like a second-hand clothes dealer who has been left a legacy.
But she spelt work.

'What did you do before the Oxford Players?'

'I had a lot of experience with the Ouds.'

I knew I should have given her the mouthful 'The Oxford
University Dramatic Society' but somehow came out with the
usual abbreviation, rhyming with 'clouds'. Not unexpectedly she
said, 'The *what*?' I gave her the mouthful. 'But,' she said, 'aren't
they amateur?' Then she added, even more accusingly, 'You're not
full height, are you?'

I went red, as if I had been caught in the act. 'Five foot eight
and a half.' I threw in the half.

'Can you play Dicky Bird parts?'

I was lost, thinking for a second, can I chirp? Twitter? She
meant Richard Bird, a leading London actor. Not full height.

'Can you play'—Miss Warner pursued, as if testing me about
a card game—'can you play Hysterical Scenes?'

My face cleared: 'Oh, yes!'

'Then call at Drury Lane stage door three tomorrow, take this
card.'

I walked out with a flourish of my umbrella as I recalled Bird's
successes; both *Havoc* and *The Ghost Train* had been toured to
death, he himself was in America. Could it be . . . that rehearsals
for a new West End play were being held up because they were

desperately looking for a young actor to play 'the Dicky Bird part'? The following afternoon, as I approached Drury Lane Theatre, the Mecca of the profession, the air seemed fresher and the bowler lighter.

I thought, there's an extra matinée: the pavement was jammed with a queue, three deep. It led, though, not to pit or gallery but to the stage door, and consisted of young men. There were many bowlers, and as I took my place I was joined by one more, higher up than mine. We all looked as if war had been declared and this was Recruiting Day.

Recruiting, for a new Dicky Bird? I turned to my companion and tried to sound light. 'What would you say we're here for?'

'Oh, one of those general calls, they're casting the juveniles in umpteen tours and this is weeding-out day. I've just done two years' hard labour, rep in York, where have you been?'

I gave my answer before realizing the snobbery of it. 'New York,' I said. The conversation wilted.

As the queue shuffled on I caught drifts of talk from front and back. 'Found two years in Nanette a weeny bit much by the time we got to the split weeks . . .'

Gradually we changed from patriotic recruits to helpless humanity on the slow boat to extermination. Comic accents flourished; 'All I sez is, 'e bitched the part oop proper, 'e did an' all . . .' We filed past a poster, SHOW BOAT THE SUCCESS OF LONDON, then past the photographs of the stars, flashing successful smiles. How had they ever got their first job?

Shuffle, shuffle; half a yard, half a yard onward, in their Sunday-best, inched the Six Hundred. But we were less a Brigade than a chain-gang: instead of picks, umbrellas. The doorkeeper could not be bothered to glance up from his paper at a procession of stage-struck rubbish.

'As for Manchester, Mrs Mort in Ackers Street's gone right off, won't do lunches and tends to lock up the bathroom . . .'

We were descending a passage, stairs which were nightly being bounded up and down by working actors, as I had once bounded.

Shuffle. 'Brighton to Aberdeen in one Sunday, what do they think we are, cattle?'

My bowler weighed a ton. By now we were on the stage. The curtain was down, the furniture under sheets and the scenery dismantled; the working light far above made us all look more than ever like a throng of convicts disguised as prosperous young stockbrokers.

Was it possible that in less than six hours music would waft up behind that prison wall—that the stage would be flooded with light and the wall rise on grace and colour and song? 'Others Find ... Peace of Mind in ... Make-Believe ...' Where was it now? In the middle of the stage four or five long flat supports had been laid parallel along kitchen chairs, the arrangement farmers make for letting sheep through in single file. Beyond the gap, at a table with paper and pencils, an impassive wardress presided with on each side, at attention, an impassive warder. Behind me I heard, 'It's Ena Lovell, dear, she's the power behind Barry O'Brien's throne, the two others are queens, watch out ...'

The queue was moving through the improvised turnstile to a businesslike rhythm. Each actor got a quick glance from the six eyes, from head to foot and back again, then a couple of questions; as each approached the barrier he clicked on a bright look: I'm happy to consider an offer but it's all a lark really ...

I thought, they can have no pride. My turn came and I did exactly the same thing. Miss Lovell looked up from her list. 'Experience?'

'I was in *And So To Bed* in New York.'

She stared at me with raised eyebrows: I had overdone the insouciance and spoken so sloppily that she thought I had said, 'I go to bed in New York.' 'Thank you,' she said, and half a minute later I was in the Strand.

I footed it feverishly to Vincent Square and coaxed the geyser into giving me a hot bath. I must have obscurely felt like flushing the episode down the drain.

Mr Higley was once more a help, over tea, honey and turpentine, 'Luck o' the game, my dear Williams, early yet.'

In clean socks, a clean shirt and old flannels I walked to Shaftesbury Avenue and *Her Cardboard Lover*. Tallulah, Leslie Howard. My second queue in one day, but this was different.

'Dear Dad and Mam, I have been so busy with my room I haven't had time for my acting plans. But everything happens quickly in London, any day now things will be on the move ...'

I must write that play.

[71]

CHAPTER SIX

ON THE MOVE

Still smarting from *A Murder Has Been Arranged* on the *Carmania*, I was determined that this one would be 'all right'. But in order to prove its all-rightness, I had to get it on, in London.

I remembered Glen's advice, to start with a star in view. But I had already planned to provide a star part for an unknown—myself. I was becoming convinced that to succeed as an actor I must do just that; and to ensure acceptance with such a handicap, at least two of the other parts must be tailored for stars.

In a play 'about real people'? It would be a tricky venture. I ventured.

I would write of the two things I knew: Wales and the theatre backstage. A country boy and girl, brought up together, run away from Wales to seek their fortune: Jack and Jill, come to fetch a pail of golden London water.

They arrive at the home of Eve Lone, famous musical-comedy star: a flat over the Leicester Square Theatre. (An invented name, I was anticipating.) She herself ran away from Wales to go on the stage, and Jill—her niece—longs for the same career.

I was conscious of the source: my favourite childhood novel *A Welsh Singer*. But all writers are influenced by what they have read ...

I kept to my resolution. I took my time, I examined, I was tough with myself, I imagined reading it out slowly to a cabinful of managers.

After four weeks of steady work done at a normal temperature —in between excursions in pursuit of tours of *The Ringer, Interference, The Trial of Mary Dugan*—the play was finished. One set, seven characters. I revised, cut—really cut, timing each act—and again turned professional typist.

The title? A word which was not then the debased coinage it would become: *Glamour*. It looked good.

Halfway through I was prodded back into being the hopeful actor by a note to call at the Arts Theatre Club, which incorporated the Arts Theatre where Angela Baddeley was to star in an adaptation of Christopher Morley's *Thunder on the Left*. They were looking for 'somebody' to play Martin, the fey young hero.

Getting out bowler and brolly, I remembered Drury Lane. Queue Day . . . But at the Arts Theatre there was no queue, and in a tiny office I was welcomed by Mr Richard Pryce, the prim, polite little adaptor. 'Do take a pew.' My spirits rose.

'Forgive me,' he said from behind his desk, 'but can you cry?'

It was a puzzling question. 'Well, I've never tried. When I've cried it was because I had to.'

This sounded sissy so I added quickly, 'Which hasn't been often, of course.'

'I ask,' Mr Pryce went on, 'because the character has to burst into tears without giving an impression of weakness.'

This was an odd one. 'Well,' I said, 'I imagine it would be difficult for a man to burst into tears and give an impression of strength.'

Then I thought, don't be sarcastic or you'll lose the part, and gave a tentative smile to show I hadn't meant it.

'Quite,' he said amiably. 'What I mean, I suppose, is that it's the actor's problem to do it without seeming girlish. Would it be too much to ask to cry for me?'

I stared at him. 'Now?'

'Now.'

I felt as if he had asked me to take my trousers down. Except that I could have had a shot at that without being too girlish about it. I thought, here goes, nobody but him to see it and if he enjoys it, good luck.

I laid my bowler on his desk, and after making sure I wouldn't knock my umbrella over I gripped the arms of my chair, shut my eyes, concentrated, opened them, gave him a wide uncomprehending stare and burst into deep sobs.

I hoped they were deep. I hoped too that nobody would barge in. Slowly I placed my elbows on his desk and slowly my head fell to my knuckles, which muffled the sobs as they died away. I surreptitiously composed my face and raised it.

'Thank you,' said Mr Pryce, 'so much.' I left. The part was

played by Bramwell Fletcher, a blond Adonis for whom the engagement led to a career.

It was my first, and last, encounter with what was to be known as Method Acting. I did feel I should have been paid a token fee for my audition. Sobbing money?

I returned with relief to my typing. Gerald du Maurier, the top West End director, would give the play his own stamp and the part of Jill, having been written for the triumphant Constant Nymph of last year, would fit her like a glove: Edna Best. For the star's man-about-town lover—du Maurier might not want to play him as well as direct—the imperturbable charmer Ronald Squire; for the star's malicious society friend, high comedienne Ellis Jeffreys.

For Eve Lone, the star? Gladys Cooper. She was then forty and at the height of her fame and beauty; might she perhaps not quite warm to the idea of being presented as a faded actress of thirty-three? Not if the part were good enough. For the boy? Emlyn Williams. I had my cast. I delivered four copies, on foot —no bowler—at the offices of Messrs Basil Dean, Alec Rea, Alban Limpus, Herbert Jay.

Nothing happened.

After three weeks I had a brain-wave: to write to my ex-pupil 'Miss Megan Lloyd George, House of Commons, Westminster.' 'Gentilissima Miss Megan, I am sending you a play about due personnaggi di Wales...' She asked me to the House; during dinner we talked Welsh, which puzzled visitors at the next table. Bluff admirers from all parties stopped to have a bright word: are you paired dear lady see you in the tea-room...

Over coffee I suggested—not entirely as a joke—that she might rope in, from Tadda's rodeo, a stray millionaire who felt like a splurge; after all, didn't they refer to themselves as Liberal?

She laughed it off. 'Now, now caro Professore, I'll think about it...'

She wouldn't, for she was as alien from the theatre as I was from this club of jovial word-jugglers. After three weeks, my savings were dwindling.

Without warning, the phone relented: a call from John Fernald, my Ouds contemporary who had directed *Vigil*. His father had put him on to Sewell Collins, who was directing a new play at the Arts. John was to be stage-manager and there was a vacancy:

ASM and walking on. Three weeks' rehearsal—no pay, of course—then five perfs. at thirty shillings a perf. I had an offer. Through a friend's father's friend. Seven pounds ten spread over four weeks meant less than two pounds a week. God . . .

Better than Queue Day—except that *The Pocket-Money Husband* was a comedy thin to the point of attrition. One of my walk-on bits involved me, as a speechless playboy, in wearing my own white tie and tails, an expensive nuisance as they had been put away after Oxford and would have to be cleaned.

And there was time to brood over the fact that *Glamour* had elicited no reaction at all.

Except for one manager. He wrote that the play wasn't quite what he was looking for, but suggested sending it to Miss Tonie Edgar Bruce. Miss Bruce had not acted for some time, but might apparently be 'intrigued' by the part of a star who lives in a flat over a West End theatre, in view of the fact that she herself lived in a flat over a West End theatre, the Prince of Wales.

I did send her a script, wondering if I might arouse a flicker of interest in *A Murder Has Been Arranged* by advertising for an actor-manager who happened to be a millionaire through having killed a relative on stage.

*　　*　　*

At rehearsals I got talking to Betty Hardy, a small solemn girl with a comic face and saucer eyes behind thick glasses, who played a tiny part. Our unspoken ambitions made a bond.

After the first night, which had gone neither well nor badly, we had coffee at the Strand Corner House, Open All Night and a godsend to actors.

She talked excitedly about the theatre. 'Have you written anything since *Full Moon*?' I told her about *Glamour* and she asked to read it; I hesitated but she was sincerely interested and next morning I called at her digs with a copy.

After the second night, we went again to the Corner House. 'Oh, I like it. I've read it twice, Jack and Jill are warm and real . . . Who have you thought of for Jill?'

'Edna Best.'

'Oh.' A pause, then with tremulous insistence, 'I know I'm not pretty but I have got good legs and this thing with dialects and with your help I could do the Welsh on my head.' I did not know what to say. She was a potential personality but as much of a nobody as I was: 'I'd never get it on without a star ...'

'Well, now business. I have a godmother. If I found a new play with a leading part for me, she'd put up two hundred pounds to get it on.'

I looked at her, and under the shock my mind worked quickly: for a star part, is a pretty face essential? The play went to Lady Hawke.

Two days passed. I tried not to hope. On our last night Betty rushed in with a telegram. 'She's said yes!'

In the Corner House we talked for an hour. In the way of backing, even then two hundred pounds was not much, but with care it would get the play on for a couple of weeks' try-out, say at the Embassy, Swiss Cottage. Betty's agent, Vera Brunt, was now secretary to C. B. Williams, a manager who, she was sure, would take the play; he was Welsh too.

That night I opened the play for the first time since finishing it. It was going to be done ... In that room where I seemed to have waited so long, I felt a wave of delirium.

The curtain rises in darkness, but in the immense window at back, a city's million electric bulbs have melted into one restless glow ... In the window-seat, EVE *sits motionless, listening. Far down, music plays, thinly and sweetly.*

ONSLOW: What is that?
EVE: The little man entertaining the queues.
ONSLOW: What are you thinking about?
EVE: A crooked old house far from anywhere, in Wales. A house hung between the mountains and the sea ...

From the corner of my mind a whisper. 'Sentimental?'

'If it is,' I answered myself, 'then all homesickness is. Anyway, it's an unusual opening.' For that time, it was. Then I looked at the arrival of the country cousins ... '*It is as if the walls of a dark house had been raised, letting in windy sunshine ...*' It was going to be done. I slept well.

'My dear Son George, Many thanks for your piece of news that you have found an acceptor for one of your plays, *splendid ...*'

John Fernald, at lunch, was impressed. 'It's going to be *done?*

Well, I knew you'd make it . . . Me? Stage-managing again, Sunday
show, help me with these props will you?'

I took his other parcel and in Poland Street, Soho, I followed
him up to the usual bleak rehearsal room. At the far end two
actors were at work on a death scene; one knelt on the dusty
floor, while the other sprawled awkwardly on three kitchen
chairs.

'Interesting play,' John said loyally, 'but too special for week-
days, they always are, damn it—but I'm glad about you, good
luck!' I felt sorry for him.

Things advanced. 'Dear Dad and Mam, I am just going up to
Mr C. B. Williams' office in the West End, I have a feeling his
name will bring me double luck, he being Williams and having
the same initials as C. B. Cochran.'

I enjoyed walking up the Avenue to Number 62 and looking
forward to plush carpets and prints on the walls. It was only
when I started to climb the narrow stairs that I sniffed a possibility: while Mr Williams' address was indeed in the West End,
he need not be a West End manager.

The office was a small back room and Mr Williams was older
than I expected, wore pince-nez and looked like an unworldly
Welsh deacon, while Miss Brunt was a blonde as hard as her
name. 'We've got to watch the pennies . . .'

There were posters of C. B. Williams productions, small-town
tours of old musical plays I had never heard of: those initials
were the only thing he had in common with Mr Cochran. Plans
were formulated, for a week out of town and then two at the
Embassy. Mr Williams liked the play so much he would direct it.

It was now that I first encountered a unique British institution
which, for an adventurous dramatist writing before 1967, had the
power to make itself a nuisance and even an enemy.

I saw Miss Brunt slipping one of my scripts into an envelope
and then grimly addressing it.

'Censor's copy,' she said, 'for the Lord Chamberlain's Office.
If you won't cut out the Christs and the bloody-hells bang goes
your bloody licence. Anyway you can thank your stars you
haven't got any Prisoners of War in it.'

This was the name of a play 'with homosexual undertones'
which had been allowed for one Sunday evening, the Lord
Chamberlain's rule being to relegate such themes—presumably

by arrangement with God—to the Sabbath. Which meant that on any Sunday, before club audiences, young men could look into each other's eyes, tell each other what they were going through about each other, and next day find themselves in a hushed *Times* review instead of in Wormwood Scrubs. I didn't even have a Christ or a bloody-hell, but I resented losing my script.

'Dear Dad and Mam, Miss Mary Dibley will play the star, I used to see her in films at the Hip, she is a little older but still beautiful.'

Her man-about-town would be Harold Anstruther, who had played small parts in the West End. The only acting salary I knew was my own, five pounds a week, and I imagined the others were not much higher. There would be no understudies; perhaps a crystal-gazer had been consulted, at a reduced fee, who had given the cast a clean bill of health.

It was clear too that the author, like the actor he had been in the summer, had lowered his sights: of the names he had visual-ized—Edna Best, Gladys Cooper, du Maurier, Ronald Squire, Ellis Jeffreys, Emlyn Williams—only the last seemed to be avail-able.

* * *

John Fernald rang: would I like to go to a party tomorrow night, Saturday? It seemed an ideal way to celebrate, and we took a 39 bus to Tite Street.

It was all a Chelsea party should be, a free-and-easy mixture of stage, art and music and given by Dorice Fordred, a South African character actress who had played last year in *King Lear* for the Ouds when John was President. She introduced me to Polly Heseltine, a mature pretty young woman with a coquettish half-veil at variance with a direct manner, and left me with her.

'I know what you're thinking, that this veil's a mistake. Well, it is, I look like an unsuccessful tart trying to pass as a lady.'

I was tickled, and asked if her name was Mary.

'No, why?' I told her my mother's name was Mary and that my father had always called her Polly.

'That's funny, my younger sister's name is Mary and my father called her Molly.' She gurgled suddenly, and again I was amused.

[78]

I asked her if she was South African too: no, she had gone out in a show. I was immediately caught. 'What was it?'

'I played Polly in *Polly*!'

'Polly playing Polly in *Polly*?'

'I met my husband on a boat out there, he was an orange farmer and I left the show to get married and he insisted on calling me Polly and it's stuck, my sister didn't like it a bit, Polly and Molly, it was a bit hard on her.'

I asked what her real name was. 'Dorothy Shann,' she added, sipping her drink. 'Oh, this damn veil—but when Mother put us on the stage she decided O'Shann sounded more winning and that was it.' I asked if they were Irish. 'Not as Irish as we said we were. Birmingham really, our grandmother was a gypsy but tell me about you.'

The mixture of poise, spontaneity and self-mockery was attractive. 'You've got a play coming on, but how exciting! We've got some people in for drinks Tuesday, will you come ...?'

On my walk back to Vincent Square I thought, yes it is exciting ... Tuesday at 6.30 I presented myself at the flat in Mallord Street, Chelsea.

Darkness inside, no voices; I rang the bell. A light came on, the door opened an inch or two; inside, Tchaikovsky on the gramophone.

Without her hat, with hair untidy and wearing a sort of housecoat and slippers, Polly was hard to recognize. She found me hard to recognize too.

'Oh, my God, it's Mr Williams. We had to make the party last night instead, how awful...'

'It doesn't matter a bit. I'm so sorry, bye, bye...'

'No, no, it's just Sonny and me and he'd love to meet you, please...'

Sonny? A red-necked Afrikaans farmer who had called an actress by the name of her part and then stopped her playing it...

I entered the sitting-room, beautifully furnished with what even I could tell were carelessly genuine antiques. The same wall-to-wall carpets as at the Philadelphia Harts'; thick lined curtains to the floor, and each window—to me the seal on a sophisticated room—crowned with a scalloped pelmet; over the mantelpiece, a painting which Mr Higley would have given his David and Goliath for.

Standing in front of it was her husband, hand extended. Sonny was tall, slim, in his thirties, with fair hair, blue eyes and a vague hospitable smile; the handsomest captain in any public school and a man who could smoke a pipe at the age of thirty-six with no air of patronage.

'I'm a bit of a dilettante, I'm afraid—dabble in furniture and houses . . . Polly's got the talent though.' He wore breeding like an invisible cloak.

They had been married six years; he was a well-born rebel whose natural habitat was Chelsea. 'I hated my school so much we're sending Bryan to a progressive one like Dartington.' 'He may have been to Harrow,' Polly said, 'but he's happy eating out of newspapers.'

A guest who had burst in on two strangers, I sat back, felt at home and stayed to dinner. Sonny opened wine—'fill up your jorum'—then Polly played the piano, Schubert or something, it seemed to me beautifully.

'She has a lovely voice, too, but won't do anything about it: restless that's the trouble . . .' When I left he said, 'To think we nearly went to a concert, we'd have missed you!'

And if they had gone out, I reflected, I would have walked home and never run into them again. As it was, I had made two friends.

*   *   *

Walking confidently to the first rehearsal, I was too inexperienced to realize that since no new play is flawless and usually needs important adjustments beforehand, it was alarming that my director had not one word with me about my script.

He had not made one suggestion, such as 'Re the gossipy friend, I'm afraid expressions like "That old cat" and "Isn't it a scream" just aren't right . . . When Eve says, "It's glorious to give, and give completely," mightn't we lose our audience. . .?' I would have jumped at such help and rewritten the play in a week.

As we rehearsed, even my optimistic eye soon spotted that something was wrong. Mr Williams had arranged the dining-room chairs and tables in a convenient pattern, and entrances and exits fell easily into place, even the standings and the sittings.

Beyond that, nothing; no discussion of the pace of an angry passage, or whether a look should be taken or not or of a point being over-emphasized or smudged.

Rehearsals limped on until one day Betty, at lunch in a Lyons, sat with hands clenched, emotional but realistic. 'He's nothing but a stage-manager. We need *telling* . . . this is like being an amateur again!' In the evenings we worked on our scenes, directing ourselves and each other.

By our last week, the play was trickling into the papers. Somebody had advised me to subscribe to a press-cutting agency. The *Flintshire Observer* carried an interview headed LONDON PLAY FOR HOLYWELL MAN, but I could not remember saying, 'As a result of my last London appearance I have turned down five West End offers.'

Then appeared such items as 'He has introduced some Welsh into his play. Help!' and a headline CLERGYMAN'S DAUGHTER AS ACTRESS. 'That,' Betty said, 'will have people storming the box-office.'

'My dear Son George, My *Liverpool Echo* gives you a good write-up except he can't spell poor fellow, writing you down as Elwyn Williams but his heading says *Noël Coward Watch Out!* with a mark after it, now to my mind that is a compliment. Your Mother and me went to St Helens to William Griffith's funeral viz my mother's brother, there was an old Welsh minister burying.'

'I can't wait to get there,' Betty said, 'for the dress-rehearsal, what with the set and the shaded lights and the curtains—it'll be like a tonic!'

On Sunday December the 2nd, we left Waterloo Station for the Theatre Royal, Aldershot.

CHAPTER SEVEN

NOËL COWARD, WATCH OUT!

We went straight to the theatre. From the wings I could see that the curtain was up and the stage a blaze of colour; Mr Williams was lighting the set. I did not examine further as I wanted to see it fresh from the front. I hurried through the pass door and up the aisle, sat down and looked.

'The drawing-room of a flat over the Leicester Square Theatre; it is lavishly and gaily appointed, as would befit a star of musical comedy.'

On the stage, in a pitiless glare, the sides and back of the 'drawing-room' were canvas flats lashed together and daubed to pass as antique oak, though the canvas looked older than the panelling it was aiming at. In places it sagged so dejectedly that the ancestral walls seemed to have been first flooded, then warped.

In the background, twin paintings which Mr Higley would have rejected with scorn. They depicted hunting scenes. To the right, where I had pictured an arch over a sweeping staircase for the star's entrance, a doorway with one shallow step up on to a platform. Behind that, a canvas wall blank except for 'The Blue Boy'.

Item, two standard lamps with metal stands and shades of brown parchment.

The fireplace was surrounded by a massive high fender topped with worn leather; presumably to make the place look lived in by a star of musical comedy, a stage-hand was inserting fire-irons and a threatening poker. Downstage a pouf, again of leather. The room looked like a provincial men's club gone to seed.

Except that one side of it was dominated by a grand piano. As the instrument does not lend itself to leather, here it was difficult to go wrong. But an attempt had been made, for the lid was draped in a sequin-fringed shawl liable to latch on to anybody who passed and bring hurtling to the floor half-a-dozen shabbily framed photographs.

Finally, facing in the centre of the back wall, the Picture Window yawned importantly. The curtains, unlined and drooping to the floor, were in a faded chintz such as one might see in a nice Women's Institute.

The one unexpected note of extravagance was a side-table groaning with every known brand of strong drink: Haig, Crême de Menthe, Napoleon Brandy, Curaçao, anything you name. From a watering-can, through a funnel, a stage-hand was filling each bottle with water which would be coloured later.

Betty came through the pass door, looked round at the set, looked at me and sat, heavily, next to C. B. Not-Cochran: by now, she and I were calling him that.

He smiled at her. 'Don't worry, dear, if it looks a bit bare, we've got the knick-knacks coming.'

Knick-knacks . . . Flying geese chasing one another up a wall? A stuffed fox?

Harold Anstruther appeared and stood next to me. I awaited his comment. It came.

He leaned over to Miss Brunt. 'That photograph of me' he murmured, 'should be in a silver frame, the script says so,' and moved on. He was right.

I sat with my eyes closed, an author without authority.

*　　*　　*

In my digs next morning, after staring at the empty grate in my back-bedroom and shivering to the bathroom, I compared to-night with the Cochran openings in Manchester: all-night re-hearsal, everybody dead with fatigue, then the glittering profes-sional triumph . . .

I seeped away the hours by walking the flinty streets; on a smirched rainy day Aldershot was as disenchanting as it sounded. Who shot Alder, and why commemorate it?

Looking at the few shoppers resentfully piloting umbrellas I thought, where will the few creatures come from to watch my play tonight? Out of caves?

After the curtain rose I descended to the stage, from a dressing-room seedier than a coal-hole, as late as I could before my entrance. The actors' voices sounded unnaturally loud as brittle chatter echoed round a theatre half-full, with many of the occupied seats unpaid for.

MRS PETTIFER: I feel so guilty I'm blushing all over.
ONSLOW: *All* over?
MRS PETTIFER: O-o-h Mr *Onslow*!

A laugh: not from the audience, from her, a shrill giggle followed by silence. The theatre might have been empty; I sat with eyes closed, while despair rose in me like a tide. I was back on the *Carmania*. Except that I couldn't close my script and retire to my cabin. I had to go on and act. Should I run? The stage-door was there, nothing easier . . .

With a mental click, I made myself switch from author to actor, and the actor said to himself, 'This part's been written for you so don't let the poor author down.'

Betty sat next to me in raincoat and tam-o'shanter and we clasped hands, babes in a shoddy wood. I whispered, 'Forget the play, just give the performance to help the author,' and she understood.

We went on, and in the first minute the audience laughed; from the dark I heard the faint beat of a heart, contact had been made. They remained mildly interested; at the end, fair applause. We had got through.

On the second night, there were fewer free seats and therefore fewer people. Walking home in the rain I faced the truth: the play was being presented against odds, but was itself built on sand.

When I had told myself I knew what I was writing about— Welsh people and the West End theatre—the first could be true, the second was not.

It was Coal-black Mammy in my murder play all over again; a few weeks of running up and down stairs in a London theatre had snared me into tackling the private life of a London star and a Mayfair man-about-town. I knew nothing about either.

If I was facing that now, why couldn't I have faced it before starting the play at all? Staring at the streaming pavement I thought, what ought I to write about, which I know at first hand?

A picture flashed across the back-street, of a composite stage

set, corridors and cubicles. The Everard Baths in New York. Now
that . . .

I imagined the Lord Chamberlain's desk, and the script lying
on it. That was a licence the good Lord would not provide.

* * *

'My dear Son George, You will be glad this week of waitin is
over but remember it is Darkest before the Dawn, we will be
with you in spirit at Embassy Theatre 8 p.m. Mon. the Great
Night. We can only hope the lords and ladies and the criticks
God bless them will have a good spread beforehand . . .'

For the Great Night, things had certainly brightened up; day
by day Betty had done wonders—new covers, pictures, ornaments, flowers, even the lighting had been worked on.

And C.B. had managed to fill the house, which included a
smattering of London Welsh. Oliver and Trixie had brought
friends, Polly and Sonny were there, Mr Higley had dragged his
old black suit from behind the Old Masters and escorted his
Promising Pupil, and my own ex-pupil Gentilissima Miss Megan
had brought a party.

It went well. The audience laughed moderately at the right
places and were unheard at the wrong ones, and at the end were
warmer than Aldershot while remaining decorous. Next morning
I was out at eight, standing with my collar up in a drizzle while
the damp pages of newspapers flapped before me.

Since nothing is easier to ignore than the spoken comment of
a witless acquaintance, why can words in print, penned by a
theatregoer who may easily be no more qualified, acquire at any
given moment the ring of finality?

There was praise for Betty, and for me as an actor—'vitality . . .
fresh . . . discoveries . . .'—but on the play the verdict, boiled
down, was exactly the one I had inflicted on myself in Aldershot.
Welsh side true, London side false.

It was expressed in terms varying from the indulgent to the
abrasive. Actors and playwrights have mixed feelings over mixed
notices; when you are both, those feelings are a welter as you
do your best to stomach the indigestible mish-mash of good and
bad.

[85]

Daily Sketch: 'This schoolboy play is apparently written in all seriousness.' I brushed the rain off my sleeve.

Guardian, Ivor Brown: '... but he does understand youth, he must try again ...' The *Morning Post* presented me with a new idea of myself: 'He is a crusader, but it is a pity he has chosen the theatre as his medium.' The pulpit perhaps?

Times, Charles Morgan: '... we had an uncomfortable time till Jack and Jill appeared ... some happy fragments ...' It was like alternately having your face shoved in the mud and being helped up again.

But the *Mail* had the last word. 'Why a famous actress should leave her man-about-town for a penniless yokel with neither looks nor physique, is a mystery which the author makes no attempt to solve.'

The rain dropped off my hair on to the newsprint which was at this moment being disseminated over the British Isles. Bastard.

It was with sagging spirits that I walked from the No. 2 bus to the second night; I felt that people were staring back at me and muttering, 'Just look at him, he's got neither looks nor physique.'

I minded that much more than the jibes at my writing. After all you can suddenly write a play better than your last, but whose looks were ever improved by experience?

But Betty seemed pleased and the play went well. Afterwards C. B. Not-Cochran sat in my room, exhausted but beatific.

'Don't be disheartened, dear boy, by this week's takings, the theatre is rather far out and it's the pre-Christmas slump. I've spent the day tramping around the West End trying to find a home for our little play.' I did not take to the idea of my manager hawking my wares ... but the West End!

And every day brought encouragement. A class-mate of mine had been at the first night: from Miss Cooke, 'Ena writes that it went wonderfully. We all rejoiced at school, everybody's face beamed ...' If she saw the play she would recognize the truth, but I was cheered by her pleasure.

Then Alan Webb turned up, whose bristling nostrils I had feared. 'Oh, yes, the whole thing's not quite right, but Emlyn you've made such strides! Come to supper at Rules.'

In the historic little restaurant in Maiden Lane, which I knew he couldn't afford, he scanned the wine list and asked the ages of the bottles, putting on twenty years himself as he did so.

Then he remembered something. 'What do you think's happening? Glen's getting married.'

'What?'

How could Glen be giving up his freedom? 'But, Alan, he's as young as us!'

'Oh, she's young too.'

'Who is she?'

'Angela Baddeley.'

I dropped my fork. 'But she's a star!'

Alan nodded sadly. 'I know. Marrying an actress, very rash step.'

'Surely.'

He raised his glass; we had turned into two archbishops mulling over dark news at the Athenæum. 'Cheers . . .'

*   *   *

The pre-Christmas slump was slumping all right. As author I received 'five per cent of the gross', and my Embassy royalties—august phrase—amounted to twelve pounds. Ah, but after Christmas . . .

'Dear Dad and Mam, I know you will be glad that after finishing on Saturday 22nd December, *Glamour* will transfer to the West End on Dec 31st, for an indefinite run at the Court Theatre Sloane Square, it is where *The Farmer's Wife* ran for over three years.'

I had not seen my family since the day I had walked out nearly two years ago, vowing that I would return only on a swell of success. And this seemed the moment; had not C.B. said, 'Nice little house the Court, yet it can take sixteen hundred on the week!' My share as author could be eighty pounds a week . . .

After the last Embassy night I took the Tube to Euston, and as in the chilly dawn the train slowed down for Connah's Quay I leant out and waved down at our back door, crowded with Mam, Job and Thomas, Mam waving a dishcloth.

I hurried down the alley—was it narrower?—past the weeds and the peeling front door, round the side to the back yard. Dad was working, six till two, Mam standing at her table, washing up. 'Well, here you are . . .' She smiled but made no move; again it struck me that I could not remember her kissing any of us.

The house was more faded, she a millimetre smaller and her hair a flick whiter, but nothing was changed.

I could smell Dad's dinner in the oven, there were frugal sprigs of holly on the mantelpiece between the tea-caddies offering a faded scowl from Gladstone, Disraeli and their Queen. The same sooty kettle bubbled on the hob, there was clean newspaper on the table and the grey years-old shaking-grass still stuck out of the two vases, Mam was wearing the brooch of coloured stones I had bought in Venice, Long Vacation three years ago, 'Wipe your feet, Job, I mean Thomas.' A train tore past, darkening the window. Nothing was changed.

For old times' sake, I enjoyed scraping soot from the kitchen chimney and cleaning my teeth with it at the tap in the backyard. Pouring my tea, mother studied me. 'Anyways, you don't look poorly.'

I produced her Christmas present, a box of soap. 'You shouldn't ha' spent the money but it does smell nice; after your father's seen it I'll put it away.' For Job I had fifty cigarettes; she tut-tutted and said nothing. I asked where Thomas was.

'Upstairs,' she sighed, 'gettin' into his uniform.'

'But there's no war on ...'

'The Salvation Army.' Tom came down, sixteen instead of four-teen, taller than me and elegant with blue-green eyes fearing God but nothing else. I knew he would appreciate his present: *The Life of General Booth*.

'This new theatre for your play,' Mam said, pouring my tea, 'is it near the other?'

'Oh, no, that was miles out by Hampstead, and now they are to move it to the Court, which is in London proper.'

'London ... well, you can only do your best.' I knew something more was coming. She added, with a sigh, 'London's the mischief. I got them cornflakes in for you.'

I sat in my old corner on the sofa and took up her *Woman's World*. I might never have been away.

'He's been better,' she said, knowing I knew she meant Dad, then the old phrase, 'considerin' the drink's been half his trouble.' I was tempted, as always, to ask what the other half was. 'Hardly ever stops at the New Inn, the doctor warned him you see, in eighteen months he'll be sixty.'

I thought with a pang, that's when he should retire, and said,

'That's a patch of damp.' Mam looked to where it was artfully masked by a chair. 'Ay, gets worse every winter, last week the tide come up again in the backyard. I don't like that, gets at your chest.' I could never forget that 314a was below sea-level.

Dad arrived like a burst of December sun and hugged the hands of the sailor home from the sea. 'Well, George, and how was the Bowery?' I had forgotten New York. I gave him his present, two tins of shag tobacco. When Mam said he was 'pleased wi' the cuttins' she was, as usual, understating: he spread them on the table as if to display a handful of uncut diamonds. At the Works they had been passed from hand to hand and were filthy. 'Well, George, so London is to have the privilege of seein' *"Clamour"*.'

'You're not sayin' it right,' said Mam.

'Neether I am, but when George first wrote about it I thought it was Clamour meanin' a big noise and we got into the habit of it at the Works.' Trying to define glamour for them I wondered if 'Clamour' was not the better title.

Thomas dived under the stairs, fished out his cornet and gave it a polish. 'Well, Tom,' said Dad, producing his betting list and stub of a pencil, 'I hope you drag a good crowd o' souls to the Mercy Seat!'

Thomas was unperturbed. 'God be with you,' he said, screwed on his peak cap, looked handsomer than ever, and departed. Mam sighed, and looked out at a passing goods-train as if it were a hearse. 'The Sally Army have got him.'

She made them sound like the Press Gang. 'I know they save souls but I don't like him shuttin' his eyes in the street an' then prayin', it's not right.'

In the train I recalled that my parents had not mentioned my finances: had they sensed that they were not flourishing? All I knew was that Dad had hoisted his flag atop the Court Theatre, London. Let it fly, let it fly . . .

Walking out of Euston Station, I saw a red bus racing triumphantly across my vision with one great word streaming triumphantly across it: GLAMOUR. With a G. I wished Dad were standing beside me; the same word was splashed across the front of the Court Theatre.

On Sunday night we had a dull rough run-through, stopping for lights. I watched the first scene from a box, a moment enlivened by a doleful old stage-hand standing at my elbow, sway-ing and smelling of beer. During a hitch he murmured, 'Excuse me, d'you see 'Arold?'

I told him I hadn't seen anybody much yet.

'I doubt if anybody's seen 'Arold.'

'What's he look like?'

'Oh, terrible. Very 'eavy, 'Arold. Red boots an' 'ats like Queen Mary, blimey . . . This looks a nice 'omely li'l show, Larry was good but 'Arold was 'orrible . . .'

He was delivering his verdict on a tragedy in blank verse by Lord Tennyson recently presented at the Court with Laurence Olivier as King 'Arold. The evening onstage offered nothing, in the way of dialogue, half as effective.

*　　*　　*

The first night, not being a real one, lacked the heart-beat of the Embassy opening; also C. B. Not-Cochran seemed to have forgot-ten that, second only to the evening following a royal demise, New Year's Eve is the worst date of the year for an opening. How is a critic to write a sober review and at the same time see the New Year in? Anyway, only a couple of second-stringers bothered.

On the second night, though, I was cheered to find the theatre almost full; no reaction from the gallery, but the rest were friendly and eager to applaud.

C.B. had explained to me that, as author, I would nightly re-ceive from the box-office a note to show me how I was faring at five per cent of the gross. After the second night I felt settled enough to study the first two notes. £15, £19!

The third night—again kind, though nothing from the gallery— £23. By the end of the week I'd have made a hundred pounds.

Thursday night, C.B. came round at the end and I showed him my slips from the box-office. He looked depressed, 'Too bad, isn't it?'

I realized, with a thud, that the figures represented not my five per cent share, but the whole of the takings. I had nothing to say.

'We're papering the theatre every night, nurses and that sort of thing.' I remembered that 'paper' was the semi-humorous word for free seats.

I thought of the gallery. 'What about the gods?' You can't

paper the gods. 'Seven people last night, three tonight.' No wonder they had been quiet.

'It's the time of year,' he continued, 'the post-Christmas slump. Too bad, nice little play.'

That evening Frank Vosper was in front, came round and asked me to supper, again at Rules. Admiring him as both actor and as playwright I was uplifted.

An expansive Rabelaisian man, he had been 'impressed by my performance'. To such a compliment an actor-playwright reacts like a mother with twins: if one of the two is praised the other is clutched to the parental bosom.

What of the play? He hadn't liked my other twin. Over the red wine, kindly, suddenly: 'Of course, you wrote it tongue-in-cheek, didn't you?'

From him, this unseated me. 'N-no, I didn't.'

'But you're not as naïve as that!'

'Well, the part I play's supposed to be naïve . . .'

'No, I mean the English characters, now they *are* out of a novelette, aren't they? Good stuff in between, but they just aren't you!'

I pondered this. No, not tongue-in-cheek: I had sincerely put together some cardboard characters and pumped in hackneyed emotions.

Sincerely? Yes, I had looked for sincerity, hard: but it is like charm, it is either there or can't be found. I had made myself believe I was sincere. Why?

Because the mental attitude of a young writer is often a complicated one: at the moment when he is thinking, 'What is it I want to say?' he finds himself asking, 'What is it my audience wants to hear?' When I started *Glamour* my mind was split: the instinctive half was determined to write a good play, but I was also bent on commercial success, and subconsciously worked out that it could be achieved by ingredients: a worldly setting and smart cocktail people faced with a pair of young rustics real but artfully naïve, the two ingredients mashed up to make a dish of happy-ever-after.

I had practised deception on myself, and I must not do it again.

'Dear Dad and Mam, *Glamour* finishes on Saturday after two weeks, it's the post-Christmas slump and quite a few theatres are suffering . . .'

To Miss Cooke. 'I am not going on the tour of *Glamour* as my agent advises me to stay in town . . . John Fernald tells me he is trying to get *Full Moon* on for a Sunday night, though it sounds unlikely, also he might find it difficult as he has a steady job, the Sunday show he was S.M. for is going on for a West End run.' The day I had followed him up to the rehearsal room over the Soho pub, the two actors I had been just as sorry for as I was for him were Maurice Evans and Laurence Olivier, preparing the death scene in the play which the world was to know as *Journey's End*.

As I addressed the envelope, my eye caught Miss Cooke's writing. 'We all rejoiced at school . . .' Under it, my father's letter, 'the heading says, *Noël Coward Watch Out!*'

Noël Coward, relax. I put the letters sadly away. My mother had had the last word. London's the mischief.

CHAPTER EIGHT

LONDON MORE MISCHIEVOUS

'My agent' was not an invention. After a performance, a visitor knocked at my door and diffidently introduced himself; he had the mild good looks of an amiable headmaster. Would I like to call at his office tomorrow with a view to his 'looking after me in both capacities'?

I had never heard of Walter Peacock but John (Fernald) was impressed. Peacock was not a run-of-the-mill agent; he ran Golding Bright, a top play agency handling Shaw, Barrie and Maugham. He was, moreover, an *éminence grise* with back-door access to the West End theatre who did not normally look after actors; the only one seemed to be Charles Laughton. Also John had fixed to direct *Full Moon* for six performances at the Arts.

GLAMOUR Last 8 Perfs. It had one champion: to my father, a critic attacking me was a wasp trying to sting a stone wall. 'The cream of them all is the *Graphic* where he says you know nothing of Stage Life, I suppose he is paid for putting such rubbish in the paper...'

During the last week I was helped every morning by striding to a rehearsal of Zola's *Thérèse Raquin* to be presented at the Arts on Sunday for one performance. Betty had taken me to tea with the Greins: J.T. was a veteran entrepreneur, nearing seventy but still indomitable, who had had a hand in coaxing Ibsen down London's gagging throat. His enthusiasm for his 'International Theatre' was shared by his portly jolly wife, and she was directing the Zola play.

The fee was one guinea but the play offered a unique challenge; it was to be given in French. While I rehearsed on the Arts stage, actor-members passing the notice board had to be impressed by any British name under 'Dimanche prochain, en français...'

Once I saw two figures drift into the dark back of the auditorium and watch for a moment: Alan Webb and John Gielgud, rehearsing upstairs for *The Seagull*.

When my voice rang out—'comme tout est compliqué avec toi, ma chérie!'—damn it they *had* to be impressed, I must tell Miss Cooke. My French was something nobody could take from me, not even the *Daily Mail*. 'Dimanche,' I said to myself, 'tu vas être superbe ...'

I may not have been superbe but I was evidently a guinea's worth, 'playing the little husband with such engaging charm that one did not accept Thérèse's behaviour ...' I showed that one to Mr. Higley.

'Well,' he said, 'if you're engaging the next step is to get engaged, what?' I agreed.

Returning to the sport of phone-watching—and a dull pastime I knew it to be—I also started a spaced-out trek up Mr Peacock's stairs. He always saw me, and was always encouraging, 'several things nearly materialized ...'.

John did get *Full Moon* on, at the Arts for five performances, but the papers were loweringly kind; 'quite a pleasant poetical fancy, even if it is on the sombre side'.

Thinking I might learn something, I went to the last night. The theatre was half-empty; as at the Oxford Playhouse my familiarity with the lines dulled any reaction and I learnt nothing.

Except when I stole a glance around: every face had the same look, respectful and utterly detached. I thought, where have I seen this before? I remembered, with dismay: sermon-time in my Welsh chapel.

My royalties, at a pound a performance, had amounted to five pounds. At the suburban Q Theatre, where the play moved for a week and I was paid five per cent of the gross, they fell to three: so the week's takings were sixty.

During that week the front of the theatre, with FULL MOON high above the entrance, must have looked forlorn. Full?

*   *   *

I was surprised, without being heartened, to find that such hard facts were hidden from the onlooker behind a smokescreen of casual publicity. In both London and provincial papers, stray theatre items still described me as 'the promising new actor-playwright (*just* twenty-three) who has had two plays on in London in two months'.

February the 11th, from the Connah's Quay Urban District Council: 'Dear Sir, I herewith convey to you our congratulations on the great achievement you have attained in your profession, A. J. Mothersole.'

'Williams,' said Mr Higley, as we sat in shirt-sleeves over our mugs of tea, 'Cabinet Ministers have been glad of less.'

But Mr Peacock gave me no time to mope. Ernest Milton, the distinguished Shakespearean actor, had ventured into management, starring at the Queen's in Pirandello's *Enrico Quarto* (*The Mock Emperor*). Having made a striking success he was following it with a play by his wife, the novelist Naomi Royde-Smith.

Mafro, Darling! was a country-house comedy, 'a bit mad', and I was to play the small colourful part of a multilingual valet for ten pounds a week. 'Mon, next 11 a.m. Queens Th'. At 9 a.m. I stood in Mr Higley's doorway polishing a shoe while he sat in his shirt-sleeves stamping his fingers along the keys as he limbered up for the day.

I divulged that this was my first West End show from scratch. 'Exciting, my dear fellow, but don't tell the others, doh ray mee fah SOH.'

As I left, a pale slip of a young woman hopped up the stairs; 'Ah, Miss Edgeley!' It was my first sight of the Promising Pupil whose contralto had convinced me that she was a towering Clara Butt; tremulously she shook hands. A booming sparrow.

Three minutes to eleven, Queen's stage-door. I said 'Mafro, Darling!' to the doorkeeper and walked downstairs. He had looked mildly surprised; yes, it was a peculiar title ... TO THE STAGE, QUIET PLEASE.

On my walk I had pictured the scene: curtain up, auditorium empty and mysterious, the stage housing one of the sumptuous *Mock Emperor* sets, its shaded lights illuminating a group of players as perfect in face and figure as the tableaux in Harrods' windows, swimming slowly from one impeccable slow motion to the next.

The first morning was not that; it was, moreover, typical. To begin with, as in Drury Lane that bad afternoon, dismantled scenery was stacked against streaked walls or hung dejectedly on wires; rugs lolled about in rolls, carpets lay protected by a stage-cloth rucked and foot-marked, furniture lurked under dirty shrouds.

Under the usual dismal working light, the stage looked like a dilapidated warehouse on the verge of bankruptcy, with a semi-circle of kitchen chairs ready for a meeting of bristling creditors.

And the auditorium was neither empty nor mysterious. It was lit by a brutal flare in mid-stalls, casting the scattered witch-like shadows of the lady cleaners, bent double and patient as Millet's Gleaners as they scavenged for cigarette-ends and chocolate wrappings.

And just as last night's modulated tones had floated from stage to stalls, so now voices travelled the other way round; shriller, and speaking dialogue rather less oblique than Pirandello's. 'My eldest is goin' through 'ell with 'ers, don't ask *me* . . .' 'I'll give you three guesses what I just found in the gallery . . .'

On the stage, people stood in twos and threes. They were as well-groomed as I had imagined; like me, they were all in what my mother would have called 'their Sunday best'. Jewels and tie-pins sparkled, while Dorothy Dix, the leading lady, was in a long swathe of dark glowing fur: I guessed I was having my first close look at a mink coat. It was needed; the stage was draughty.

They were all talking, which bewildered me: with more experience I would have known that no animal could be more nervous than an actor, in the London of that time, on the first day of a play—nerves stemming from stark uncertainty: about the play, the part, the rest of the company, oneself—and the result was chatter as inane as at any cocktail party.

People whose normal behaviour was simple became unrecognizable: any two actresses, whose usual speech was good straight-forward stage English—and when it was good, there was none better—would exchange greetings in purposely excruciating Cockney which made the cleaners sound like Court dressmakers. Accustomed to waving decorously across street or restaurant at least four times a year, they now became Livingstone and Stanley face to face at a jungle crossing. '*Yew?* What abaht that dress? That ain't off the bloomin' peg!'

It went on until Mr Milton clapped genial hands and reared the head of a majestic oriental eagle. 'Ladies and gentlemen, shall we get at it?'

At the voice of the magician the cocktail party had vanished, ousted by a group of professionals solemnly settling on the chairs. I remembered hearing that West End plays always started with a Reading, and watched scripts rustle nervously open as if to unveil a fragile gift.

The curtain was lowered, cigarettes were lit, and the stage-management carefully placed large rusty tins to serve as ash-trays. There was a crackle of importance in the air.

I enjoyed the reading; everybody, determined not to 'give a performance', murmured their lines with a languorous grace just right for a well-bred inconsequential comedy. 'Don't be an idiot, darling. I'm calling your bluff, do you mind...?' It was a good morning.

I had lunch with Freddie Mell, playing a footman, his first West End job: a lively Cockney gadabout. 'I'm thirty-five ducks but wi' slap on me face and a spot o' surprise pink in the floats I can get away wi' twenty. Oh, it *is* a relief to let me 'air down! Show looks good, don't you think?'

By the end of the second day though, I could not agree with him. The early moves were set enough for the actors to begin acting, and the lazy lines which had caught my fancy were acquiring a brittle gloss; 'I'm calling your *bluff*, do you *mind*!' It was worrying.

Next morning Mr Milton, as Mafro the flowery young ballet-dancer, began to acquire confidence too. We watched a distinguished actor become vivacious. Not quite forty and in his prime, he was still too old to make his first entrance inside a skipping-rope.

Sitting in the wings, Freddie the footman whispered to me a comment which reminded me of Pierre the Count, and which included two expressions unknown except subterraneously, though years later they were to thrust themselves above ground and thrive like nettles which have lost their sting. Mr Milton had just jumped on to a stool and thence on to a table, 'Un, deux... *trois*!'

Freddie looked to see nobody could hear. ' 'E doesn't know it,' he said darkly, 'but 'e's *camp*. What's more, if 'e's not careful, on the first night the gallery's goin' to send 'im up. Let's pray my Dennis doesn't get wind of it. If 'e does, we're all for the roof.'

I asked who Dennis was. 'Gallery First-Nighter, dresses hair in the day, can spot camp a mile off, bein' camp 'imself you see. Funny, the only time 'e isn't camp is when 'e's givin' a first night the bird. When 'e boos 'e goes bass. You'd think it was Wallace Beery up there; I 'ope to God it's 'is off-night.'

The more Mr Milton built up his part, the more the play's foundations frittered away under him; it was the work of an intelligent woman who had mistaken frivolity for humour. I should have been warned by the exclamation-mark in *Mafro, Darling!*

'Now *that*,' Freddie whispered, 'is camp too.'

From Mrs Milton, a daily delivery of paper covered with frenzied scrawls: a disease had set in, a galloping one. Rewriting.

But the automatons stayed automatons. 'Doin' their best,' Freddie muttered, 'all as bright as bloody buttons. But are they goin' to shine *on the night?*'

On the night the cast acted more like bloody buttons than ever —I more than any in my explosive little display. I did not know what else to do. But the audience was bright back and Dennis's boo went unheard. Steady as a ship though, the play sank. In the last act it listed and disappeared without trace.

'My dear Son George, I see by the papers that the Criticks have taken the stick to the lady for her play.'

They had wielded it so well that on the second night we read on the notice-board: THE MANAGEMENT REGRET THAT 'MAFRO, DARLING!' WILL TERMINATE ITS RUN ON SATURDAY. ON WED. NEXT 'THE MOCK EMPEROR' WILL RESUME ITS RUN.

I was to play Berthold, 'one of the boys', and understudy Mr Milton; the 'boys' were the equivocal group whom the mad 'Henry' had engaged as his retinue. On Wednesday afternoon—we opened that night—there was a sketchy dress-rehearsal for the replacements, who included John Fernald.

Somebody said to him, 'You've left *Journey's End*? But it'll run for ever.'

'That's why I've left, couldn't stand that gunfire eight times a week.'

'Accordin' to that, mate,' said an embittered old walker-on in the corner, 'you wouldn't ha' been much good in the last conflict.'

Both John and I had the right figures for mediaeval pages with hair in a brown fringe and falling behind the ears, puffed sleeves and tights up to the waist. 'Listen,' Freddie murmured to me, 'I'll give you a tip. Twist a couple o' pennies into the top of 'em to fix your braces on to, makes tights stay up tighter. Can make the front row sit up tighter as well.'

He had been cast as fifth boy, in a fair wig. 'I'm 'is lordship's only blond dear.' It was, needless to say, a silent part. Looking at him in my mirror, I saw him narrowing his eyes and asked him if my make-up was all right. 'Not too camp?'

'What's that?' John said. 'Camp?'

'I'm never sure,' I said, pulling on my wig. Freddie scrutinized me, 'You'll do, p'rhaps a tidge less lipstick. You look a bit like Clara Bow.' I looked at him coldly and thought of New York, of those corkscrew curls. Then it had been Mary Pickford. I was at least catching up.

'Sorry I spoke, dear,' Freddie said. 'Dress-rehearsals bore me stiff even if they're a drag show like this one, so I get a teensy bit pixie-ish. I was only sendin' you up.'

'What was that?' said John. I toned my lips down, fixed the couple o' pennies and wished Freddie were dressing next door.

The rehearsal proceeded. Mr Milton was his cheerful self— 'Yes, you new lads look spiffing'—but during the break for a lamp to be adjusted, I looked at him.

In costume, he was sitting straight up on his throne, while hands drooped over its arms, eyes closed: having forty winks and oblivious to all. Off his guard he looked deathly tired, utterly withdrawn and more a king than royalty. I felt my preoccupations slide from me as I considered a man, fresh from a failure which he was bearing for a loved wife as well, trudging now through a play already written off as a *succès d'estime* and in a few hours to be coaxed back into life.

Facing a respectful non-first night, Milton, bone-weary and dis-illusioned, gave a wonderful performance. In the second act I joined the others round him in the half-light and listened to his great monologue. 'It's getting dark ... When I was a child I thought the moon in the pond was real, I believed everything I was told and I was happy ...'

Next afternoon, walking in the sun in Battersea Park, I learnt it. On every side, activity: pale skinny Londoners sprinting round a track, football, tennis, and as my feet and lips moved together, I was part of it all.

That night on the notice-board, a fresh bit of paper; the revived *Mock Emperor* would re-expire tomorrow week after thirteen performances.

My immediate task, self-imposed, was a tough one: to finish

learning Henry as if I knew the star was going to break a leg after the last matinée and I would be playing for him that night. I was a bricklayer feverishly building a wall which is to be blown up in a week.

In between, sitting nightly at Milton's feet, I learnt more about holding an audience, with face and voice and hands, than I could have in ten years from a drama school; I learnt too about professional behaviour in the face of adversity. I should have written that to him. For me they had been two fruitful failures.

* * *

But financially, barren. And without meaning to, my father made me feel doubly guilty. 'I am at home with a slight accident at the Works, I fell on my knee but can walk nicely now—now about Thomas, your Mother saw an advt that Mr Jack Dodd wanted a Youth to go out with orders and as soon as Master Tom told him whose lad he was he engaged him so now he will be a High-Class Grocer, 15/- a week to start with. Better than the Works as trade is not so brisk but it don't interfere with my work as I am always engaged . . .' I wished I could write back the same.

With April coming up, the end of the financial year, I bought a small account book and totted up my income for the two years since I went on the stage. Excluding America it amounted to £98; during one year the promising actor-playwright had earned an average of two pounds a week, little more than his young brother would soon be bringing home as a grocer's assistant.

I tried looking at a couple of press-cuttings: 'an actor to be watched'. Where is he to be watched from, the top of a bus as he tramps up and down Shaftesbury Avenue looking for work?

But in Number 34, top floor, the dry bread was spread with gold: thanks to Miss Cooke, there was honey still for tea. And Mr Higley was still a rumbling well of comfort.

'Don't worry, Williams, you won't be long out of a shop.'

Where did he get his lingo from? 'Shop' must have gone out with Irving. Once he said, 'Getting short, are you?'

'I'm not any taller, if that's what you mean.'

Better laugh than cry.

* * *

Each time I had played at the Arts Theatre I had been automatically a member of the Club and now sometimes sneaked in, read the papers and looked around at the well-known young players hurrying in and out between shows: Robert Douglas, Adrianne Allen, Maurice Evans, Ursula Jeans, Jack Hawkins, Ann Todd, Roger Livesey, Jane Baxter, Laurence Olivier, who looked —with a black Ronald-Colman moustache and a black Anthony-Eden Homburg—like a smouldering Under-Secretary.

They all seemed sociable, with the easy movements of success, and at many moments I could have drifted into conversations which might have led to friendship. But friendship might have led to the solicitude of prospering contemporaries—poor old Emlyn, I must ask him to a meal—and I avoided their eyes.

It was with the obscure that I felt comfortable: Freddie Mell, chatty, impecunious and outrageously himself, tripped up and down my musty stairs between his travels. One Sunday he rang up, en route from Brighton to Huddersfield in *Bird in Hand.* 'Pays the rent, ducks. I could go on touring for ever, born to be a landlady's darling!'

I envied him and yet I didn't; you *could* go on touring for ever. Then he said, 'You must take a half-page in *Spotlight.*' This was a new bi-annual publication with photographs aimed at prospective employers, and he knew two girls who had a studio off the King's Road. 'They've just started and they'll give you a price.'

Judging by the photographs the girls took of me it seemed doubtful if they had even started; the only possible one duly appeared, under 'Juveniles'. They had done everything to make me eligible, short of surgery. Out of focus and less touched up than smudged up, I looked as if I had been snapped at the bottom of the sea; my eyes swam off the page, please give me a part ... Intent on looking winning I had come out winsome and had forked out two guineas for the privilege.

A message from the indefatigable Greins: Mrs was to direct Sarment's *Pêcheur d'Ombres* for one Sunday afternoon at the Arts, would I play a lead, for the guinea? Besides which, I would be showing off my French again. I jumped.

Five characters, the leading one a boy of twenty, a dreamer not right in the head, a Fisher After Shadows. It had been created in Paris by the young author and I felt it was made for me.

Mrs Grein phoned about rehearsals, adding that the boy would be played by the director George de Warfaz, a sharp-faced Belgian actor established in the West End in small foreign parts, aged forty. I was to be his elder brother, morose and unsympathetic. And forty. On the Sunday, I affixed a false moustache as if it were a mustard plaster.

The following week Miss Cooke wrote that 'in the evgs' she was deep in Teach-Yourself-Spanish prior to Easter and a student bus-trip in Spain, which would entail a night in London.

I wrote back that since when I was fifteen she had arranged for Thomas Cooke and Sons to meet me at Euston, settle me into the Wilton Hotel and see me on to the boat-train for France, it was surely poetic justice that the other Cook (e), Sarah Grace, should be met by me at the same Euston, put up at my London residence and seen on to the same boat-train.

But how to put her up?

Passing ghostly old Mrs Mellowfield in the lobby I was surprised, after a year of invisibility, to be greeted with a grey smile. When our landlord had described her as a refined lady he had understated; her accent had been shredded through a grater.

'Ay understind we hev a budding authah on the primmises?' Before the cresh came, when we had footmen and such, Ay was once taken on Mr Disraeli's knee and he was kaynd enough to pet my ringlets.'

For something to say, I told her I was looking for a room for my aunt: 'my aunt' sounded better than 'my old schoolmistress'.

'Would the lady,' murmured Mrs Mellowfield, 'partake of *may* humble abode? Ay can easily slip ovah to my daughtah.'

I was about to insist on payment when she added, 'Ay do miss not being in touch with her. Ay understand you have a telephone?' It was a ploy impossible to parry; Mrs Mellowfield would have an extension, keep a list of her calls and re-imburse me once a month.

I had never seen Miss Cooke in London. 'See here, George, lug that hat-box down but be careful, the bottom's nearly out, maybe I shouldn't have put books in it then hail a taxi. Well, how are you?' I imagined directing the driver past a theatre which featured my name, but it was a consolation to show her the programme of *Pêcheur d'Ombres*.

As we drew up at Number 34, I made her chuckle with the

news that she was to spend the night in the bed of a lady who had had her curls toyed with by the Earl of Beaconsfield. Unexpectedly tactful, she waited on the doorstep while I paid the driver with the air of a property owner.

Preceding my guest into the house, I saw it through her eyes; I knew she abhorred dirt as much as my mother did. The lobby and staircase looked grubby. I opened the door of Mrs Mellowfield's humble abode.

It was tidy, with every ornament and frill as carefully placed as the accent, but the abode smelt. Not strongly, it was just that the window was tight shut and the smell made you wonder if it had been like that since the demise of Mr Disraeli. It seemed possible that the exalted hand which had once fondled a little lady had been cut off, inefficiently embalmed, and left under the bed.

I put down my visitor's luggage and hastened to precede her upstairs, wishing I had taken her to the Wilton. But I had a good tea waiting and my accidentally dappled walls still looked fresh.

After a café meal and seeing the latest Maugham play, *The Sacred Flame*, from the pit, lying awake I realized, too late, that I should have given her my room, pretended to install myself in the abode downstairs and tramped the streets till daylight. I imagined her rising from her musty bed and striding up and down Vauxhall Bridge all night, ignoring the stare of a curious bobby.

In the morning, taking tea down to her, I detected a dash of eau-de-cologne. After seeing her off I realized we had not discussed the theatre or my future; instead she had talked of old pupils—'Take Millie Tyrer, writes a jolly good letter, Rica Jones is another...'

From Spain, 'Now my boy why not go home for a week? It'd please your parents and be a change of air.' Perhaps she was thinking of the lobby downstairs.

I forgot about Mrs Mellowfield until the morning I picked up the receiver to make one of my rare calls and heard two female voices in a spate of chat, 'No deah, Ay'm wrong it was the Friday and she was in her *blue* het...'

The daughter sounded as disembodied as the mother, as if they were on separate clouds having a ghost-to-ghost natter. Mrs Mellowfield was certainly keeping in touch. With Sevenoaks. A toll call.

*   *   *

All Quiet on the Western Front had just been published; in May I borrowed a German copy from Mrs Grein and dug grimly into it. This may have given her the idea of asking me to play opposite her, for fun, in a comic duologue, in German, for the Anglo-German Society, as a doddering old man. She would understand if I thought it infra dig ...

I didn't. My part involved talking to a stuffed dachshund. I would willingly have played the dachshund. So one evening I found myself on a tiny platform in front of the immense horseshoe of an Anglo-German banquet at the Criterion Restaurant, Piccadilly Circus. Waiting for work, I played—appropriately—a waiter: 'Jawohl, mein Herr!' and wore another false moustache, capped this time, with a bald wig.

I was making a fool of myself, for nothing, in the very middle of London. All round me the dazzling slogans, C. B. COCHRAN PRESENTS WAKE UP AND DREAM ... and under me, in the Criterion Theatre, paid actors were playing—around my Yvonne—in *By Candlelight*.

But the thought did not depress me. On the contrary, this was so far from what I wanted that it was grotesquely amusing—how much more unhappy I would be on tour, grinding away in a carbon-copy of the same play! And Mrs Grein's high spirits infected me; we made the diners laugh.

In the Gents I changed into my dinner-jacket, left over from Oxford—the one Miss Cooke had sent me which had been her cousin's—then had the free dinner in lieu of the Guinea. I sat next to a member of the German Embassy, a pleasant man of forty with an empty sleeve; I talked to him in my halting German about *All Quiet*.

'It is good,' he said, 'to hold this dinner. I was in the war, it can never happen again and it is good to know.' As I sampled my Rhein-wein he made me feel that the world was not a bad place.

So long as I got a job ... In the meantime Miss Cooke's hint worked: leaving my door unlocked so that Mr Higley could take phone messages, I went home. To write: without that I would have slipped back into post-Oxford failure.

If you could call it writing. Any project would serve, and I had hit on one which would at least be good practice. Cleaning out a drawer, I had felt something lurking at the back: *A Murder Has Been Arranged*. It was the only copy left, the others having lost their way for ever in the mouldering vaults into which managements toss rejected plays. When the vault is full, they brick it up. This copy looked mouldy too, though still fat.

I told the family I had a rush job, to put the finishing touches to something 'for people who are interested'. As I settled into my parlour corner and looked out past the aspidistra at the back-yards of High Street I felt I was back with my school homework: task, revision.

Starting from scratch I made caustic notes, the sort Miss Cooke would scribble in the margin of a pretentious essay: cut out dire comic relief, never lose sight of fact you've called your play 'A Ghost Story'. . .

The theme I had chosen, one which would continue to possess me, was a supremely difficult one at which my first shot had so signally failed: the counterpoint of the mundane and the macabre, involving the maintenance—in a realistic setting—of a super-natural atmosphere, until in the last scene the two faces of the play will merge. That atmosphere must grow until the whole theatre is brooding with it: not through a ridiculous vase straight out of Rider Haggard, but through people.

This all meant major structural alterations; also as I went along I cut ruthlessly and trimmed until the shape was streamlined.

Typing the final copies, though, I faced the fact that the two obstacles against acceptance were as salient as ever: genuine ghost, and murderer as leading man.

I heard heavy footsteps down the alley and a shadow crossed the window. 'George, your father's back and your egg's gettin' cold.' I had done my healthy homework.

❉   ❉   ❉

Mr Higley welcomed me with a mug of tea. No, there were no messages. He was cleaning a new masterpiece; the priceless David returned my look, mischievously.

Suddenly he sighed and stared into his tea. I asked if anything was the matter.

'Williams, I'm in love.'

It was as improbable as if my father had said it: I had never thought of him as anything but an eccentric recluse. He sensed my amazement. 'You're looking at my bald head but believe me that's no sign that life is over! Just because a house isn't thatched, does it follow that the door-knocker doesn't work?' It was a striking simile.

'I mean I'm only fifty and that's not old these days, is it?'

I said I agreed but of course I didn't, to me he was a healthy-looking old man. Then I added, with a mechanical smile, 'Am I to congratulate you?'

For one dire moment I thought he was going to cry into his tea. 'It's my prize pupil. Miss Edgeley.' The booming sparrow. No wonder I had heard 'Softly Awakes My Heart' so often.

'I fell in love with her voice, then with her. Wrote to her father asking for her hand in marriage.'

The Victorian phrase sounded splendidly right. He produced a letter from his waistcoat. 'From her pater. Now, Williams, don't you think this is a bit much...? "It is out of the question, our daughter is twenty-four next birthday."'

I saw Pater's point. 'Where would you have lived?'

'Here, of course!'

I looked at his folded camp-bed; to open it at night he had to cram the rest of his furniture even closer together. 'Easy,' he said, 'she loves this room and with another of those we'd be as happy as larks.'

Larks they were too, with soaring voices. 'He won't let her come for any more lessons, we're broken-hearted.'

Gone those blissful hours with her lusty contralto pouring out of that timid throat, to mingle with his mighty bass, 'Softly Awakes My Heart...' As their eyes meet in song, his face grows younger and younger: two larks, in a nest of creaking canvases. It was not to be.

*　　*　　*

With the advent of July I called on my Sole Representative. 'Several people have read the new version and find it most ingenious, but they're put off by...'

I knew. Well, it had been an exercise; any plays being cast?

Very little till the autumn, but he was keeping his eyes open. The autumn! My savings were dwindling.

I read in the *Stage* that William Poel was planning a matinée of *The Tragedie of Biron*, an obscure Elizabethan drama; it would mean a guinea. I applied and was allotted two parts, with six lines each.

Poel had a formidable reputation as an eccentric genius who worked doggedly, in the celebrated teeth of Irving and Tree, at presenting Shakespeare as he imagined it had been done originally, and had in the process discovered Edith Evans. 'Mr Poel is interviewing the cast, Friday at four.'

At three, I was opening the door of my room to walk to Dean Street, when a figure appeared from below, hauling itself up slowly and surely by the banister: a tall incredibly bent old man in his late seventies, with long straggling white hair round a bald pate. He reached the corner, saw my trunk, clutched at a coat-hanger, and toiled up towards me.

I stood aside, taking him for a new pupil of Mr Higley's. Scales, at that age? He blinked up at me, 'Mr Williams? I fear I'm an hour early, got a bit muddled. I'm William Poel.'

Disquieted, I hurried him to my armchair; considering the climb, he seemed in not too bad shape. Clutching to his bosom a tall stiff-backed script as if it were Holy Writ, he looked like an absent-minded Moses who had lost his way to Sinai. The eyes were vague and watery.

But it was firewater, the look of a fanatic. 'No tea, thank you, shall we read?'

Out of a mediaeval portfolio, he fished two copies of *Biron*. Did he think I was to play the lead . . . ? No, he opened the page at my first bit, and gave me the cue in an unexpectedly strong voice. 'I wish your migh-ty race might mult-ip-ly, Even to the pe-ri-od of emp-ery!'

I spoke my six lines, which he countered with a speech of his own, considerably longer, about the Poel Method. It was to do with breathing, and he illustrated it by reading to me both my speeches. It sounded very unnatural and I thought, I may be conceited but I'm glad I never had to go in for Voice Lessons. And thought too, Edith Evans would have been all right anyway.

I preceded him slowly down to the front door as he wavered down the banisters, thanked him profusely for the honour he had done me, as indeed he had, and watched a grand old man wander uncertainly towards Victoria. I wondered which obscure young actor he would surprise next.

I was glad my rehearsals were few; they depressed me. In the stuffy room, twenty strapping older Shakespeareans and seedy young bit-players like me hung around waiting for cues.

One stifling afternoon I seated myself dejectedly at an open window, the boom of blank verse behind me. From the pavement far below I heard strains of sweet music, and felt myself retreat gently into childhood.

Craning to look, I saw a handful of men round a lamp-post: workless Welsh miners, singing their hearts out. They were harmonizing 'Y Gwenith Gwyn', the rapturous melody I had heard the village colliers sing under the moon: O Na Byddai'n Hâf O Hyd, Would That It Were Forever Summer ... The actor next to me threw a penny; from my pocket I drew a penny and a shilling, hesitated and threw the shilling. One of the miners retrieved it, turned his face up to the sun, smiled and waved, I waved back. Would That It Were Forever Summer ...

It would bring me luck. It must.

I hated my few lines in *Biron* and my mind refused to absorb them. 'I will observe how he stands attractive to their ends, That so I may not seem an idle spot in train of this ambassage.' What did it mean?

'Dear Miss Cooke, I am rehearsing *two* parts in a special performance and have four or five irons in the fire.' She must have wondered if it wasn't rather a lot. Enough to put the fire out ... ?

The shilling had made me reckless, and one night I queued up for the pit for a revue at the Victoria Palace, *The Show's The Thing*, where London was nightly discovering thirty-one-year-old Gracie Fields from Lancashire.

As I sat watching the auditorium fill, then heard the orchestra tuning up, I thought, she's in her dressing-room calmly getting ready, this is the theatre, and *I* am in the theatre too. I took out my miserable scraps of paper and stared at my cryptic lines as if they were 'To be or not to be'.

As the orchestra burst into its overture, I made them mean something. By the time the curtain went up, I knew them.

By the end I was bewitched by the glorious voice, the clowning, the poignant simplicity with which an inane ballad was interpreted so as to hold a couple of thousand people mesmerized by the tenuous thread of a top note.

'When whipperwills call...Molly and Me, and Baby makes three...in my Blue Heaven...' Was it possible that a gawky young woman with a black plait coiled and clamped round each ear, could make an audience accept the news that she was a loving husband and father? It was.

Finding myself back where I belonged, I glimpsed again what the wear and tear of material worries had, for months, blurred for me: the Grail of the theatre, the moment when stage and audience are united by a current as magic as any electricity. I looked forward to tomorrow's rehearsal. The next evening Freddie said, 'But you've got tastes as common as me ducks, you just like music-hall!'

Betty, over out-of-work cocoa: 'But Emlyn you're *versatile*, you can do comedy and pathos and play a strong scene, and then your foreign accents, it's a shame...'

Determined to turn the heaviest stone, I asked her where I could borrow a funny hat. She had one, a deerstalker she had worn in some prank as an eccentric spinster. I went to the cheapest photographer I could find and was snapped in five poses.

First, square on, true blue and chin jutting out; second, an extravagant smile; third, reading an unpleasant letter with a face 'drained of emotion'; fourth, eyes staring into camera, features distorted with fright.

The fifth was the comic one: three-quarter face, chin tucked back to make teeth protrude, eyes fixed on the camera under the deerstalker hat, intentionally too small and perched on top—a hodge-podge of Chaplin, Keaton and Harry Langdon.

It was one of the saddest photographs ever taken. I showed none of them to anybody.

* * *

My dumbstruck telephone did not endear itself by constantly presenting me, when I lifted my receiver, with Mrs Mellowfield's private life: a privilege for which I was paying. When the last bill had come in, I had ringed-in-red twenty or so toll calls and slid it under her door. I had heard nothing since and never would.

But she enjoyed her extension—'No, deah, it didn't commence

raining heah till fave o'clock. How is your blistah?' Once as I listened—and fought a desire to shout, 'Get off my phone, madam, and into a debtor's prison where you belong'—she interrupted herself, sharply—'My deah, Ay hev an idea that we hev an eaves-droppah on our lane. Ay'll ring latah'—and clicked off. My face as I hung up must have been a baffle of rage.

By August, out of the £190 I had brought from New York £15 were left in the Holywell bank. Then I was in bed for a week with acute flu and too depressed to write letters; Mr Higley nursed me like a nurse. Convalescent, I wrote to explain and the responses were swift and characteristic.

I had been consistently careful to give 314a the impression that I was doing well, hoping they were not wondering too hard why I scarcely ever sent money home. The first letter was from my mother.

'Dear Goerge, your father at work, i was thinkin there was something wrong, if you think you will get better at home come at once, i am enclosin this 10/- note so you can gett some nourishment love from all at 314a ...'

By then my eyes could not see the ruled paper, and it took a walk round the Serpentine to restore me.

Next day, my father: 'It is no use your overworking your brains and body, you have a long way to go yet, here is Dad being the preacher. Something is sure to turn up so keep on smiling *there's a good boy* and dont you be short of anything as you know it is there for the asking, please keep in close communication with us ...'

Miss Cooke's letter felt ominously thick and I postponed it till I was sitting in Hyde Park. I was right. It was a broadside straight between the eyes.

'Now you're over flu I can talk with no holds barred. First, I have never felt I was ever particularly good to you, most people would find it hard to realize how impersonally I live ... D'you know, even if I won that problematic £250,000 on the Stock Exch., I shdnt want in the least bit to back a play for you!!!! I have no patience with people in a hurry. If you tell me that for you London has to be postponed indefinitely & you will have to go on tour for X years my heart will not ache for you. These are my feelings, or lack of feelings.

'In the meantime, down to brass tacks. If you're worried about money, you have no need to be. I see your acct. here is v. low, here's the procedure. I am today paying into your acct. £100, & if in time that gets low—God f'bid—I'll send you £10 or £15 a mth as you need it.

'In short I'll see you don't go short of bread & butter, & for g'dness sake don't feel oppressed with gratitude, I don't have a bit the sense that I'm giving you money, as a matter of fact I'm not, it's your next year's income you'll be using! !

'To get things right in my mind—I'm helping you because you've got the quality I admire: risking all on what you believe in. (You realize, don't you, it's the same quality as yr successful business man has—you are not such an ass, are you, as to despise the Sir Alfred Monds of this world—you, if your mind had turned to business & not drama, wld have made your way all right there, because you have 'stick' & attention to detail.)

'Oh I do thk the human mind is funny: I like Rebecca West (at times) she too is interested in those labyrinths. You know that in politics I am an unrepentant Tory, well here I am with several members of my family poor—but I feel no desire to help them; more than that, I feel I OUGHT to help you rather than them because you work & they don't. And that is pure Socialistic theory! ! Well, that's that. Gd luck, Yours affectionately S. G. C.'

Through the languor of the city summer, her spirit blew like a sea-breeze with a tang of salt. And of solvency.

Polly and Sonny phoned. Back from Italy, where Sonny had persuaded her to have singing lessons, they had rented a bungalow on The Island, Thames Ditton.

From a train from Waterloo, I walked in the holiday heat through the village to the old Swan Hotel and took the ferry across the few yards of backwater-Thames to the colony of bungalows forming the Island, small enough to swim round at leisure of a morning with a view of Hampton Court thrown in.

The bungalows were rickety, the inhabitants rackety, forming a contented colony living a cut below respectable suburbia without becoming disreputable. They wandered over the tiny lawns in stages of undress, tottered into punts swinging portable gramophones, held their noses before springing off home-made divingboards and sipped coffee and beer on peeling verandahs, lounging low in frail old deck-chairs stained with bathing-costume damp. The Heseltine bungalow was named 'Hickidoola', with on one side Dorice in 'Ouimaidit' and on the other a touring comedian in 'Takiteezi'.

Polly and Bryan, six, were on their bit of lawn, he solemnly winding up the gramophone and she sunbathing while Sonny swam between the punts. Polly rummaged in a drawer and produced a stray bathing-costume which roughly fitted me: the conventional 1929 model, black, cut slackly across thigh and not tight up over hip. From there it rose decorously to a high U neck-line and shoulder-straps looped under the arms.

I changed in my cubicle in the rear, next to my folding-bed. Thrashing up and down the water on my back, I heard from one bungalow after another quavers of matey music, 'I Want To Be Happy', 'Louise', 'Tip-toe Through the Tulips'.

My week-end lasted three weeks. In between picnic meals on the tiny verandah, with beer or sherry, I lay in the sun with my eyes shut, imprinting on my lazy mind such details as Polly peeling potatoes of Bryan tranquilly making mud-pies. Continuously with friends, I realized what a lonely life I led in London.

There was the occasional twinge, such as a call from the retreating dinghy, 'See you all late tonight!' 'Poor Dorice, matinée on a day like this . . .' She was in *Murder on the Second Floor*, by and with Frank Vosper, a great success. *A Murder Has Been Arranged On The Second Floor*, poor Dorice my eye . . .

I had been frank with Polly and Sonny about my finances. One bedtime she appeared at the door of my cubicle: 'Would you like to come to Bordighera with us and tutor Bryan in Italian?'

I sat on the bed touched to the quick, but as I heard the creak I knew the answer would be no. Because I had a plan. To be a success in the theatre. I told them I would not forget their offer; like the miner's shilling, it would bring me luck.

It did. I thought I had better check about work, and travelled up into the city heat. But the autumn was on its way, with its promise—to the successful—of great projects; to the others it would mean a chill in the air.

'Ah,' Mr Peacock said, 'I was just going to wire you, would you like to play bits in the new O'Casey play Cochran's putting on, I've suggested you to understudy Laughton. Cochran's known for paying well, they're offering twelve.'

CHAPTER NINE

THE CHANCE

The faces bustling through Waterloo Station looked friendly, and the train full of light: not only was O'Casey at the peak of his success, with *The Silver Tassie* I would at last be under the right C.B.: Cochran the Showman. In the train I picked up a newspaper and read about the play: 'Our astute Mr Cochran has evidently realized from *Journey's End* that the war is at last box office.'

And to understudy Laughton would be marvellous. Short and fat, he had become—only last year, at the age of twenty-nine—the most talked-of actor in London. Remembering that he was subject to laryngitis, I felt a heartless glow; he was to play a wounded footballer, and I could look much more like a half-back than he could, provided no ball was laid at my feet. The tang of autumn was no longer apprehensive.

At the first Apollo rehearsal the stage was milling with actors, from Ian Hunter and Beatrix Lehmann to the Irish players headed by Barry Fitzgerald and Una O'Connor; in their midst, unmistakeable, was the star of the play. Laughton was massively crouched in an old wheel-chair, knuckles white round the arms of it, eyes protruding wildly in a pale pudge of a moon-face. He looked nearer fifty than thirty.

Without warning, he started to spin: back and round, round and back, frantic with frustration. While the others chatted and pretended not to notice, he was unselfconsciously getting the feel of his last act: a procedure, at this stage of rehearsal, then unknown.

I crossed to a corner to join the dozen other young people walking on. They were staring at Laughton, caught without being impressed. 'Footballer my eye,' one muttered, 'looks more like the football.'

When the understudy list was posted up, I was disheartened to read that Laughton's had gone to a tall good-looking nobody who apparently 'covered' the star of a play automatically. I was to understudy four small parts and walk on 'as required': one minute a Stretcher-Bearer (Third), the next among the dozen guests dancing the tango.

While the principals rehearsed, we the crowd sat interminably. The play was too intense to move me, except when the band off-stage played 'Avalon' and 'Whispering' while the broken soldier whirled among the dancers like a maimed bull on wheels. With a dance tune and an invalid chair and the mask of a great actor, the moment encompassed the tragedy of war.

Every day after rehearsal we spent a tedious hour standing round a piano, repeating over and over again the Catholic chants, in Latin and in Greek—'Kyrie eleison...'—which we were to intone offstage in the weird second act; a posse of professional wailers at a wake. I also seemed to spend helpless hours sitting on the stone stairs wrestling with khaki puttees, trying to wind them trimly round. They always ended up coiled round my ankles, and I thanked God that when the war ended I was twelve.

Laughton we never saw offstage except as a brooding baby in a wheel-chair, obsessed by the difficulties of his part—his Irish accent was up against the real thing all round him—or as a wild beast charging into his dressing-room to gargle and spit. But it was not unsociability, for in the wings he would suddenly cast off his troubles and wheel round at anybody who was there, it could be any of us.

Then something would bubble out; once it was to Clive Morton and me. 'Christ these Irish parts, but it can happen the other way round—when I went to Dublin recently to get the feel of this, I saw a tremendously Oriental play which started with the Muez-zin in the market place and weird Arab music—fine until one of the hooded figures on his knees turned to his neighbour and said, "Methinks the wind of Allah boiteth mighty cold in the bazaar tonoight."'

This exploded him into helpless laughter which transformed the smouldering sufferer into a mischievous fat cherub. Just as swiftly there was a dissolve back to the sufferer: he sighed, lumped forward and started to glower, ready for his next entrance. Then a hoarse near-Irish mutter of despair, 'Will Oi ever get it roight, damn an' blast...?'

One day I mentioned Walter Peacock and he said abruptly. 'He told me you're a good actor'. I was surprised that he knew which I was. Then a relapse into torment.

Though I still enjoyed the prospect of being overpaid twelve pounds a week, the fact that I was in the middle of a seething top London production with no share in it induced, from day to day, intense frustration. Ironically, if you walked on in a West End show as opposed to being locally acclaimed in provincial rep, at any minute you could be physically within inches of success. Once, at the stage door, a voice thin and high, 'Mr Laughton rehearsing still?'

It came from a waifish gypsy of a girl in a skimpy cloth cloak and sandals, with frizzy red hair, a snub nose and enormous golden eyes whom I recognized as Elsa Lanchester, the star of a satirical cabaret *The Cave of Harmony* who turned out, improbably, to be Mrs Laughton. Not so improbably, though, for he had wrenched free of his family's stolid Scarborough hotel to become himself a gypsy.

Another time I was walking with Clive past His Majesty's, where the queues snaked round the theatre for *Bitter Sweet*; a young man hurried past us. 'Look,' Clive said, pointing to the slim trim back disappearing in at the stage-door, 'that was Noël Coward!' If he had turned round and approached us, I would have stared at him as at a ghost, and scuttled.

He was six years, less twenty days, older than me. I had six years to go.

Rehearsals alternated with a private plan. One day I met Freddie in Soho, back from his *Bird in Hand* tour. He stopped at a door in Old Compton Street. 'That's my room, ducks, up there, means you're marvellously central.'

I had a sudden longing to be the same. 'I'd suggest sharin' a flat,' he went on, 'but my Dennis wouldn't like it, you know how it is ... Listen, why don't you suggest it to one of the boys in the show? A flat for two's no end cheaper, and more value for your pennies.'

A flat ... And shared with a compatible friend, each coming and going as he pleased but always with the other to chat and have coffee with—life would warm up! I felt my way gingerly.

All the walkers-on were fixed but Clive knew of a chap playing a small part at the Queen's in *The Apple Cart*, Paul Tanker. He seemed pleasant and serious, and declared himself sick of digs and anxious to share till he got married. We settled on 12a Wellington Mansions, at the top of Upper St Martin's Lane.

They were far from being mansions. A dark stone hall led to a small stone staircase: at its foot, up one step, 12a. We were shown round the flat by an eager sharp-faced lady from upstairs. 'It's a sub-let you see . . .'

The front door opened on to a large room, with beyond a tiny passage leading to a smaller room, a lavatory, and a small kitchen with a bath in it: all for thirty shillings a week unfurnished, *and* there was electric light. Paul would have the big room for a pound and furnish it, I the back room for ten bob. And in a flat!

The drawback was that the walls were filthy and the bath even rustier than in Vincent Square, but the lady assured us that she would have 'the workmen' distemper right through and enamel the bath, no charge, and the day after my first night we could move in. As a housewarming present I bought myself a portable gramophone and a couple of records.

After our last late Saturday night rehearsal, I thought I would show 12a to Clive. After bacon and eggs at the Corner House, we walked up St Martin's Lane and into the dark hall of the Mansions.

As I took out my key I was puzzled to see a light under the door. At one a.m.? I peered through the letter-box. On a ladder held by the lady, her son of fourteen was sloshing the wall with an old paint-brush; I could see the dust flying. It seemed tactful to walk away.

The *Daily Telegraph* described *The Silver Tassie* as 'puzzling', *The Times* as 'a great stumbling failure', but of course it would run.

Later in the morning I piled my bits of furniture on to a cart, said goodbye to Mr Higley—'Jolly good luck, Williams!'—didn't bother about Mrs Mellowfield (that phone bill), took the bus to Trafalgar Square and walked up past the Coliseum to my new home. W.C.2 . . .

That night Paul and I decided to have our first bath. It was satisfying to watch the steaming water trickle over the new white enamel. We tossed up for first go, he won.

Suddenly, from the kitchen, 'Oh, my God . . .' I ran in to find my flat-mate standing naked in a cloud of vapour and when he turned round, his calves and bottom were splattered with white: hot,

blistered paint. Our landlady's son and foreman, after sloshing the walls, had sloshed the bath. I was glad to have lost the
toss.

Next morning, after shaving at the sink, I spent an hour sand-
papering; the bath ended up more mottled than when I first set
eyes on it. To enamel it would cost as much as a new bath, so
we settled for what we had: a flat in the West End.

* * *

On the first Monday night, empty seats. Cochran the infallible
had been misled by *Journey's End*; this was a war play that was
not going to succeed. And while the arranging of the flat had
been fun, once it was over . . . the fun was over too.

Going in and out I became more and more depressed; the hall,
shapeless and empty, led by the stairs to a sordid compound of
what must be tiny rooms with a floating population of tarts and
near-tramps. Once, at midnight, I found a shabby woman slumped
against our door, dead drunk and looking as if she had been
murdered by Jack the Ripper.

My dim top bulb was dismal and I went back to the old
Aladdin lamp, but no glow could disguise the walls: the edges
were jagged and grime showed through everywhere. My window
overlooked a warehouse roof, with a skylight in the shape of a
dirt-stained coffin humped against the corner of a grey sky. I
might be living anywhere.

The front room had the same view. On its opposite side, next
to the front door, an embarrassingly large window afforded us the
prospect—through another window a couple of feet lower and
four away, bang-on and stereoscopic—of another flat, semi-
basement.

It sounds sociably bohemian, but what we faced was a sombre
room inhabited by a furtive man-and-wife who gave the continual
impression that they were hiding from the law. Whenever they
saw me pass our window, they would start visibly as if I were a
policeman in uniform. We decided to keep those curtains permanently closed. No such problem with the kitchen window. There
wasn't one.

One other thing I became conscious of: that as I had to go
through the front room to get to mine, or to get out, we were two

strangers deprived of privacy. A more serious realization was that we had nothing in common. Not meant to be an actor, my flat-mate was ambitious 'in the management field' and pontificated plummily, 'the pros and cons of the proscenium arch ...'.

One night I brought Freddie back for coffee. 'Sorry 'bout me 'air ducks, my Dennis tidged it up but he'd 'ad a couple an' it's gone a wee bit goldilocksy ...'

My flat-mate was drinking beer with two clumping chums in the front room, and after stiff introductions Freddie and I hurried through.

As I closed my door we heard a loud laugh. 'They're sending me up,' Freddie said cheerfully, 'through the roof. Couldn't care less, I got a 'ead for heights ... He's terribly wet ducks, what 'ave you let yourself in for?'

As I made the coffee, he sensibly remarked that as neither I nor my wet friend could cook, the kitchen was wasted.

On Sunday it rained. I longed for Vincent Square, for the mason's yard and the cheerful chords of Mr Higley's piano, and went for a walk. On it I understood, too late, that for an actor Central London is a week-night affair plus two matinées: all around me I felt the Sunday emptiness.

The drizzle drove me back, and in the echoing dark hall I collided with a burly Bill Sikes of a drunk: glazed malevolent eyes, tottering legs. 'Sorry, old boy ...' A typical lost lodger from upstairs.

I put on Gracie, but today she failed me. 'Thoughts of you ... when you are far away ...' Thoughts of whom?

* * *

A letter was forwarded from 314a: 'Dear George, Remember me, Holywell County? Fancy you on the stage, how thrilling, I'm teaching and have a flat near Paddington, Yours ever, Dilys Pugh.' She had been a commonplace girl but it would be a nice change to swop school memories and I went to tea.

The plain schoolgirl had blossomed into an alert bouncy-breasted young woman: no make-up, healthy red lips. We had our tea and scones on the rug in front of the fire and reminisced, 'Oh, George, I *was* scared of Miss Cooke, you felt she could read your thoughts, oo-er.' She put on a record of 'You Were Meant for

Me' and sank down again beside me, hands crossed behind her head. Our eyes met. I was expected to make love to her.

With an immediacy which surprised me I rolled on top of her and kissed her ravenously. As I fumbled among a thick jumper for the two sensitive areas, the question darted across my mind— was I expected to travel with one of those things in my wallet?

As I fumbled lower she fumbled lower still, but—alas—not in my direction. She was pushing my hand away and murmuring, 'No, George, no . . .'

Whether her motive was prudence or false modesty, her reaction was a bucket of water on a small but roaring fire. And my childhood name had not helped. I sat up, rumpled and foolish, while she pulled her skirt down and said, in a little-girl voice, 'That was naughty of us, wasn't it?'

Then she did something I recognized from old-fashioned novels: she pouted. 'You Were Meant For Me' was running down, and trailed into a sullen growl. My fire was out. We talked politely of Holywell, she asked if I knew Noël Coward. I said yes, I'd seen him only recently. I longed to get away, and pleaded a rehearsal.

In the Tube, wondering if I had been expected to whisper sweet nothings before suggesting Sunday night dinner and a film, all paving the way to victory, I was back to my self-searching in New York. I tried to see myself sharing 12a with her, pouting all over the place. No, better the flat-mate I spent my time avoiding . . .

In the meantime, what I called the C.L., the Cooke Loan, was being eaten into; the future was parlous. Freddie said: 'What about that swanky degree you got? You could go back to bein' a school-teacher.'

I said indignantly, 'But I've never been one!' Then I remembered my Criccieth night-classes. No . . .

Out of the blue, whence all things hurtle towards actors, came the chance.

❊　　❊　　❊

On a Sunday night a war play called *Tunnel Trench* had been well received; sparked again by *Journey's End*, it was to be put on for a run. The author had seen *Glamour* and I was wanted for a secondary part, they would pay my present salary. Mr Peacock had checked that since I earned over ten pounds in *The Silver Tassie* I was entitled to give two weeks' notice.

An hour later an envelope arrived at 12a: my part in *Tunnel Trench*. It was in one scene in the last act, only four pages but tightly typed. Private St Aubyn is discovered, mortally wounded, by his eldest brother (Brian Aherne, the star of the play) and talks deliriously to him.

My eyes picked out stray sentences. *'Why doesn't somebody come to see me...? I'm so damn thirsty...I want to get through! There are people—millions of people! People to have a good time with...to bathe with, all the squalor washed away...I'm not going to live, I know it now...Some water...Never fight again...'* He falls back, the lights fade.

I stared at the page. For an actor with no worries it was a gift: for one in my state, a miracle. There was not even the hazard of finding oneself in a star part and unable to bear the weight. I looked at the drabness around me and floated above it as if to drift out of the window, over the wet warehouse roof and up through dirty grey clouds into the sun.

In the dressing-room that night, although I understated—'quite an effective bit'—Clive and the others were envious, 'lucky bastard'. Paul Tanker echoed them and so did Freddie, *St Aubyn,* what a posh name...

Next morning I took the part out of its envelope as if it were four bank-notes and talked to myself as if I were a director: don't try to act young, you *are* young—if you're a boy dying in a trench the audience will be moved by just looking at you—so don't reach out, don't *know* you're dying...

At the reading, the large cast included a rabble of one-line parts, young men in the Flying Corps; how easily I might have found myself one of them! During the hour and a half I spent waiting for my scene, I found that apart from Aherne's there was no outstanding part except mine. By the time we came to it, my fingers had tired of clenching.

The stage manager muttered, *'Scene, a shell-hole.'* Aherne, in his reading voice: *'Ronnie...Good God, is it you, are you hurt...?'* I spoke quietly too, pencil in hand, indicating the torment of the dying boy with the faintest catch of breath. *'Why doesn't someone come to see me...?'* I felt inattentive heads turning my way, but held back. *'Am I in pain?...Only a*

little ... I'm not going to live, I know it now.' At the end, the
director Reginald Denham smiled and said 'Fine.' I had cleared
a hurdle.

To 314a and to Miss Cooke I did not understate: 'It's a big
chance.' After several days while the rest of the play was being
set, I was called; alone in a rehearsal room with Aherne and the
director, I thought of the day I had seen Evans and Olivier preparing a similar situation.

I stayed tentative, Mr Denham's directions were few and help-
ful; a progressive start. He said there was a lot of work to be
done on the rest of the play, three more days till my next go.

Times: 'Tunnel Trench will be the first play to open the newly-
built Duchess Theatre, on November the 25th. The cast, headed
by Brian Aherne, will include Reginald Bach and Emlyn Williams.' November the 25th would be the eve of my twenty-fourth
birthday.

My last week in *The Silver Tassie* started with a couple of
straight run-throughs of my scene, the second almost smooth; I
felt I was beginning to create hallucination. *'Bright sun, beautiful
horses, thousands of them ...'.*

Next day we 'had a bash' again, straight through twice, just us
two and the director. 'Right,' Reggie said; by now he was Reggie.

I got into my overcoat and said a cheery good afternoon. It was
still early, about three. But I had forgotten to ask about my next
rehearsal; turning to run back I heard footsteps coming down.

'Sorry, Reggie,' I said, 'I didn't ask when you want me.'

'Awfully sorry, Emlyn'—he pronounced it perfectly—'but I've
got some not very good news.'

I thought of 314a, somebody had died ... He coughed. 'I'm
sorry, but I've regretfully come to the conclusion you're not quite
right for the part.'

[121]

CHAPTER TEN

CHARLIE IS ME DARLIN'

I stared at him and my mouth went dry. A couple of walkers-on squeezed past us on their way up.

He rattled on, uneasily apologetic. 'It's just that you're—well, not believable as Brian's brother, you can't help being emotional and . . . well, Welsh. Nobody feels worse than I do, I'm sorry—and of course if you want to stay, walking on and under-study-ing . . .'

Another actor hurried by; I coaxed my well-thumbed part from my pocket. He said again, 'I'm so sorry.'

'So am I, to have wasted your time.' 'Oh, that . . . I only hope you stay.' Returning upstairs he must have felt relieved to have weathered the nastiest ordeal a director can be subjected to: sacking an actor.

Finding myself in the street, I wheeled round a corner. Then back on my tracks and round another corner. Cars and buses loomed up and growled past me as masses of nothing, while pedestrians were a procession of limping winter masks, the blank background to my own disintegration. Through Cambridge Circus, Shaftesbury Avenue, Piccadilly Circus, it was a tramp round and round the West End which I had wooed and just been slapped by, hard.

As I veered past Leicester Square Tube, a face swam into focus: C. B. Williams, who had presented *Glamour*. My eyes bounced off him and I walked the other way.

Halted by traffic, I felt a sharp tap on the arm and turned to find the same face close to, infinitely sadder and older, with a spark of anger added. 'I'm the chap who put your play on and did his best for you, remember? Are you ashamed of me?'

I looked at him stupidly. Instead of saying, 'I've just lost my job and don't know what I'm doing', I shook my head and walked blindly across the street. I could have been run over. I never saw him again. When he died, he must have nursed a poor memory of me.

I had to go back to 12a some time. I ran past the dividing curtain and sank on my bed. On Queue Day I had thought I was touching rock-bottom; I was now lying on it, grinding my nose into the crevices of failure.

For five minutes I stared in front of me, and halfway through thought this would make an effective film shot. Then I burst into tears, rose and was faced in the mirror with the distorted face of a spoilt baby.

Pride had to be swallowed with no regurgitation: a decision must be made. To stay in *The Silver Tassie*? I would sooner make a pilgrimage, on my knees, down Shaftesbury Avenue and up the stairs to Miriam Warner's office—can you play Dicky Bird parts?

No, it would be *Tunnel Trench*, walking on and understudying. But first, with darkness the Apollo had to be faced: the communal dressing-room, the khaki puttees and the chat, hello chaps anything new on the Rialto?

'Well, yes, I'd been uneasy for days about this part and today I finally persuaded Reggie ... Oh, I'm staying on doing bits and pieces, interesting play and this isn't going to run ...' There is such a thing as professional pride. There is dishonesty too.

At the next morning's rehearsal I took my place among the walkers-on. One said, 'What happened?'

'Reggie and I talked it over ...'

Besides 'bits and pieces' I was to understudy my ex-part, Private St Aubyn. Freddie had been right, it was a posh name, perhaps that had been the trouble ... But I would be allowed to play it in an emergency, when an actor labelled as inadequate is better than no actor at all.

I was numb enough to feel nothing and obey orders. In the first act, as Captain Sandys—in being demoted as actor I had been promoted as airman—all I had to do was sit in the Flying Corps Mess, cross-legged among the others, and listen.

Later I had two lines: first, 'Four are still in the air, sir' and— watch out, mustn't miss it—'Come on chaps, let's leave.' In later scenes, I was 'an Observer' (speechless) and '2nd German Private' (speechless). Versatility.

In a lull Aherne came up: 'I thought you were going to be jolly good, but of course Reggie has the last word.' I was touched but nothing could help.

Who would be the new St Aubyn? I hoped he would be attractive enough to damp my jealousy. Somebody whispered, 'Wetherby's playing it.' I looked.

He had sandy hair, was no better-looking than me and not fresh from the public-school mint either, having superimposed an immensely correct accent on an Australian one. We ran into each other on the stairs and I managed to say, 'Good part, isn't it?'

'It is rawther, isn't it?', and he passed on. He could have said, 'Sorry I got it this way ...' Sod him.

'My dear Son George, Your Mother and me have no doubt whatever that you will fulfil your obligations in your new capacities to the satisfaction of all concerned.' From Miss Cooke, 'What a fearful business casting must be! My word, when all else fails, you can sit in the street with a notice-b'd saying STORIES TOLD & the coins will drop on you like manna ...'

During the run-throughs, when it came to the St Aubyn scene I was careful to get out of earshot and join the walkers-on. A dull lot they were, and not overloaded with looks; sitting listlessly around, I became conscious of the absence of female society and got the illusion that we were a minor school with Aherne as the clean-cut Head Boy.

The new little Duchess Theatre, only just finished in time, offered a hundred steps from the stage to the dressing-rooms, one of which I shared with five others. The march in file, up and down, down and up, again belonged to a school.

The play stemmed from heartfelt experience, but on the first night the audience began to cough. Next day, my twenty-fourth birthday, the play was a failure.

I needed the money, but I would have found a lengthy term at this pseudo-school unbearable: particularly after an incident which seemed to me, even then, bizarre. In later years, it would be incredible.

The curtain had fallen on the first matinée, would the walkers-on report in Mr Aherne's room. 'It's the old dodge,' I overheard, 'salary cuts to keep the show going.'

We crowded in. Aherne, like all of us, still wore his uniform and looked more than ever like the Head Boy addressing a scruffy

O.T.C. He cleared his throat, 'I'm afraid a delicate situation has arisen.'

A hush. Money missing from dressing-rooms, can you believe it ... ? We waited.

'One of you did something at the dress rehearsal.'

I glanced round; Maitland was missing, a slight hang-dog kid who never spoke. A thief ...?

The Head Boy continued. 'And I have been asked to do this by the other person concerned, to put you on your guard. The chap who isn't here made an indecent suggestion to him.'

Silence at the court martial. Then a mechanical voice, 'Oh, I say ...' Then another, 'Good God ...'

Not believing my ears, I thought of the poor repressed nobody upstairs, wondering where everybody was and little knowing that he was to be shot at dawn. Everybody was looking nonplussed except Hudson, a tall smug boy with insipid good looks.

I was back ten years and tasting what it would have been like at a public school. But we were grown men—not one under twenty-one—Aherne twenty-seven—and earning our living in a sophisticated metropolis. I was enraged, and as nobody else spoke I did, and did not care what came out.

'You mean he raped him?'

A nervous titter. 'No, no,' Aherne said, 'not quite that!'

'He put his hand there?'

Sniggers. 'Er—I imagine something of the sort ...'

I had never before taken a floor and held it. 'Anyway, aren't we all men and able to defend ourselves?'

A last nervous laugh; Hudson had gone red. Aherne's face cleared—'I agree'—and they trooped out. I turned back. He had been kind to me and I hoped I hadn't rattled him.

'I'm glad you said that,' he said. 'It was awkward for me, he was so insistent.'

'And I'm glad you agree. If this happens after a week, what will it be like after six months?'

I needn't have worried. The following Saturday the school closed.

❀   ❀   ❀

I sat in my room, put on the other side of Gracie—Toselli's Serenade—and brought my little black book up-to-date. Silver

T. £54, Tunnel T. £24, Sunday Shows £2.25. £80 earned in nine months. £2 a week.

'Dear Miss Cooke, the Cooke Loan is in a bad way, a bath with water trickling in and streaming out. I have made a decision: if no work turns up by Christmas Eve, I shall write to the firm of Gabbitas and Thring (to both jointly, in case the other might take umbrage) to see what teaching posts are going...' That blackboard, those desks... The first morning I would age ten years. But might the embittered young schoolmaster, in the intervals of correcting grubby exercise books, burn the midnight oil and write a searing masterpiece in three acts about an embittered young schoolmaster correcting grubby exercise books? Daydreams are incurable.

December the 13th: eleven days to go.

From Miss Cooke: 'I don't like a depressed letter from you. The stage has its swings and its roundabouts, this is a roundabout.' But she was soon herself again. 'Take Baldwin, decent I grant you, and like many decent folk, futile...'

On the 14th, passing the great window of Keith Prowse the major theatre agency, I stared at the rows of posters plastered with the names of the thriving. I was an orphan savouring hot food through glass. Ten days to go.

On the 15th, a phone call from Walter Peacock. Archie de Bear, a well-known revue producer, was reviving *French Leave* for a limited season for Charles Laughton: a light comedy set 'behind the lines'—it seemed that I could not escape from the Great War —and nine years ago a healthy West End success. Would I read, at the reading, the small part of the French interpreter, originally played by George de Warfaz? He was not free.

I had been so bruised that I was unable to be optimistic. Suppose that during rehearsals de Warfaz suddenly became available?

Such useless surmise was cut short by a knock. 'Sorry to intrude,' my flat-mate said, 'I'm getting married next month.'

'Congratulations, means you'll be leaving?' I failed to keep the relief out of my voice.

'Afraid so,' he said, doing the same thing.

'Mon. 17 Dec, Vaudeville Th, Stalls Bar.' Laughton greeted me as a friend. 'You'll be pleased to hear, my dear chap, that I've been promoted from Private to General.' A startlingly radiant girl turned out to be our leading lady, Madeleine Carroll. The cast was small: besides them, two young officers, two Cockney soldiers, a landlady, and me.

The landlady was to be played by May Agate, whose French was so good she was bilingual. When she and I got to our big scene and the stage manager read out, 'Here they embark on an altercation, in French', Miss Agate screamed at me, impromptu, 'Tu es un cochon!' 'Toi aussi,' I shouted back at her, 'merde alors!' Laughton and the others roared with laughter; I knew then that she and I could work up something special and that it would take more than George de Warfaz to do me out of this part. My salary would be twelve-ten a week for eight weeks. I was reprieved.

At rehearsals we all felt proud to have in our midst the prettiest girl for miles; the two juveniles were friendly and civilized and Charles—in this cast he was 'Charles' by the second week—became a happy enfant terrible as he prepared his caricature of a top-brass idiot. He beamed on us all.

For me, a break at Christmas passed as unnoticed as did New Year 1930. It couldn't be worse than 1929.

One day Charles turned to me suddenly, like a sincere child and with a near-stutter which seemed a symptom of embarrassment, 'Emma-lyn, you're very g-good you know'. It was what I needed. Another day we got to a scene in which I had to say to him, 'Mon Général, I have my suspicions.'

Studying the evening before, I had decided, since the French for suspicions is 'soupçons', to try something out. At the rehearsal I drew myself up and said, 'Mon Général, I have my soupspicions.'

Charles turned to the director, 'But that's perfect—exactly the way a Frenchman would say it!' I could have kissed the moon-rubber face, right on the button of a nose, for helping my self-confidence to stagger to its feet.

The play opened to easy light-hearted success, there were sunny notices all round, and I had a dressing-room to myself with a sofa. I spent my long waits on it, a French soldier studying a German grammar, which I only set aside in February to study my part, for the Sunday Greins, in *Das Blaue vom Himmel*; it was short but in German, and I was glad of the difficulties. After the last two engagements, this one was a frolic.

But returning to the flat at night, I dreaded that dark hall; once or twice the same burly Bill Sikes loomed and lurched, typical of the slum we were all trapped in. I had bought my ex-flat-mate's double divan and slept in the denuded front room. I was lonely again.

Freddie buzzed in and out. 'My Dennis got a friend, acquaintance reely, they met in the Bargain Basement, a boy we call Miss Curtis who's an assistant at John Lewis and madly looking for somewhere to kip. What's wrong wi' him havin' the back room and running the flat for you, he'd be out all day and you out all evening, what about it?'

I said I'd like to see Miss Curtis first. And I was reassured; he was slight and pasty with frog-eyes behind glasses as solid as paper-weights, and only spoke some time after being spoken to. In his brown suit and tie he moved noiselessly into the back room for ten bob a week.

On his first night I got back to find he was in bed. There was no sign that he was there, except that he had washed up, cleaned the kitchen and placed a bowl of water in front of the gas fire with a note: 'Stops the air getting dry, goodnight.'

But he *was* there, and when I heard strange footsteps stagger past our front door I was glad. Next morning I was woken with a cup of tea, and by the time I had finished it he had silently vanished, on his way to 'business'. It's non-living, I reflected, but a good arrangement.

March. New sofa-study in my dressing-room for the Greins, this time in Italian, a longish part in *La Piccola*, and rehearsals were a marvellous exercise. They were alternately brought to the boil by a lovable explosive old Italian actor, Vittorio Rietti, then calmed by the benign presence of the director, Beerbohm Tree's immensely tall vague daughter Viola.

Amiable and urbane, she knew little Italian and met the situation halfway by directing in musical terms drawled in uncompromising English. 'Don't you agree dawlings, that that was a little *too* vibrato? And now my dears, what d'you say to da capo with a *twinge* of allegretto?'

'This month Mr Williams will act in his fourth language in eleven weeks'; I was acquiring a sub-reputation as a linguistic freak, and not sure that I liked it: a Berlitz mime-of-all-work.

The next week, though, brought the offer of an English-speaking part. Would I like to play, Everyman Theatre, one short scene in Kaiser's *The Fire in the Opera House*, Sybil Thorndike, seven performances, a guinea for each?

Next morning, another: would I like to play, Prince of Wales Theatre, one short scene in Clifford Bax's *Socrates*, Lewis Casson, two performances, a guinea each? The Casson family was on my side.

'Sat. March 8, FRENCH LEAVE last 2 perfs.' 'Dear Dad and Mam, Charles has to leave to star in the new Edgar Wallace thriller about the Chicago gangsters, all the Wallace plays have been winners, *The Ringer*, *The Squeaker*, *The Flying Squad*, *The Calendar*.' Not only was Wallace front-page news, he was a fanatical racing man and constantly figured on Dad's daily back page.

French Leave had renewed me, and Sunday's morning tea was flattering. I brought my little black book up to date: from April to April 1929, in spite of the first barren six months I had earned £200, an average of four pounds a week. A bit better.

But by Monday afternoon I felt—as many actors do, post last-Saturday-night—that I had not worked for weeks; I was glad that tomorrow afternoon I would be rehearsing for *La Piccola*.

The sun was out and I went for a West End walk. Cutting through St Martin's Court, I caught a glimpse of Charles hurrying in at Wyndham's stage-door, where the Wallace play was in rehearsal, his second day. I sauntered past, killing time.

*   *   *

The next morning the phone rang, would I come at once to Wyndham's, they were replacing somebody in Mr Wallace's *On the Spot*, a small part, and Mr Laughton had suggested me.

Within three minutes I had raced down St Martin's Lane, swerved right at the New Theatre, and dived down the steps at the stage-door and on to the stage.

Nothing seemed to be happening. The bare stage faced a darkened empty auditorium in a silence complete except for church-like whisperings from dim corners. Only one figure was discernible, picked out under the working light, centre stage: Laughton.

As when he had swung about in his wheel-chair, he was feeling his way to something, alone and absorbed. But this was different:

he was pacing to and fro like a caged hobbledehoy, glaring and growling.

First he experimented with a clumsy waddle, from which emerged a walking gait, lithe, graceful, tigerish; then the hobbledehoy stood stock-still and scowled into the dark, blubber-lips pursed. He might have just been told that for the school play he had been turned down for the part of Cupid and was settling for a sulky Bacchus.

Then he would prowl again, muttering phrases to himself, a hotch-potch of imitation Italian and broken English. As before, the actors in the shadows studied him with the amusement of bystanders at a fair: weird way to work, rum cove, make a good story in the Green Room Club . . .

A tall gangling young man bustled in from the stage door. 'Sorry, Charles, it was Edgar on the phone.' He was hurrying past when he saw me. 'Mr. Williams is it? I'm Carol Reed, stage director.' He looked younger than me; I had read that Wallace swore by him and it was not hard to see why, his enthusiastic charm was infallible.

'Sorry this is so sudden—you know?—I'm afraid all the scripts are out but here's the part, you've time to get the hang of it.' I retired into a corner. I had not yet recovered from the phone call, and was taking things as they happened.

The pages were mostly filled with short sentences, but after gathering that Angelo was Perelli's right-hand man, I soon knew that the scarcity of the lines was out of all proportion to the importance of the character. It was one of those golden parts which are constantly just east or west of centre-stage and in which every line tells.

There was one difficulty: the assumption was that Angelo spoke in an idiom completely American, and I was not at home with any unfamiliar accent in English. 'Say, Tony,' I whispered to myself, and it did not come easily.

From the back of the shrouded auditorium, a stir. I scrambled to my feet. Laughton stopped pacing as a figure strode squarely down the aisle, followed by others: the King of the Jungle, the long cigarette-holder trailing a cloud of Staff. Edgar Wallace.

I remembered the report—and it fitted the legend—that after a couple of days in Chicago he had written *On the Spot* in the train. 'Sorry, Charlie'—he called him Charlie!—''ad to go an' see

a bloke about a racehorse.' He was a dry, curt, amiable realist of
a man's man, at pains to show he was still a Cockney. Laughton
saw me and hurriedly presented me, across the extinguished
footlights, to 'Edgar'.

'Ah,' said the legend, 'I hear you're an Italian scholar?'

'I don't know about that, sir, but I'm playing on Sunday in
Italian at the Arts.' God bless Mrs Grein and Miss Cooke.

'Well, that sounds the ticket. You're E.W. are you—well wi'
those initials your future's in the bag!' His joke gave me a fillip,
must tell Dad...

'Half a mo, while I catch up wi' the serious side o' life.'

Everybody waited while he stood—with his back to the stage
to get the light—flicked open the early edition of the *Evening
Standard*, and immersed himself in the racing outlook. Laughton
resumed his prowl, while Reed came up to me.

'The position is this,' he whispered, taking my arm and making
me feel like an important friend, 'Mr Wallace had pictured
Angelo as a big older Middle Western thug—you know—and cast
Roy Emerton. But Charles got to feel he was too like the other
gangsters and sees Angelo as a different type, young, dark—you
know?—so he's been switched to a smaller part, you know how
these things can happen?' I did indeed.

But Emerton rehearsed only yesterday; and being Canadian he
must have a passable accent... 'Right,' Wallace said briskly,
making a mark and throwing the paper down, everybody conscious that he had just decided to risk a couple of hundred pounds,
'let's have a look at the stable, mm?'

I took the plunge. 'Mr Wallace, would you like me to try empha-
sizing the Italian side, implying that he was born in Italy like
Perelli, which helps the bond between them?'

Laughton looked at Edgar; 'I like that.' 'Fine,' Edgar said. I
said, 'Thank you, sir', opened an imaginary door, script in hand,
and embarked on a conversation with Perelli. It had to be casual
and swift, I was reading the lines aloud for the first time and at
the same time conscious of a group of burly gangsters watching
me, among them the one who had lost my part.

I was too nervous to be nervous. Phrases I brought out in
expertly Italian broken-English—Welsh vowels, with soft con-
sonants—got entangled in American insecurely mumbled; I
seemed to be thrashing through bushes and tripping over boul-

ders which I had not seen coming up. Laughton was a help by being as yet unaware of his lines and himself mumbling and fumbling after the right accent.

The scene was over at last. A hush. Somebody looked at a watch, it was lunchtime and I half saw Wallace making for the pass-door. He went up to Laughton, said something, then came to me. I stiffened. 'That's O.K., as we say in the play. See Bill will you—Carol, a couple of things—two thirty?'

Bill was S. E. Linnit, his business manager, a handsome affable young man sitting in a little office next to the stage-door. 'Well,' he said with a twinkle, 'how much are we to pay you?'

I thought, like lightning, Wallace pays well, suggest sixteen and come down to fifteen.

Then I attempted a twinkle myself. 'What would you say the part is worth?'

'Twenty?'

'Fine.' I heard the word come from behind my face, and sounded a little bored as I added, 'It's what I had in mind.'

'You'll have your contract on Friday.'

'Mr Linnit, there's one snag. I can't let Miss Thorndike and Mr Casson and Miss Tree down.' I explained.

'God, you're a busy beaver . . .' He was sure they would all fit my few rehearsals between my priority calls at Wyndham's.

By the time I came to, I was sitting in a café staring at two poached eggs, then out of the window down one of the alleys I had stumbled along after being sacked. Could it be only sixteen weeks ago? I hurried back to the Mansions and sat down to have a better look at Angelo. 'Dear Dad and Mam, An incredible thing has happened . . .'

In the afternoon I met the rest of the cast, first the gangsters and the police: Ben Welden, Dennis Wyndham, Roy Emerton, W. Cronin-Wilson, they were certainly big hulking brutes. Shaking hands with Cronin-Wilson, I recognized him as the Bill Sikes I had seen zigzagging in and out of the Mansions; at the moment he looked the worse for wear but dead sober. The coincidence might bring luck. Gillian Lind I knew from *Mafro, Darling!*; next I was presented to Gladys Frazin, who was to play the 'vamp'.

A moment before, Gillian Lind had been a beautiful young girl; now she looked like the vicar's daughter. For Miss Frazin added up to more than an actress. 'She's no Bernhardt,' I had overheard earlier, 'but she amuses Edgar.'

Miss Frazin was a grande cocotte, Broadway version. Drowned in mink, she looked radiantly happy in her immersion; as she swayed, the mink parted to show the glitter of diamonds at every chink, from ears to shoe-buckles, while behind the buckles were the highest heels I had ever seen, every step was a hazard. It was also my first encounter with false eyelashes, on a face wearing what could only be called an overcoat of make-up: a pearly mask, with scarlet lips cradling a great smile.

From tiny toe to tiny hat sparklingly pinned above a bang of black hair over one eye, she was enamel and jewellery and fur. Freddie would have crowned her with the garland of camp, and everybody liked her.

* * *

Next day I worked hard, and at home harder still. I must think of Angelo as Italian, then gradually superimpose the colour of the American accent . . . And as I worked, I realized more and more how effective he could be: subtly insolent, with the amused cruelty of a heartless child.

I got Miss Curtis to hear me. He cooked a nice dinner, I put on a new record from *Cochran's 1930 Revue,* 'With a Song in My Heart' and felt happy.

All next day Mr Wallace forgot his horses and gave the play his whole attention. Like his writing, his directing was happy-go-lucky with a base of common sense; the rest he left to his players. The play had an impudent life of its own and with Laughton as the hub, illuminating his part and all around it, *On the Spot* directed itself.

Third day, a stroke of luck. A direction in the first scene ran 'Perelli and Angelo argue in Italian'. 'Emma-lyn,' Charles said, 'will write it for us.'

I did, an urgent spate of dialogue—'ma caro, è troppo pericoloso per noi'—'ascolta ascolta'—'non ascolto più, sono qui il maestro . . .'. In corners, syllable by syllable, I coached an eager bumbling pupil who immediately bumbled ahead of teacher. To see Laughton catch fire, and set fire to me, was intoxicating.

All Sunday I worked alone. On Monday Miss Frazin and I were

sitting at the side waiting for our cue. 'Christ,' she said, 'hope my maid packed my part...'

I watched her click open her capacious handbag, which like its owner was encrusted with jewellery and emitted a cloud of perfume. She fished out what looked like a squat script. 'That's not it, shit...'

She peered further. 'Here we are...' The first 'script' had been quite different, and fatter: a bulge of five-pound notes. She saw me looking.

'Guess what I'm gonna buy myself with this lil load. Poker chips!'

I had a brainwave. 'Would it be a liberty to ask you to read me some of my part?'

'Honey,' she breathed, taking my arm with a big scented smile, 'take any liberty. You name it, I got it...'

She squeezed the arm, gave an affectionate giggle and took up my script as if it were a naughty novel; as she read I noticed that she held it at arm's length. The perfume, expensively bold and spelling luxury, also made me wonder what she would be like in bed. Would she have removed the make-up? Or would there be, halfway through the exercise, a resounding crack?

She read on. 'In this racket, buddy, a guy gotta jump around, we ain't sellin' chewin' gum...' It was a great help, provided I could drain off the sexual content.

I was getting into the part... wasn't I? 'My dear Son George, Re Mr Laughton, they used to sing a song Charlie is me Darlin and he is certainly that to us lot. Your Mother is washing today and Job on nights...'

As the days passed the nervous excitement fell to slogging level: a dangerous time, before the temperature rises again, for better or for worse, towards the first night. In every actor at this stage of rehearsal, somewhere along the pedestrian hours there should be the erratic heart-throb of a life preparing for the throes of birth. As well as in Laughton, I could feel it in the other players, but not in myself.

Everybody was nice to me, but I had a sense of ebbing. And as I sat offstage there rolled into my mind the stony fact that I should have been given my contract last Friday.

On Wednesday I said to Carol jocularly, 'D'you think it might have slipped somebody's mind?' He reassured me but looked vague. I went on for a scene. Wallace wasn't ignoring me exactly, but he was paying more attention to the others. Rehearsal dismissed. I wouldn't be wanted tomorrow.

That night I lay awake. The signs were unmistakable. I was to be sacked.

As soon as it happened, I would start the machinery. 'To Gabbitas and Thring, Dear Sirs . . .' G. E. Williams, M.A. (Oxon) assistant Fr. master at Somewhere-in-the-Marsh. Towards dawn I slept, and was grateful for the Curtis cup of tea. Poor Miss Curtis but he was secure, John Lewis would never let him down.

The day stretched empty before me, I kept busy by cleaning my room. At noon, the phone rang; I was wanted for rehearsal at two and my contract would be at the stage-door. It had all been in my imagination.

It hadn't. Several years later Carol told me that Wallace had developed cold feet. 'Sorry, Charlie, but I still can't get to see what he's going to do, I think we should make a change.'

And Charlie had said, 'Edgar, I promise you he'll be all right, let him stay.'

CHAPTER ELEVEN

RIDING A WAVE

During my mounting anxiety, my mind had been switched off by a couple of rehearsals for my Thorndike stint in *Fire in the Opera House*, when I dived into the Tube for the Everyman in Hampstead, worked for twenty minutes—'You're a dear boy to spare the time'—and dived back.

The same procedure was followed for the seven shows: Tube, a scramble into my uniform as 'The Usher' and down to the dark congested wings where Miss Thorndike joined me for our entrance, phosphorescent with friendship. By the time she was launched on her indefatigable part, I was Underground.

I never saw anything of the play and had no idea what it was about; all I took in was that, as 'Sylvette', she was in Chinese trousers and a coolie hat. Was she dressed for an opera? '*Turandot*'? some time later I asked her. 'I don't remember, dear. Gosh, I must have been nearly fifty then. "Sylvette", I ask you, I must have looked like English mutton dressed as Chinese lamb. Strange little play, I rather loved it...'

One afternoon in Piccadilly Tube Station, creeping up the moving staircase through the light and noise of the Centre of the World, I saw a poster glide past—ON THE SPOT—just in time to catch, among the large names of the supporting cast, my own. I travelled down again and back, then bobbed up into the Circus like a jubilant cork.

It was a friendly company, most of whom had worked for Wallace before, including my Bill Sikes neighbour Cronin-Wilson, whose first name really was Bill. He chatted acceptably but in jerks, keeping hands down which were not quite steady. He had a bit of a cough, he was a bit of a wreck.

I guessed him to be a shy character who needed drink to unlock him. One night after a late rehearsal I accompanied him back to the Mansions; in the doorway he hesitated, 'Think I'll nip over to the Club for a nightcap', and his heavy footsteps died away. It was the tread of a lonely man.

My last Everyman night—Saturday, ten days before April the 2nd, the first night of *On the Spot*—I scuttled out as usual, surfaced at Warren Street Station and by nine was in Percy Street, climbing to the Laughtons' top-floor flat.

It was tiny, shabby and crammed with books and paintings, 'that's a John Armstrong . . .'.

Elsa poured out wine, then sat on the floor holding the script while Charles and I quietly went through our scenes, rattling through our Italian bit over and over again. All over London, plays were in full swing; by two weeks tonight we would be caught up in it and the rumpled overweight sixth-former would have turned into something else . . .

Next day, at the dress rehearsal of *Socrates*, I exchanged Mrs Casson for Mr, starting my Sabbath in a line of Athenian youths shivering in the wings in our underpants. After we had planted bare feet in basins of thick brown soup called bole, a female ASM in unsmiling glasses dipped a sponge in the soup and poured the icy contents down wincing arms and legs. The Glory that was Greece.

The day of the first night of *On the Spot* was a jumpy one. I had an absent-minded lunch and walked over to the Carlton in the Haymarket: Maurice Chevalier and Jeanette MacDonald in *The Love Parade*. After a couple of hours of voluntary stupor, I returned to the dump to lie in the diseased bath like a Roman emperor: tonight I must be extra clean.

Emerging at seven I ran into Bill Wilson—dead sober, no cough —and we walked down to Wyndham's, as formal as two clerks setting out for the humdrum City but soon to face a Wallace–Laughton first-night audience, glittering and narrow of eye, while from the Wallace box would protrude the long cigarette-holder, unwavering, confident. We were monosyllabic and as nervous as cats.

First-night nerves, on a big occasion, are a compound of iron control, quaking fright and bravado.

Once the curtain is up, the player's mind becomes a supersensitive plate precipitately exposed to light and sound and registering every second's variation—tempo, intonation, audience's laugh, cough, silence—and most of all, the sudden crisis: the match which won't light, the cork which won't pop, when an interior alarm goes off and every corpuscle rushes to the rescue.

In dressing-room and wings, though, the nerves are translated into behaviour which would puzzle an onlooker by its trance-like simplicity, resembling the unnatural calm of the toreador, his mind—with love and fear—on the bull. Measured movements, low monosyllables, spare and practical—everything subjected to the minute-to-minute demands of an operation as delicate as any in that other theatre, the surgeon's. Let me try that buckle again, steady, good luck . . . make sure you have the glass of water ready but not too full, good luck . . .

In between that behaviour, and just as puzzling, the bravado spurts through in jets of childish frivolity. As I stood on stage, having answered the call of Overture and Beginners Please, the music struck up: not an ordinary orchestra, but—specially engaged for the first night—the Band of the Metropolitan Police. Through the curtain, the blaring music had a circus effect which was overwhelming.

A strange figure emerged from the wings. It had emerged before, at the two dress rehearsals, but now, on the brink of battle, Laughton was nervously and supremely in control. Every detail was definitive: flashy tight black-and-white suit, olive complexion, jet-black hair, dago moustache and—a bold cue from Miss Frazin—false eyelashes. He gave us all a triumphant leer and said in his Capone voice, 'Who said-a I couldn' be sexy?'

He was, in a new way. It made him as happy as an infant and we all laughed. It was bravado, good luck, good luck . . .

Curtain up: there seemed to be the right tension, there were certainly both laughter and applause, but like everybody else I knew that you cannot know, for better or for worse, till next day —not only from the Press but from the air around you. All I could be made sure of was that I had the best line in the play.

In the first act, after a Perelli gang-murder, Angelo lugs in an immense harp of lilies ordered by Perelli for the funeral. Curtain. At the height of the last act, Perelli comforts his hysterical mistress over his murder of her lover while Angelo stands by for orders. 'Get him the swellest funeral ever; roses, orchids, everything . . .'

Angelo reflects, hands crossed: then, thoughtfully, 'It would pay us to grow our own flowers.'

After a split second, the house roared with the delight of surprise, revealing—as only the first audience can—that gold has been struck. Afterwards there was the famous Wallace party at the Kit Kat, and at three a.m. I walked home not in a completely straight line.

❋   ❋   ❋

In the morning, having bought the papers—I had learned not to study them in the open air—I walked up to Bill Wilson's room. It could have been in a quayside hotel let by the hour; here was the homeless actor who keeps his few belongings in a great travel-beaten trunk in his dressing-room.

He stood hugely in the mean little shack, coughing and then stooping before a cracked mirror to shave; his long, thick, shabby dressing-gown looped round him, hair in disarray, from the back he looked like Balzac, 'Come in, old boy.' There had been a rough couple of small-hours at the Club. 'Have a glass of beer.' His hand shook so much that the beer spilt. The room smelt stale.

But once we opened the papers it became a jewelled cave: 'Success...'... 'Triumph...'... Detective played with force and naturalness by...' 'As Angelo...a most ingenious mixture of innocence and guile...' 'Triumph...' 'Success...' Bill said, 'Means we're good for a year. We must celebrate. Cavour twelve-thirty?'

Before that I had an errand. I walked to the Midland Bank, Shaftesbury Avenue, and opened my first account: I could hardly think of my 'arrangement' with Miss Cooke's Holywell bank as an account... I told the man that every Saturday morning I would be depositing fifteen pounds and that every week, for ten weeks, ten of them should be sent to Miss Cooke.

The Cavour was a small plush late-morning resort of supporting actors and stage managers, 'What about a snifter at the Cavour?' I joined Bill Wilson in a group consisting of some of *On the Spot* plus a couple of hangers-on: in a gathering as conventional as a business-men's get-together I realized that I was the youngest in the cast.

There was a lot of 'yarning'; all seemed to be members of the Green Room Club, a stronghold of well-bred drinking and male straight-from-the-shoulder gossip. 'Funny story I heard from Beau—Hannen, of course—about Barrie and Fay, stop me if you've heard it...' Except for Bill Wilson, a contented listener

[139]

holding a glass, they were heavily voluble. But that morning I would have basked in a nest of Welsh revivalists.

As Julian Andrews, our stage-manager, was toasting the play, we were joined by his girl-friend and an affable man whose name I knew well: Bruce Cannon was an important touring manager to whom I had written more than once, 'if you could spare the time . . .'. He was very complimentary and left.

'Poor old thing,' whispered Julian, 'you realize he's handled Edgar's tours for years and hasn't yet been told he won't be handling any more?'

I asked why. 'Edgar's rumbled him. He's a sod, and was putting the nancy-boys he was keen on into the tours. Some woman put Edgar on to it. You should have seen his face, white with rage. If there's one thing he can't stand, it's pouffery.'

I looked down at the bar at the looming tough-guy profiles of Roy Emerton and Dennis Wyndham, then next to me, tough-guy Cronin-Wilson. Wallace would never have to go white over any of them.

In the evening there were queues round Wyndham's. But without mentioning the name, everybody waited for the *Sunday Times* and the most powerful critic of the day, wise, witty and wilful: Agate. 'A success . . . Mr Williams reminds us, as Angelo, that likeableness and a naïve, almost cherubic degeneracy may be combined . . .'

By June the theatre list read WYNDHAM'S ON THE SPOT LONDON'S TRIUMPH. From the Hart sisters in Philadelphia: 'We read in our *Variety* that you are in a smash . . .'.

'My dear Son George . . . The Rev. D. M. Griffith told your Mother that he knew years ago in Chapel that you would enter the Theatrical Proffession, how's that for second sight, I must get him on to the Horses. Somebody brought the *Daily Mail*, players with a Future, mentioning the names John Geilgud Dina Winyard Cella Johnson and your good self, your Mother and I are proud of these reports . . .'

One morning, after Miss Curtis had noiselessly placed my tray by my bed and just as noiselessly disappeared for work—to sell socks, poor devil—I sipped my tea and opened *A la Recherche du Temps Perdu*. I was sampling Proust for the first time.

I closed my eyes: my future was assured, for months. And sitting back, I looked forward. What did I want?

As always, to write a new play: a play with truth. Which meant it must have a theme of my own, it must be about a person or persons whom I knew. But I didn't know anybody except my family, and Miss Cooke whom I counted as family. A saga of Welsh peasants? And what audience would ever summon interest in a play about a forceful spinster with a passion for teaching?

A love story? But I had no love: no Circe, all wiles and whims, who had driven me first to madness and now—to make up for it— to my typewriter. Neither was there a beautiful youth, with the same treacherous charms, whom I could transform—I looked at my book, it had been done before Proust and would be again— into the same part for a magnificent actress: wave a wand and cheat the Censor.

Next on the agenda, my personal future. I would be the inde-pendent bachelor, with a flat in—say—a shabby house in Soho Square, eccentrically small, but with every unobtrusive luxury; pelmets.

When I was not alone, reading and writing, there would be a procession of friends in for drinks, early and late. I would be elusive while remaining popular, popular while elusive. I would employ a charwoman: no dining-room or kitchen, solid entertain-ing would be at the Ivy, buon giorno Mario ... In the bedroom, a double bed.

But no love. And no play.

Waiting for inspiration, one or two mornings a week I tended to drop into the Cavour, rationing myself to one small gin. Then 'The other half, what's yours?' After the jocular chat, I accom-panied Bill Wilson to the cafeteria across the road and then to a film, where—so long as his cough left him alone—he was a restful companion.

Meanwhile our play was 'the rage'; one night in the royal box, taking a breather from rehearsals for *Private Lives*, Gertie and Noël. Once coming downstairs to go home, I ran into Charles ushering out a dim timid-looking bespectacled old gentleman. Charles presented me to 'Mr Rudyard Kipling'.

He murmured, 'How do you do.'

I said, 'A great honour, sir.' He turned back to Charles. I went on.

Next day Bill Wilson: '*What?* How did you feel?'

I said I had been very interested. He got quite shirty and said, 'Interested? You should have been bowled over!'

'I suppose it's the difference between our generations.' That made him shirtier. Then he laughed. 'Good God, I'm not as old as Kipling, it's my forty-third birthday next week!'

He looked older even than that. But he was a nice fellow. Poor old Bill.

One Saturday, after the matinée, early dinner at the Perroquet, a chic little restaurant in Leicester Square, with Charles.

It was the first time for weeks I had seen him outside the theatre; and without the glossy Perelli image he looked more the pudgy washed-out cub than before. It was also the first time I had ever been alone with him. For all his sporadic friendliness, might he be difficult?

I had guessed right. A glass of wine was permissible between shows, and he took a long time to choose the bottle; he seemed anxious to prove, to himself as much as to me, that he was a man of the world.

Then I noticed that whereas on the stage, regularly, the two of us fixed each other in the burning eye, with the complicity of instant understanding, now, in private, his look slid away. He was self-conscious, almost shifty, with sudden bawdy guffaws which did not ring true and left me hot and wondering what to say next.

Puzzled too. Since my gratitude to him was only matched by my admiration, why could I get no nearer to him?

Because he was the complete actor, who needs an audience to make him real; I was sitting opposite a schoolboy mask. Did he long for affection? If he did he waited for it crouched behind a barricade of hoarse clownish intellectualism, and his very urge to prove himself a thinker seemed to prove that he was not one. 'To me, my dear Emma-lyn, the whole shitty theory of—er—God being the excuse for that sort of crappy conservative point of view . . .'

He also went on about his own profession, and no actor was ever less equipped for dissection than this instinctive wizard. He could never be a bore but the challenges, continuous and vehement—'But you *must* agree, the fact that in this country actors are simply *not allowed* to rehearse for a year, like the Stanislavsky people, is bloody disgraceful!'—were fatiguing.

I nodded and smiled both at the arguments and at the noisy

jokes, some slanted towards sex, an area in which I sensed complexity. He and Elsa had built a weird wooden house in a Surrey forest, with a tree growing up in the middle of the big room through the roof. I could see him lunging from branch to branch, naked and heavy with childish blubber, while her stripling body sailed from one lofty perch to another, and without wires: Ariel wed to a genius of a Caliban.

✿   ✿   ✿

That night, walking back to the Mansions after a week of crammed Wyndham's, I wished I were celebrating. Meeting people.

But peering my way to my front door I was not unhappy: was I not now self-sufficient? It was comforting to hear little Curtis tinkling about in the kitchen, making Ovaltines. I lit my gas-fire and looked into it. If I was self-sufficient, why was I restless?

Why did the dream of the bachelor flat sometimes look bleak? As on many nights, I sat soberly working it out, and that led to more dreams, vague personal ones of a shared life.

First, I imagined living with a woman: she would be plump, sensual, fond but not possessive, prone to stray affairs and amusing about them, down-to-earth and yet house-proud.

But she was missing: somehow all the women in the plays, weekday or Sunday, were impersonally pleasant, or intense, or attached, or all three. I did not see Polly and Sonny regularly enough to meet any of their circle; if I had, might I have made contact with an adventurous bachelor-girl, a painter, a model?

Remained the Friend: the same age as me, simple, clean-cut, male and at the same time broadminded, affectionate; not a writer, and definitely not an actor. But where was he? There was nobody.

It was not worth moping about, I would improve my mind for an hour. I took down *Madame Bovary*, wound up the gramophone and put on 'With a Song in My Heart'.

Sipping my Ovaltine and turning the pensive page, I hopped outside myself—not for the first time—and studied myself from there.

How could anybody who had seen *On the Spot* this evening connect me, the Student on the Hearth, with that amoral gun-boy?

The music trailed away, and there was no sound but the hiss of the gas-fire. A domestic hour passed.

There was a knock at the door.

PART TWO

The Friend
1930–1934

CHAPTER TWELVE

STILL RIDING

It was a heavy knock, followed by a cough. Poor old Bill. I laid down Flaubert and heaved out of my chair.

With his hat on the back of his head and a foolish smile, he was not too far gone. 'Lo 'ole boy, still up?'

'Come in, take your overcoat off.' I opened the half-bottle of whisky I kept in case, and decided it was dull not to join him in a nightcap. He sank into the armchair, I sat on a stool.

'Mind my smoking?'

'Of course not, sorry I don't.'

'Lucky, wish I didn't.' He wheezed and coughed but was holding his drink, even if the conversation wasn't riveting. 'Nice place you've got here, just this and the kitchen?'

'Plus a small bedroom. A friend's got it for the moment, he's gone to bed.'

'Cheers.' We might have been sitting in the Green Room Club. Then he added, 'Is he your lover?'

It was so unexpected that I sat upright. 'Good God no, a business arrangement.'

'I'm glad to hear it. Passed him the other day, looked a bit obvious.' Poor Miss Curtis of the mouse-brown tie. One of Wallace's toughs had caught up with him.

'I'm sorry,' I said coldly, 'I wouldn't know about that.'

I drained my small whisky. This was taking a boring turn, I'd as soon have Charles. I stooped and put Gracie on the gramophone. Would he be disparaging about her? That would annoy me.

'Great artist, so I'm told . . .' A bout of coughing. 'Sorry . . .'

Then he leant over, placed a hand on my knee—the foolish smile—and spoke again, slowly, impersonally. There were the verbal hesitations; but in his mind, none. 'One day at rehearsal —er—I thought, that kid's an actor an' what's more—er—he's attractive. An' what's more—er—the little devil knows it . . .'

I was staring at him as much as I had at Mr Higley when he told me about his pupil. It hadn't sounded right and yet it had been said straight from the half-drunken shoulder. Gracie's voice soared '... thoughts of you, when you are far away ...' I switched her off, she didn't fit.

Once I was over the surprise my eyes met his, and I felt immeasurably easier than at dinner with Charles. He watched me as I looked into the gas-fire. 'What ye thinking?'

'Not only have I never been told that before, I'd never have expected to hear it from a man like you.'

'Why not?'

'For one thing, the Green Room Club.'

He smiled crookedly. 'I see what you mean. What about Jekyll and Hyde?' New Hyde was more interesting than old Jekyll. I looked at him for the first real time.

Not that there was a physical transformation, he was still a burly middle-aged man, an innocuous drunk who happened to be a good actor. In that second, though, I noted that the worn brown suit was uncrumpled; and even I could tell it was from a first-class tailor, probably unpaid, while the collar was fastidiously fresh and the shoes, again not new, had a mellow sheen. As he took up his glass, under the nicotine and the tremor it was a strong fine hand.

I saw too that he was indeed younger than he looked at a first glance. The hair was brown, straight and fine, neatly parted and brushed back from a good brow. Mouth full, mobile and mettlesome; teeth which could have betrayed an unsightly gap were cared for. It was in between, and below, that the damage lay: the puffy bloodshot eyes were cruelly underscored by dark pouches, the chin which ought to jut out was ruined by jowls.

Inside the man, though, there was nothing common; his present approach could not have been more direct, and yet, behind the whisky boldness, there was a male diffidence. What was his background? Like Sonny, he spoke the perfect English which passes unobserved.

'Do you agree,' he asked, 'this calls for another?'

I poured two drinks and sat again. Cigarette in hand, he swayed to his feet. From my stool I might have been looking up a mountainside. I smelt stale smoke.

His rising wafted me the scent of fresh whisky, and that turned him into another man: for the smell must have lingered with me from long ago, when my father had once or twice picked me up for a bibulous hug. The vague downward smile held no evil; mischief only, and behind that, loneliness. The mischief put me in mind of paintings: of Bacchus lying vine-leaved and content under thick trees, being ministered unto by nymphs and shepherds.

I didn't want to hurt his feelings, and I was lonely too. I smiled back.

*   *   *

My mind stayed void of ideas for a play, and its inactivity was emphasized every week by Miss Cooke. '. . . Glyn Davies, bright but lazy, admitted he thought he didn't need to work for his exam. I walked into him; then I remembered his mother drinks but it was second nature to rap him over the knuckles. When I stopped, tears were in his eyes, he wrung my hand & said, "Miss Cooke, I'll never forget you." It was like an epitaph, George: for at times I worry lest I trounce those scamps too much & I was grateful to him.'

I, nearly half her age, was not living anywhere near that level and felt myself to be what she called a shirker. I spent much of my time with Bill; accidentally together in the Wallace current, we drifted down it side by side. After our midnight meeting either of us, when alone, could say anything without regretting it, while the haphazard physical interlude kept striking me as nothing more than odd, comic almost.

He cared little for food, being as much at home with a cafeteria lunch or a pub snack as I was. After the matinée he usually came back to the flat to sit about and smoke and read, then we would walk over for dinner at the little Alexis in Lisle Street, or eggs in 'Mary-and-Mum's', the café in the court behind Wyndham's, run by a jolly ex-wardrobe-mistress and her daughter.

Once, between the shows, Freddie dropped in; he amused Bill—they had met in bars—and chatted away. But the door had hardly closed behind him when Bill turned to me coldly.

'Where'd he pick you up?'

I was in court. 'He didn't, we were in a play. Anyway he seems just as much a pal of yours . . .'

'Nothing to do with it, old boy. No harm in Freddie but *you* can't be seen about with that hair of his, you've got your career. You ought to drop him, you're too special.'

'You're special yourself,' I said; 'let's admit it, we both think we're special. I hope we're right.'

I caught his eye, lifted my teacup and added, 'Chin-chin, old boy.' He broke into a smile.

Those were the sober times. Once, at two in the morning, I was woken by the familiar knock; I waited, then heard uncertain footsteps in retreat. Sinking back into sleep, I was troubled by a sense of pity.

But poor-old-Bill was ousted from my mind by a phone call.

The Greins had a friend who had promised them he would 'do a little paragraph' mentioning me. Over the theatre of that time a formidable power was exercised by a skinny parsonic-satanic journalist who wrote, in the *Daily Express*, a weekly page called 'Hannen Swaffer Looks At The Theatre'. At a period when the Press was unchallenged by other media he could make or break; his weekly Look was long, and violently for or against prominent people in the limelight. Once, in the Savoy Grill, Tallulah had slapped his face and left no bruise on either reputation.

The morning I was summoned to him I pretended to Bill I was calling on Mr Peacock. He made coffee and asked me to tell him 'the story of my life'; as I left he said there would be a paragraph tomorrow. When in the morning I hurried to the newsagent's to find that this week Hannen Swaffer was Looking At THE SMUTTY TREND IN MODERN DRAMA, I was glad I had told nobody about the interview.

The following Wednesday morning Bill called in, waving an *Express*. 'You mean you haven't got it?'

The first thing I saw was my photograph. Round it, the whole of Swaffer was devoted to me. In telling him the truth—I had missed out Miss Cooke, knowing she would not appreciate being brought into it—I had given him rich material; while the legend of self-made success was a cliché in politics and business, in the theatre it was rare. It was all there—'his story is a wonderful romance'—but exact: FATHER A GREENGROCER, BEAT THE HARROW BOYS. And it ended: 'I prophesy for him a brilliant future.'

Face to face with the first personal publicity I had ever received I felt hot all over, a heat which turned quickly into exultation. Backstage at the matinée everybody had seen it. One thing was certain: never, in any restaurant, would I slap Hannen Swaffer's face.

* * *

One Monday, after a week-end with Polly and Sonny at Hicki-doola, I was surprised to see Bill on the Waterloo platform, wel-coming me as if I were returning from abroad. As I wheeled towards the Tube he hailed a taxi; seeing me lean forward to examine the meter he said, 'What are you thinking?'

'That except for when I met Miss Cooke this is the first time I've ever been in a taxi.'

'Good Lord . . .' Then he grinned and patted my knee. I was puzzled. 'What's the matter?'

'Nothing, just a wave of affection. Edgar's apparently left for the States,' and we talked, leaving the pauses which pass un-noticed because they spell intimacy. I spent a couple of them wondering why I had been so struck by his words: again it was something which had never been said to me before, by anybody. 'Just a wave of affection.' I tried to detect artificiality in the phrase, and found none.

On the following Sunday morning, a glorious one, I suggested a Green Line bus to Box Hill. 'Haven't done this sort of thing,' Bill said en route, 'since I was younger than you, in Lewis Waller's company and taking the girls out.' In the bus coming home, sun-flushed courting couples clutched bunches of wild flowers.

Walking back to 12a, he was greeted by a conventional-looking middle-aged man who walked along with us; when he had gone Bill said, 'That's Duggie Fairby.'

Apparently an inveterate picker-up and at the same time a dreader of 'incidents', Duggie had lately found himself caught up in more than an incident: more than a scandal even, a sensa-tion.

A year ago, in the Long Bar at the Troc, he had got to know a presentable young man, bought him a good suit, dropped him and left him to his own devices, which were to take an unusual form: one morning last October, when Duggie opened his morn-ing paper he sat bolt upright. In a Margate hotel his protégé, Sidney Fox, aged twenty-eight, had murdered his invalid mother by setting fire to her bed, for the insurance: a *cause célèbre*. Duggie spent a bad couple of days, appalled and denying he had ever heard the name Fox—'Wait a sec, isn't it something in Hollywood?. . .' But during the front-page trial so many people sidled up offering drinks—'But, Duggie, what was he like to *know*?'—that he could not get away with it. 'Actually, my dear, Sidney was a charmer, seemed to *adore* his old Mum'—and Duggie found himself under a spotlight.

Of notoriety, or of fame? He settled for the latter, switched overnight from remorse to self-esteem and sat in the Long Bar holding cautious court, basking in a glory reflected from the Old Bailey dock.

He had not been so cautious, though, one evening only a month ago when he got maudlin, 'Such a nice boy was Sidney and after I gave him some links he wrote such a sweet note with a P.S. love from Mum, he can't have done it, oh dear, oh dear . . .' At nine next morning, in Maidstone Jail, the nice boy was hanged.

I was struck by all this. Then Bill said, 'It's after six, I think I'll walk over to the Club,' and I spent a dull evening alone. Why wasn't I down on the river?

I was glad to play in two Sunday shows on end—*Ruth* and *Search*, each as bad as the other—but I had the star part in both. In the former, as a young cripple who spent the whole evening in a wheel-chair before falling out of it, I could hardly fail.

Even in *Search*, miscast as a clean-limbed Raffles, I was let down lightly. How much easier it is for the newcomer to win praise, than for the old hand! The *Observer* observed that 'Mr Williams lent to the part his liquid voice.' It was never to be described as liquid again.

* * *

'My dear Son George, Your Mother and I appreciate your kind idea of sending us five pounds per week towards family expenses but plays do not go on for ever so please reduce to Three.' I guessed that Mam would hide the weekly notes in her mysterious tin-under-the-bed of which only she had the key.

One morning in the Cavour, Bill and I were sitting with Julian our stage-manager when Bill saw a friend and walked down the bar. 'Poor old Bill,' Julian said, 'hope to God he'll tighten his belt now he's got this long run. No sign of it yet I'm afraid, he's still subbing every other week...'

I asked what 'subbing' was. 'Hope you never find out, means drawing part of your weekly salary in advance, damn bad habit. His bill at the Green Room must be astronomical, he'll lend to anybody, poor old Bill...'

Why did it depress me to hear fair comment which did not concern me? Julian chatted on. 'Edgar's been marvellous to him, of course, with all that making a bond between them.'

I asked about 'all that'.

'The fact that they're both illegitimate. Didn't you know? Bill's mother was a Gaiety Girl, died years ago and the father in Debrett and not far off the Royal Family, he's got a complex about it, never brings it up...'

I looked over at Bill and having seen him lately with new eyes, now turned another pair on him. His friend, a white-haired baldish older man was telling him a story; he was listening almost deferentially, and yet there was something indefinably superior about him.

I was impressed. He returned. 'Sorry, old boy; old Ben Lamb, haven't seen him since Australia with Lady Forbes-Robertson. He's got a small part in something and taken a furnished flat, only a fiver a week and I'm going to share, how's that for quick work?'

I looked over at Old Ben, red of neck and face, lifting his glass—'Cheers, old boy'—to another red old face opposite him. 'Come over, old boy,' said Bill to me, happily—the second drink was oiling the wheels of hangover—'and meet my old stable-mate, he used to bowl the girls over like ninepins, still does.'

I followed him. Was Old Ben poor old Ben? No, it was the weathered healthy face of a stupid man radiating elderly self-confidence. After another drink I ended up having lunch with them both next door at the Café Anglais, only a notch below the Ivy.

More gin-and-its; Bill was host, and the prices on the menu startled me. I had no need to talk... 'Bill, d'you remember that juicy little married woman in Melbourne sitting at a window in the Outback Club and she was up in my bedroom before you could bloody well say...'

And Jack Robinson it was. I thought sourly into my third gin-

and-it, I'm in the bloody Green Room Club without having to pay the bloody subscription, Bill's too good for this and yet he looks quite happy sitting there . . .

Out of anger I had ordered smoked salmon and deserved the embarrassment of not knowing what to make of it, having vaguely imagined it to be my favourite tinned salmon rolled up into a sort of cigarette. I had never had so much to drink in the middle of the day and hated it.

'Those two barmaids in Auckland, God . . .' Old Ben was weaving down Memory Lane with contraceptives dangling from every hedgerow. 'What about that night in Cape Town, old chap, no Jo'burg . . .'

I looked at my watch; I had spent two hours in the cradle of boredom, endlessly rocking. Bill paid with a five-pound note, left a lavish tip and suggested the Club. I excused myself and walked morosely home to sleep it off.

Why morose? Two old friends had had a reunion and bored me. But I had often laid myself open to boredom—it is a hazard of professional life—and then, with a sigh of relief, extricated myself. What was the matter with me?

*　　*　　*

During Bill's last days at the Mansions he came in a couple of times for tea; the steady hand never looked right clumped round the saucer. 'We got yarning after lunch . . .'

I asked if Old Ben was broadminded. 'What? Good God, no, told me once if he found any son of his was that way inclined he'd wring his bloody neck.'

'But Bill, won't sharing a flat rather cramp your style?'

He had thought of that, 'It's a good thing, it'll stop me getting out of hand and dragging people back.'

'But it'll be in order for *him* to drag people back?'

'Of course.' Then he chuckled, 'He might get her to bring back a girl friend for the lodger.'

I looked at him much as I had when he made it plain that there was a side to him not to be suspected in a burly drinking man. 'You like women?'

'Oh, yes, not easy to arrange—but what about you, Rouen and Canada and all that?' I asked him when he had last had a woman.

'Oh . . . D'you really want to know, old boy?'

'Yes, I do, old boy.'

He was diffident but factual, 'Let me see . . . Diana Sapley, it must have been four or five years back.'

She was a statuesque, well-bred beauty whom we had seen in a play one matinée. I said, 'She looked pretty ladylike on the stage.'

His eyes twinkled, 'She wasn't very ladylike in bed, thank God . . . I liked Di, she was a good sport, lasted a whole tour.'

I asked why it had stopped. 'The old trouble, she got intense, I hope I didn't hurt her feelings. She got—you know—possessive.' He was more complicated than I had thought.

Was I complicated too?

But there was nothing complicated about his move to Greycoat Place: one evening, as we walked down to the theatre, in the late summer light, he carried a sponge-bag.

I asked him what he did about laundry.

'Laundry? Locke looks after all that'—a dresser at Wyndham's—'he takes it up to the wardrobe and it goes with the theatre stuff.'

He might have been a Scottish laird dealing to the best of his ability with an inquisitive question about the estate. Passing his dressing-room I heard him ask Locke to nip out to the pub for a bottle: the laird was planning to sit up with his old pal, getting blotto, old boy, lots o' yarns.

I rang Polly and asked myself down for Sunday; it was a good idea, two young married couples were staying too, all interesting and light-hearted, though there was no sign of the friendly bachelor-girl I had envisaged. After Bryan had gone reluctantly to bed I read to him from one of his picture-books. Once again I had enjoyed company.

Back in the Mansions late Monday afternoon, I met Miss Curtis home from work; as he poured tea he murmured that he had met a new friend and would be leaving. He took his own tea into his room as Bill arrived, sober, pale and dejected. I asked him about his Sunday.

His lips began to quiver. As at another hot moment with Mr Higley, I thought he was going to cry, and felt as hopeless as if I were watching a wall about to topple; he controlled himself by taking tight hold of my knee.

It came out in fits and starts. Old Ben had gone off to Brighton with one of his girls, so on Sunday Bill was alone in the flat. Pre-lunch bitter at the local, never meant to go further than that but ran into old Alec Something, rattling good sort he hadn't clapped eyes on for years.

Bill had the widest circle of cronies, if not the deepest: Old Alec had nothing in common with Old Ben. For Alec had, from the age of fourteen, nursed a passion which he vowed never to lose: a love not of the sea but of her children. Sailors. Trousers hitched as tight as a drum on a bum and then impudently flaring sent his blood on a race without end; so Bill found himself accompanying Old Alec to a pub in the Waterloo Road awash with seamen, most of whose bodies, according to Alec, were not only able but willing.

After crisps washed down with Johnnie Walker, at three o'clock they piled into a taxi and back to the flat: Alec, Bill and four of the navy lot. More drinks, and things got fairly rough.

'They were a healthy bunch of lads out for fun . . . No, all in the sitting-room, the flat's got an old gramophone and one put on "No, No, Nanette" and he and his buddy started to dance together, arsing around, you know . . . No, in the buff, except for socks and shoes, hats on the back of their heads.' I was taken with the idea of two near-naked stokers fox-trotting to 'Tea for Two'.

But my smile was soon wiped off. 'Then the door opened.'

He stared down at the rug, his face was grey with worry. I was afraid to ask, then did. 'The police?'

No answer. I saw a flash of Bill in the dock, then another, of a large face glaring at the *News of the World*: Edgar Wallace.

Bill collected himself and looked back at me. 'The police? Good God, no. Old Ben.'

My reaction was relief, 'What happened then?'

'One of the kids roared out, "Come right in Guv an' join the prayer meetin'!"'

I laughed out loud, but Bill's face was as stricken as before, 'No, it just wasn't funny, poor old Ben's face had gone as red as a beet-root'—could it have gone any redder than it was before?—'He just looked at me and walked straight through to his bedroom. Put the kybosh on it I can tell you.'

I said deliberately, 'Bloody old spoil-sport.' He said I didn't understand, I asked him to explain and he tried.

'Ben and I have been chums for twenty years, pub-crawls and all that and he passed girls on to me, wanted me to share the fun.'

'Threesomes?'

'Good God, no . . . I'm afraid this has been a tremendous shock.'

'Has he taken to his bed?' Once again I was at public school, where a master—Old Ben—had been given incontrovertible proof that his prize pupil was a swindler.

Bill looked at me, 'You still don't understand, I suppose it's the difference between our generations.' Perhaps it was, hadn't I said the same thing about Kipling?

I asked if Ben would tell.

'Never, he'll persuade himself I was so pissed I hadn't the faintest what they were all up to.' In Old Ben's memory, four harmless lads were to be labelled for life as male Delilahs; the simple mind can be as elastic as any other.

Bill went on.

'When I was seventeen Oscar Wilde had only been dead four years, you've no idea the effect any mention of him had on the profession, and still has on anybody over forty. Normal young actors, members of the Green Room, were terrified of being mis-understood at some point, and then branded.'

He lit a fresh cigarette. Over the years this had sunk deep, and this was a rare chance to talk. 'There was one good-looking young chap, you've seen him'—he named a beefy charactor-actor of his own age—'well, I happened to know that when he was twenty a fairly brazen old piece in the company had once got him drunk and disorderly. What's more, he suspected I knew, so for years in the Club, at the sight of me he'd blush, you've no idea.'

I asked if all that still held good. 'As Charles puts it in our play, you can say that again . . .' Which reminded him, 'Did you ever hear the story about Charles?'

I welcomed a ray of levity through the gloom. 'It was when he was sent for by du Maurier with a view to doing *Alibi*, he'd just been in *The Man With Red Hair* playing that very pouffy part. Du Maurier congratulated him, then tapped the ash off his cigar and said, very off-hand, "Laughton, are you a bugger?"'

I asked what Charles did then. 'Shot up in his chair and out of nerves spluttered out, "N—no, Sir Gerald. Why, are *you*?"'

But we were soon back in the shadows. 'The Garrick's worse

[157]

than the Green Room. One member—an actor, I'm afraid—told me the Committee's just waiting for the fool who's going to put up any name out of a list they have, of certain authors, actors and lawyers. Said there'll be so many black balls the box will look like sheep's droppings.'

We were silent, in the tawdry room; it felt as if the giant fingers of powerful forces were waiting to close the walls together. I reminded him that he had chosen to share with Ben.

'I know, my dearest boy, but you see I can't be alone, and I haven't got anybody. That's the reason for everything.' He put down his cup and looked at the rug again.

'My dearest boy . . .' He had said it unconsciously. I got up, walked past him, turned, put my hands on his hunched, defeated shoulders and said, 'Bill, it's not true that you haven't got anybody. You've got me.'

The gas spluttered. He lifted his hands, felt for mine and held them hard. I moved round again and sat opposite him.

'Bill, there's no future in this for you. Why don't we take a flat together?'

CHAPTER THIRTEEN

SLIDING

His heavy face lit up. 'You mean it?' It was as if I had found a child on my doorstep and carried it to a fireside: an old, abandoned orphan. That night Carol said, 'I hear you're going to share with Bill, you're a Good Samaritan.'

'Dear Miss Cooke, Re settlement of Cooke Loan, the thanks are the other way round . . . I'm hunting for a flat in a pleasanter district, and so is another actor in *On the Spot,* it often happens in a long run.'

Dalton's Weekly provided me with Marchmont Street W.C.1, a busy minor thoroughfare on the fringe of Bloomsbury. Number 60 was a first-floor flat, decently distempered, in a house over a butcher's shop run by the landlord; the bath was in the kitchen, but enamelled.

Shopping in the Market for the extras I ran into Mr Higley, jogging blissfully along with under his arm a filthy new masterpiece. 'Top o' the morning, Williams, you're going strong I'm told!'

I *was* going strong—'Sat Evg June 28, 100th Perf.'—and began to take pleasure in the knowledge that during certain hours in the week, for months my family and Miss Cooke knew exactly where I was; it gave me a feeling of professional tidiness.

But precisely on that 100th Perf., the tidiness was smudged.

*　　*　　*

I always looked forward to my five minutes with Miss Frazin in Act One, sitting in the wings on the Act Two ottoman; there we waited for the moment when I ushered her into the Perelli apartment, to meet him for the first time and pave the way to his bed. Every performance she appeared slowly from under the stage, swathed in fur and her face even more coated and rouged.

Wreathed in the usual dizzy scents, she was outlandish but cosy too; she would squeeze my hand in her warm slippery glove and purse her lips an inch from my cheek as if I, and not she, were the oil-painting, then with the dazzling smile came a whisper, 'Hello, honey . . .'

I was learning a little about glamour, after *Glamour*. At the matinée (99th Perf.) she had given her usual smooth amusingly weavy performance.

Sat. Evg. Sitting on the ottoman, just as I realized she was late she appeared, advanced, stumbled and sat carefully beside me. Even in the half-light the oil-painting looked as if it had been left out in the rain; the truth was that it had been finished in a happy hurry. She pressed my hand, but instead of, 'Hello, honey,' there came a gurgle of joy as her mink coat slid open. Under it she was naked, and gloriously drunk.

Her husband was Monty Banks, an Italian film director, small and insanely jealous; for days there had been murmurs of Mediterranean tornadoes in their Claridge's suite. After the matinée she had gone home and entertained a friend.

To tea? Who knows? Her lord had burst in unexpectedly, locked up her wardrobe, collected her clothes from the floor, hurled them out of the window and strutted out. Did a startled commissionaire collect them off the pavement like variegated manna and take them home to his wife?

We discovered later that she had swept in at the stage-door in mink and high heels, stalked up to her room, sat at her mirror and given herself the impression that she was perfecting her make-up. Her dresser had then entered and was on her way to the wardrobe to extract the first-act costume when Miss Frazin said—it was her only utterance—'I'm ready, dear', and since the mink was the coat she wore for the first act, the dresser believed her.

And here she was. I heard my cue, opened the door and walked on. As I did so, I registered that Miss Frazin would soon stand on the same platform, in three-inch heels, with two steps to follow. I turned to Ben Welden. 'Your woman Maria's in the hall waitin' for you.'

She was doing nothing of the sort: the door hurled open and Maria teetered triumphantly past me. I was just in time to hold her arm to save her from sailing off the rostrum into thin air. Holding her coat to her chest she somehow managed the steps, then her walk to the middle of the stage, except that in those heels the teeter had become a totter.

Charles swung round, advanced as usual and effusively kissed her hand, 'Maria, I am Tony Perelli!' Maria should have rejoined, as usual, 'I've heard a lot about you Mr Perelli. Ain't Mrs Perelli a Chinese lady?'

But Maria was not in the mood to be usual; she looked at him, coolly amused, as if waiting for him to finish with a *bon mot*.

But he *had* finished. It was appallingly clear that her vow of silence in the dressing-room was to be sustained on stage, and no silence is more utter than the sudden stage pause. Moreover, when a player is incapable it is the others who look guilty: Charles gaped at his visitor in astonishment while sweat flooded his olive brow. Miss Frazin took her hands from her chest and laid them provocatively on her hips. The coat opened.

Only for a second, for I was able to swing her sideways and coax her hands together to close the gap. But Charles had seen.

In repertory, actors are conditioned to emergencies; Charles had never been in repertory. I knew too that it was out of the question for him to speak his next line, 'Let me take your coat . . .'

Making my exit, I caught a flash, downstage, of a startled peering face: Mack the ASM, to prompt or not to prompt? From the wings, I watched Miss Frazin smile and sway.

The audience must have been puzzled, but there was no sign of the fatal giggle. Charles, sleep-walking in floodlight, came out with a later line, 'You like Chicago?'

After a pause, Maria spoke. 'Oh, *Charles* . . .'

From the audience, the giggle. Then a few more, but they might have died away if Maria had not made a sudden stab at the text. 'I mean, oh, Tony . . .'

The audience laughed. Heartily. The first act, which ninety-nine times had glided as confident as a Rolls-Royce, had gone into a spectacular skid. Not only would Miss Frazin not speak, nothing would budge her from centre-stage; she might have been nailed to the floor by those three-inch heels.

As Charles did his best to improvise—'Maria, my darling-a bambina, ecco nice-a chair'—I heard him turn from a bullying gangster into a terrified Italian waiter who had worked at the Pavilion Hotel, Scarborough.

Finally he took her by the arm, sat her in a chair and darted down to drape her mink over her knees. And, there, with her hands miraculously back together over her chest, she stayed.

It posed problems of stage movement but given ingenuity, those could be skirted; the snag was that while she smiled endlessly, her vow of silence was inviolable. As the act lurched on, her contentment grew so rapt that she made you believe in the physical impossibility of smiling and speaking at the same time.

At last, at last, her exit. Charles had helped her to her feet. She should then have delivered her parting line, which would have brought the house down: 'I hope I make that party of yours tonight...'

Instead she nodded, smiled and made to put her hands on her hips again. Charles gave a convulsive jab at her elbow, clamped his other hand on her bottom, and in one second she was up the steps and out of the door.

But the relief did not last. He had propelled her into Julian offstage and her lips were unsealed; out of sight, she was not out of earshot; I could hear her from the other side of the stage. 'Julian, honey, I gotta get back to Charlie, I never said my *lines* to him!'

Poor Charles was at that moment trying to say his own; then as Julian made the mistake of pinning her by the arm, her voice rose. 'Lemme go, Buster. What you tryin' to do, you son of a bitch, rape me?'

From the first rows, a healthy murmur. Charles battled on; he told me afterwards that he was praying for her to come back onstage, anything to keep her quiet.

Gradually, under the stage, her voice died away and at last the curtain fell on the longest first act ever endured by a cast outside China. The audience might just as well have been in China too. We were all soaked in perspiration, and Charles almost fainted.

The exception was excited Ben Welden: his wife understudied Miss Frazin, who was the only person in the theatre to remain both cool and unpuzzled as she sauntered up to her room looking forward to her favourite costume, the transparent nightgown. Instead she was gently bundled back into her mink and by the time the second act was under way she was in Claridge's, smiling into her mirror and ready for a nap. Did she first throw her husband's clothes out of the window...?

Meanwhile her understudy was fighting a rearguard action: uncertain, terrified and not always audible. But sober. At the end, between the calls, her husband turned to Charles and grinned from ear to ear. 'How d'you think she made out?'

'Wonderful,' Charles beamed back, 'she *said everything*!'

* * *

Mrs Welden played for three nights, then was replaced; I missed Miss Frazin. The incident was not reported to 314a or to Miss Cooke, I felt it would have detracted from the image of respectable theatre I was aiming at.

More Sunday excursions, Whipsnade, Epping Forest; two lives joining in one salubrious stream. But streams are capable of frothing into a whirlpool.

Miss Cooke was due through London, beginning of the summer holidays; she would stay one night for *On the Spot*, then the boat-train to the city she still called 'Parry'. I booked her a room at the Kenilworth in Great Russell Street, and as I arranged to pay her bill I felt a nip of satisfaction.

The night before her arrival Bill muttered to me that Old Ben had gone to Edinburgh and would I come back to Greycoat Place after the show.

We had a quick whisky in his dressing-room; as we emerged into Charing Cross Road, Bill's hand went up for a taxi. I said lightly, 'Look, there's a 29 bus, take us nearly to the door.'

For a second he hesitated, then 'All right,' and we walked to the bus; I raced as usual to the open top, he came puffing up behind me. How long since he'd been on a bus?... Rounding Nelson's Monument he squeezed my knee. 'The Welsh certainly have their heads screwed on!'

The nondescript furnished flat already belonged to the past. Bill would make scrambled eggs. 'My batman taught me in the war. A snifter?'

I hesitated. Hell, we must drink to the new flat! While I poured out the drinks, Bill got into his thick old dressing-gown and scuffed carpet slippers, I into my shirt sleeves. We settled on opposite sides of the gas-fire, and talked.

He was anxious to hear my history, and impressed by Miss Cooke; I was careful not to ask him about his own antecedents. We got on to books and found a mutual admiration for Maugham and Dickens, especially *Bleak House*. He said I must read Saki, a name I did not know: a strange, witty, quirkish writer, killed in the war. His *Collected Stories* was the only book Bill possessed.

He picked it up, put on black-rimmed glasses and read out a couple of favourite and funny passages. It struck me how distinguished he looked. 'One more drink,' he said, 'and I'll do the eggs.'

As I started to read a story there came a full tumbler to my elbow; I read while Bill glanced through the paper. For the first time in my life I felt I was sharing something.

'No thanks, Bill, I'm doing nicely . . .'

'Just one before I break the eggs.'

As he poured, an unimportant lurch, then into the kitchen. I closed my eyes. How pleasant this was going to be in Marchmont Street, sitting around, talking, reading, writing . . .

He returned, draining his glass. As he picked up the bottle I said, 'No, I mean it.' While I was muzzy, he was over the hill. 'Bill, don't you agree we've had enough?'

'Wozzat, ole man?' The smile faded, 'Speak for yourself.' He poured himself another swig, and took his glass back into the kitchen.

I looked at the half-empty bottle of whisky and said aloud— I had had enough for that—'Well, this is it.' I rose, took the bottle, went into Old Ben's bedroom, laid it under the bed, came back and leafed through Saki.

The cook returned, empty glass in hand, 'Eggs on.' He looked round, like a puzzled lion. 'Where's bo'le?'

I looked up. 'Bill, we've had such a good evening . . .'

'Where's bo'le?'

'I've put it away, have you any beer . . . ?'

'You've *what*?' He was standing feet apart, glowering down at me. 'You've *hidden* it?'

I stuck to my guns, the not-so-drunk versus the drunk, 'Yes, I have. I'm fond of you and I want you to wake up feeling like a human being.'

His face was a mask of hate. 'You little shit, fetch me that bottle or I'll wring your neck . . .' He advanced on me.

I was too obstinate to be frightened, but I had a grotesque vision of Sikes and Nancy; the only thing missing was the dog.

'Taffy was a Welshman, Taffy was a thief. You *pinched* it!'

The one thing a Welshman hates to hear, even in jest, is that tatter of doggerel. I said, 'You drunken bastard,' walked into Old Ben's room, banged the door, and remembered he really was a bastard.

He wrenched it open immediately, with the quick cunning of the besotted. 'Earlier on'—the voice was coated with glue—'that door was shut, and jus' then it was open, you been in here you bloody sneak.'

He staggered in. Nowhere much to look; the wardrobe yawned open. I started to undress; he heaved me aside, crouched down by the bed, then swayed triumphantly back up, clutching the bottle. 'Sucks to you, Lady Astor!'

I squared up to him, calm and cutting. 'Better Lady Astor than a fourth-rate Falstaff.' I thought I wasn't doing badly, till I saw that my trousers were all over my shoes.

He took a swig from the bottle. 'What *you* know 'bout life, you post-war upstart, you lily-livered loon?' Apprenticeship in Shakespeare with Lewis Waller had had its uses.

'My liver isn't lily,' I said, 'and I can drink you under the table.'

'Can you, by Jove?' He held out the bottle. I took it, and gulped two mouthfuls as if it were water.

It was fire, and only pride stopped me choking. I handed him back the bottle. 'Now get out and make a pig of yourself.'

The obscenities flew, meeting in mid-air as thick and aimless as dung flung in the dark. Sober quarrels can be undignified but drunken ones are bestial; the last expletive hurled, my host clutched his bottle to his belly, gave his Sikes glare and lurched out. I shut the door carefully, sat on the bed, disentangled my trousers, heaved slowly sideways and glided into oblivion.

*　*　*

When I awoke, from a sleep as thick as treacle, the first thing I saw was the electric bulb above me, still burning and spotlighted by the blazing morning sun.

My head throbbed spasmodically like a wonky heart, while my mouth was a pan of raked-out ashes, still warm and dry: I had not felt like this since my first Oxford party, when at the age of twenty I had been sick on a strange bed.

I was now twenty-five but felt too ill to be ashamed, as my body creaked to its feet of its own accord. I had passed out in the good old way, with socks and shoes on, and my trousers lay in a heap as if cast aside for a jumble sale. I trudged carefully into the sitting-room.

It was an oven. Every light on, while the gas-fire spluttered happily in the sun in the home of a slumming millionaire. In a corner, the empty whisky bottle lay as if in a gutter. I turned off the lights. I knew beforehand the torment it would be to bend, but my mother's thrift forced me to do so in order to switch off the fire.

I crept out, caught the bus home, was sick, and after hours of cleansing sleep woke at five, to sobriety and to misery. Not the right state for Cooke Day, and on my way to meet the bus from Chester I bought some Listerine.

For the first time ever, instinctively, Miss Cooke and I kissed each other on the cheek; I was glad of the Listerine. She was wearing a surprisingly smart hat. It was only a few minutes' walk to the Kenilworth, but I found it an effort to keep up.

Over tea in the lounge she was bursting with the news of a pupil who had just missed a scholarship to Newnham. 'She took the knock very well, fair play, and what of tonight, are you and Mr Wallace to sup me full of horrors? . . . Now listen here, George, what's the ultimate effect of the evacuation of the Rhineland? I wouldn't trust the Labour lot any further than I could throw 'em.' Quite a distance though, I thought, my head pulsing with hangover.

We walked, the air did me good. In Charing Cross Road Miss Cooke stopped to examine the bookshops before they closed, and picked up three or four secondhand Spanish texts which she let me pay for. We had an early dinner at Lyons' and walked round to Wyndham's.

At the stage-door I pointed out Delysia going in at the New Stage door opposite—*Topaze*—gave her the stall ticket I had bought, and left her. I knew she would examine the great painted sign for my name, then the photographs, then saunter up St Martin's Court to peer at more books.

In the play, I had no scenes with Bill: in the wings, the occasional mechanical nod, no contact till the three minutes in Act Three when he joined me on the ottoman, waiting to arrest Perelli. Tonight we were polite strangers. 'How is Miss . . . Cooke is it?' 'Fine, is it true Steve Donoghue's in front?' It was not enjoyable.

Having asked beforehand, I took Miss Cooke into the star dressing-room. Charles emerged from behind a curtain, scrubbed and in dressing-gown, and went into his Yorkshire, 'I 'ear you're from Leeds, lass, d'you know Scarborough?'

She did indeed, and the family hotel. 'But if I may say so, your performance is an experience.' I had never before heard her pay a formal compliment; I could see that Charles was taken with her, 'A drink, do?' I was about to say, 'No, th...' when I heard her voice. 'A little whisky, thank you, undiluted.'

Had she said it? 'George tells me you've met Kipling?'

Charles looked puzzled, 'George?'

'I mean Emlyn, have you the feeling that "Recessional" is not entirely sincere?'

'Interesting you should say that,' and they were off. But only for a moment; she interrupted herself. 'But you have a train to catch, please continue to give excitement to so many people.'

'Miss Cooke,' I said as we got to Cambridge Circus, 'whisky, what would the Headmaster say?'

'I'd heard so much about it in books and such, I thought I'd sample it. Tastes like medicine, I must give gin a try... isn't the detective good, a nice touch when he read the suicide note and his hand shook with emotion.' It did, did it?

All she said about me was, 'Little did I think when you were a youngster and I arranged those Italian lessons in Geneva that you'd be spouting it on the London stage, life is rum... Isn't it the detective who's going to share the flat with you?'

'It's fallen through.' At the Kenilworth, I kissed her goodnight. I was proud of her and I felt she was proud of me.

Walking to the hotel next morning I found her waiting outside, holding a long piece of string to tie round the Spanish books. It was good to sit back in the taxi without the nag of extravagance. At Victoria the train receded down the station shadows; waving and smiling, she slid out into the sun, as alive as the summer light around her. She would now sit down to her Spanish.

It was Saturday; I walked to Greycoat Palace. My knock was followed by a barrage of coughing, 'Who's there?' It could be a creditor... He was in the old dressing-gown, his usually groomed hair in spikes and his eyes sore: he looked terrible. 'C'min, ole boy.' I went in past him like a stranger.

He cleared his throat. 'Show went well, didn't it? How did Miss Cooke . . .?'

'Bill, I'm afraid the flat won't work.'

'You know best, old boy.' I was not prepared for polite acceptance. He looked at me with a shaggy smile and said, simply, 'I've lived nineteen years longer than you have, and I've experienced all kinds of people. But I've never met anybody like you. Nobody's ever wanted to do anything for me before. It's a pity.'

He clasped my elbows and pressed them to me, I felt the tremble of his arms. As he kissed my cheek he smelt of tobacco and whisky, but it was not unpleasant. 'Good luck,' he said, 'my dearest boy.' I turned and went. How did I get into this?

Normally my summer walk through St James's Park would have raised my spirits. Suppose I had been told, a year ago, that today I would be dragging myself to a theatre, to play a marvellous part in a long run . . .

I phoned Polly, asked myself down for the week-end and put on my cheery face for the matinée: the same politeness. Between the shows I went back to the Mansions, already a place of troubled memories, and lay on my bed. The evening was harder still.

Another Sunday of sun and swimming and friendship. At four it started to cloud over, we had tea indoors, and Polly put on the gramophone.

Sentimental music, and I knew the effect it would have on me. I saw him shuffling round that borrowed flat, pouring drinks he could not afford for strangers he would never see again, a man whose only strength was his refusal to fight his weakness. The strangers leave and he sits, glass in hand, staring at the rug.

'Anything the matter?' It was Polly.

'No, no . . .' She would have been sympathetic but I nursed a prejudice against understanding women, who are liable innocently to confide to girl friends—sometimes to men—how understanding they have been.

Happy in my surroundings, I thought I would sleep. But my mind, aching with longing and sorrow, wandered wilfully. It was a hot night; I got up, pulled on my bathing-suit, padded round the bungalow in the moonlight, settled on the edge of the lawn, and stared down into the water. I was still able, like a feverish patient, to examine my case. The old committee of one.

First, I had seen myself as a solicitous young man pulling a defeated older man up out of his slough of despond. When Carol dubbed me a Good Samaritan and I felt self-satisfaction I deluded myself. The first days—true—I had been no more than sorry for him, then subtly the whole thing changed until it became . . . this.

And 'this' was possessive love. I wanted—for the first time in my life, and the last—to own another human being, to dominate a man potentially superior to me and who, unflawed, could have dominated me. I craved to rivet the broken pieces together, to coax the rusty watch to tick.

Probing further, I acknowledged it as a love imbued with the physical: over the weeks Bacchus had somehow acquired the pipes of Pan and the tunes were growing on me. I dwelt on the fact that since he was nineteen years older he could have been my father; to me Freud was only a name but I recognized the flavour of incest and it refused to repel me. There was danger here, a danger which meant that yesterday I had been right to break loose . . .

Then, out of the luminous dark, I heard his voice: 'Nobody's ever wanted to do anything for me before . . .' I must live up to that. Next morning my self-examination might never have happened. I returned to London and walked to Greycoat Place.

When he answered the door everything was the same: the sagging dressing-gown, the unshaven face, the eyes empty of plans for the day. He closed the door and put his arms round me like a bear, reeking of smoke and drink. We sat opposite each other. I said, 'Did you have a good Sunday?'

'The usual.' He coughed and took a half-smoked cigarette off the table a second before the cloth would singe. As he fastened his frayed pyjama collar his hand was shaking. Below his dressing-gown his feet were bare: beautiful long feet, different from mine, which were strong and stubby. Yesterday's *Observer* was scattered on the floor.

He coughed again, winked and smiled. 'You remember what you called me on Friday?'

'I was provoked to it. Then you called me a runt.'

'At least it rhymed. Actually you're not a runt, you've got a good compact body and you'd make a good half-back, I'm all in favour of you as a half-back. 'Smatter of fact I'm all in favour of you.' I put down my cup, crossed to him, bent, kissed him lightly on the head and sat again. Then I said, 'I'm going to ask you something. Do you need me?'

It was a vital question. We exchanged a look: the look you give yourself in the mirror. 'We've got used to each other,' he said, 'haven't we? I've never loved anybody before. And I love you as a friend, and as a son.'

I felt emotion rising and resisted it. 'Does that mean—you do need me?'

'The flat you mean? D'you want to be saddled with an old crock with a chest?'

'You've got a chest because you smoke too much, and your liver is because you drink too much. I'm talking like a doctor, but I could help.'

He nodded his head. 'All right.'

The pact was made.

CHAPTER FOURTEEN

MY FATHER'S KEEPER

In the bus he did not light a cigarette, and in the Cavour he had a bitter; the barman smiled. After a cafeteria snack, on our way to the Empire he stopped for chewing-gum. 'It helps.'

This reminded him of Cochran's wife, an enchanting woman with a drink problem. 'Darling,' a well-meaning friend had said, 'it's simple, if during the morning you feel a craving for a martini, eat an apple!'

'But, my dear,' Mrs Cochran had answered gently, 'I can't eat twenty-five apples before lunch . . .'

During the film he got restless a couple of times, made for a pocket, hesitated, and took the gum from another pocket. After tea in the Mansions I said, 'Bill, have a cigarette, the warder says you can.'

We sat reading for an hour, he was dipping back into Saki. The scrape of a key; it was little Curtis home from work. 'Oh my feet . . .' Ten minutes later he tiptoed through with his suitcase, whispered goodbye and left my Mansions life as unobtrusively as he had entered it.

On Sunday, an excursion to Virginia Water. Sitting under a tree Bill said, 'I haven't been here since before the war.'

'When you took the girls out? I'm glad you weren't killed in the war.'

A shadow crossed his face. 'What made you say that?'

'I was just glad you're here. Just a wave of affection.' It was a clement summer day: a clement summer relationship.

Then a danger signal.

Sitting next to me in a Tube station, he turned to me, ill at ease, 'Emlyn, I don't think we ought to go through with this.'

He had taken me by surprise. 'Why not?'

'Because you ought to be meeting people, you're on your way up—and I'm meant to mooch around and meet my pals at the Club . . .'

'You've been doing that because you hadn't a home to go back to. Now you have.'

It was true, but even between two honest people the important part of the truth is often below the surface. He was not only thinking of me. A friend curbing your bad habits may be good for you, but when they are the habits of a lifetime ...

He was chafing: alarmed and realistic. I was not.

'Bill, all I want is to see you happy.'

Again it was true, but I was angry as well, at the prospect of losing possession. 'So, Bill, let's drop it, shall we?'

He smiled. 'All right, I've got it off my chest.' He lit a cigarette. I could never cure that, the coughing and wheezing would have to be accepted. The train came in and no more was said.

The double divan furnished the living-room and we shared it, which meant that the little bedroom was never slept in. It was ironical that after the Paul Tanker awkwardness, here I had the privacy and was to make no use of it.

That first night, after the play we got into the Tube: including a call at the delicatessen for tinned soup and eggs—for Bill to scramble—we were back in twenty minutes, door to door. This was to be our routine, the eggs to alternate with cold meats.

Our daily timetable was set as well: breakfast at ten prepared by Mrs Atkins, my first charwoman, and then we would sit around and read. Bill had suggested joining the Times Book Club: *Cakes and Ale, Angel Pavement, Farewell to Arms*. Once, he looked across and said, 'Marvellous to have you with me all the time.' On rainy mornings, with outside the bustle of the street and the whoosh and hoot of cars, two new table-lamps gave out a homely glow.

Twice a week I walked to the Book Club and back. Then at 12.30 we would take the Tube 'down West', for a beer at the Cavour, the cafeteria, a film, tea at Mary-and-Mum's. There he would sit on while I walked in one of the parks; I knew the impending performance was keeping him out of temptation. It occurred to me that I should take him to meet friends like Polly, but with his shyness of feminine society it would have been hopeless. It was a funny non-life. I was happy.

'My dear Son George, Your Mother and me are delighted you have dropped anchor in another bit of sand up there in the Smoke as the sea-faring folk speak of London. And Mr Cronnin being a gentleman that much older than you judgin by the photos will keep you to the Strait and Narrow, now your Mam.

'Dear Goerge, Be careful of them geysers in the new place, i of seen in the Dispatch about one blowin up and markin two men for life. PPS from your Dad. Re geysers, your lovin Mother is referin of course to the Baths and not to the Ladies.'

❋   ❋   ❋

Bill's new way of life was paying dividends. 'But it's unbelievable,' somebody would say to me, 'he looks ten years younger!' He stood straighter, walked lighter, and the blood had drained from his eyes into his cheeks.

I even made a concession: the cutting off of 'the hard stuff' was bound to make him suddenly lethargic, so we agreed that every night he would look forward to one good whisky-and-soda in the flat. After supper we sat in the middle room: he in his dressing-gown, upright on a hard chair and treasuring his drink, I cross-legged on the lino.

I talked, and that made him talk. We ranged from the dubious existence of God to the unchallenged reality of literature, from Dostoievsky to Daisy Ashford. Then he would ask me questions, and he was the first person to whom I gave a complete picture of myself. Nothing was outside his understanding.

Every day he became more of a companion, and a valuable one. On Thursday mornings he would cross to Wyndham's box-office and arrange free seats for that afternoon's matinée of some other play. These visits meant that behind the diffidence which fell upon him when sober, I recognized more and more his sensitive intelligence and freedom from pretension.

His taste in acting, unimpaired by the costume plays of his youth, was infallible. Whether in comedy or in tragedy, he recognized simplicity: the seemingly effortless player who conveys the truth which tells the audience more than it seems to.

All else he rejected: performances hailed as great he often dismissed as meretricious. At an abrupt false note—a grimace, a clamour of sobs—I would hear a sharp intake of breath, no . . .

Chance remarks stayed with me. I asked if he had any one test by which to measure fine acting.

He looked perplexed. 'Not really . . .' Then, 'It's a performance when every sentence sounds as if it's being said for the first time.'

After seeing one matinée, we ran into an actor who was in the play. 'Frightful lot out there,' he said, 'half a house, not one laugh out of 'em, what can one *do*?'

Afterwards, I said it was surely a defeatist attitude. 'Of course it is, what one can do is to try and give an even better performance than when it's a full house, you can't blame people for the empty seats next to them.' I learnt a lot about my job from him.

I also learnt about behaviour offstage; his lack of pretension enabled him to spot it in others and afterwards prick the bubble. He had an odd and commendable habit of never using the first names of great ones with whom he had worked: it was always Miss Lawrence, Miss Titheradge, Mr Lang, Mr Galsworthy. 'Did you notice the way she brought in Miss Vanbrugh's name as if she knew her, even called her Vi, damn cheek . . .'

He's like a ship, I thought one night as I went to sleep, a big ship adrift but with its searchlight working, picking up every flashy bit of paint on the smaller more specious craft who know exactly where they are going. Could I chart a course for him?

It seemed so, but plain sailing does not last: and under thirty it shouldn't. One day I discovered, with displeasure, that I was jealous: not of the present, of the past. Searching in his drawer for a household bill he had mislaid, I came across two grubby snapshots. The first was of a little private soldier, eighteen at the most, a uniformed cherub standing at attention against a painted glade. 'Who's he?'

Bill looked. 'Lord, it's little Gareth my batman, beautiful boy, Welsh. And damn good value, as I remember.'

'Was he?'

I had tried to sound indifferent and turned to the other snap. It was another figure in khaki, older, twenty-seven or twenty-eight: a tall, slim officer, cane under arm, looking into the camera with clear challenging eyes, the mouth sensuous but firm, with a humorous curl of provocation. The most attractive photograph I had ever seen.

'Who's he?'

Bill drew on his spectacles. 'Good God . . .'

I asked if he had found this one good value too. He gave me a

curious look. 'Only when there was nothing else on the agenda.'
Then he smiled. 'It's me.'

'You?' It had caught me unawares, and he flinched as if I had
flicked a hand across his face. There was no way I could put it
right. I tried with, 'Well, it was years ago . . .'

'Fifteen, not that long.' He went to have his bath, and I studied
the photograph. The eyes looked into mine, unquenchably young,
ready for post-war London, ready for success. What had happened?

Mrs Atkins came in to 'do the lounge' and hearing the kitchen
curtains clatter open, I went in to take over the bath. Bill, naked
and drying himself, was turned away from me, and I was used
enough to what he called his 'paunch' to be amazed.

As in a museum you catch an exhibit from the back, so now I saw
him, a statue as perfect as the young man in the photograph.
The long legs were smooth and unblemished, while the straight
back broadened up to the shoulders from narrow hips. He turned
round, shuffled into his dressing-gown, bent down for slippers,
and had a bout of coughing.

I was face to face with the tragedy of the passing of time.

❋　　❋　　❋

I fitted the photo of the young officer into my wallet, and when
alone I would take him out and study him. I waited for his knock.
Perhaps, one night, he would be standing at the stage-door, tall,
straight as a ramrod, shining of hair, tooth, skin and eye. I felt
again the stab of jealousy: then thought, since I now possess this
man, why am I jealous?

Because—I was talking to myself, so could hurt no one—because nobody else wants him. Whereas the postcard of that lucent
young male, looking out at me as if he knew me, gave proof that
he was wanted by everybody: and was to be mauled by woman,
man and demon drink. 1918, it could have been my thirteenth
birthday. Time had cheated me. I was angry, and ashamed.

But I did my best to know him: one night, after supper in the
middle room, I asked questions. Not about the childhood in the
gilded Mayfair cage, which was a locked book; and there is no
doubt that this unattainable side of him helped to sharpen my
interest.

I did ask him if he had loved his mother. 'I suppose I'd have liked to but she was rather bored with me, hated me being called Bill . . . No, she called me Will.'

I liked that, then I asked him about his adolescence. 'What? . . . Oh dead normal, girls in the company and all that, it was all part of the game. Till I was twenty-seven, then the war came and that was that.'

He was closing up again but I persisted. 'That was that?'

He was silent. I waited.

'Nothing normal any more.'

It was my turn to be silent. He went on. 'But it's all been gone into by Sassoon and Graves . . .'

'Everybody's different, this is you.' I was not only the friend straining after participation, I scented the rarity which every writer seeks, the first-hand impact of life. If I got him to talk a little now I would remember his words for good.

'Nothing normal any more?'

He had finished his drink and it loosened his tongue.

'I was old enough at twenty-seven not to be taken in by that King-and-Country balls, it was all a bore, bang bang and home by Christmas. Actually at first it was fun, the uniform and no responsibilities, just orders, like school, but always on the move. Then France, the real thing, wham . . .'

There would come a pause to light a fresh cigarette but he never lost the thread.

'. . . I'd never seen a dead body before. Every other day you found yourself in some sort of butcher's shop, that's why I hate that display downstairs . . . Looking at it you said to yourself, ten minutes ago he talked to me and I can't work out which bits are him. The shock of that went right through you, top to toe and front to back. The body got to be special, the living healthy body.'

His voice vibrated close to me but his eyes, sated long ago with grief, were veiled and far away; he had never spoken like this before to anybody.

'You saw it all the time, the body I mean. When it wasn't in the butcher's shop, it was in the sun diving nude into the river, or in the dug-out by the light of a lantern, standing bollock-naked in a hip-bath. You started to latch on to those moments so tight it was like being mad, the booze helped. There were the knocking-shops behind the lines, but queueing up for three minutes of oo-la-la . . . no thanks . . .'

Another cigarette.

'D'you know the thing I remember about the war? No, not the Union Jack flapping in the breeze or the Angels of bloody Mons either. I was crossing a field once after a stifling hot night, it was the most perfect morning in creation. At the end I passed a dozen Highlanders lying there, lit by the rising sun. All sorts of positions they were in, arms flung out, heads on elbows . . .'

'Dead?'

'Good God no; fast asleep, knees up to the chin, knees up in the air and sprawled apart, so that the kilts had ridden up over their bellies and the summer dawn was kissing a row of the biggest cock-stands anybody's ever set eyes on. The attack was next day, three-quarters of them went west.'

There was nothing to say; I waited.

'Then there was my batman little Gareth, talked like you when you get worked up, it's what I first noticed about you. The day he enlisted he got engaged to a girl in the next village, always wore a ring on his left finger, once I saw him kissing her photo . . .' He got lost in thought. 'What was I going to say . . . oh, yes, this is a funny bit, I'd forgotten it . . . We'd got to a nasty night, the guns going like one o'clock, I was standing in the old hip-bath—you did your best to keep clean, for the kill—and there was Gareth running in and out with fresh water like a French farce.

'"Soap me," I said, "will you, old chap?"

'"Certainly, sir." Inevitable result. The guns helped.

'"Fair's fair," I said, "get your togs off and I'll soap you."

'"Oh thank you, sir, that feels lovely"'—not a bad Welsh accent, the actor in him had remembered—'and it wasn't a minute before we were both "feelin' lovely", and by now the shells were whistling like one o'clock when suddenly—this is the bit—the kid suddenly said, "Excuse me, sir, is it all right for me to let myself go?"'

I started to laugh—of course it was funny—then saw that Bill had tears in his eyes. He said simply, his voice beyond emotion, 'The reason I've remembered it so well is that a week later he was killed, I identified him by the ring.'

* * *

At the end of August a development quite unforeseen.

Bill had asked to read *A Murder Has Been Arranged*—'But it must be done, this is original, what they're frightened of is exactly the reason it might go!'—and had then prodded me into sending it to the Repertory Players, the Sunday society which had discovered *Rope*. I had sent it, then forgotten I had.

A phone call from Henry Kendall. He was trying to persuade the Players to do the play with him in the leading part and directing, but they were frightened of—I waited for it—the murderer-hero and the ghost.

I had no hopes but was flattered. Kendall was a very well-known actor in his thirties; was I free for lunch on Tuesday? I was free for every meal.

At the Ivy I wore my best dark suit, to sit in the same room as Isabel Jeans, Ivor Novello, Phyllis Monkman, Marie Löhr, Dorothy Dickson, Owen Nares: what Dad would have called a high-class lot. Kendall ordered dry martinis, mine was my first. I felt rich and wanted, what the hell was I doing walled up like a nun over a butcher's shop?

With the fish and white wine Kendall said, 'It's now as definite as these things can be before rehearsal, which will be in six or seven weeks. They want to do *A Murder Has Been Arranged* on Sunday, November the 9th.'

I looked over at Jeans, Novello, Monkman, Löhr, Dickson and Nares, they were all merging and looking identical. Then I concentrated. We discussed Sunday shows: too few rehearsals, no set till the day, too little of everything, the impossibility of a first-class director.

Then Kendall said, 'What about you?'

I said I would agree to whoever he wanted.

'I mean what about you directing it?'

'But I've never . . .'

'All the more reason to start. What gave me the idea is that you write the right stage directions, think about it.'

Within half an hour I was opening my script, seeing it not as author but as director: an immensely new field where I would surely confront problems only solvable by the expert—idiotic but vital queries, how can she answer the phone when she is carrying a tray out and the phone rings the other side of the room?

I took a sheet of paper, drew an oblong and started fitting in furniture: sofa, armchair, desk, table for drinks, dining-table ...

A memory crossed my eyes like a curl of smoke: I was a child of six who had never heard of a play, squeezing bits of cardboard into an empty Woodbine box, for my cut-out fashion plates to be piloted around talking to one another. Then—vital to the last act —I placed the long dining-table to run up and down stage, so that the ghost could sit at the head of the table with his back to the audience. That was easy.

I realized why. While writing the play, I had unconsciously plotted the all-important ghost effect and worked back from there: the host is murdered in the alcove so that the black alcove-curtains can be closed to hide the body until at last the black dinner-jacket will materialize out of the dark of the curtains.

It was the same all the way through. I had been directing the play as I got it on to paper: it was now a question of manœuvring the people to look and sound natural. I could cope. Next morning I started marking my script with little childish crosses, moves ... Then I reminded myself it was not for weeks yet, and anyway there might be a hitch; I would get my mind off it till the time came.

My mind did not need all that persuasion, for towards the end of August the tick-tock of Marchmont Street-Wyndham's was once more interrupted.

* * *

Even as a child I had hardly ever been ill; overnight, my throat became agonizingly swollen.

I remembered Doc Mervyn, a rosy little Welsh G.P., not much older than me, with whom I had made friends in the Cavour; he diagnosed acute tonsillitis and put me to bed. There was no question of playing, and the idea that the show would go on tonight without me was intolerable.

Bill rang the theatre, hurried to the chemist's for pills and made me some broth; he burnt the first lot, but the second was all right. Turning at the door at theatre-time he said, 'I'll take a taxi straight back, have you got the water next to you, see you eleven-fifteen at the latest ...' And he was gone.

But I would not be alone here tonight, even while he was away. For he would be back.

Lying with neck throbbing and fists clenched, I looked round. I had only ever been alone in the flat for a few minutes, and never once at this time on a week-night. The few objects in it, from the too-few books lolling along the book-shelf to my depressed closed desk, too small for its wall, and the uncovered armchairs with the Woolworth ashtrays, seemed to be staring at me like nonplussed pets, what are *you* doing here?

I clenched my fists—what indeed was I doing here?

Under Doc's pill I sank into a stupor, came to with a start and lunged at my watch: five minutes to eleven, the curtain was coming down.

Eleven, eleven five . . . and that means he was on his way; as I said it, aloud, I started to listen to cars. There would come a swish, which got louder and then died away; then a wait, then another swish which got louder and died away.

At last I heard a car stop, and the smart ring as the taxi-driver flicked up his flag. I looked at my watch, it was eleven-ten and he must have raced through his dressing; the taxi door banged shut, the empty taxi revved up and drove away, I heard the door close downstairs, then footsteps heavy but brisk.

I sat up, so as to look as if I were better; I had left my door open, and formed a welcoming smile. The footsteps reached the flat and went on upstairs. Our landlord was also a heavy man.

At eleven-forty-five the curtain had been down nearly an hour. At midnight, I would give up hope. A swish becoming louder and dying away, then another, then—at longer intervals—others. Mostly a silence deep enough for me to hear, from the wireless upstairs, Big Ben striking twelve.

I turned off my light and lay staring up into blackness; even in fever, I was realistic enough to think, as I had once thought staring down into water. Making my mind a blank, I let it fill up of its own accord. I thought for two hours. Even with a temperature, that is a long time.

Eight months ago, I thought, I was on the brink of the gutter and in despair; tonight I am poised on a ladder, and again in despair. At a moment when I was having enough success to open a door to a social life with a circle of close friends, I had let it

swing shut and made myself a prisoner. I was in a quicksand up
to the knees, was it too late to squelch out?

What was more, I had known this situation before: that face
on the dark ceiling was turning into another. My mother's.

I am in 314a, where for the second time my father's dinner has
gone back into the oven: she sits, hands folded in her lap, within
her eyes the ashes of anger. She hears a sound, and stiffens: a
train approaches, clatters past and in silence she sits back.

Can there ever have been a more grotesque repetition? It was
a bitter two hours.

I must have dozed again, the light woke me. He was in the
doorway, hat on the back of his head, smiling.

'Hello, ole boy, berrer? Sorry, ole Ben came round, Club ...'

I said, 'You're in the other room.' A minute later I heard a thud
and a creak.

I looked at my watch, which said two-thirty, and turned out
my light. I knew I could never trust him again.

＊　＊　＊

Re-opening three nights later I felt a truant, and a shaky one
at that, but got through; the same great laugh on 'It would pay us
to grow our own flowers'. At the end one of the understudies said
of my understudy, 'He got the same big laugh, isn't it a marvellous line?' In the theatre, it is not hard to keep one's head.

Life resumed its tenor. I had learnt, as a reformer, not to count
on anything and perhaps because of that Bill seemed happy to
come straight back at night and sit around, off the beer and on
the whisky but seldom beyond the glowing stage, while I worked.
The first rehearsal of *A Murder Has Been Arranged* would be
October the 11th and I was back at my script: stands, moves,
crosses, sits. Then I moved on to concrete preparation: furniture,
props, clothes. Most important, the set.

At rehearsals of the most lavish West End presentation, sooner
or later the cry is heard ... oh, when do we get the set, not till
Friday ...?

'The scene is laid in whatever theatre it is being played in'...
Could there be a theatre with a permanent set which was con-
ceivably right? If so, I would be the first London director, ever,

to enjoy the luxury of rehearsing in his set from the very first day
—was such luck possible?

As I eagerly turned over a paper they phoned that a theatre
had been fixed for my Sunday: the Strand. Week-nights, it presented Leslie Henson in *It's a Boy!* A farce, bad luck.

But since it was in one set I thought I had better check, and at
noon next day I was groping my way through the wings. The
curtain was down, a stage-hand turned on the working light and
I walked to the middle of the stage.

I was standing in a sumptuous drawing-room. The designer had
decided to 'do it modern' and his choice of colour, right through,
was a mixture of stippled pale blue and grey. Flooded by farce
lighting, it probably made a jolly background for belly-laughs;
as I saw it now, drained of dazzle and in the morning silence, it
looked dead. Haunted.

Under the dust-sheets I peered at sofa and armchairs, all in
an expensive colourless pattern: a vast French window, downstage, could be made into a draped alcove. I walked to the middle
of the curtain, drew aside the folds and looked out into the empty
auditorium. The front row of the dress circle looked a few yards
away and even the gallery, soaring above, was friendly and near.
A beautiful theatre. My theatre, for my play.

CHAPTER FIFTEEN

AS NEAR AS DAMMIT

Even with a month's rehearsal we had to chop off evenings and two afternoons a week. I decided to dispense with a reading, we would plunge straight in.

And this plunge was unique. The curtain was down, and to start the action Ann Codrington as Miss Groze, script in hand, ran to the middle parting, opened it, looked down at an imaginary orchestra and shrieked, 'Stop!' She told me afterwards that half-a-dozen cleaners had shot up and stared at her.

Rehearsals were happy, and happiness is difficult to report: they absorbed me so intensely that I hardly noticed that a new Wallace play *The Mouthpiece* was also in preparation. All my players—rare in a Sunday show—were perfectly suited; a cast tends to take its colour from the principals, and Kendall and Margaretta Scott were fun. Eighteen, she had a few lines in *The First Mrs Fraser* and I had been doubtful whether she would be capable of tackling a leading part. From the beginning she glowed not only with beauty but with talent.

They trusted each other and me, which meant that the others trusted me too, knowing that as one of them I would never forget that actors are as easily frightened as any racehorse. They were eager to work not only through the mornings of their matinée days, but even to hurry from those matinées, meet me on the Strand stage at 5.30, and rehearse for a couple of hours before a snatched dinner.

Nightly *On the Spot* almost made me forget the daytime, but sitting offstage I let my thoughts wander. Could my play end up with the same impact on an audience as this was having at this minute?

There was no way of knowing. The cast seemed sanguine, but actors are not good judges of a production in travail, optimism can be because they are interested: no outsiders came to rehearsal and at our Friday all-day rehearsal there were only a few mute shadows in the stalls from the Repertory Players, joined by Walter Peacock for half an hour from his office. 'It looks good to me.'

To check audibility, I had felt my way to the gallery and saw the play from the front row. Between me and the lowered curtain, the house-lights were out and I felt alone in my haunted theatre. When the band rehearsed, I leaned over the rail as keyed-up as I had been as a schoolboy in the gallery of the Royalty Theatre, Chester, waiting for my first pantomime.

On my way to Wyndham's I wondered again—will it go? Impossible to tell . . .

On Saturday morning we rehearsed bits, and again between the shows. That night, I was glad of *On the Spot*. Sunday, notes and a relaxed word-rehearsal, then a disbanding before the first and only night. Bill had wanted to go but I had discouraged it, eight o'clock on Sunday evening was not his best time.

Getting into my dinner-jacket I remembered with relief that after the performance—if there would ever be such a time—I was going to Polly and Sonny's, to join a birthday party.

Would I watch from the back of the pit? In case I couldn't face it, I slipped a small German dictionary into my pocket, then walked to the Strand stage-door to wish the cast luck, I would be 'around somewhere'. There was nothing more for me to do.

I walked up to the Opera Tavern, sat with a small whisky and made it last till five to eight, when I walked to the theatre, remembered the *Carmania* and felt giddy. But I had rewritten it since then, it *had* to have improved . . .

The foyer was seething. I turned on my heel past the Waldorf Hotel. I had five heart-beating minutes and spent them walking round and round Aldwych, getting back just as the last of the audience were trickling in.

I darted to the back of the pit. The band was playing 'Mountain Greenery', the theatre was packed and buzzing, you could hardly hear the music. That was right, the audience was accepting it as the usual overture.

The music finished, the house-lights dimmed, the chatter died away; expectant silence. Out of it came 'Zulu Wail', a weird blues number I had chosen in a record shop. My heart thumped, the music soared. Through the curtain, a bolt from the blue, Miss Groze: 'Stop!'

I was out of the theatre like a pickpocket.

* * *

Back in the Opera Tavern I ordered another whisky which I gulped, and a sandwich which I could not get down. I was glad of my dictionary, knowing that the best way to unwind, for me, would be to memorize some difficult words. I made my whisky last an hour, then ordered another. They'll have got to the murder ... they'll have got to the entrance of the Dumb Woman ... they'll have got to ... I drained my glass and left.

Too early at the stage door, I stalked up and down the deserted pavement. Was this how expectant fathers pace, outside the hospital?

I looked at my watch, went inside and hovered on the stairs. From where I stood, I could hear nothing of the vital last minutes of the play, though in my mind I could watch them as in a dream: the murderer blurting out his confession, then the silence while they all stare at the ghost—slowly it rises from the table, slowly it walks across ...

A dresser passed, shaking out a powder-puff while her high heels clacked across the silence. From the stage, a crash. God, has the permanent set toppled over?

It was the safety curtain hurtling down, to prevent the murderer from escaping into the auditorium. All over.

I went down into the wings and heard tremendous applause which could be meaningless, topped by a shout from the gallery of Marvellous-Marvellous which could be sarcastic—Freddie's Dennis? Then a surge of people through the pass-door; I fled. It had certainly 'gone well, good reception' but those can be the phrases a friend falls back on to describe your non-success.

The party was a big one, with Polly and Sonny at their easy best. 'Fill up your jorums!' A mixed crowd of attractive people; it had got around through Polly that I had come straight from my play, how did it go, how did it go ... Went quite well I think, thank you, Sonny, a whisky ...

Flowers, lights, gramophone music, 'Falling in Love Again', 'Dancing on the Ceiling', a whirl of smiling faces, good-looking men, pretty girls, a stream of names, well-known novelists, playwrights, actors, publishers, composers, Emlyn this is William

Gerhardie Moira and Warren Chetham-Strode Eric Portman who
lives upstairs my cousin Philip Heseltine I mean Peter Warlock
Jo and Alan Bott Molly and Jack, how did it go . . .

I guessed who Molly and Jack were: Polly's young sister and
her husband. He was tall, cadaverously good-looking, distinguished and a good fifteen years older, about forty, with an easy
sardonic sense of humour. Knowing she was a barrister's wife I
had expected her to be on the grand side but she was warm and
friendly, a pretty girl smaller than Polly—'Mother always called
me the dainty one'—with beautiful ankles. I liked both him and
her. How did it go . . .

Early next morning I sat stiffly and slammed open *The Times*.
'Here is a dramatist who can throw over the theatre an icy and
continuous spell.' *Morning Post:* 'fresh, original, imaginative'. The
Telegraph produced a jumping headline, GHOST STORY THAT GRIPS,
YOUNG AUTHOR'S SUCCESS. 'Unless all the theatre-managers in London are stark mad, it will be transferred . . . Not for many years
has any author made my flesh creep so goosily . . . An ovation.'

Bill said, 'They're the best since *Journey's End*.' I remembered
myself in the parlour of 314a, labouring at the play 'as an exercise'. Exercise is good for you.

Mr Peacock phoned. I had never heard him excited before,
would I come to see him.

When I did, he was on the phone and making notes, 'Yes . . . ,
yes . . .' After ringing off he said, 'I've never known anything like
it, how many managements would you guess want to put your
play on? Eleven!' Harrison of the Haymarket, Firth Shephard,
Howard and Wyndham, Reandean of the St Martins, Maurice
Browne, the Daniel Mayer Company . . .

He gave me details of last night. 'They were with it from the
word go . . . On Kendall's entrance, first act curtain, immense
applause and at the end of his monologue, a salvo . . . When Peggy
Scott came on as Juliet, applause and when the Dumb Woman
finally spoke there was a stillness that's very rare . . .'

Walter—he was somehow no longer Mr Peacock—had sorted
out the offers, weighing one against the other. It was a pleasure
for me to confirm that at last he would be making money out of
me: ten per cent of my royalties, and he deserved it.

An important issue was the type of theatre; a delightful but
brand-new one, like the Duchess, would damage the atmosphere.

Howard and Wyndham wanted stars engaged, Fay Compton for
Peggy Scott's part, Frank Lawton for 'the love interest', but I was
adamant that the cast which had contributed to last night must
be offered their parts. The choice fell on the Daniel Mayer Company. While West End playwrights were usually paid 5 per cent
of takings up to £1,000, 7½ per cent between £1,000 and £1,200,
and 10 per cent over £1,200, the Mayer Company was offering
a flat 10 per cent all through. 'Do you realize,' said Walter, 'that
only Shaw commands that?'

Going down the stairs, I remembered how often I had mounted
them in dim hope. On my way to wire 314a and Miss Cooke,
Charing Cross Road was paved with gold.

I bought the evening papers. 'His play compels a shuddering
attention.' Finally the headline 'WILLIAMS OUT-WALLACES EDGAR'.

By next evening all was signed and sealed: the play would open
in two weeks' time—on the 26th, my birthday—at the St James's,
a beautiful old playhouse which, under Sir George Alexander,
had presented the first night of *The Importance of Being Earnest*.
An added detail seemed too good to be true: the theatre had the
reputation of being haunted. Once more the set, by arrangement
with Leslie Henson, created a unique situation: the scenery of
one London play was duplicated for another which would run
concurrently.

At Wyndham's, from Charles on, everybody expressed a family
pride which touched me. From Miss Cooke came the first emotional letter she had ever written to me.

'After I sent the telegram, I thought of such a lot of things I
might have said, I know that the ship will come home welcomed
by all who have good hearts to understand . . .'

'My dear Son George . . . Before this I was well-known in the
Works but now everybody knows me. Even the Welsh religious
magazine is praising you with DRAMODYDD WESLEAIDD ENWOG,
Celebrated Welsh Dramatist, your only criticks being the Sally
Army, Tom says Commander Watson is sorry you gave your play
such a Murderous title. I expect they would like it better if you
called it "A Salvation Has Been Arranged" but I think you would
lose custom that way.

'Fancy the *News Chronicle* printing the little photo of you that
you asked us for, a good headline too *The Famous When Young*
but your dear Mother is giving them socks here she is.

'Dear Goerge, I hope you of not been overstrainin yourself, they of made a big mistake with your age you were not 7 years old but 4, in the photo you look simple for 7 please gett them to correct this your lovin Mam.'

From the Hart sisters: 'Our *Variety* informs us that "The opus is a melo stuffed with plenty hokum but Williams is a smart scribe", this may not be English but it's gratifying.'

On a Sunday evening Peggy Scott's parents gave a party for us both; it was like one of Polly and Sonny's. Peggy's mother, in a corner with me, whispered, 'We're thrilled to bits, but I have an extra reason to thank you, you've got her away from *The First Mrs Fraser.*'

I looked suitably curious.

'You see, she's developed this immense admiration for somebody in the cast—I may as well tell you, it's Henry Ainley ... Oh hero-worship really, but he apparently has a roving eye, what's more he's fifty-one to Peggy's eighteen, and one knows of these cases of young people getting entangled with men old enough to be their fathers, *and* the drink problem—Emlyn my dear, being a writer I know you can understand ...'

I nodded my head wisely, 'I can indeed.' I got home late. Bill was later.

*　*　*

A phone call from E. P. Clift, one of the managers I had wooed with *Glamour*. In the New Year he and Gilbert Miller intended to present *Etienne*, an adaptation of the great Paris success by Jacques Deval (*Mademoiselle, Tovarich*) and wanted me for the name part, I said thank-you-very-much-I-look-forward-to-reading-it.

These days, one after the other, were so unreal that having just been offered a miraculous star part, I was taking it as much in my stride as if it had meant another Sunday guinea from the Greins. They were not made any more real when I read in the papers that last night the new Wallace play had opened and was a failure, WALLACE MAKES A SLIP, EDGAR EASES UP.

Bill was as surprised as I was but did add, 'Look at the titles— which play would you book for, *The Mouthpiece* or *A Murder Has Been Arranged?*'

Next day he said, 'I've been talking to Bill Linnit, you must have two new suits.' This other Bill, next to Jack Buchanan, was the snappiest dresser in London.

I said, 'But I haven't the figure to interest a good tailor.'

'The best reason for going to one.'

I met Bill Linnit in Savile Row; afterwards he said he had never seen anybody more restless than me choosing two patterns and being measured.

As we left he gave me a message from Edgar to congratulate me on the fact that his and my initials had brought me luck and to say he had a box for the 26th. If I had been informed on my last birthday that on my next the Cigarette-holder would be watching a first night of mine ...

The price of the two suits was outrageous. 'But, Emlyn, you can afford it!' It was delightfully hard to get used to.

Since I was unavailable in the evenings, the St James's dress rehearsal was an afternoon one, and public. Just before the overture, taking my stand at the back of the pit to take notes, I saw that the audience, impregnated with the casts of other plays, was packed and over-excited: the notices and the publicity about managers fighting for the rights had acquired for the play a fantastic reputation.

Would it live up to it? The performance went smoothly, the set and lighting were if anything improved.

But it was not the same. Following the monologue, a murmur of appreciation and a dozen hand-claps. After the Sunday night, hadn't Walter spoken of 'a salvo'? The reception at the end was good, but the over-familiar word 'polite' recurred to me. There was a feeling of anti-climax.

Bill had been seeing the play for the first time; sitting in Mary-and Mum's he said, 'Mind you a ghost story can never be a matinée play, and of course a very critical audience. They were certainly held.' He had not been carried away.

Anti-climax ... I felt it in the air. The first-night audience evidently reacted well, but there was no shock of discovery.

The play had been over-praised and several of the notices said so, with encouraging riders. 'A hundred faults, but it is promising ...' 'He displays a devil-may-care energy, however, which renews one's hopes in his future.' Agate wrote, 'The capital is seriously divided as to the merits of Mr Williams' play ... He will forgive me for saying that my own pulse never at any time beat faster.'

The play did pretty well but the theatre stubbornly refused to be full. Would it have made the difference if the play had been initially put on for a run and made the same thrilling impact as on that Sunday night?

There was a more perplexing question: if I had not been 'obstinate' and had consented to Fay Compton and a brace of other high-powered names ... All I knew was that excitement had inexplicably turned to ... anti-climax, the only word for it.

The day after that Sunday night one would have thought I had written the best play since *Saint Joan*. I hadn't, and knew without being told that audiences were not leaving the theatre saying, 'You *must* go.' On December the 10th Arnold Bennett wrote in his diary, 'An evening of claptrap, I was disappointed.'

I was disappointed too. Could it be that the play was a clever trick, and that even the clever ones are found out?

'Too bad,' Bill said, 'and it was as near as dammit ...'

But the cast were happy, and my royalties amounted to a hundred pounds a week: a year ago I was earning twelve. The London streets may not after all be paved with gold, but there was a definite glint of yellow dust. And I enjoyed spending money: Christmas drink for the cast and presents to 314a and Miss Cooke. Dad's best present was that plump body of cuttings.

'My dear Son George, We note with pleasure that in this new one *Etienne* you will be playing a Starring Part in the Smoke, viz LONDON. You have set this locality on fire with your Brilliant Career.' His eldest was a genius.

On January the 24th (1931) *On the Spot* closed and Bill left for an eight-week tour of the play, headed by Charles. Waiting for *Etienne* I had four days, and went to Berlin.

CHAPTER SIXTEEN

A TRIP TO EVIL AND BACK

'The wickedest city in Europe ducks,' Freddie Mell had whispered to me, his Dennis having returned from a riotous German holiday.

I had said I'd like to go, and Dennis had sent me an introduction to Roger Davilion, Berlin correspondent of the *Morning Post*. 'He'll show you *everything*.'

As I stepped out of the station, I felt I was moving into exoticism: across the street, in electric lights, THEATER, and I made up my mind to go, tonight. Underneath, the name of the play, AUF DEN FLECK. I looked again: *On the Spot*.

I signed in at the grandest hotel, the Adlon, and studied the theatre list. I was tempted by *Im Weissen Rossl*, a new musical spectacle Dennis had swooned over—*White Horse Inn*—but duty won and I walked to the Deutsches Theater, to see a brilliant production of Brückner's *Elizabeth von England*. Then a walk round the corner, for my rendezvous with Mr Davilion at the Bar Cozy-Cozy. In my good mood—I was glad I had spent a sensible evening—he sounded dashing and the bar welcoming.

The latter turned out to be small, dark and furtive, with dusty drapes: the former, an accommodating bald man in pince-nez more suited to advising at Thomas Cook's on family holidays than to whispering 'Open Sesame' to Sodom and Gomorrah. Chaperoned by the usual sphinx-barman, two sickly boys sat in a corner chattering quietly like harmless birds.

'Early yet,' Mr Davilion said, then took me to '*the* place, has to be seen to be believed'. But the El Dorado, much bigger and spattered with balloons, had not filled up either. The gaiety was on the sluggish side, whipped up at hectic intervals by a noisy sleepy band, jocular male clients and women of all sorts and sizes, very made up.

A couple passed us, a nondescript careworn older man dancing with a tall haughty girl, respectably gowned, with brown hair parted down the back and drawn to each side to form plaited circles like large ear-phones. She looked like Gracie Fields' un-talented sister. They were striding to a decorous snarling tango.

'Well?' Mr Davilion asked eagerly, gleaming at me from behind his glasses like a broadminded uncle with cloven hooves, 'What d'you think of her?'

Surprised, I said, 'She looks rather respectable—*is* she a tart?'

It was the reaction he had hoped for. 'She?' he said happily, 'It's a man, they all are! They're in *drag*!'

It was then a rarity, and I had to look again. 'What's more,' he added, 'it's their *own hair*!' The band played 'White Horse Inn' and the couples fox-trotted with mechanical abandon.

Why had I come? For I was old enough to know that 'night life' is a delusion which will never add a new dimension to enjoyment—to know that adventure, whether of the body or of the mind, either floats to you by chance or is of your own making.

No, if the shocking is to be examined at close quarters, the back must be firmly turned on such dispiriting travesties of wickedness. Let's go to the real thing. Next morning I bought a street map. Not of Berlin, of Hanover. And in the afternoon, I set out on an adven-ture of my own making: a macabre excursion, of the mind.

* * *

Something must have told me that Berlin would not live up to its legend, for in my suitcase was my copy of *Murder for Profit*: in the Christmas lull I had read William Bolitho's masterly account of five mass murders. One of them had lingered to visit me in the small hours, in dreams from which I woke in childish fright. Then beside me I would hear Bill's regular breathing and relax into relief. The relief, though, remained shadowed with the evil of the nightmare.

Sitting in the train, I felt the evil at work: half against my will, half on purpose. I studied my street map.

From my compartment—where I sat alone, which seemed right, no apple-cheeked hausfrau to distract me—I watched the Ger-man January afternoon wither into dank twilight, and by the time the train was bumping through the respectable suburbs of Han-over it was dark.

And as the dark settled, so my nightmare settled too: into its own reality, based on the facts which I knew by heart from the book in my luggage.

I am no longer—I said to myself—a twenty-five-year-old actor-playwright from London: I have turned the clock back seven years, to March 1924, to my Easter vacation from Oxford. But instead of having won a travelling scholarship in French, and so sitting in a train in France, I have won it in Germany; my Hanover connection to Frankfurt does not leave till morning, so tonight I plan to doss down in a corner of the station waiting room.

The train slows down and the big sign slides past—HANNOVER with the two Ns—as it has slid past hundreds of adolescents before, students or homeless drifters—they are legion, in this depressed Germany of 1924—who look forward to the warmth of the waiting room.

As the train halted in the busy Hauptbahnhof, the imagined undergraduate melted back into my present self. I crossed to the station hotel, booked a room, went up to it, took out *Murder For Profit*, sat down and re-read the chapter.

I laid the book open, went to the window and looked down. Hanover Station. In the dim spill from lamp-posts it looked the terminus, by night, in any city. Cars crept up, black figures seeped into the station like shadows, seeped out like shadows. But they were real people, like me, carrying parcels, luggage, umbrellas, stopping to buy a sandwich, a newspaper. Real.

Then, as I peered fearfully down, there crawled up the smell of horror. I took up my street map and walked down into the station. There it was, WARTESAAL, Waiting Room. I opened the door.

It was exactly as I had imagined from the Bolitho book: large, high, bare of any furniture except benches. People sitting here and there, older men, a few women with children. Weary transient night-faces waiting blankly for the time to pass. This was the place, and as I sat on a bench I willed the picture before me to fade slowly out as if it were a film, then I made it fade in again: the same room, but seven years ago.

It is crowded now with adolescent boys, some dozing, some looking vacantly at the floor, all cold, hungry and adrift, and all German except one: my imagined self, the undergraduate in the corner. And I watch myself raise my head as the door opens.

A man. Neither cold, hungry nor adrift. Fritz Haarman. He is nondescript, forty-five, heavily built, of peasant stock, shabby but decent. Overcoat, woollen gloves, plain brown hat: there is nothing to distract from the image of the respectable citizen. He scans the room with purposeful eyes. A fatherly detective.

Which he is, in a way. A tradesman by day, by night—in these lawless post-war times—he helps out the overworked police, investigating dubious goings-on among the vagrants, even doling out advice.

His eyes pick their expert way over a couple of sleeping figures and alight on a boy near me. He sits and asks him questions, the boy unbends and smiles, nein he has no home but he is with the two asleep over there, excuse me mein Herr . . .

The police agent rises, sees me and walks over, your papers, bitte, are you hungry? I am, he lives not far and the stove is lit. It will be a face to talk to and good for my German, warum nicht?

Then my present self got up, and—in my dream—trailed the imagined man and boy of nineteen: and it was not entirely a dream, for I knew the route by heart, from the map in my hand. Also the dream was not difficult to sustain, for the dim little streets must look the same as they did seven years ago: the same little square here, the same lone lamp-post there. I tagged along, stalking the two silhouettes: the heavy citizen, the slighter Welsh undergraduate improving his German. From the map I recognized a turning, wheeled into a short street and looked across at the narrow high houses. Rote Reihe.

There it is, the seventh along. Sieben . . .

I watch the two figures saunter up. The man stops at the door, takes out keys, unlocks it and melts into the dark of the crumbling old house. The boy follows him, and he too is swallowed up in the darkness. Never to be seen again.

I stood in the deserted street, looking up with drugged eyes, half waiting for the dark to glow from an oil-lamp being lit in the attic. A shadow, as a threadbare curtain is pulled across . . .

I stared at the black window: yes, it could have happened to me. And as I stood and stared, rooted in fright of the fantasy I had wilfully encouraged, in my mind I drove my phantom undergraduate self into the pavement, stamped on him as if to extinguish a fire, and hurried back to the hotel.

Getting into bed I saw the open book beside me. 'A rumour arose like a wind from nowhere: "There is killing in the Old Town..."'

The honk of a car. An engine grumbling to a halt, then hoarsely expiring. I slept badly; once I was woken by a scream and lay quaking. It had been a screech of brakes. I was glad to open my eyes to daylight. My morning was planned.

＊　＊　＊

I walked to Police Headquarters—Polizeihauptquartier—explained to a uniformed man, in stilted English, that I was an author preparing a These about die Kriminalpsychologie, showed him my passport, and mentioned the Haarman case. In any part of the globe, on the subject of any local scandal which has passed into history, the police are inclined to be on the defensive. The official bowed smartly, ushered me into a room like a cell and disappeared.

Ten minutes passed. I was beginning to visualize arrest when he returned, placed something before me, bowed, left the room and closed the door. Before me lay a folder with on it one word, in immaculate Gothic: HAARMAN.

I untied the cord, opened the dossier, and scribbled telegraphic notes. 'Series of discoveries of which people talked in hushed tones...' I turned the page and was faced with the first of the commonplace illustrations with which the transcript was interleaved.

We are, more and more, flooded with photographs. Whether they are personal and of every sort of banality, or public and of every sort of brutality, we look without seeing.

My situation, however, was special. I had come upon a story in a book, and like a stone that cannot be rolled away it had lodged itself in my imagination: a story of real life, and my grown-up reason had of course accepted the fact that seven years ago all this had happened.

But looking now at a perfectly ordinary photograph I realized with a shock that in my heart I had not been able to believe that such things had come to pass. And the picture spoke to my startled eyes, 'You see? It did happen! Look, this cloud in the background, it was there for that minute, *it happened!*'

[195]

It was a snap of the river. Along the far bank, fuzzy trees in a row with in front of them a curious passer-by, hands in pockets, and next to him a dog: a real man, living in this city at this minute. You could put this picture in tonight's paper and trace him from it.

In the foreground, on the near bank a long row of what looked like pale skittles, neatly arranged. Bones. It was they which, washed ashore by a storm or worried out of the water by dogs, had started the first fearful whisperings.

'Written confession, involving accomplice Hans Grans aged 21 ... Claims that experiences on Western Front altered his character ... First offence night of September 27th, visited waiting-room ... took home Friedel Rothe, aged 17 ... sexual offence ... at moment of climax took knife from table and cut victim's throat ...

'By day butcher by trade, knife from his own shambles ... will hear evidence of Frau Seeman who lived underneath ... heard chopping ... at dawn, passed her on stairs with buckets ... swilling in back yard, whistling at his work ... "working overtime, Herr Haarman?"'

Opposite, a photo with underneath 7 ROTE REIHE: Haarman's room, a bed-sitter pitted with poverty and cluttered with the details of monotonous daily life, each spelling reality more clearly than the last. Peeling wallpaper; two old-fashioned Gothic texts, I could just read the word GOTT. 'God Bless our Home'?

My eyes went back to the typed page, 'during 1923 and this year, 1924, average of one murder a month, 27 murders in all ...' Then a list, like a school roster: '1923, 20 Marz, Wilhelm Schulze 17. 17 Mai, Hans Keimes 17. 23 Mai, Roland Huch 15. 25 Juni, Ernst Ehrenberg 13. 24 August, Heinrich Struss 18 ...'

I looked back at the photo; sagging from a nail behind the door, a worn overcoat and in a corner, a battered stove. I stared at the bed. It was single, with sagging mattress and iron-work at head and foot, like my old bed in 314a, with a coverlet neat and threadbare.

On the little table a pipe, I could almost see the teeth-marks. The home of a sad penniless tidy bachelor, in a sad dignified historic city. I turned the page, and a face confronted me: it had to be his.

It looked like an enlarged passport snap, except that unlike the dead eyes of passports his were living and as keen as knives: and looking straight at me and saying—when you saw my room just now, where I respectably lived while you were growing up in your foreign country—you must have believed *then* that I am real! ...

You still didn't quite? Well, will you believe it *now*? I exist. To prove it, I am looking into your eyes. And don't I look like anybody else? This old shirt I am wearing, I buttoned it absent-mindedly this morning just as you buttoned yours. Last night you imagined me in that waiting room in a plain old hat, didn't you? Well, d'you like this smart little Tyrolean one, see the feather. Don't ask me where I got my hat from, ah ha! ...

I am an ordinary man, don't I look it? And believe me—no, no, mein Freund, *look me in the eyes*—believe me, nothing that they all talk and write about, God and kindness and evil and ideals and repentance—nothing of all that exists. But I do. An ordinary man, what's all the fuss about?

'... will hear evidence of boy's father Oswald Rothe ... Father travelled to Hanover, heard that boy seen with H., then 4 p.m. called on H. in his room, learnt nothing. H. since confessed that 3 ft. from father, stuffed behind stove, was boy's severed head ...'

It had been an afternoon call. 'Coffee, Herr Rothe? Made from acorns, but still ...' Water boiling in the kettle on the stove.

I looked back at the room: at the peeling wallpaper, the overcoat, the texts, the pipe, the stove. And there was the kettle.

'... Frau Seeman will testify ... He stopped her on the stairs ... opened sack ... full of bones ... As H. was butcher it was natural, she made soup of them but says soup was too white, threw it away ...' I remembered the German for 'butcher': Fleischer. A dealer in flesh.

The last item was a photo taken in the police station, and whether it followed criminal procedure in Germany or was taken specially as an insult to a creature whose body had ruled his head, I could not know.

It showed Haarman, standing at attention, in profile, staring indifferently at the wall, and naked. You saw the hands and feet and sexual organs of any other man of forty-five: you half expected these last to bear some weird mark of the horror but they did not, being as indifferent as his look.

Behind this page there were two sheets of twenty-seven tiny blurred snaps, culled from shabby family albums: a gallery of young faces, some callow and bewildered, some brutalized, all defenceless and as pale as paper. Wilhelm, Ernst, Heinz, Friedrich, Willi... Cold, famished children of the Apocalypse, who had never savoured the faintest whiff of life.

On the cover behind them, in careful Gothic, ENDE.

Emerging into the watery winter sun, I felt I was staggering and had to make sure I was not. My mind, certainly, was out of kilter. Sitting back in a train, I closed my eyes and like a diver rising from the murk of a monstrous sea-bed, felt myself surface to the light of a beloved common day. I was going home.

But I had a lot to think about.

First, what a play this could have made! Horrifying, compelling and what a part for Laughton...

'Could have' is what my mind automatically formed, not 'can': in 1931 there was no point in contemplating, even for a moment, this particular play, because on the basis of a three-line synopsis it would have been banned. But that address, 'Sieben Rote Reihe' —what a title, in any language! *'Seven Red Row'*.

The Lord Chamberlain, however, held no licence to censor thoughts. He was powerless to prevent me, seated in a train with absent eyes glancing off the comfortable sunny countryside, from indulging in speculation of an unorthodox kind.

Disquieting thoughts.

They started with my mind being drawn back to *Murder for Profit* and my first introduction to the Haarman case. Sitting there, I relived the couple of nights in Number 60 when I had woken in fright, to be reassured by Bill's presence, peacefully sleeping beside me.

But had I not—before dozing off again—gone through a moment of... unease? As I lay there, that presence had slowly become sinister, for my imagination was turning his breathing into the breathing of another man, a man of his age and build. Fritz Haarman.

And now, as a result of an extraordinary visit, I took a look at the subject of sexual licence in relation to murder.

*   *   *

I thought of Bill: of my knowledge that he had a wild side to him. So had I. We were both liable, at moments, to try anything once. Twice. And in 1931 'anything' shocked many people.

My thoughts crept deeper. Like Haarman, in the war Bill saw sights . . . Little Gareth, identified by a ring. Eighteen . . . I recalled something, and it startled me: had not Bill described the carnage as 'a butcher's shop'? Vicious Haarman was hardened by it, had it hardened Bill too? Vicious Haarman . . . WAS Bill also vicious?

Streaked with it. I winced at the memory of a 'juicy bit of old gossip' from a crony of his, then examined it.

'One boozy night old Bill got involved with a woman who was mad on flagellation. He said not on your life, but she begged him to beat her and after a couple more drinks he obliged. Next day he looked really shaken up and I finally got it out of him that with the drink and her egging him on he damn well might have killed her, snapped out just in time . . .'

He might have killed her . . . It was not out of the question that this gentlest of men, who would have felt remorse over boxing a dog's ears with a newspaper, could have ended up in the dock. And looking at him, you knew that no woman on the jury would have been on his side. No man either. He would have been hanged.

The gentlest of men . . . Could Haarman perhaps, at his trial, have been presented as just that from the witness box, by shocked unbelieving associates?

No comparison. Yet . . . did Bill not describe himself once, jokingly, as a Jekyll and Hyde? And the double life he was referring to—does it not in many ways match the daily life of the consistent criminal? The cool subterfuges, the bold deceptions; the dark side streets, the door carefully locked, curtains checked for the fatal chink of light . . .

Then there stabbed into my mind the picture of Bill, greyfaced, telling me about the four sailors, how the door opened . . . Then my staring at him, 'The police?' Did the young accomplice ever stare at the murderer and say, 'The police?'

Possibly. Probably. Certainly.

Yes, it is near: the nearest any citizen with no inherent harm in him could ever get to contemplating, through a wall of unbreakable glass, the yawning pit at the bottom of which Haarman breathed with ease and luxuriated. Near enough to pitch headlong in.

Except for the unbreakable glass wall. Why is it there, in front of some and not of others? It was certainly absent when young Sidney Fox stepped forward into matricide.

The question, bringing up the mystery of personality, heredity and environment, is unanswerable. But the wall is there.

Fortunately. At Ostend, I roused myself and walked on to the boat, a reserved correct-looking young actor with his next part in his suitcase.

At 60 Marchmont Street, holding my key in the gathering dusk, I stopped and looked, through the panes of a locked door, into the butcher's shop. Dimly guessed at under the one bulb, the mangled corpses lay shrouded in gauze.

I rammed my key in and raced upstairs.

CHAPTER SEVENTEEN

A STAR IN THE SMOKE

Sitting up, I re-read *Etienne*. 'He is a sixteen-year-old French schoolboy, gauche, inarticulate . . .'. After a star entrance, it was a star part. I could draw not only on being non-English but on my fifteen-year-old summer in Haute Savoie. I would write to my mother for the béret which, on my return, I had hidden away for ever after she had said, 'Where shall I put your French hat?'

'ETIENNE Co. Dress Reh. 8 p.m.' Smooth, except for two absurdities.

The first was to do with a scene in the second act which had scraped past the Censor. The father's mistress arrives to find the boy alone, in dressing-gown over a pyjama jacket, and seduces him on a chaise longue. As he sits back in an agony of embarrassment she undoes his jacket, starting at the top button and working down, then slides her manicured hand inside.

In 1931 it could be bold enough to provoke nervous giggles, plus a bass boo from Freddie's Dennis. But the scene faced me with a more pressing problem, one which now sounds ludicrous.

My seducer was a beautiful young French actress, but we had made no personal contact; at the last run-through before the dress rehearsal, she sensibly got near the important gesture by pulling aside my tie and undoing a couple of buttons. As she inserted her hand I made a confused mental note.

There was hair on my chest. Not enough, on a beach, to make me look like an ape, but enough to be visible from the stalls. Surely not a bad touch, the adolescent accidentally revealing a harmless sign of pubescence? Not in 1931. Before the dress rehearsal I lathered my chest and shaved it. The Lord Chamberlain may not have censored the scene but I had.

The operation left the chest sore, and me foolish. When we reached the scene at the dress rehearsal, it seemed to proceed with the right comedy suspense. She undid my buttons and coolly inserted her hand. Then she gave a puzzled frown and raised an eyebrow which said, 'Mais chéri, pourquoi?' I did not need to act embarrassment.

If we had known each other better she might have murmured afterwards, over a drink, 'Ecoute, mon petit poilu, if tomorrow I make you a present of a li'l toupet-pour-monsieur, will you—for the première, just pour moi—attach it to your poitrine?' But she never did.

The second absurdity was even more disconcerting. My under-study, a handsome boy of twenty, five years my junior, was very friendly. Affable. Since the part entailed many delicately mumbled moments, I had asked him to sit in the gallery and check my audibility.

I was taking off my make-up when his head popped round the door. I steeled myself for notes—'dare I ... not *quite* enough pro-jection?'—but no. 'Heard every word.'

I was relieved, went on rubbing my face and invited him to help himself to a whisky. He toyed gratefully with his drink. 'You don't mind if I mention something personal?'

I stiffened. 'Of course not ...'

'It's a question of hair.'

Could he mean the hair missing from my chest? 'Yes?'

'It's just that from so high up, under the lights you can see.'

'See what?'

'The thin patch on the crown of your head. You don't mind?'

Whether in the Thirties or the Seventies of this or of any other century, there has never been a young man whose spirits have not plummeted at the hint that he is losing his hair. To intimate the possibility to a young actor is to plunge a dagger into him; to break the news to the same young actor when he is twenty-five and it is the night before he is to present himself to a London first-night audience as a schoolboy, is to twist the knife slowly, thrice.

I was still looking at him in the mirror. 'I am not going bald.' My voice was flat.

'Oh dear, I've offended you ...'

I offered a second drink, to mark the end of a non-existent friendship. He declined effusively and went.

As the door closed, I seized the hand-mirror and manœuvred it till I could see the back of my head in the big mirror. Yes, I could see my scalp: not much of it, but I could. I combed carefully and it was better. But the poison had worked. From an understudy not averse to undermining a near-star, it was a fiendish ploy. The mirror was to be up and down for a week.

While the play went well it was 'too French'. But I knew Dad would approve of the Criticks, they were more than encouraging: Agate not so good (he had seen the beautiful Paul Bernard in Paris): 'Mr Williams looked like an out-of-work Welsh miner but overcame natural disadvantages ...'

The play limped on till Saturday week: fourteen performances. It had not turned me into a Star in the Smoke, but I had made a creditable success. And my chest could now stop prickling and get back to normal.

❊   ❊   ❊

The next evening, Sunday, the *On the Spot* company was en route from Leeds to Brighton and Bill had suggested I should travel down to Brighton for the night. Determined to be strong, I had compromised by meeting him at Victoria for half an hour, at the station bar.

He looked battered but not too bad, and was as proud of the *Etienne* notices as my father. I gathered that in Leeds he had stayed not in digs but at the Queen's, so was unlikely to be saving a penny, forget it ...

'Am I going bald?'

He stared at me. 'Good God, no; whoever told you that? When I was your age somebody told me the same thing—no, men start going bald at the temples and your hair's practically in your eyes. You won't go bald.' I didn't.

We had been happy to see each other, but for me the meeting, in a severe bar with one eye on the clock, was a mistake.

I knew it when I arrived at Number 60 in the rain, hurried past the butcher's shop up into the empty flat, slumped on to the double divan and looked past the black glistening panes at the chill dark. Why had I never bought net curtains? ...

Beside me lay a letter from Walter P.: a tour of *A Murder Has Been Arranged* was going out with Donald Wolfit and Margaret Webster, and in the repertory and amateur fields there was enormous interest: 'In spite of the play having run only ten weeks, don't be surprised if you have a small gold-mine on your hands.'

So why was I depressed? Why had I not asked Polly and Sonny to dinner, or Peggy Scott and Harry Kendall?

Just as once, in this place, I had found myself alone and had looked round it, now I looked again. That first time, I had dwelt on the depletion of it; now, conscious of my bank balance and more acquainted with the comfort of other homes, I filled the room with the things which were not there.

A fire. Lined curtains. Pelmets... Over the mantelpiece, a framed oil painting: a landscape with Italian trees and blue sky. On it an ornamental clock—a Market bargain—with on either side some good china. What *was* good china? One can ask... Snapshots, invitations... I looked at the Woolworth ashtrays.

I had only ever lived here alone during the *Etienne* rehearsals, but those evenings had crackled with preparation. I was now out of work, a Star in the Smoke without a part, and even a thriving actor is only as successful as the play he is in. That over, he waits: from limelight to twilight.

I sat grimly on, thinking once more of the little Vincent Square room in which, with no prospects, I had cheerfully spent hours alone. *All Quiet* in German...

Why couldn't I make a plan—get a new reading ticket to the British Museum, wasn't I supposed to be an intellectual Oxford graduate? I might even find an idea for a play...

No, I faced the fact that, materially well off as I felt, I was without resources. I remembered Miss Cooke's 'You've never had a hobby': no golf, no fishing, not even chess.

And no people either.

A phone call from Freddie Mell. 'It's my Dennis's birthday, like to meet us at the Long Bar?' Within three minutes I was in the Tube.

Having known of the Long Bar since *And So To Bed*, I had been newly curious about it since hearing it was where Duggie Fairby had met his murderer friend Sidney Fox. It was located in the Trocadero, just up from Piccadilly Circus in Shaftesbury Avenue.

In what was outwardly the most respectable rendezvous in the most respectable of all capitals—No Ladies Permitted—two inscrutable barmaids, presumably not Ladies, waited on little tables clustered with Gentlemen Only, all in the old uniform of bowler, dark suit, rolled umbrella and starched collar. Earlier in the evening, the talk was as starched as the collars; but as the whiskies mounted so did the voices. Barriers melted and by closing time impulsive friendships tended to burst into bloom.

It was exactly as I expected; I spent a pleasant hour with the birthday couple, then they had to leave to dine with Dennis's Mum and Dad. Sitting alone at the table, I ordered a small whisky and looked at the small groups, all looking as if they were waiting to catch trains. I hoped I didn't look as if I hoped to be befriended.

Perhaps I did hope to be, at that...

By the mysterious young Friend? In the Long Bar? I drank my whisky; the smell and taste could only be the most vivid of reminders. I gulped it down, walked out into the Tube and walked from Russell Square to a café where I sat morosely munching. I might have been a penniless tramp.

In between the dull days there were the dreaded evenings. Between them there came one agreeable one: Mrs Atkins had written down that a Mrs Carus-Wilson had phoned. I still tended to think in terms of *Glamour*—a Mayfair hostess? I rang the number.

'This is Molly, Polly's sister.'

'I'm so sorry, the message said Mrs Carus-Wilson.'

She laughed. 'I am Mrs Carus-Wilson, isn't it a pretentious name? I'm afraid I married above my station! We've moved to South Ken and having people in for drinks and Polly thought you might like to come along.'

No. 3 Rutland Street was a tiny house in a tiny street near Harrods, furnished simply but with the warm comfort I was missing so acutely. The company too made me feel welcome: Polly and Sonny and half-a-dozen others.

I told Molly I had expected them to be living in grandeur. 'Heavens, no, we haven't a penny but I hadn't a penny before so I'm used to it.'

I asked her about her stage career—'Well, you could hardly call it that'—but I persisted. Her first appearance had been at the age of nine before an audience of wounded Tommies, her mother having dressed her up as one—complete with bloodstained head-bandage—and persuaded her to recite something called 'Spotty Was a Pup 'E Was'.

From that she had graduated to 'The Cocky-olly Bird' and as

Molly Cottontail in 'Brer Rabbit'; then, the drunken father having walked out, her mother had got a job playing the piano at Etlinger's Academy with free elocution lessons for Molly from Dame May Whitty.

I saw what she meant about her subsequent career in musical shows—'I wasn't very good but I *could* dance'—though some of the titles were memorable. When she was fifteen her mother had pretended she was eighteen and she had toured in *Chu Chin Chow* in transparent harem trousers. 'In Birmingham the Watch Committee made us wear tights underneath.'

Then she had gone into *Battling Butler* with Jack Buchanan, at the same time playing in the Midnight Follies at Rector's, then as an Athos Beauty at Prince's and walking home at three in the morning. 'Oh, no, we only got chorus money but I made enough to furnish a little flat I had with Mother in King's Cross.' Then came *Clo-Clo, Riki-Tiki* and *Enter Kiki*.

I enjoyed every word; I needed people. Jack didn't drink but was an affable host, urbane and dry. I noticed he called her, with a sort of teasing affection, 'my little Mole'; I tried to imagine myself calling a wife by a nickname, and couldn't. I thought, married life is funny . . .

It was marvellous to get outside myself. I stayed till nine and was loth to leave for the tedium of nothing after nothing, day after day, evening after evening.

The night came which brought things to a head.

*　　*　　*

I knew the Long Bar could do little for me, but I was by now so low that I was willing to be leered at by the Hunchback of Notre Dame. In Shaftsbury Avenue, blazing with THE BARRETTS OF WIMPOLE STREET, STRANGE INTERLUDE and YVONNE ARNAUD IN THE IMPROPER DUCHESS BY J. B. FAGAN, I ran into Duggie Fairby going in.

He was no Hunchback and I was glad to join him, though he was no golden boy either, a scraggy, balding forty. He talked freely of his late protégé, the murderer, and I was a good audience. Over our second whisky he said, 'How's poor old Bill? Oh, I've known him umpteen years, once we got pie-eyed together— mind you he was young then and a knock-out—and we picked up a tart and there we were thrashing about in one big bed, what a night!'

'Duggie,' I said, 'I feel like going on the town.'

'O.K., what d'you fancy my dear?'

'A woman.'

I had caught him in mid-swallow and he nearly choked. 'A woman?'

'Why not?'

'Let's see, I'll consult the li'l ole scandal sheet.' He leafed through his address book. 'Got to think up a wench who'll take on a threesome, mm . . .'

I hadn't got as far as that but what the hell . . . After another whisky he said, 'I'll give somebody a tinkle, nice creature, house-keeper to an old lady by day but gets on her scooter by night, hangs out at a club in Archer Street . . .'

He was off, and back from the phone in three minutes. 'Vi'll be on the corner in a quarter of an hour.'

She was too: a buxom woman of forty, quietly dressed, black turban, brown coat with fur collar, friendly refined smile. In the taxi, her voice was as refined. 'You're Welsh, fancy, so am I, well, half, born in Mountain Ash, fancy . . .'

In Number 60 the living-room looked as blank as ever, but I quickly lit the gas-fire and wound up the gramophone. The one Bill had given me, for Christmas, with records, La Boutique Fantasque, Scheherezade, The Swan of Tuonela . . .

I put on 'Falling in Love Again . . .' The suggestive throaty voice serpented round the room like aphrodisiac smoke.

'What I like,' Vi said, 'is a nice musical show, *Rose Marie* was lovely.'

I brought in the whisky and there was the familiar swish of the siphon, the glow of cigarettes. Duggie and Vi chatted, 'Oh, I remember her, Doug, worked in the Alhambra stalls bar I think it was, had two kiddies . . .' I might have been sitting in a train entangled with a couple of loquacious strangers.

'Emlyn here,' Duggie said, 'wrote that *marvellous* play *They've Planned a Murder.*'

'Oh, that does sound exciting, tell me, dear, what was it about?'

I got up, caught Duggie's eye and went into the kitchen for a siphon. He pattered after me. 'Don't worry, my dear, I'm told it's the drink that does it with her, works wonders.'

I opened the cupboard and took out a second bottle of White Label. We went back. As I poured out for Vi, she gave me a pretty smile. 'Isn't Duggie a naughty thing? Cheers.'

An hour passed. I had played every record I had, from Gracie to Scheherezade and back, and all the music did was to remind me. The room was thick with smoke and the fresh bottle half-empty. Duggie was drunk, I half-drunk and Vi, who had had as much as the two of us, showing no signs whatever.

And showing nothing else either. She started arguing with Duggie about whether St Ives was in Devon or Cornwall, until she rose to get another cigarette and he gave her a push. She fell on the double divan, bounced and lay flat on her back: a move less promising than it sounds, for as she fell she closed first her eyes and then her legs. Then she said, in an unrecognizable infant voice, 'Nice daddies, I'ze so *sweepy*,' and placed an index finger between her pursed lips. She was Baby Peggy of the silent films.

But Baby Peggy's other hand was holding something out. An empty glass. I filled it, full, with neat whisky, 'Ta, ducky.'

She drank it all. 'You two *is* slow!'

Duggie and I had another, he slipped his hand up her skirt—'No, dear, oo mustn't, don't oo dare violate me!'—then he started taking my trousers off. I had half-guessed it: he was no violator, he was a voyeur.

Except that it didn't look as if there would be anything to voir. I handed Vi another glass of neat whisky. 'Ooh, ta, oo *is* good to Vi...' It was polished off like a thimbleful of iced water on an oasis. Which was she, Baby Peggy or Falstaff in drag?

Before turning away again, she saw I was in my shirt, said, 'Ooh naughty,' and closed her eyes. Somehow it infuriated me. I whipped off my shirt, winked at Duggie and we set to.

It was like undressing a thrashing whale. A whale with the giggles. When I came to dealing with her brassière, it snapped smartly off and nearly hit me in the eye. I stared.

My solitary dreams had been intermittently rosy with smiling big-breasted women: what faced me was something else again. Two moons. More than moons. Balloons. An *embarras de nichons*. Suspecting that Duggie had never before been afforded an uninterrupted view of even a normal female bosom, I looked at him: he had gone ashen.

Vi was again lying on her back, legs apart, but her eyes were once more sealed and she seemed in for a good night's rest.

I had been well put off, but by now it was only fair for Duggie to try to give him something to remember the evening by. I did my best, until I turned my head to find that he had gone to bed in the little room. My performance had failed to hold, and the audience had walked out on me.

I rolled over beside my captive leviathan, pulled the sheet over us and foundered into sleep.

Soon after daylight I heard her step out of bed, get into her clothes and tiptoe out. I got up, parted the curtains, dressed, straightened the bed, opened the door and stumbled into Duggie, half asleep in his shirt and with his trousers over one arm. He looked as if he had seen a ghost.

I heard a step on the stairs. 'Charwoman,' I whispered, propelled him into the big room and on to the bed and covered him with the blanket.

As Mrs Atkins let herself in I hurried into the middle room. From the kitchen, a sizzle of bacon which reminded me of my mother. A plump housewife emerged in Mrs Atkin's apron; she had laid the table, breakfast for three. I had forgotten our guest was a housekeeper.

'Mrs Atkins,' I said, 'this is Mrs Fairby, Mr Fairby's not quite awake yet.'

'Pleased to meet you, Mrs Atkins, isn't it *warm* for March?'

I returned to the big room to get Duggie into my dressing-gown. 'Your old Dutch is asking for you.'

The three of us had a pleasant breakfast party, then Vi said she had to hurry off to work but first could I sign a copy of my play for her and her little girl. I found one and wrote, 'To Vi and Edie with lots of luck from the Author.'

She called to Mrs Atkins in the kitchen, 'So long, dear,' then kissed us both. To me, 'See you sometime, lovey.' To Duggie, with a wink and pointing to the open kitchen door, 'Hubby, darling, you *will* be home in time to kiss the kiddies goodnight, won't you?' And she was off, heels tap-tapping down the stairs.

A whale with a heart of gold.

❁   ❁   ❁

On the mat, a long envelope addressed to W. Cronin-Wilson Esq. The flap was only just stuck; I fingered it open and drew out a contract for Drury Lane, to support the immensely popular Austrian tenor Richard Tauber in *The Land of Smiles*. Salary fifty a week: fifteen more than I had got for *Etienne*.

An actor in a success, particularly at Drury Lane, finds he has many more friends than he knew, let's all go up to the Club... No more coming home to cold food and rationed drinks; the tame bear had gnawed at his chain and it was ready to snap. Only I was involved, suffocatingly: the quicksand, long past the knees, was at the waist.

I looked at the ravaged bed. It was too soon for the ridiculousness of last night to be funny, and I let the squalor of it swamp me. Duggie had appeared in the doorway and was looking at me with concern. 'My dear, what's the matter?'

I had not realized that I was breathing hard and my fists were clenched. 'I'm all right,' I said, 'bit of a hangover.'

'Nice wench. Shame it was such a failure.'

For the first time in my life I felt old. I went to see Doc Mervyn in his digs. He frowned. 'You look awful, what's the matter?'

'I don't know.'

He told me to sit down and describe how I felt. I told him I had no desire to see anybody or to do anything. Yes, one thing: to write a good play. And for that you have to have something driving you, some direct electric current running between you and the world around you. I wasn't living. As for sex, I was standing stock-still in the middle of the road, and that's as good a way of getting run over as any.

'You've got to get away. I tell you what you must take'—he sounded as if he were prescribing—'a cruise.'

I looked up at him. 'A cruise?'

'To the Far East. To the sun.'

It was like hearing an orchestra strike up. I went to offices in Cockspur Street and booked my passage, for April the 19th, from Tilbury to Gibraltar, Marseilles, Egypt, Ceylon. A new life.

CHAPTER EIGHTEEN

WHAT THE DOCTOR ORDERED

The *Ranpura* had an orchestra, they told me, and a swimming pool; there would be strange lolling girls and boys who, to music, would not be strange for long. Ceylon evoked a white hotel fronted with palms; from my terrace corner I would look down over tawny sands, type END OF ACT ONE and join a group plunging into the cool orient sea.

The boat was bigger than I expected. I walked smartly down to my cabin, wound up my portable, put on 'White Horse Inn', lay back and felt the ship of adventure begin to throb. As the afternoon light streamed past the porthole, I fell asleep as if drunk.

At seven, the dinner gong. I put on 'The Peanut Vendor', dressed carefully and slipped a notebook into a pocket, for when I would overhear something interesting, Hadn't *Private Lives* been written on a trip like this?

I sauntered up to the dining saloon, sat at a table for one and gave the room the bold indifferent gaze of those who dine alone.

There were mixed couples and tables of four males, but the younger generation must be dawdling in the bar. All who were not middle-aged were old, the glitter of cutlery chiming with the gleam of spectacles and of balding brows.

They were pleasant people, English and well-behaved: 'nice' was the word, a nice lot. The married couples seemed fresh from modest hotels in such elysiums as Harrogate. Many of the men wore toothbrush moustaches and the fact that they mostly knew one another by sight did not rob them of a shamefaced look. I took my napkin out of its ring.

The misspelt menu—propped against the vase of faded arti-ficial roses screwed to each table—announced, in dim duplicate, leek soup and boiled mutton with chips. The travellers applied their spoons to the soup like convicts. The stewards were ship-soiled figures in crumpled black. The zest of departure seemed to have ebbed from them, they looked soured and stationary.

The married couple next to me nibbled a roll; I laid my notebook beside me in case they said something. I had to wait till the mutton. He said, 'When they saw us off, her name's Marjorie and you called her Edith.' She said, 'Did I? Well, I wasn't far out.'

I wrote it down, but it puzzled me. Were Marjorie and Edith identical twins? I never knew, and the exchange was never to be spoken on the stage.

Nobody arrived late. Halfway through my apple dumpling I realized that I was the only passenger under thirty, that all the others were pining Empire preservers and that the vessel which was to spirit me to a new life was a P. and O. liner plying grimly between England and Australia as a Tube train shuttled between Edgware and Morden. Those who were not returning to rubber in Malaya were on their way back to tea in Ceylon.

I rolled my napkin into its ring, went down to my cabin—my home for the next three weeks—and put 'White Horse Inn' on again. I had brought no books, how was I to spend the next few days?

I had forgotten the Bay of Biscay.

In the night I woke up to the sharp shudder of a door and felt unreal—where was I, who was I? The cabin was straining and groaning and there was a wind, giant, implacable. I thought of the leagues of treacherous water around and under, dark with wreckage and carnivorous jaws: of the bones of the dead swirling round the world for ever.

The next two days and nights were fiendish. Several times I tried to slide into a permanent faint. Could my father have ever been a seaman?

Once I clawed my way up to the streaming deck; there was a sudden mammoth roar as a vicious slap of water heaved towards me, a lash of the tail from a marine monster on the run. I staggered back to my cabin, through a barrage of hot rancid oil which made me sicker than before.

With Gibraltar, however, we entered the peaceful warmth of the Mediterranean. The name was wrapped up with my young reading—Monte Cristo, Quo Vadis, Pompeii, Leander swimming and Shelley drowning, the galleys, the mermaids; that evening, from the moonlit deck I heard music and low voices, this was more like it . . .

But as I approached I could make out the words: 'Oh, yes, all the ships look the same but you get to know which one you're on by the stewards; nice to get into the Med and put away the stomach powder . . .' Under a couple of fairy lanterns a dispirited three-man band was rendering 'Zigeuner' while several couples bustled dutifully to and fro.

Looking out at the shimmering sea, I remembered a recurrent dream. Swimming in a mill-pond sea, I glance to where water melts into sky and steer myself contentedly right round. As I do so, I observe that the melting is not confined to one horizon; it is on all four, and my minutes are numbered. I longed for a walk in the country.

In the library, between the Marie Corellis and the Dornford Yateses, I found *Bleak House*. A lady in the next deckchair asked if I was having a nice trip, I said it was nice to see the sun.

'We dread it,' she said, 'the one thing we miss away from the U.K. is the grey skies,' then closed her eyes and fanned herself. Could Maugham have done anything with her? I tried to imagine a dead lover at her feet and a smoking revolver between her fingers: the nearest I could manage was a smoking cigarette.

I wandered to the bar and sat near three sociable bachelors, two planters and a doctor with fortyish faces transformed by the magic East into leather. 'Who's for another snort?' Somebody shouted, 'They've organized the pool!'

I followed them to the top. The pool was a big stained tarpaulin full of sea-water and the sea-water full of the nice middle-aged lot: bathing-costumed figures shrieked like children, ooh, if you splash me again I'll give you a good ducking, ducking I said you filthy cad . . . I went to bed.

On Sunday, Protestant Service in Top Lounge All Welcome. I looked through a window at a dozen of the couples sitting in winter best for church in Welwyn Garden City, while the ship's padre prayed for them. 'Lord watch over those in peril on the seas.' It made you wish you were really in Welwyn.

Notorious seaport coming up, what's yours old top? The three bachelors had, of course, gone ashore at Marseilles before, on the Med run, but could never cope with the lingo, Williams what's your Frog-talk like?

Although I had never been here before I was promptly elected as housemaster-guide to three lubricious elders. At a café in the Cannebière, over mid-morning Pernod and bad whisky, I showed off negligently by asking the garcon 'où l'on pouvait s'amuser'.

My boys—by now I thought of them as that—stared as he scribbled down a discreet address where the door was opened by a maid in cap and apron; behind her, a lady in black with hair scraped back and pince-nez.

The doctor's face fell, 'Haven't we come to the wrong place?' Half-a-dozen girls appeared and we paired off into elegant little rooms. My choice chattered away, and once again it was agreeably uncomplicated. Lying with my head on her breast I thought, am I only ever to find fulfilment in brothels?

When the doctor emerged he looked dazed. 'D'you know what mine did? Sat on top of me, marvellous!' It was comic, I expected a doctor to be surprised by nothing.

*　*　*

The more friendly the sun, the more they all retreated under canvas as if from a bombardment.

Port Said overpowered me with the sounds and smells of a hideous sore of a city trapped between two hemispheres; the night heat steamed with evil, little windows squinted at one another like the eyes of rats. In the cafés, our drinks looked dirty.

The boys got into conversation with a little misfit of a man in a tarboosh who looked Arab and could be selling anything from indecent postcards to hashish, but talked Cockney and plainly saw himself as English.

'Every sod in this bloody place 'as got a bit o' Turkish, Jew, Greek, or nigger, I know one woman 'alf English an' half Arab, had a do with a pukka sah'b Britisher an' got the idea 'e'd marry her an' ship 'er back to the old baronial 'all. 'E ditched 'er an' she knifed 'im, lovely woman too...' I was glad to climb back into the ship, up a ladder out of a cesspool.

The Suez Canal was straight as a die and about as interesting, and entering the Red Sea I understood what they meant about the heat. It was suffocating, lethal. On both sides the ship was hemmed in by giant ash-heaps. There was no glimmer of green, no movement of man or of beast; the earth crept by as dead as the moon.

Behind me I heard, 'See over there, dear? That's Mount Sinai.'

I concentrated on my wet eyelids and prised them open; it looked like all the other ash-heaps. How could he have toiled up—and then down—in this weather, that armful of Commandments must have weighed a ton . . .

Another time, passing a lounge I hear a voice. 'You don't hold any mystery for me, darling; do you mind?' It was Noël talking to Gertie, *Private Lives*. Three of the couples were hunched round a gramophone, limp with sweat and nostalgia.

Out of the furnace and into the Indian Ocean. With the heat assuaged by breezes it was still hot enough to moon-bathe on the top deck. Lying half-asleep up there during the small hours of May the 8th to 9th I peered at my watch. In Drury Lane Theatre the orchestra was playing the first-night overture to *The Land of Smiles*. Good luck dear Will. I felt a melancholy not unenjoyable.

Then came the morning I was waiting for: May the 10th meant Colombo, Ceylon, and a gliding through a beautiful dawn into a great port and a new life. Rickshaws were evidently the thing and I sat back in one while the morning breeze seemed to bear me along and made the journey perfect.

Up to a point. The sun began to hot up, but slunk behind a sulphurous cloud. I was travelling along a severely straight tarred road, with on my right a concrete pavement shelving down to a sea of grumbling grey.

And I was not being borne along by a breeze. Between the shafts of my carriage there pounded a barefoot bag of bones in a damp loin-cloth, fighting for breath.

Social inequality had never aroused resentment in me, or conversely guilt, but sitting back in that rickshaw I was soaked not only in sweat, but in shame. The white Maharajah descended, paid and tipped his beast of burden, heard him panting, and hurried into the Galle Face Hotel. The best.

At the desk the clerk—a beautiful ebony man with a thin proud moustache—said in Welsh-English, 'Some communications for you, dear sir.' They were the two regular letters I knew would be there. I had not expected a third, yet found myself bitterly disappointed, and angry at my disappointment. The knots I had put between me and London were in vain.

There was a rustle of white robes and another employee preceded me up the stairs. He had the same looks, attractive as a portrait in a museum is attractive.

I was bowed into a vast featureless bedroom where I heard a squawk and a clap of wings: a large black crow had flown in and was banging resentfully against heavy furniture. It found a plate with some fruit on it, clamped on to something, squawked again and left. I leaned over the sill. The sea was grim and restless.

I was restless too. I walked downstairs and back into town, along the same road. Dusky figures slid past in the rain. I had never thought of a palm tree as bedraggled; I passed twenty such slatterns. The sea snapped at the concrete. I had travelled six thousand miles to get wet walking along the front in a black Bournemouth.

* * *

I walked into the first bar, clean but dingy. Several men sat about in crumpled tropical suits, drinking whisky and talking in tight-lipped murmurs. They might have just come ashore from my boat.

I ordered a whisky from a hard-bitten white barman and drank it with the same dejection as the others. I was not going to leave this bar until I had done one thing: settled on the subject of a play.

Nothing to be got from the *Ranpura*. Ah, Port Said: ... the misfits, some half-French, some half-Cockney, that could be funny. The beautiful woman, hang on to that, and to the pukka sahib who went home. Why should she not have a child by him, who is taken to England and brought up by his childless wife? Boy is never told he is not hers, sent to Harrow—arrives in Port Said—fair, English—and meets real mother. The supposed mother pleads with her not to tell him the truth, she relents, boat leaves her with the other flotsam and jetsam, in the port from which there is no escape. A woman half primitive, half gentle: and that gave me a title, *The Savage Dove*.

Falsely warmed by whisky, I felt better and walked back to the hotel. The rain had stopped but there was still no sun. The enormous deserted dining room was an Oriental hydro whirring with fans and haunted by silent gliding waiters.

After lunch I went for another wander and found what looked

like a Nonconformist chapel: Colombo Public Library. It was empty, except for the same books as on the ship plus dozens of bound copies of *Punch*. I pulled out one which covered April of last year, sat down and looked up the notice of *On the Spot*. There was a caricature of Mr Charles Laughton, another of Mr Cronin-Wilson.

I stared at the page, walked out and back to the hotel desk where I asked what I should see. Neuralia is jolly fine, dear sir. As I wrote the name, guessing at the spelling, he added that it was high up, 'with not only misty climate but also heather which delight British with memory of Scotland'.

I crossed out 'Neuralia', which anyway sounded like an ailment. 'A jolly nice walk, dear sir, up to Mount Lavinia.'

I set off. The sun had disappeared again, leaving no air.

I climbed past strange-smelling bazaars with gleaming black eyes as impenetrably watchful as cats in the dark, and toiled up to an extensive golf course, English except that the first green faced a huddle of huts, with rusty corrugated roofs sagging to the ground. Next to a flea-bitten dog, three naked brown children scrabbled in the dust. I walked back to my expensive hotel.

That night I lay awake comparing the cost of my return ticket with my father's weekly wage.

❊   ❊   ❊

'Dear Mr Williams, Dr Mervyn Lewis has written me, I'd be glad to put you up, bachelor quarters I'm afraid. Just arrive, herewith route, Yours sincerely, Fergus MacWhaley.'

I consulted the desk, 'The only transport, dear sir, is hired car.' I sank back in a luxurious limousine, with at the wheel yet another smoothly beautiful Singhalese in uniform and peaked cap, I was glad Miss Cooke could not see me.

Dusty roads wound between green feathery trees, up hills and down valleys, all monotonously picturesque in the sun. At intervals, staring from the roadside, the same dark face.

I looked down at my note; Doc Mervyn had a mixed address book, and this was more likely to be an amusing friend than one of the patients whom he called 'my bread-and-butter lot'. Would he be young or old?

I had not been speculating long before we reached miles and

miles of what I imagined from novels to be 'scrub', and the
Oriental skies closed over the sun like a trap, opened again and
poured out water.

Not just rain, a ruthless endless flood. Solid sheets pounded at
the windscreen; the road was a spluttering torrent of dust churn-
ing into mud. I asked the driver how far we had to go. Forty
miles, dear sir, and he crawled indifferently on.

We were in a submarine bumping along the sea-bed. It bumped
for three hours, one more mile, dear sir. As we crawled to a halt
on a hill, at a small gate, I said I assumed he would be coming in
with me. No, dear sir, friends in village neighbouring.

I tipped him, seized my suitcase and lunged out into the rain.
As I opened the gate I could just see 'Kirkcaldy' before I tore
up twenty steps. By the tenth I was as drenched as if I had
walked out of the sea; a French window opened and I dived
into it. The Ark at last.

'I'm Fergus MacWhaley, how d'you do.' I found myself in the
middle of a sitting-room, shaking formal hands in a pool. 'I've
some dry clothes laid on.'

I squelched after him, dripping like a drowned dog. 'It's the
monsoon, I'll get you a whisky,' and he disappeared.

I dried myself, got into a shirt, khaki shorts and enormous
sandals, gave my hair a quick comb and flapped back. It was
student digs in Scotland, with shabby furniture handed down
from one bachelor to another. I sat down, gratefully grasped a
tumbler and looked at my host.

He was my age and height: but thin, with sharp reddish
features under ginger hair, knobbly elbows, and below the same
shorts as I had on, sore scraggy knees which lived in fear of the
sun. One of Doc's bread-and-butter lot.

The opposite of my three 'boys', he was forty fifteen years too
soon; a reserved, kind, lonely young man with responsibilities
who suffered, tight-lipped and in permanent exile, from chronic
homesickness. On the mantelpiece a photograph of his dead
parents, his father in a kilt; another of football groups with rows
of arms aggressively folded; another of a house. 'It's in Kirkcaldy,
that's why my grandfather called this Kirkcaldy.'

I made a guess: that he would call me Williams. 'Williams, here
for long?' And I knew he would not join me in a whisky, he had
the bleak teetotal look. He was the savourless salt of the earth.

But he was not difficult company. Every word he spoke was one he wished me to hear and there were not many, so I was spared the Ranpura jocosities. He was having a rare day off, and I got the impression that he was committed for life to long tough hours with low returns.

He was disappointed that I had never been to the Highlands and so was I; it would have given him pleasure to hear me talk of them. I mentioned 'Neuralia'; his eyes brightened, he spent his short leaves up there.

No wireless, no telephone, no books. With every window locked against the lashing elements, the room was close and dark. Were we to sit here till the waters rose and engulfed a little corner that would be for ever Caledonia?

After lunch, served by the expected noiseless white-robed figure, I made notes for the play while he tore the wrapping off a newspaper—the *Scotsman*—and sat engrossed, starting at the beginning with the advertisements and reading it like a book. It was restful. On the sideboard, a clock which looked like a twenty-first-birthday present struck the quarters as if it were beating a native.

We sat until tea was borne in. Oil lamps were lit, the Ark looked cosy. The ginger head was still stolidly bent over stolid news from home; I tried to melt the sore face into the most beautiful I could think of, remembered the photo of Bill as a young soldier and the shadowy features formed before my eyes.

The clock struck and shook me free. I returned to my notes.

*   *   *

By the next morning the inscrutable East had changed again, and as unexpectedly: the sun was brilliant. The 'bog' was up the garden, a steep area of rubble and weeds. Mid-morning, I thought I would try a stroll down the road thickly bordered by green trees.

'Be careful,' my host said, 'take my topee.'

I soon knew what he meant. The green was deceptive. The heat was as malevolent as the rain had been, and when I toiled back up the steps of Kirkcaldy I was as wet as I had been on delivery.

After lunch my host took his shirt off. I followed suit. It was

hot enough to take shorts off as well, and for a second I thought
he was going to. He lay back in the armchair, 'A siesta, good habit
out here.' I lay on the sofa, where heat and somnolence conspired
to work on me: if my host's eyes had been open, he would have
gone a deeper shade of brick.

He was as alone as an old maid in a Highland croft. What did
he do for sex? What could he do, except fall back on the obvious
safety valve? Even that I could not envisage: that closed correct
face distorted with self-made delight, those pale correct eyes
rolling up to the ceiling—no.

I looked at the folded pages of the *Scotsman*, then at the picture
of his parents, and felt a wave of sorrow for him. Then another
wave for myself, was it possible I might end up like this? I
wriggled sideways and fell asleep.

The evening temperature was merciful enough for a drive to
somewhere-or-other where they did something-or-other to the tea
before it becomes tea as we know it. I nodded and hoped to look
interested; I was making up an Arab name for my half-caste
woman—Narouli Karth, that was it, and Mary Clare, my mother
in *Etienne*, would be perfect, you mean the leaves are subsequently dried? I decided *The Savage Dove* was not stark enough
as a title, I would call it *Port Said*, all those tons of tea a month,
hard to credit . . .

After dinner MacWhaley looked up from his studies—he had
exhausted the *Scotsman* and was working through the *Illustrated
London News*—and asked me if I'd care to pop into town tomorrow for the weekly shopping. I accepted. At that moment I had
decided to cut my losses and take the next boat home.

In the unbearable damp heat—I was glad—we drove down into
Colombo-super-Mare. I got out at the Galle Face to ask mail.
There was none but I returned to the car to report a non-existent
cable calling me back for immediate rehearsals. My host looked
deeply disappointed and I felt remorse.

The *Maloja* was sailing in forty-eight hours. At the end of my
six thousand miles, I would by then have stayed put for six days
and nights before covering the same six thousand miles again.
I shut my mind to it.

We drove to various suburban stores. I bought half-a-dozen
exercise books, having worked out that my cabin would not be
right for work and that typing on a crowded deck would be in-

advisable. MacWhaley carried a shopping bag, which did not go with the khaki shorts. He ought to be married. I again felt sorry for him, but it was too late for communication.

I took him to lunch at the Galle Face; he was delighted, it was obviously the pukka place. Each British dish which steamed up, each drop of sweat which streamed down—all was a salve to my conscience. Driving back we ran into a dust-storm, a new horror which I faced with a smile.

MacWhaley saw Williams off. 'Remember me to the U.K.' The last I saw of the exotic Orient was ginger hair, long limp khaki shorts, bony red knees and a red homesick face. As I waved to him, he looked forlorn.

CHAPTER NINETEEN

MORE THE RAGE IN THE
ACTING LINE

In a corner of a deck as busy as a railway station, I opened Exercise Book One.

By Aden I had illegibly reached the end of the first act, and even the Red Sea was powerless to deter me. While others lay gasping, only one interruption could have raised my eyes from the ruled lines: the waters parting and necessitating a long puzzled walk.

By Port Said, I had written two-thirds of *Port Said*. I had three hours, just right, and I walked the streets with notebook, pencil, and new eyes.

Much of my guesswork had been near the mark, a dozen details fell into place: the distant wail of an Arab song, the bark of a mongrel. I noted the names of streets, a stray advertisement—Majestic, Janet Gaynor et Charles Farrell dans L'AMOUR EN REVE—and searching for my stage café I found it up a side street, with baby palms in pots and yellowing posters, Bière Bavaria, Thé Lipton, Pharmacie de Lesseps . . .

But work could not override the other obsession, and I asked the Purser if I could get off at Marseilles and continue by air. He looked at me as if I had suggested chartering a dolphin. 'Air?' I did not tell him I had never flown.

'I suggest the Radio Officer.'

The Radio Officer scratched his head and looked something up. Yes, there was a sort of service, a plane leaving at ten and supposed to land at Croydon late afternoon. I noted 'supposed'—which sounded as if the plane might end up in the Channel—wrote out a cable and from then on almost enjoyed the Med.

In Marseilles one beautiful morning I took a taxi to the plane, which was outside the city in a field. Had it two engines, or one?

I never thought of it. It looked as I had imagined: like the machines in the silent war films, a big, clumsy eagle.

There were only two other passengers, both men; a woman would have been unthinkable. It was like having a private plane. As I strapped myself in I was as excited as when I climbed into my first train. The goggled pilot banged the door, then turned round to us like a paternal robot. 'Ready, gents?'

The eagle cleared its throat deafeningly, gave a violent lunge and swayed forward. We were up. I had resigned myself to Biscay nausea, to the vertigo of towers and cliffs: it was glorious, and below me in the sun Marseilles unfurled itself with a slow dignity which I knew it did not possess on earth.

At that time there was no question of zooming up through clouds to hurtle along an eternity of desolate vacuum; our magic eagle-carpet creaked and ambled low over a perpetual motion of lakes, mountains and roads crawling with cars driven by insects. Lunch was sandwiches I had brought from a ship which was now a phantom, and I munched them in a haze of levitation.

Seen from above in the afternoon light the sea lost its menace, the Channel steamers looked as if you could pick them up and rearrange them; toyland England streamed under me, then the jostle of nursery roofs which was outer London. At Croydon Aerodrome the plane wheeled and dipped; I felt no fear. I knew the bird would swoop to earth, as birds always have.

A small bus took the three of us to somewhere in the Haymarket, and as I walked across Leicester Square between eight and nine, in the cool evening light of the London summer, I thought of the Red Sea; at Drury Lane stage-door I thought of Queue Day.

''Allo, sir,' the same stage-door keeper said, 'you're the young gentleman that wrote the show at the St James's, Mr Elmo Williams, that's right! ... Mr Tauber's on, just goin' to start 'is fourth encore, never known anythin' like it.'

I tiptoed through the darkness behind the backcloth as frantic applause died into expectant silence. Then, soaring through the theatre, the glorious voice. 'You are my heart's delight ...' I stood and listened. 'Where'er you are, I long to be ...'

In a welter of personal and professional emotion, I crossed to the tiny room where Bill dressed alone; stooped before the mirror to check on his drooping Chinese moustache, he looked remote and authoritative. It was a reunion in backstage whispers; he was self-conscious to be meeting me in his make-up and that made me self-conscious.

'In Marseilles this morning? Incredible . . .' Like all actors I was a nervous visitor; I did not belong. As I started to say something, he opened the door to hear what point the show was at.

The call-boy's tap was a relief; when he rose the long robes made him look thinner, and to a waterfall of music he was gone.

I looked round. No telegrams, no family photos, only the old trunk. I looked at the worn good suit hanging behind the door, then at myself sideways in a mirror. After days and nights of exile I was sitting in a cell staring at the empty clothes of someone who had not been out of my thoughts.

And at this moment of return he was standing, in rich unapproachable disguise, a thousand miles further from me than I had lately been from him, which is the distance from a dressing-room to the stage when the non-working actor is in the dressing-room.

I looked again at his suit; it was as divorced from him as if he had died. I opened a drawer and a half-full bottle of whisky rolled cheerfully to greet me.

A faint 'God Save the King' and he was back from the distance and from the dead. Off with the mandarin grandeur, on with the grubby dressing gown. The dresser handed us each a whisky and went out.

Bill turned and squeezed my knee. 'God, I've missed you.'

I was pleased, and yet watching him as he wiped his face I saw him once more for what he was: a nice man with a diffident charm who had wasted his life. On my hideous holiday, what had I been haunted by? Is one's own imagination the ultimate love-potion?

We called at the delicatessen and bought cold supper; after it, we drank whisky, not too much, and talked. When I told him about Duggie and Vi, he laughed hard.

I had made the gesture of escape and it had not worked. The flat was as empty as before—I sensed that he had spent only sleeping time in it—but I was as near home as I would ever be, and I had a play.

I never called for him at the theatre again. Not ever counting on his coming straight home, I found that he usually did; when

MORE THE RAGE IN THE ACTING LINE

he didn't, I was engrossed enough in my revising of *Port Said* not to be irritated. I finished my play, *The Land of Smiles* closed. We took a bus to Cornwall and wandered about St Ives, two actors out of work, until there was a phone call for Bill.

'Edgar wants us both for his new play.'

✿   ✿   ✿

The next evening, a script was ahead of us at the flat: *The Case of the Frightened Lady.* Bill read it first. Closing the script he said, 'It's Edgar at the top of his form.' I asked what his part was like.

'Small but effective, why don't you ask about yours?'

'What about it?'

He squeezed my knee with a smile, 'You lucky young devil,' and settled into the big room with a book.

I looked at the list of characters; against several, pencilled initials. Inspector Tanner, A.D. Alfred Drayton. Sergeant Totty, G. H. Gordon Harker. Lady Lebanon, C.N. Cathleen Nesbitt. Lord Lebanon, N.B.—E.W. I wondered why I was made so special.

Act One, an office in Scotland Yard, where the Inspector is investigating a mysterious strangling at the Lebanon country seat. Young Lord Lebanon arrives to confer with him: a silly young man, a nicely-written scene of naturalistic vagueness. 'The whole thing's very unfair, and when your own mother's in it, you know, it sort of gets you ...' Enter messenger; a second murder has been committed, curtain.

Act Two: in Marks Priory the Inspector is a guest of Lady Lebanon, neurotic and evasive; the young lord is under his mother's thumb, twice he has been drugged by two footmen who are obviously in league with her.

As actors will, I riffled pages to find my next scene. I was not in Act Three Scene One at all, the last scene opened with the policemen on midnight watch, with frayed nerves. Clearly the mother is the key to the mystery and will now be confronted, does that mean Lord L. will not appear again?

I put 'The Bronze Horse' on the gramophone before finishing. Lord Lebanon was a pawn in the game, a nothing. A bad joke of Bill's? It wasn't like him.

[225]

No, here comes Lebanon, racing in fright down the stairs; finding the Inspector alone, he is more the ineffectual lordling than ever: 'I heard a sort of choking noise, where's my mother? . . . Do sit down, won't you? You make me nervous . . .' The Inspector sits opposite him.

Then the change: he begins to babble of the family heritage, while the other man sits frozen. After a speech which proves him to be hopelessly insane—his mother has done everything to shield him, the footmen are his keepers—he draws a loaded revolver and continues his speech, ice-cold, reasonable.

'You're pretending you're not frightened, but you are . . . When I'm quite well, I'm mad. It's only when I feel excited that my brain is clear . . .' The others come in, he tears to the staircase and is halfway up when his revolver goes off and he topples to the foot.

The music near me swelled to a climax and clicked off.

A lucky young devil.

*　　*　　*

In such a two-handed scene the partner is all-important, and I asked Bill if Alfred Drayton was prepared to play a stooge. 'I don't know, he's a good actor.'

On Sunday morning we put on Sunday best; Mr Wallace wanted us all down at his country house, Chalklands, Bourne End, for luncheon and a reading of the play. I felt not a tremor, I knew I could do it.

A large car called for us, then for Bill Linnit, then for Drayton; I understood his success in cruel parts when I took in a bullying corpulence surmounted by a bullet head completely bald, cold eyes and rapped-out sergeant-major syllables, 'Why the hell has Edgar saddled me with the dullest part and at the last minute it's whisked from under my bloody nose by Nigel Bruce?'

Of course, the N.B. had been pencilled in and then replaced by E.W. . . .

'Oh,' Bill Linnit said, 'Edgar started the play with him in mind, then realized he was wrong for the last scene, Emlyn's playing it.'

Drayton sat bolt upright and stared at me. 'Good God.'

'How d'you mean,' I said as lightly as I could, 'good God?'

'Well, I meanter say, you're a topping little actor but dammit, this chap's a Lord.'

I looked at Bill next to me. I had never seen him glare before.

Losing my Welsh temper would only mean gaining my Welsh accent. How would Dad have dealt? 'Mr Drayton, you have made a misunderstanding, my son George resided in the same college with Cardinal Wolsey and Sir Philip Sidney and Lord Dunglass and will take a Lord's part as to the manner born.'

Bill weighed in. 'But you can't have type-casting to that extent, old boy. Before Paul Robeson came along wasn't Othello played by quite a load of white trash, Irving and all that?'

A neat upper-cut, which spurred me to what I knew would be below the belt. 'My one strong card is that I did go to Christ Church and can only hope it'll pull me through. Did you ever play Oxford?'

Bill said quickly, 'It's a brilliant last scene.' As we entered the front door of Chalklands, behind the fat back of Drayton's neck I thought, God in that last scene he'll do everything to upstage me, he'll ruin it . . .

After luncheon at a baronially long table we trooped behind our host into a library stacked with Wallaces, sat round him and read him his play.

I was so concentrated on sounding well-bred that the rest of the afternoon passed over my head. Just before my first line I looked over at Bill; the cousin a couple-of-times-removed of the King of England, masquerading as a carefully-spoken Wallace footman, winked at me.

I thought, it's a funny world and sucks to Alfred Drayton, spoke my first silly-ass scene as nervelessly as if I were obliging an absent actor and aimed at my usual speech with the faintest drawl. 'Not that I approve of the House of Lords, I'm a democrat you know . . .'

We reached the scene everybody was waiting for: impervious to Drayton's sulky interpolations I was determined to read flatly, madly and with breeding. Or rather, not madly: with the matter-of-fact clarity of the insane.

Next morning, I answered the phone; Drayton had asked to be excused, a grumbling appendix.

It sounded just right for him. Bill would play the part.

✳   ✳   ✳

The play may have been dashed off, but the drive of it was so true that rehearsals were easy. 'You will be interested,' I wrote to Miss Cooke, 'to read in the programme that Mr Williams is dressed by Preston's of Mayfair.'

I asked if I might play the first two acts in horn-rimmed glasses and keep the naked eyes for the last scene, also if I might enter Scotland Yard holding a bowler hat—I still had it, it would come in useful at last—and with a book under my arm. It would somehow look good.

Though we had not reached the crucial scene, one early morning at home Bill and I decided to grapple with it; as we read across the table, I was dismayed to discover a serious flaw.

After the most normal conversation, the scene took off with the boy's beautifully unexpected and cryptic 'Don't you think the Lebanon line should be wiped out?' followed by the Inspector's 'Line? I don't understand...' Then followed the turning-point of the play: the moment when Lebanon draws out the scarf with which he has committed the murders, and the audience realizes the truth.

But between that first exchange and this revelation there was lodged a diatribe including a railing against heraldry—'It's all these treasures and gules and trefoils, *they must go!*'

An audience at a who-dun-it, as the climax approaches, becomes quicker and quicker in the uptake: it would be obvious, from the moment Lebanon started to enlarge in this way, that he was insane and therefore the murderer. By the moment of the scarf, the audience would be ahead of the author.

The scene should be reversed: the Inspector's 'I don't understand...,' then the flourish of the scarf, then the speech going into madness. If it were played as written it would be killed.

But it meant a major transposition, what about Edgar? The scene was the best he had ever written and his attitude must inevitably be 'I know you've written a thriller yourself but hands off mine.' And it would be only the first night reaction—too late— which would prove I had been right.

As the days passed we never seemed to reach the scene. In the end Bill and I learnt it with my alteration incorporated, and rehearsed it meticulously at home across the table, directing ourselves. I even included an idea that at the moment of revelation —after 'Don't you think the Lebanon line should be wiped out?'

—the boy, before bringing out the scarf, fixes his eyes widely on the Inspector's and slowly smiles.

The afternoon came when the director said, 'Right, now the big moment, everybody can go except you two.' This was it. The curtain was up, but as he was tackling the scene for the first time he came through and settled into a chair facing upstage. 'Right...'

I said, 'I've been studying it, Mr Wallace, it's a wonderful scene but there's one bit...'

'Oh, you've been working on it, have you?'

'Yes.' O God...

'Have you learnt it? Can you show me something?... You can? Right, I'll go in front. We need some light, Carol, throw me up a couple of floats.' He prided himself on knowing the jargon.

As he lumbered through the pass-door I hurried to Mack in the corner and whispered that we had changed a couple of things and not to prompt and also to simulate the revolver shot. As the author-director settled into a stall, the holder looked longer than ever. He was a chain-smoking Caesar surrounded by his court. 'Right!'

Mack's voice rang out, 'Ferraby and Gilder have left, the Inspector is alone.'

Bill sat as we had rehearsed. Those sunny mornings in the flat... I ran down imaginary stairs, as we had rehearsed. And as we had rehearsed, Bill keeping carefully downstage so that my face was to the audience—where would I be if Drayton were still with us—we went through the scene without a hitch. I even struck the match and firmly lit the detective's cigarette.

The run to the stairs, and at exactly the right second Mack shouted 'Bang!' and I crashed to the floor; he knew his job. I scrambled self-consciously to my feet, brushed myself, wandered to the table, sat and waited.

Mr Wallace called out, 'Carol, get Jim from the office, will you?'

Mrs Wallace—'Jim'—came hurrying into the stalls and sat next to her husband. 'Right!' and we went through again. 'Bang!'

'That's magnificent,' Mr Wallace said, 'never play it any different.' I heard the music of the spheres.

The big night was August the 18th; in the afternoon, I went to the Plaza, Maurice Chevalier in *The Smiling Lieutenant*.

At six, my usual opening-night second bath of the day; then, since I lived once more outside the West End, I formed another habit I was to continue. I walked, alone and unhurried, to the theatre, thinking of my family and Miss Cooke and Bill: they were all thoughts to soothe me, and my walking legs steadied my mind.

During the show I was nervous but sure; again the match did not tremble. At the end no hysteria, a healthy glow which stayed to hover over the Wallace party at the Kit Kat. But again I knew enough to be wary.

Next morning, MR WALLACE DOES IT AGAIN! And in one of the most effective parts ever written, I had made a success. Two reviews gave me more pleasure than seemed possible. The first, 'There was one moment of silence, during which the face flowered softly into madness, which was more genuinely blood-curdling than all the pistol-shots...' The second, 'As a peer, he speaks English purely, as it was meant to be spoken.'

"My dear Son George, Once more your name is on all lips... Tom has just come in from a good night at the Army, they got seven sinners to the Penitent Bench, well they won't get Edgar and yourself because at the moment you got nothing whatever to be ashamed of...'

*　　*　　*

And success meant that journalists rang up for interviews; I always suggested the dressing-room, making it an hour before the show as in this play I dressed with Bill and wanted to get it over before he came in. They were mostly polite shadows, and I was careful to be polite back.

One evening, yet another shadow. 'It's only for the *Era* I'm afraid, it's a theatre weekly and I don't know if anybody reads it. My name's Clowes.' It was a colourless, classless voice. In dark, striped suit and long, old-fashioned overcoat, he was any age from thirty to fifty, and thick: thick of body, of crinkly hair and of spectacles astride a prominent nose. It was to take me time to know that here was a special person disguised as a grave solicitor come to read out an unfavourable will.

Earlier interviewers had put their questions eagerly and inaccurately, and I was ready with my answers: no, I was never a miner; no, not nine languages; no, I never proposed to Megan

Lloyd George; goodnight and thank you so much . . . Ready for the routine, I put on my unspoilt face. 'Yes?'

'Are you tired of being asked if you were a miner when you weren't?'

This was not routine; missing too was the eager manner, replaced by a timid directness I was unfamiliar with. I was not sure if I liked it, then decided I did. I said, 'Yes, sick of it.'

'I was the opposite. When I was twenty-one I was a lumberjack in Canada and when I mention it people just laugh, you can't blame them. Tell the truth and nobody'll believe you.'

I invited him to take his overcoat off. 'No, thank you, it makes people think I'm going to stay. When you wrote *Full Moon* did you realize how much Chekhov was influencing you?'

This wasn't routine either. The answer was easy, 'No, I didn't, and he was.'

Then I remembered, 'Was it you who wrote the *Era* notice, that it was lovely and true and a new experience in the theatre?'

'It sounds a coy thing to have said but I did, yes . . . It was a beautiful play.' He said it absentmindedly, blinking through his glasses as he looked round the room almost resignedly. He had spoken with such simplicity that he made it a beautiful play.

'I think,' he added thoughtfully, 'you might write such a good costume piece, they don't have to have all that fustian. Jimmy Agate told me you'll write a really good play one of these days. He can be wicked but he does know.' I found this, spoken flatly and with again the resigned look round the room, extremely invigorating. 'How's Bill?'

Still less routine. I told him Bill was fine, and waited for 'Poor old Bill, still knocking it back?' It did not come. 'A nice man, beautiful hands. Well, thank you, you've been most co-operative as we say in dear old Fleet Street. I hope we meet again.' I hoped so too.

From Miss Cooke . . . 'A teacher's salary is not munificent & this is a begging letter. I'm v. anxious to advance £50 to an ex-pupil doing Spanish and needing Salamanca Univ . . . I've got some insurance due next yr & can repay then, with interest of course.'

It was an inspired way, at this moment, of helping me to do something for her. Enclosing a cheque I wrote, 'I remember a schoolteacher of mine saying, "Never lend, *give*", and I'm taking her advice. I note that you intended paying back "with interest".

I appreciate the close attention you have always paid to my welfare, but this kind of interest would be unwelcome.'

My next special visitor turned up before a matinée. "'E's up in your room, sir,' the stage-door keeper said, ' a young guardsman.' Bill looked at me in surprise. 'Says 'e's your young brother.'

Tom sat in my place, peaked cap on knee, a Galahad of eighteen in the armour of Salvation, on four hours' leave from the Army College at Denmark Hill to which he had been posted. He was the first member of my family for me ever to see in London, and in a dressing-room it felt doubly weird. He was mesmerized by the make-up tables. I said I would ring through and fix him a seat.

'I'm not allowed.'

We both looked at him. 'Not allowed?'

'The Army's got a rule, no theatres, no films.'

'But, Tom, you're in a theatre at this minute!'

'Yes, but not watching anything.' He went off happily for a walk in the park.

I said, 'After that, serve the Army right if somebody tries to pick him up.'

Bill's reaction was unexpected, 'I don't like to think of that, I've never seen any lad with such beautiful innocence.'

Cathleen Nesbitt was as indignant as I was. 'Do you mean to say this boy's allowed to loiter in the wings at the Folies Bergère pressed between two nude ladies, and forbidden to see *The Sign of the Cross*?'

I wanted her to put that into writing and send it to Field Headquarters.

* * *

One night at the flat, after supper with Bill I happened to say I hadn't known that Edna Best had two children.

'Oh, yes, twin boys.' Then he added, 'Like me.'

'What was that?'

'I've got twin boys too.'

'You're joking.'

It had been before the war, when he was nineteen and on a tour of one-night stands. At Newton Abbot he had taken the landlady's daughter for a walk in the woods, and three months later there was a letter from her mother. Later still, another to say it was twins, and that the girl's uncle was adopting them and emigrating to the States.

'Did you hear again?'

'Once.'

It had been about six years ago, when her mother read he was playing in something and wrote enclosing a snap; he saw the snap before the letter. 'I thought, good God, who's sent me a photo of the two most beautiful American sailors anybody's ever set eyes on? Identical they were, face and uniform, arms round each other's necks and grinning straight at me, Hello there, Pop! Marvellous American teeth.'

Did they look like him? Hard for him to tell, perhaps they did; yes, their names were on the back, but he didn't remember what they were and he'd thrown the snap away. 'When there's an American ship in I think, walking down Shaftesbury Avenue, why shouldn't I come face to face with two identical sailors with their arms linked, pardon me, sir, but could you direct us to a hot night-spot?'

'What would you do?'

'I'd ask them back.' His face was alight with mischief. 'By now they're just your age.' Then he put on his glasses and opened the evening paper.

I imagined us sitting opposite him at this table, drinking: me and my beautiful American brothers. And as he read on, the glasses melted into the face of the young officer in the snapshot which had not been thrown away. The four of us . . .

As his features reassumed the ravages of a bad middle age, my forbidden excitement merged into pain. Pain at the dissolution of youth: would the two Apollos on each side of me coarsen too? Pain at the squandered fatherhood, at the years that would be darkened by a loneliness into which I had strayed.

He put down his paper, started to cough and then to wheeze. 'I think a whiff of Friar's Balsam.' Five minutes later his head was under a towel.

*　　*　　*

From Miss Cooke, 'see here George, have you thgt of Life Insurance? In yr profession surely invaluable, think abt it.'

Bill Linnit put me on to the Gresham Company and a beaming

[233]

courteous man called at the theatre while Bill and I were making up. He looked so like a doctor that his brief-case could be crammed with the elixir of long life. I agreed to a hefty policy. After he had gone Bill nodded sagely as he put out a half-smoked cigarette and lit a new one. 'Jolly good idea at your age, glad you took her advice.'

Sitting one morning in the kitchen bath behind the curtain—Mrs Atkins was washing up—I pondered resentfully over *Port Said*, turned down four times, too sordid, too sordid . . .

I remembered the Wallace posters, MRS EDGAR WALLACE PRESENTS; she might hesitate over a West End gamble, but for one Sunday night . . . I was right; she agreed to present the play on Sunday November the 1st at Wyndham's.

I sent a copy at once to Mary Clare, who telephoned her enthusiasm; much encouraged, I asked her to lunch. Bill said, 'She's a fine actress but don't you need a star?'

'Isn't the play the thing? And it'll be a leg-up for her and may even *make* her a star.'

Waiting at the Ivy, I felt powerful and kind; she arrived in a flurry of excitement. Over sherry she said, 'My dear, I've been having such bad luck, isn't it a tantalizing profession we're in? Oh, I loved reading your play!'

I remembered Harry Kendall and ordered wine. Over the main course, as I was about to get back to the play she put her hand on mine. 'My dear, something rather exciting's happened to me.'

A bequest in a will? Her voice had the gentle glow I remembered from *Etienne*. It would sound beautiful in *Port Said*.

'Really?' I was pleased for her, 'tell me . . .'

'This morning Noël asked me to play the star part at Drury Lane in his *Cavalcade*.'

We drank to it. A tantalizing profession indeed.

After supper I told Bill, adding, 'Drury Lane, ever heard of it? And she's playing the star part. You said she wasn't a star.'

'She isn't. Noël's the exception.' For a man who led a foolish life, he could be disconcertingly wise.

'Noël?'—I was out of temper by now—'You usually refer to the great as Miss Compton and Sir Gerald, you know Mr Coward?'

'Met him not long after I was demobbed, I was in *Bird of Paradise* at the Lyric, showy little part. This rather pimply lad came round and said, "I'm Noël Coward and I'm terribly, terribly, impressed by your performance." Must have been nineteen but looked fifteen, said he wrote lyrics. He was so complimentary and sort of showing off, I was embarrassed.'

I could see the poor boy trying, and failing, to impress a reserved and suspicious young man, thirteen years older, who had been in a war.

'Pity,' I said, 'if you'd played your cards you might now be signed up to star opposite Mary Clare at Drury Lane. You missed the bus, old boy.'

He looked up, a smile in his eye. 'Old boy, I think you mean the Rolls.'

* * *

But what of Narouli Karth—what star would be willing to shine on one Sunday night? An audacious move was indicated, like casting Caruso as Lear.

One day in the Cavour I overheard, 'I'll never forget her singing as the half-caste in *Show Boat*.' Marie Burke was playing twice daily at the Alhambra in an enormous spectacle called *Waltzes from Vienna*, but I sent her the play and asked her to lunch—again at the Ivy—on the chance that in the meantime she had not been engaged by Sir Thomas Beecham to sing Carmen at Covent Garden.

'No, *nothing*'ll stop me playing this part, we'll start at nine every morning. Are you game?'

I knew then that as with *A Murder Has Been Arranged* the hard work would be fun.

Act Two opened with the café deserted except for the spectacle—fairly astonishing in 1931—of two raddled old Toulouse-Lautrec prostitutes, one half-Cockney and the other half-French, dancing dejectedly together to 'You Were Meant For Me'.

'Gawd, my feet... Where's the men?'

'Eet eez not amusing to dance weez a woman. Nothing fits, one bumps...' They were in and out of the action, and important.

May Agate was delighted to tackle a 'vieille fille de joie', and for the half-Cockney I had what I knew was a good idea: Amy Veness, the cook in *A Murder Has Been Arranged*. Matronly, respectable, tight-lipped, she would be funny in a new way.

With the script I enclosed a jocular note: something like 'I have to warn you, dear Amy, that you'll be breaking new and not altogether hallowed ground, but I have a feeling you'll enjoy it'.

I heard by return. 'Dear Emlyn, I'm a broad-minded woman but I cannot understand (a) a nice boy like you conceiving of such a revolting part, (b) offering it to me. I'd love to be in another play of yours but not *this* one.' Why do the narrow-minded always draw attention to the broadness of their views? I could not believe such a letter from a good actress, it could have been from the wife of a Welsh deacon. It was my first—and last—professional contact with something out of date.

At rehearsals, the cast displayed the same zest and swift professional application as my other. With one exception. W. Cronin-Wilson.

I had written the leading male part for him—an Anglo-Turkish drifter, cultivated, embittered, in love with Narouli Karth—and he worked as hard as anyone, and soberly. When I heard him read his part in the early mornings he was alert and natural and I could tell he would be first-rate.

Once he got on to the stage among the other players, however, with me standing in the front row directing the detail of the play, he became markedly nervous. Not only had he never worked with a very young director, the very young director happened to be me and that seemed to paralyse his faculties.

I tried to forget I knew him, and only succeeded in sounding distantly friendly; it seemed as if at any moment I might say, 'Mr Wilson.' Then I would hear myself call out sharply, 'No, no, walk to the *counter*, and more relaxed.'

He seemed unable, from day to day, to remember his moves— 'Sorry, old boy, I should be over there'—and he would cross like a bewildered performing bear. The situation was worsened by our being together twenty-four hours a day; we might have been handcuffed together with the key lost.

It was a damp October, and during the Thursday night performance before the big Sunday the inevitable happened: Bill lost his voice. Next morning Doc's verdict was that he could play neither Wallace nor Williams. In his heart, was he relieved? Was loss of voice induced by loss of nerve?

In the meantime I had to make a command decision: at sixty hours' notice I would play the part myself. There was no reason why a middle-aged Anglo-Turk should be more disillusioned or more enamoured of a woman of forty than an Anglo-Turk of twenty-six, particularly in a production crisis.

I started learning as I shaved and was on my feet for most of the sixty hours, till the moment—half an hour before the performance—when I sat before my mirror and set a red tarboosh at a rakish angle. The dusky make-up certainly brought up the white of one's teeth.

Due to *A Murder Has Been Arranged* and Marie Burke, the theatre was packed and expectant, but I was so intent on remembering my lines that all through I had no idea how the play was going. After my last exit I sat in my room engulfed in a tidal wave of tiredness, as the mirror told me that heat and emotion had rendered an Egyptian complexion enough tones lighter to get into South Africa.

At the end the usual crowd backstage. It had been such a strain that I jumped at the suggestion of a drink at the Arts with Jessica Tandy and Jack Hawkins, who had played the girl and boy. On our way out we passed Lilian Braithwaite. The great lady of the theatre said, with a couple of nods and one weighty intonation, 'an *interesting* evening . . .' It prepared me for the next day.

Not a disaster. No triumph either, except for Marie Burke. 'He crams a quart into a pint pot . . .' 'A quality of restless imagination . . .' 'I doubt if in twenty years' time Mr Williams will wish to be reminded of *Port Said* . . .' 'Wants cutting . . .'

A week ago I should have done just that: the play had run three and three-quarter hours. I reflected dolefully that I must be the first dramatist whose play, on its first night, has run a quarter of an hour longer than the time he spent on the spot getting the local colour for it.

Overweight, and over-complicated; I should have re-remembered Miss Cooke's warning, 'simplify, my boy, simplify'. The reaction hit me so full-on that I could hardly drag myself back to Wyndham's, but performance is the actor's medicine. It was for Bill too; he was back in the show, recovered.

During rehearsals I had once or twice imagined, with trepidation, a withering judgment on *Port Said* from somebody who had lived there for years. Among my Woolgar and Roberts press-cuttings, there it nestled, like a bomb through the post. 'I left after the first act, which seemed interminable ... To anybody who knows Egypt at all, this play is a farrago of preposterous nonsense.' I cancelled my subscription.

'My dear Son George, ... judgeing by the Criticks you are more the rage these days in the Acting Line.'

On Wednesday at breakfast Bill looked up from his *Telegraph*, 'Mack's play opened at the Arts.'

I had to remind myself that Mack was our ASM and that to eveybody's astonishment he had written a play. Bill handed me the paper: 'NEW DRAMATIST'S SUCCESS ... Brilliant ...'

I was silent for some moments.

Agate on Sunday: 'the best first play by any English playwright in the last forty years'. Ronald Mackenzie's *Musical Chairs*, as soon as John Gielgud was free of *The Good Companions*, would open with him and Frank Vosper at the Criterion, where it was to run for thirty-nine weeks.

*　　*　　*

After all that, I needed a diversion; it came, an unexpected one. From Miss Cooke.

'Look here, will you do something for me? For a c'ple of yrs I've had an ambition, to have a bust done of you, I've written asking what would be the fee, wld you kindly post enclosed having verified address?' I looked at the stamped envelope. 'Jacob Epstein Esq.'

He was the best-known living sculptor, admired, vilified and —aged fifty-one—at the height of his powers. Miss Cooke had perpetrated a few bold things in her time, but this ...

I tracked down his address, 18 Hyde Park Gate—did he live in a *house*?—but hesitated before posting. I did not like the idea of Miss Cooke being snubbed.

Three days later, 'Hurrah, see encl.!'

The encl. was a careful scrawl. 'Dear Madam, I acknowledge your kind letter. My fee for one cast of a bust is Two Hundred Pounds (£200). I await hearing from the young gentleman concerned, Yours faithfully, J. Epstein.' It could have been from a modest tradesman.

Miss Cooke continued, '*Isn't* it a good letter? One stipulation I will write to him'—I imagined her starting with 'Now see here, Epstein'—'viz, I don't want anybody to know who commissioned it. If you are asked, even by Bill C.W., kindly say that Epstein was so impressed by yr acting he wanted to sculpt yr head.'

I wrote back, 'I bow my head and will tell a lie, I imagine Mr Epstein will do the same.'

I took up the phone with some trepidation. 'Could you put me through to Mr Epstein, please?'

'This is Jacob Epstein.' It was a shy, gruff voice with a German-Jewish accent overlaid with East End English: 'Mr Williams is it? May I suggest about ten morning sittings, starting ten a.m. Friday, collar and tie?'

I told Bill—as I had once before, on my way to Hannen Swaffer—that I had an appointment with Walter Peacock. At Number 18, a large respectable house, the front door was opened by a coatless caretaker with sleeves rolled up who seemed to be engaged on some job in the shabby hall. He smiled and bowed. 'Please come in.'

It was Epstein: a burly man with curly dark thinning hair, teeth ragged and discoloured, and a manner as diffident as his voice.

I followed him down a couple of steps into a large high studio crammed with sculpture. Mixed up with heaps of wood, piles of clay, stacks of old newspapers and the dust of years, there was every sort of head and limb at every height and angle, from the ruthless stares of statesmen to the writhing thighs of agonized Titans and the swollen hungry lips of giantesses with corrugated wings of hair caught in midstream and in between the wings, fierce caverns for eyes. It was hard to reconcile the gentle care-taker figure with the welter of frozen power around him, till I noticed in a corner the golden-brown bronze head of a sleeping infant.

He asked about Miss Cooke. 'She sounds a fine woman, how kind of her to write to me. Excuse me while I walk round you.' He then took me gently by the elbow as if I were a breakable object and led me to a gnawed high stool in the middle of the studio. I climbed on to it and sat immobile, determined not to look at him. Straight in front of me, a criss-cross contraption had been knocked together from raw wood mixed with a shapeless grey mass pitted with holes: tiny snails of clay rolled and pressed together between finger and thumb.

He did as he had said, he walked round me. I could not resist quick sidelong looks and saw the shy host give way to a cool detached professional with narrowed eyes. He proceeded in his continuous circle on feet suddenly light; abruptly he would stop, squint, then dip his knees to scrutinize a new plane of my face from another angle.

He was even more of a surgeon than the actor is, as he felt his way towards an operation of the utmost delicacy. I felt that with every second my face was becoming more and more transparent, until there was no secret which was not known to him.

He took up a palette filthy with the stains of old clay and slapped fresh stuff on to it which he rolled briskly into more snails and slapped on to the mess on the stand. 'Relax, please.' After studying my face with the cold absent stare of an adversary, he set to work with lightning dexterity: no sound but the rapid breathing which I was to hear for nine more mornings, alternating with the sharp unconscious grunts of creation.

Every morning the same metamorphosis: from the clumsy courteous host into the absorbed implacable creator with the hands and even the toes of a dryad.

For me the sittings were never a strain; during his silences I had my own thoughts. One was that the face steadily evolving from a cloud of clay was soon to become bronze and live indestructably on after I would be dead. The silences would be broken by a commonplace remark so absent-minded as to convey an idea of ventriloquism. 'What a prolific writer Wallace is! ... Warm for November, would you say?'

We had agreed that I should not examine the bust till it was finished and cast, and he only spoke of it once. 'Strange,' he said, 'I have always found that the face of every male sitter has one profile masculine and the other feminine. I've rarely seen it so marked as in this one.' 'This one', as if he were discussing his work with someone else.

As the end approached, the hammer-gossamer hands took to hovering stealthily above the work, as if about to pounce and destroy it, while the eyes bored into my face and then into the clay, darting with increasing speed from one to the other. Then two fingers would slowly descend, stubby and yet feather-light, and flick the clay with the last vital touches. They would press it a thousandth of a millimetre to left or right: a stroking which, if it had not been professional, would have been a caress.

The rhythm of his movements—of the fanatical jerks of the head as he stared from me to the clay and back, of the airy touches—began to accelerate; the grunts grew sharper, the breathing more frantic, as if this were a sex ritual and an act of consummation were taking place.

And that seemed splendidly right, for what is more physical than the phenomenon, as simple and mysterious as birth, of a pair of human hands, over hours, moulding dead clay into the eternal semblance of a mortal man?

After the very last brush of a finger-tip coaxing a last edge of clay-flesh one hair's breadth into perfection, the hands rose slowly together from the work and turned back into the peasant hammers. Then came the long expulsion of breath, as final as the end of life. It was done.

He broke a packet of cigarettes and gently, over the head he had created, draped a frayed dishcloth with a cigarette-burn in it.

'I think that's all,' he said, striking a match with a timid smile which showed the broken teeth. 'You have been very patient, children are the most difficult sitters, of course.'

It was less than a month since Miss Cooke had written to him. A quick business deal between two great people.

CHAPTER TWENTY

A NEW FILM FACE

The Case of the Frightened Lady was to be filmed, starting two weeks from now and they wanted Miss Nesbitt, Harker and me. Bill's part had gone to Norman McKinnel. 'I see what they mean,' Bill said, and his passivity saddened me.

'My dear Son George, Little did we think when we took you in the threepennies to see Charlie Chaplin with an orange each that prior to your 26th birthday you would be launching as a Star, the Flintshire Observer puts it that you are a new Film Face.'

The two weeks when I was not at the theatre seemed long. For Bill the best time was the morning; even if he had been late at the Club he would sit reading and talking, and the flat was warm with affection.

But there were danger signs. I was becoming more and more conscious of the unfinished cigarettes, of match after match held between brown-stained finger and thumb, of the coughing, sorry old boy . . . He was getting on my nerves. The night came up which, in all my life, I was to be most ashamed of.

I had asked Freddie Mell to supper after the play, and Bill said he would follow on. Freddie was playing in *Britannia of Billingsgate*—'two nice little scenes, ducks, I arrive on a motor-bike and potty about this girl, I love character parts'.

Bill did not turn up, and after leaving the small bedroom ready, I was asleep in the double divan when the light snapped on. Hat back to front and swaying from heel to toe, he looked like a stage drunk. After fifteen months of sterile devotion capped by sterile overwork, I saw red: I leapt out of bed and struck him in the face.

He stared at me like a wild, unbelieving animal, and the blood-shot eyes filled with such rage that I knew he was going to kill me. As he lunged I ducked into the hall and then into the small room, hurled the plywood wardrobe against the door and leaned against it. After a second of silence, a pounding to shake the neighbourhood.

A knock at our front door. 'Is anything the matter?' A stagger of feet and a bang as Bill shut himself in the big room: I had proved myself a physical coward, he a moral one. I pulled away the wardrobe and opened the front door to our landlord, extremely alarmed in a dressing-gown.

'I'm so sorry,' I said, 'Mr Wilson had an old friend in who'd had a couple, did you hear us get him down the stairs?' Being an actor can come in useful.

In bed in the little room, I calmly watched the smoke of battle drift away to reveal crossroads irrevocably sign-posted. In the morning I left my case at the stage-door, remembered that Freddie's Dennis had moved up North, phoned Freddie and arranged to have the other bed for a couple of days.

Little Curtis was also footloose again. The three of us made a lightning plan to share, and found a house which suited perfectly: three pounds a week for three years from the first of January, we would allot the rent in proportion.

Then I phoned Carol. Next to the dressing-room which I shared with Bill there was a tiny unused office. Since I was hatching a new play and needed to be alone during my long waits, would it be all right if I moved into it?

I got to the theatre early and transferred my things. In the middle Bill arrived, ravaged but nervously friendly. 'A three-year lease? Sounds very sensible.' Old Ben was going to put him up. 'See you later, old boy.'

I was glad to feel relief, but the observer in me opened the window and looked down as he sauntered aimlessly to one end of the alley, hesitated, returned and disappeared round the other corner. To the pub.

It is always strange, in a city, to see a loved one walking unaware of your look. I watched a lost man, rejected by the only friend he had in the world, wander along wondering what to do next. I shut the window sharply.

But my boats were burnt. They had been leaking and creaking, and it was time.

* * *

At six a.m. next day I sank into a hired car, hideously expensive but essential; at eight, in the British Lion Studios at Beaconsfield, I was lying back in a dentist's chair being made up by an American.

I was not called before the camera till after lunch. In the middle of what looked like a dim warehouse thronged with workers and intermittently ablaze with light, I enjoyed sitting in a canvas chair with my name burning into the small of my back.

When they reached my scene—an easy walk down a corridor with the Inspector, one question, one answer—we played it without rehearsal. McKinnel was rattled. 'God, why are films always like this? You're the lucky one . . .'

I saw what he meant. The talking picture was only two years old, and in a film taken from a play major scenes were left mostly intact. And my first film was not only from a play I had been in, it was from a play I *was* in: not only did I know my part, but when a scene came unexpectedly along I knew exactly where it fitted into the jigsaw. Which left me free for a daily task: to shrink the stage performance until I was in a real-life room which happened to have a camera in it.

This problem was not helped by the American director, Hayes Hunter. An ageing but enthusiastic recruit from the silent films who had graduated to the spoken word without an exam, he had an approach which recreated mornings when sleepy cowboys and Indians with hangovers had to be galvanized into instant snarling action before the camera in the form of a fight to the death.

As soon as the clapper-boy had clapped his chalked board in the nose of the camera—DEAD MEN'S GULCH, Scene 99, Take 3—and ducked out, Mr Hunter had been accustomed to roar a wake-up call to be heard in Beverly Hills. One could see how it had worked then, but it proved disconcerting, the minute before a subtle exchange of dialogue, to be deafened by 'Emil baby, gimme the MELL-ER-DRAMMM-AH ! ! !' You got used to it as to the bark of a dog.

On top of this he had been so used to spurring his actors on in the middle of soundless scenes—'This is great, baby, kick him twice, *now!*'—that only immense self-control stopped him ruining the take with running pep-talk. Once or twice he failed to contain

himself—'That's swell Cathleen, you're givin' me that *subtlety*'—
and swell Cathleen had to give that subtlety all over again.

I enjoyed it all: the long hours, the chilly early mornings my
father was still enduring, the heat from the immensely powerful
lamps—much hotter then than later—the getting to the theatre
and re-adjusting to the stage presentation of a scene shot four
hours earlier.

The sets gave me particular pleasure. Mark's Priory was striking in Wyndham's, but in Beaconsfield it was gigantic: rows of
Norman pillars, great bowls of real flowers, corridors of panelling,
ancestral furniture, paintings, suits of armour. As I sauntered up
and down my immense carpets with the camera obediently following, I felt imbued with careless grandeur. I only wished
that Dad could be sitting in my canvas chair watching his titled
son in his ancestral home.

❋ ❋ ❋

The film over, my reminders of the cinema came from an unexpected quarter: from my father, who now subscribed to *Film
Weekly*. 'Would Miss Jessie Mathews be a Welsh girl?'

'We are told that in Hollywood they put the blame for this
Trouser Craze on Marlene, would this Miss Detrick be a foreign
lady, nothing about you this week we live in hopes...'

Bill and I, in friendly exchanges backstage, kept off personal
questions. He had moved into a little furnished room over a mews
garage in Victoria. I knew it made him happier to be near me.
I was always to feel responsible for him.

Over the New Year, 1932, Freddie and Miss Curtis and I moved
to Ebury Street, a long thoroughfare near Victoria with a flavour
both literary and theatrical, ranging from Number 121, which
still harboured George Moore, to the erstwhile Coward home at
Number 111.

71a was an old-fashioned house composed of a three-storey flat
over a shoemaker's shop. A little staircase led to the first floor; an
L-shaped room with tall leaded windows in the front and with
the back overlooking a tree. Freddie had the room above next
to the bathroom; on the top floor, Miss C. had the maid's room
next to the kitchen.

Three friends independent of one another, we fitted in. I enjoyed communal breakfast up in the kitchen; returning home at night I would hear laughter and the gramophone, and if Freddie was giving a bottle party I often took up drink and stayed for bacon-and-eggs and funny people.

He was full of housewifely suggestions, besides producing his charwoman Mrs Tilley, a meek conscientious worker who put me in mind of my mother. And for the first time I had a coal fire. After a week my quarters looked more lived-in than Marchmont Street had after a year.

Soon after the Wallace play closed in February I joined Celia Johnson in an adaptation of Maurice Rostand's over-emotional war play *The Man I Killed*. One evening in mid-rehearsal I was on my way to Wyndham's to join Bill for the first night of the new Wallace play with du Maurier, *The Green Pack*, when outside the theatre I was faced with a poster: EDGAR—GRAVE CONCERN.

He was in Hollywood writing films, and a cold had galloped into pneumonia. A cloud hung over play and theatre.

Lunch-time next day I hurried from the Apollo to the Cavour Bar, to find that half-a-dozen others had gravitated there, looking for one another; Bill, Carol, Julian, Bill Linnit. We were like a family with father away and in danger. Later, I hurried from rehearsal to buy an evening paper. I did not need to, a poster read EDGAR WALLACE DEAD.

I stood, stupid with shock. When I looked at the faces round me, staring at the poster, I knew that it was not only people like me who were hit. I was watching the man in the street, literally, as he took in the news of the loss of a myth; it was as if a titanic engine, red-hot and roaring and cheerfully inexhaustible, was over on its side with its fires out for ever.

Passing placard after placard on my way to the Cavour, I ran into Bill outside the Empire; he looked stricken. I remembered his special bond with Edgar, and felt very close to him. For us it was the end of a reign.

* * *

The first night of *The Man I Killed* was a familiarly enigmatic experience. At the end of a long, long part—how I had hankered after one for years!—which was too high-pitched, I heard respectful applause.

Would Miss Braithwaite have described it as 'an *interesting* evening'? Definitely. A female first-nighter billowed past my open door, called ecstatically, 'Emlyn, lovely, lovely, lovely, where's Celia?' and vanished for good.

I had posted first-night tickets to Molly and Jack, and when they came round I was happy to see two friends. They were nice about the play, I gave them a drink and they left, obviously thinking I was off to a first-night party. When I got back I went up to Freddie, who had been in the gallery. 'What a *depressing* show, French indeed. Well, ducky, it's got what we in Angleterre call longueurs, ooh la la . . .'

The run of the play, though, had no longueurs. We lasted till Saturday. I went home for three days with my parents. I had a plan.

CHAPTER TWENTY-ONE

THE INNOCENTS AT HOME,
AND ABROAD

It was Monday, washing-day. There was Mam as usual, wearing Dad's cap and scurrying in an icy wind between the back door and the dolly in the shed. In the kitchen, except near the fire, it was chilly. Below sea-level . . .

I looked at my parents. Age, the tireless tortoise, was gaining ground. I worked out that my father was rising sixty-two, my mother sixty-three. He was becoming hard of hearing in one ear: 'what they call boiler-makers' deafness', brought on by working for years near blasting.

Mam sat with a pile of socks. 'There seems to be more colds about this winter.' Job was getting married, 'beaten you to it, George!' As Dad said it I reflected for the first time that they must be wondering if I had 'ideas'.

They asked if I had seen Tom again, I said the Army seemed keen on keeping him to themselves. 'Fancy them not letting him see the play,' Mam said in an access of worldliness, 'the cheek . . . So you have been a murderer in this last one as well?'

'In a way, I shot a German in the war.'

Mam looked up from her needle, 'But that's not murder, there was a man in Cable Street who got the Victoria Cross for it an' there was a big reception and he took to the drink.'

She asked what happened in the play. I did my best. 'It preys on his mind and he goes to visit the boy's family and it ends with him playing the boy's violin.'

Dad looked up from his racing, pencil in air, and spoke over his glasses. 'The lad sounds on the nervy side, eh George?'

Next morning I went for a walk that took me back to school-days. Up the disused railway line and along the remembered lanes and short cuts until I reached the main road descending between fields from the hill village of Hawarden to Queensferry and the Dee estuary.

Ever since going on the stage five years ago I had had my eye on those fields; distant mist softened the Steelworks, which were the background to us as a family. As I walked I looked to the right into a field where there was an embryonic road and a row of unfinished little houses. Nailed to a tree was a sign, ASTON HILL, BUNGALOWS FOR SALE, £500, APPLY ROBERTS AND WILLIAMS, QUEENS-FERRY. Could I have seen it five years ago, in a dream?

I knew my parents would never accept exile to a remote countryside and I was glad to see, on the road outside, a bus leaving its stop. In Queensferry, a mile downhill, I called at the builders', was shown a plan, and chose the site of a detached bungalow high in the field, backing on to another field with beyond it a couple of friendly houses. I signed as deposit a cheque for fifty pounds.

On the walk home I planned details, having made up my mind that apart from the few things of sentimental value the bungalow would house not one stick of the senile scarred rubbish my mother had guarded for thirty-seven years. There would be new bed-steads, new mattresses and on from there . . .

Sitting at home, I was almost glad my teacup was chipped.

'That was a long walk you went?'

'Yes Mam, up Hawarden way.'

'They say it's nice up there.' For weeks on end she never ventured beyond her backyard, except for the weekly excursion of three hundred yards up into High Street and to the Co-op. Now, before I could forestall her, she was out into the back for coal for the fire she had kept warm all those years.

My mind was made up.

Job was out courting, Dad home in a minute from work, so a tricky interview was upon me. I asked about Dad. 'Oh, he's been very good, only calls at the New Inn for a glass of beer so he can show any new cuttin's.'

I asked what he did about the unfavourable ones.

'He reads those out loud to make fun of the people that writes them.'

Dad arrived and started his dinner, with Mam opposite mending a threadbare pillow. I took something from my pocket and spread it out. Dad peered across. 'What would that be now, George?'

I had prepared my part. 'The plan of a house, I'm having one built.'

Mam looked up. 'Are *you* getting married?'

That was quick, I thought . . . 'No, no . . .'

'A good idea,' said Dad. 'Don't they say, put your money in property and you can't lose? In London, would it be?'

'No, here.'

'Here?'

'Aston Hill, a nice spot.'

Dad said, 'For your holidays you mean?'

'It's not for me.'

They looked at each other. She left it to him.

'Then who is it for, George?'

'Anybody that wants it. You two can have first refusal.'

They understood. He began to glow. She seemed to pale.

'Good life,' she said, and she only said it when she was startled. Then, 'No, thank you,' as if I had placed a glass of champagne before her. 'I'm not used to it.'

She looked at Dad, who was by now on a cloud and unable to help her. 'We're too old,' she said, 'to start shiftin' about. All the arrangements . . .'

'Nothing to arrange. You'll see it, then you can decide and if you want it you can pack everything in that trunk upstairs.'

Dad's smile was from ear to ear. She went on, 'What about all these? Tables, sofa, beds . . .'

'Burn them.'

'*Burn* them?' We might have been discussing babies.

Dad winked at me before saying, 'I like a nice bonfire. What's this word upside down, George?'

'Bathroom.' To make it sound less grand, I had pronounced it with a short a.

'We've lived here fifteen years,' Mam said, 'since you was eleven. How much is this goin' to cost?'

I had been waiting for that. 'I'm not eleven any more and that's a personal question.'

'And how would we get up there with the trunk?' I told her I would hire a taxi.

She frowned. 'And what is a taxi?' I was touched, and irritated.

Dad helped her out. 'It's like a horse-and-cart only it's got petrol in it. Wait till I tell them in the Works!'

*   *   *

A message from the Leon M. Lion office. He was putting on a new play by Sutton Vane, the author of *Outward Bound*, a freak success of ten years ago.

Man Overboard was even more of a fantasy, about a young man who makes a symbolic life-journey from the source of the Thames to the open sea. It was pedestrian and at the same time obscure, but I had not the strength to turn down sixty pounds a week.

One afternoon I came home from rehearsal to open a heavy crate: the Epstein. I got my arm round its neck, gave a heave, lurched it up, staggered over to the gramophone, placed it on top, walked to a corner, turned round and looked.

Bronze, dark and gleaming. Like all sitters I found it impossible to judge, and waited for Miss Cooke's letter.

'J.E. v. kindly had 2 photos taken, they are before me. Ye Gods! One is you at 50, the other you at 10, with that childish look of trusting confidence, it thrills me the way the man has got you as you were and as you will be; I shall never tire of looking at the 2 alongside.

'Both have one thing in common—intense determination. No-one knows better than I do that you have that, but I've never seen it in you. Ye Gods . . .' An eccentric gesture had been justified for ever.

The day before the opening I saw something being taken round to the Garrick foyer: a bust of Lion by a sculptor friend. I mentioned the Epstein to him, and he was magnanimous enough to say, 'Why can't we have it opposite mine?'

Next morning I brought it in a taxi, and just before the first night I wished Miss Cooke could have been watching the crowd examine her commission.

She would have enjoyed the foyer more than the show; it was another failure, but the second week brought an event of importance.

On the evening of May the 14th, at the Albert Hall, the Salvation Army would hold its Annual Ceremony for the Commissioning of Men and Women Officers. In front of thousands and to music, our Tom was to be taken into the high-bracket fold and had written that he would like Dad and Mam to be of the multitude. Dad had obtained two days' leave from the Works; Freddie was on tour and they would have his double bed.

My father had docked at Tilbury forty years ago, but could only have had glimpses of the East End; Mam, as a young wife, had made rare excursions to Wrexham or Liverpool for funerals. On Friday, in London, they would watch one son perform at the Albert Hall, on Saturday another at the Garrick Theatre: the occasion of their lives.

'The tale is spreading very nicely about us going away, they even challenge your Mother in the Co-op about it . . .'

For her it would be a plunge into the unknown. 'I will bring eggs and butter with me, if we get short of anything I suppose you are near to some shops. We will pull through D.V. . . .'

Having laid Dad's best suit on the parlour table and brushed it thoroughly, she would bring out what she had worn for Sunday chapel all my life: the tiny fur tippet with the little fox's head. I went to Harrods and bought a proper fur: not showy, but conservatively handsome. Then flowers and oranges, beer for Dad; clean sheets on Freddie's bed.

At Euston, seeing them advance among the crowd, I saw them as strangers. Who was the timid little white-haired lady in old-fashioned grey hat and long black coat, linking her arm through that of her companion and walking gingerly as if across a mine-field?

And who was he, the broad-shouldered, black-hatted elder statesman approaching with measured tread—grey moustache and gleam of steel-rimmed glasses—carrying a suitcase as if it were the diplomatic bag? The station might have been named after him, it could have been Lord Euston himself. Could I ever have seen him in his shirt-sleeves?

They saw me. My father's face opened wide and we shook eager hands. He greeted me in Welsh, which told me that he was moved. 'Wel, ymachgeni, dyma ni wedi cyrraedd; well, my boy, we have arrived!'

Then, for the first time, I kissed my mother. She was trembling a little. I noted the tippet, took the suitcase and walked them to the rank.

'This, Poll,' said Dad, sitting back, 'is a taxi, there's the petrol in there. And next time we come it'll be a car with a shawfer!'

I explained about Tom not being free. 'Poor lad,' Dad said, 'I expect they don't let 'em out during prayin' hours.'

I pointed out Hyde Park as we bowled through it in the sun. Their attitudes were, as always, typical: she peering apprehensively out at a foreign capital, he leaning at the open window as if to bow to crowds lining his route.

They followed me up the stairs into the flat, which I knew—what with the flowers and the oranges—would spell luxury. 'Well, George,' Dad said, 'you got your quarters shipshape!'

They followed me up to the bathroom. She had not seen one since she was in service in Liverpool and he had never seen one at all. I went up to the kitchen to prepare a high tea; when they joined me Mam scoured everything with a practised eye. It was fairly tidy.

We descended again to the shipshape quarters and Tom arrived, the apple of his mother's eye, tall and resplendent in his uniform. When he went up to make himself tea I said, 'That's a smart outfit he's got.'

'I can't take to it,' Mam said with a sigh. Then she made the only comment I ever heard from her which seemed on the bright side. 'There's one thing about the Sally Army uniform. He can't get killed in it.'

'Don't be too sure,' Dad said cheerfully, 'if one o' them big Bibles drops on his head, he'll be in trouble.'

But he was careful not to tease Tom, and asked him solicitously about his studies. While our parents were upstairs I gave Tom a pound to take them to a Lyons before the great event; I knew that anything grander would scare our mother into a hunger-strike. After the Albert Hall, he would have to hurry back to Denmark Hill; we arranged that he would first drop them at 71a by taxi, I told him how much to give extra.

When they came down again, my mother in her tippet, I went to the cupboard and brought out the fur from Harrods. She went scarlet. I undid the tippet and replaced it. 'There you are,' Dad said, 'your Mam was always a lady and now she looks one as well.'

When I got back from the theatre their light was out. They had made cocoa in the kitchen as instructed. It must have been the first time ever for them to share a strange bed. We breakfasted up in the sunny kitchen, I making the tea and boiling eggs; the extent of my repertoire. I distributed cups with an abstracted air. My mother kept giving me puzzled looks. Our roles were reversed.

I asked about Tom at the Albert Hall. 'When he went up for his degree,' Dad said, 'he looked fit to eat and as for the do, the Lord Mayor's Show must be nothing to it.' There had been medals, drums, gold braid, searchlights.

I could tell from Mam's face that she had been proud of Tom but had found the rest vulgar. The Project—their new home—was not brought up, but Miss Cooke's letter was a reminder.

'Good luck to Aston Hill, you are on the right tack there! Somebody said the autumn of life is the best season & you're planning a gd autumn for them both...'

At tea, a visitor. He was shyer than they were, Dad greeting him as an old friend—'Mr Cronnin I presume?'—and putting the West End actor at his ease. 'What a shock for us all, sir, poor old Edgar kickin' the bucket so sudden!'

When Bill raised his cup his hand was shaking slightly. Dad noticed it too. He can have known nothing of Bill's weakness but his quick look was almost professional: he was like an ex-convict sizing one up who is out on parole.

'It must have gone to your heart, Mr Cronnin, after doing him such good service in his plays...' When Bill took his modest leave and was seen warmly out by my father, it would have been difficult to guess which of the two had the blue blood.

I thought a bus would be a nice change, and from it I pointed out Buckingham Palace. After high tea at an ABC I handed Dad the two tickets and the programme I had acquired, then I strolled them through Leicester Square to the Garrick: on purpose, because at the end of Green Street we were faced with the façade of the theatre.

It was still daylight, but right across the front, in lights, LEON M. LION EMLYN WILLIAMS IN MAN OVERBOARD.

My father saw it first, and stopped. 'My word...'

'Good life,' said Mam.

Then Dad said, 'Who's Leon M. Lion, George?' and we crossed the road.

* * *

Making up, I imagined them sitting in the foyer, close together on a seat opposite the Epstein, and glancing from it to the smart people arriving. Except for *Romeo and Juliet* at the Shakespeare Liverpool when they were courting, and our excursions to the Chester pantomime, they had never been in a theatre. They would now see a modern play from the stalls of a London playhouse.

Luckily it was a Saturday night, the theatre was fullish and the play went with a swing. I committed no murder but did nearly strangle my mistress across a bed, knowing at that moment that Dad would give Mam a nudge of enjoyment and that she would go, 'Tut-tut . . .'

At the end they waited in their seats until my dresser came out through the pass-door to fetch them. To enter my dressing-room was for them as strange as being ushered into a cage at the Zoo. Even Dad was silent for a moment, over his glass of beer.

I felt he should be able to tell his mates at the Works that he had travelled by London Underground. As a last Sunday fling, carrying the family suitcase, I preceded them to Victoria and into the bowels of the earth.

On the platform Dad turned to me like a starry-eyed school-boy. 'The last time I did this it was nothing like so bright!' I was at a loss, then remembered that before I was born he had for a couple of years been a collier under the River Dee.

At Euston, the handshake and again the kiss. They were tired and so was I, but it had been worth it.

CHAPTER TWENTY-TWO

BUILDING FOR SPRING, BUILDING
FOR AUTUMN

The following Saturday *Man Overboard* came up for the nine-teenth and last time. Having had two failures as a Star, I found myself not even the rage in the acting line.

But by a quirk I was also a playwright, and a playwright is often like a woman who has no proof that she is pregnant, but knows she is.

'You might write a good costume play,' Dick Clowes had said. I happened to read, in an article on Shakespeare, about his theatre life and the actors who created the female characters. Lazily I began to think about this, and made the usual hurried notes.

The Globe Theatre, Shoreditch . . . company headed by Bur-bage, romantic, virile, bawdy, the Eliz. Man . . . Wife buxom, shutting eyes to his escapades, one being a glorious courtesan . . .

Shakespeare himself? Duck the trap of putting genius on the stage, he will not appear . . . Yes he will . . . At the end of Act Two a perfectly ordinary man enters from the street with a script under his arm—'Is Master Burbage within?'—and goes through. 'Who was that?' And somebody answers, indifferently, 'Master Shakespeare'. Curtain.

Story: there must be a character in perturbed relation with B . . . Not boy actor—a girl seeking adventure in London, for safety dresses as boy, applies for heroine's part, creates Viola in *Twelfth Night*, falls in love with B., confesses, he sends her home.

I went to the British Museum and renewed my ticket. I had not been since my *And So To Bed* studies, and it was satisfying now to be both student and playwright. In an exercise book I scribbled detailed notes of dates, playhouse, players, Elizabethan habits and phrases.

Keynote must be optimistic freshness of the age. *Twelfth Night* was first played about the turn of the century. Title, *Spring, 1600*.

'My dear Son George, Words fail me as they say, after London the Quay will never look the same, we cannot decide which gave us the best show you or Tom. A shame he could not see you in that play, it was as good as a Sermon, perhaps that is what made people go past the Theatre instead of in. It was an honour to meet Mr Cronnin, your Mam says he should watch that cough.

'Job and me tried to persuade her to wear the Fur to the Co-op but it was in the drawer by then, it will turn up D.V. on Judgement Day.'

Then my mother. 'Thank you for everything you done in London, what a big place it is, i did nott expect your place to be so nice with you being absent-minded.

'Your father liked the statue of you in the theatre but I didnt fancy it, I thought at the first it was a Black Man and you look as if you eaten something that has dissagreed with you but I suppose the gentleman that did it knows best. I hope the Sally Army is giving Thomas enough to eat, the godfearing ones need the nourishment same as the sinners, thank you again your lovin Mam.'

❉　❉　❉

Polly and Sonny were in Italy, but Molly and Jack had rented a cottage by the Thames, at Oakley Green near Windsor. I went down for a week-end.

It was tiny and meanly furnished, but Molly had done wonders with flowers and bits-and-pieces from Rutland Street. I had never met them out of London, and the barrister looked relaxed in flannels and open shirt. I felt as much at home with them as with Polly and Sonny.

On Sunday morning, after I had made my bed, I had early breakfast with Molly in the shabby garden, then she sat cutting up beans for lunch. She was in a sort of dirndl dress and looked very young.

I said, 'I keep expecting Jack to be the pompous barrister, and he isn't.'

'Oh, no, I wouldn't have married him if he'd been pompous.' She added with a sigh, 'I do sometimes wish he'd have a drink once in a while.' I remembered how much older he was than us.

'He doesn't seem to fit into a cottage like this.'

'Oh, Jack can have big ideas, especially when he gets into a casino, Le Touquet was very tricky . . . No, we're here because we haven't any money.' It was a cheerful statement of fact.

I asked how they had met. It had been on the first night of *Nicolette*. I plied her with questions.

'At the Duke of York's, my first real part in London, I was what Mother called the soubrette . . . Yes, I made rather a success, Agate said I sang flat, Mother said it was first-night nerves but he knew better . . .

'Well, there was this man leaning out of a box with a monocle and he came round with chocolates just like in the novels about actresses. We got married and went to live in a tiny flat in the Temple, I was twenty-one and Mother was furious, she said, "He's years older than you, and anyway a soubrette in the Temple, I ask you!" Both she and Polly said he wasn't to be trusted, I didn't know what they meant, then.'

The man she spoke of was about to come downstairs from their bed, and I knew she would only talk like that to a close friend. They had been married six years; at our age it was a long time. And he was not to be trusted.

She asked about my family, I told her about the London visit.

Jack came gangling downstairs, in sweater and sandals. 'Emlyn, I do hope you slept, the frogs on that side didn't keep you awake?'

Molly handed him his coffee; he bent his head and kissed her on the cheek. 'Thank you, my little Mole.'

Yes, he had charm. I wondered why Sonny didn't call Polly Pole.

Molly had discovered she was a good punter, and Jack and I sat back cushioned like two gigolos. We tied up under weeping willows, and as Molly prepared cold lunch I opened my exercise book and wrote *Spring, 1600*. To the lapping of summer water, I followed it with '*A Romantic Comedy*'.

'Mole, tell Emlyn about your pram at Christmas.'

When she was small in the London suburb of Wallington, on Christmas Eve her father used to take her for a walk, wheeling the old family pram carefully prepared for the outing. It never crossed her mind that he was already fairly drunk, and she loved it.

Once, as an old lady approached he stopped and leant into the pram, 'Isn't Diddums looking sweet?' The old lady, happy to bend down for a Yuletide peek, found herself face to face with a dead turkey sitting bolt upright in baby clothes. She ran. Dad would have enjoyed Mr Shann.

I wrote 'Act One. The scene is a garden in Ongar, Essex. Music, played on virginals ...' After lunch I worked and they read the Sunday papers. Once he took her hand and squeezed it, she smiled happily. I was with friends, and content. I scribbled.

By June, just as I finished the first act, again a decisive phone call: Leontine Sagan having made a great success directing *Maedchen in Uniform*, a daring German film about a girl's school, Alexander Korda had engaged her to direct a film about Oxford. The plot of *Men of Tomorrow* was as banal as its title: two undergraduates in love with two undergraduettes, in itself—at that time—a formidable improbability.

I went to Elstree, made a test and got the part of the hero's comic bespectacled friend. It meant that *Spring, 1600* would have to be put away, also that I found myself in a unique situation. On the spot where I had spent nearly three years as an undergraduate, I was to spend two weeks as an actor playing an undergraduate: the locations included not just Oxford, but Christ Church.

It was the Long Vac, and emerging from the empty station I ran into a tall, handsome, auburn-haired young man. We recognized each other, he had just made his first success in the play *Precious Bane*. 'I'm Robert Donat, hello ...'

We shared a taxi to the Randolph, the grand hotel in which, when I had been 'up', I had never set foot. Donat had 'no side', as Bill would say, and I knew I would enjoy the company of a normal, high-spirited young fellow-actor who was not a bore.

'What about this script, isn't it a stinker? But it's my first film and I need the money so what the hell—but there's this age thing. D'you realize we're supposed to be not a day over twenty, how old are you?'

I told him twenty-six, November 1905.

'I'm eight months older. How the hell are we going to manage?'

I mentioned a critic who had described him as a half-Greek god who had winged his way from Olympus. He sighed, 'They keep printing balls like that. I'm actually a half-Pole who's winged his way from Withington, Manchester. A voice teacher bullied me into talking posh and the Benson Company finished me off, they opened me vowels they did an' all ...'

The call-sheet for tomorrow read 'Mr E. Williams, Make-up, Randolph Hotel, 7.30 a.m. Second-Unit Crew moves to Ch. Ch. for Set-Up in Tom Quad.' Why couldn't they have picked Magdalen?

I arrived at Tom Gate disguised as a Commoner; my short gown felt strange, being a Scholar I had worn a long one. The same porter at the Gate now stared at me, not only with no recognition but with ill-concealed contempt. In the sun my tanned cheeks betrayed a tinge of yellow.

'Yer film lot's all over the Quad, just be-ind Mercury, that's the fountain.' I knew it was the fountain.

They were indeed all over, thirty of them: camera, boxes, folding chairs, cables and portable canteen for elevenses, next to the Cathedral. The continuity girl munched a bun, 'I rather fancy these old-fashioned locations, don't you?'

The second assistant came up, a boy of sixteen. 'O.K., Mr Williams, I'll take you up, it's some old geyser's quarters, Professor Thingummyjig, you 'ave to lean out of 'is winder an' do some funny business.' I followed him, a tolerant snob.

As I rehearsed at the window—a bit more to the left, Elwyn; could you oblige Sound by shoutin' a bit louder, thanks, Elmyn —I could see, far across Tom Quad, my first little bedroom, over the Lewis Carroll rooms.

Who was I, what was I? *Men of Tomorrow*, Scene 879, Take One, Action ...

In the Elstree studios, away from the authentic open air, it became clear that *Men of Tomorrow* would be a dreadful film. Here again my Oxford life was grotesquely repeated, first a dinner scene in a replica of Christ Church Hall, then when I sat in Schools, frowning in close-up at my exam paper and biting a nail. When I remembered that I was being paid twelve pounds ten a day to sit for an exam which would never be examined, I cheered up.

We worked many evenings, when Robert, Maurice Braddell and I were put up at a luxurious road-house near the studios. During the dinner break, provided there was little dialogue to prepare, the three of us would toast one another in white wine and sit around being irreverent about the film.

Our employer also employed his brothers Vincent and Zoltan; we set ourselves the task of inventing more Kordas. By cointreau-time we had enrolled Con Korda, Dis Korda, Whip Korda, Sash Korda, Miseri Korda, Umbilical Korda and—swept away in a Magyar revolution—Lost Korda.

Another evening Robert, till now the shoulder-shrugging Lancashire philosopher, burst out. 'God, this mucky film's getting us all down, it's so bloody dreary! Why can't the Frau let her hair down and do another Maedchen?'

Maurice took it up. 'Why can't us chaps be in love with each other, dons and all? *Men of Tomorrow*, Christ what a title. Why not *A Queer Kiss in the Quad*?'

Another cointreau and it was a musical film. Solemnly I copied out one suggestion after another, as if we were shooting next week. I made a note of a Chorus of Fellows, singing 'At the High Table, Fumble if you're Able', then of the title number, 'A Queer Kiss in the Quad, from an Anonymous Sod, Is Worth Two in Florence, From D. H. Lawrence'.

It passed the time.

*   *   *

Mr Guthrie McClintic would be delighted if I could have a drink with him in his suite at the Ritz.

I knew the name from New York, where he was an immensely successful director. Expecting a heavy business figure, I was happy to meet a volatile amusing man much younger than his fortyish years. He was planning to present *The Case of the Frightened Lady* on Broadway—there to be called *Criminal at Large*—and wanted me for it, I would sail in six weeks, who was my agent?

When Walter rang up to say he had got me five hundred dollars a week—a hundred and eighty pounds—I rang Molly and Jack and went down with whisky, champagne and flowers, then pondered what big splash to make.

A married couple were coming for dinner: I rang the Café de Paris at Bray, the grandest out-of-London rendezvous in the country, and booked a table for five for dinner in the name of Carus-Wilson. On the phone it sounded better than Williams. It was a tremendously expensive and happy party, exactly what I wanted.

[261]

Before New York, a priority: three days at 314a.

Coming out of Connah's Quay Station I was faced as usual by the enormous cinema hoarding which I had visited many a Friday afternoon to watch a man on a ladder unfold next week's silent pleasures: Theda Bara, Charlie Chaplin, Lillian Gish...

I stopped short at the sight of ALHAMBRA SHOTTON EMLYN WILLIAMS!!! SEE YOUR LOCAL FILM STAR!!! To the Quay, Cathleen Nesbitt, Gordon Harker and Norman McKinnel were insubstantial shadows.

Over tea and tomatoes, even Mam was excited. 'I went with Job on Monday, you never seed such a crowd, and when you shot yourself at the end I was glad it was not you only your photo...'

With Dad working two till ten they had arranged a special showing, for him and all the men on that shift, at eleven one morning. 'Your father went in his best and they put him where us lot have never been before, front row middle upstairs, they told me in the Co-op that at the end they clapped till the lights had to be turned on and your father got up and did a bow, can you believe it?'

I could.

I waited till she was out shopping, fished out her tape and whipped round the house, measuring the few objects I had singled out for nostalgic survival: the family chest-of-drawers, the grandfather clock, the corner-cupboard with the sacred wedding china, the horsehair sofa, the framed 'God Is Love' and 'Jesus Wept'.

Then I made my own rough plan, fitting in the furniture as I would for the set of a play, and left for Aston Hill. I felt apprehensive turning into the field, but the bungalow was far enough advanced for me to see what it would be, and plan accordingly.

There would be a low gate between white railings, a short path across a tiny flower-garden, five steps up to the front door, then the hall. I went straight to the bathroom: yes, there they were next to the bath, shrouded in brown paper and about to be cemented in for ever: the washbasin and the lavatory bowl.

On the way back I rechecked my shopping list, and next day took the train to Wrexham: to Aston's, The Store Which Sold Everything. With my cheque-book in my pocket next to Mam's tape I bought. Everything, from beds through crockery and cutlery to soap and dusters.

Then a long list of strangenesses, large and small, which my
mother had never known: carpets, wardrobes, table-lamps, lamp-
shades, electric fires—Dad would deal with those, they would
scare her to death—dressing-gowns, eiderdowns, Hoover, hot-
water bottles, waste-baskets, lavatory paper—gone the neat
squares of newspaper tied to a nail—bath-towels, coat-hangers,
tea-cosy, tea-strainer, lavatory brush, door-knocker. I even bought
a large packet of match-boxes.

After a childhood continuously aware of money as a potential
enemy, my delight now in treating the enemy as a slave was
almost sensual. By five o'clock when I signed the cheque, I was
exhausted with pleasure.

That evening Job and I retired to the parlour for a business
conference. Once the bungalow was complete he would arrange
with Aston's to deliver on one of his free days, so that he could
be there to arrange my purchases according to the plan.

My one defeat was when I suggested 'a lady' to come and do
the rough work. My mother's eyes flashed. 'Another woman in my
house, no thank you.'

Leaving for my train I stood in first one room then another,
looking a farewell at the rubbish which had been round me all
my life and which I had just condemned. My parting words were,
'Job will look after everything.' Dad called out, 'Give my love
to the Bowery!'

For the last time, I stood at the train window and waved down
to them crowded at the back door, waving up to me.

Goodbye, 314a, goodbye.

*　*　*

Freddie had settled a year's Australian tour and Roy Curtis's
short-sighted life had somehow gone into orbit again. I bought
Freddie's bits of furniture and since the flat would be empty, lent
it to Bill. He accepted eagerly. 'With you all those miles away,
it'll make it less.' There would be many cigarette-burns, at the
least, but I was touched.

'My dear Son George, We note with thanks the idea of an
annuity (the name is new to me) in the form of a weekly order
of £8 to us, your Mam says it is too much but I have given her
expert medical Advice viz to put some Sugar on her Pride and

swallow it. Also we have been talking things over and decided that since I am 63 next birthday the time has come to put my feet up.'

I guessed that his retirement would coincide with the move, and was glad.

From Miss Cooke. 'Look here George you must have quite a sum sitting in your bank, why not consult an expert about safe investments so you can reap the advantage of dividends? Please note I have underlined "safe".'

I had never thought of it, and only knew of dividends from my mother's 'divvies' from the Co-op. I called in on my bank manager, whom I had seen only once—I remembered he had a kind face—and was ushered in with what I recognized as considerable deference.

He advised me, and I took his advice: not only on War Bonds 'gilt-edged', which sounded good—but on Shell, Woolworth's, Daily Express and Marks and Spencer. Some years later a stockbroker friend exclaimed, 'You have the face to say you know nothing about business and then tell me you put money into those gold mines in the early *thirties*?'

'May I speak to Mr Williams...? You won't remember me, it's Richard Clowes from the *Era*, could I come along and ask a couple of dreary questions so I can misquote your answers?'

He arrived at the flat at six, declined to remove his overcoat, sat solemnly down and accepted a whisky. I asked how he had been.

'All right,' he said, blinking round the room with a sigh, 'just keeping my head below water... How will you feel, arriving in New York after five years, promoted from Pepys's Boy to the House of Lords?' He had again done his homework.

He asked if I was writing. I said yes, a play about the Elizabethan theatre, but superstitiously went into it no further.

'You should send it to John Gielgud, he's always looking for a play of quality to direct.'

I asked if he knew him, 'Slightly, yes, I saw quite a bit of him when I used to pop in to see Frank in *Musical Chairs*.'

Vosper. No trace of boasting; like everything he said, it came out simply, almost grudgingly. The owlish solicitor had more interesting friends than one would think.

He had another whisky, took off his overcoat and talked,

reservedly, picking his fastidious way through the unexplored field of a new friendship; he was a jackdaw encyclopaedia of Fleet Street, of literature.

'I was telling John it's about time for a new stage version of *A Tale of Two Cities* ... Somebody ought to start adapting Henry James, there's marvellous stuff there ...

'Oh, yes, Agate's very entertaining except on the two things he's mad about, French actresses and horses. Alan Dent, his secretary, says Jimmy's idea of bliss would be to see his horse win the Grand National ridden by Sarah Bernhardt...'

Dick knew the figure every show was playing to: what was packing them in and what was playing to 'paper', the free seats which were sent surreptitiously to drama schools and hospitals.

'Must be a dreary life for a London nurse, emptying bed-pans all day and going to flops at night...' We had been sitting for two hours. I helped him into his overcoat, we had sandwiches in a pub, went to the Palladium second house, and stood at the back of the dress circle for the Crazy Gang.

I had made a life-long friend.

*　　*　　*

'My dear Son George ... Wm. Peters from Cable Street told me he is the man that put the slates on the house. One thing—*what name will we give it?* We have had quite a confab, Bryn Hyfryd, the Hill of Peace, then your Mother thought of the lady's house in Liverpool that she was in service with, Briercliffe, too swanky I think, then the perfect name came in a flash—with the house being built off of your Film Career, our home will be named *Hollywood!*'

My answer had to be tactful. '"Hollywood" sounds fine but I think as I have never worked there the neighbours might think we were showing off—what about the house you lived in in Ffynnongroew before I was born, "Glasdir", since it means "green earth"?' Glasdir it was.

The evening before I sailed Bill said there was a public dress rehearsal at eight of the new Coward revue *Words and Music*, and he knew the front-of-house manager. It would make a perfect last night out.

We arrived at the Adelphi at ten to. Through the glass doors, the usual crowd, friends of cast, staff, a sprinkling of actors. Bill said, 'I can see him'; I waited outside while he went in and up to a forbidding Cochran minion who looked like a warder in a dinner-jacket.

The man shook his head and Bill came out red in the face, 'Sorry, old boy, no go, he didn't recognize me.'

Dressmakers and understudies hurried in, I felt we were refugees who had been refused a landing permit. In the middle of the foyer, a luminous figure in slacks and blazer, blue shirt open at the neck, scarf impeccably tied at the throat, a brilliant smile: a host receiving at the party of the year. Noël Coward, through glass.

I looked at Bill, 'You go in and say, "You remember me, I'm Bill Cronin-Wilson, I'm with a friend who's sailing tomorrow. Could you fit us in?"'

Bill looked at me, took one step forward, looked back at me and said, 'Would you do it?'

'No.'

We walked down the Strand in depressed silence and took a bus to 71a.

As we walked in, the phone rang: Jack Carus-Wilson, they were at the Chetham-Strodes' at Number 153a and wanted to take me out for a farewell dinner. I said I had Bill with me, 'Bring him too.'

They arrived ten minutes later, and over introductions we touched on the branches of the Wilson family, Carus and Cronin. Bill's couple of drinks had relaxed him and he talked easily, but when it came to leaving he hesitated. 'Very kind of you but I have a date at the Green Room Club.' I was glad he was realistic.

Jack and Molly gave me a beautiful dinner. We came back to my fire and talked, played records and talked again. By two o'clock it was too late for a taxi and I begged them to stay; the double bed upstairs was newly made ready for Bill, and I hated the idea of being alone in the three-storeyed house on my last night.

They agreed readily and put on clean pyjamas of mine; they looked grotesque, 'We're both the wrong size the other way round!' Molly made us all early breakfast in the kitchen and they waved me off; I felt I had known them a long time.

I had not much heeded Bill's farewell to me last night, but

there he was at Waterloo. I said, 'They were nice last night, weren't they?'

'I thought he was a bit smooth.'

'They're both rather special.' I had to stick up for the few friends I had acquired.

At the barrier he said, 'Goodbye, my dear boy, look after yourself won't you, and write every week?'

They had been Dad's words as he saw me off to France when I was fifteen. We shook hands.

CHAPTER TWENTY-THREE

SECOND WHACK AT THE GREAT
WHITE WAY

On the *Berengaria* my only contact was the privilege of a short exchange with a transatlantic institution: a Daughter of the American Revolution. Seventy, with a lorgnette and stately white hair high on a head which gave an occasional gracious nod, she spoke with such breeding that she was almost inaudible.

'Mr Wulliams, I understand that you are to play under the banner of Miss Cornell?'

I broke it to her that she had understood wrong, that I was to act under the direction of Katharine Cornell's husband Mr McClintic, and that Mrs McClintic was on holiday in Austria.

'*What* a disappointment! Miss Cornell is the First Lady of the American Theatre, you know.'

I knew. I learnt that a grandson at Groton—'our best preparatory school, Mr Wulliams'—was just crazy about the theatre and had some very lovely friends. Which reminded her of a very lovely story. 'David had been granted special leave and gotten back late on the Monday and the master sneered at him in front of the whole class.

'"I suppose" he said, "you've been spending a week-end with the Astors?" We smiled at the story later because, you see, Mr Wulliams . . . David had!'

She owned a house in Newport. I asked if it was a nice place to live, not knowing that it was like putting the question to Queen Victoria about Windsor Castle.

'Newport, Mr Wulliams,' she breathed with a smile which was kindness itself, 'is a series of beautiful homes.'

After five years the New York skyline was nobly the same but I was different. No longer anonymous, I was sought out by three reporters and happy to spend three minutes under urgent fire.

'I've read your hand-out, so you're *Welch*, huh?' Always Welch, to rhyme with squelch and belch. 'How's it feel to be above ground, huh?' 'Gimme a quote on the Prince o' Wales—on Marathon Dancin'—on Mae West—are you single?'

For old times' sake, I put up at the Bristol. When I arrived for my first rehearsal the others had been working for ten days; Mr McClintic caught me walking quietly in with the shy manner I felt was suitable, stopped in mid-direction, put out his arms and delivered a wicked imitation, 'Aw, our B-r-ritish staw!'

Rehearsals under him never sagged for a minute. I watched him jump from his chair and with a frenzied concentration which reminded me of Laughton, show both actors and actresses how a line should be played. In mid-spate though, the frenzy would shatter into fun. Bill Harrigan, solidly handsome and solidly dedicated as the Inspector, said one day, 'Guthrie, something's bothering me. When I walk down the staircase smoking my pipe, what do I wear?'

The answer came without a flicker. 'Deah boy, you'll be in a long, tight, black evening gown trimmed at the neck with mink, next question?'

Harrigan went red and said, 'No, *seriously*, Guthrie . . .'

October the 10th. Before the opening night I went over to the drug-store opposite the Belasco and ordered a big chunk of ice to be sent over later. It was still Prohibition, and I was directed to a 'cordial store' on the corner where a bottle of Scotch was produced from an open shelf and wrapped up for me; the transaction seemed to have little that was Prohibitive about it. Except the price.

After the play I had a new experience at the McClintic house, on top of mixing with the youth, beauty and talent of the New York theatre: I'd like you to meet Judith Anderson, Margalo Gillmore, Moss Hart, Ruth Gordon, Clifton Webb, Dorothy Stickney . . . Only Mrs McClintic was missing, still in Austria.

Guthrie came in from his study, called to me—'They just phoned the reviews, we appeah to hev a jolly hit, deah boy!'— crossed to a worried-looking older man and told him the news. His friend nodded and looked more worried. Guthrie introduced me to Mr Conger Goodyear, his backer. I had met my first millionaire.

*　　*　　*

I moved to the Saint Hubert, an old-fashioned little hotel on West 57th Street, where my room had a French window opening on to the roof.

Just before curtain-up on the second night the Belasco was noisy with success, and the Saturday matinée—the first, and one of the tests of a 'hit'—buzzed with matrons in hats studded with sequins. After the performance I was visited by a young man, a few years older, swarthy, heavy of jaw, and sulky-looking.

'Hello, just wanted to say I enjoyed your show.'

I told him I had seen him in *Saturday's Children* five years back. 'I've been playing the same God-damn part ever since, the perennial Broadway juvenile an' getting older an' uglier by the minute, what d'you think the play's called I'm rehearsing for? *I Loved You Wednesday*, I mean *Christ!*' Humphrey Bogart, 1932.

After the evening performance two young men stayed behind for a Scotch. They had the rugged good looks which advertised hairy tweeds in the *New Yorker*, and low, vibrant hairy voices to match. 'Oh, boy, you're just great . . .' Would I drop in for a drink tomorrow, six-thirty on?

During a quiet Sunday I kept recalling them with pleasure, and at seven p.m. turned into East 72nd Street. After the still-hot reviews—there had even been a headline EMLYN IS A SENSATION —this was the Sunday people would really single me out: I was about to take a deserved swallow-dive into the warm water of adventure. I looked for the house.

I did not need to, I could hear it: a distant buzz which changed, as I got nearer, to a shrill hullabaloo varied with cackles of parrot-laughter. As I entered, a cop on the corner gave me an old-fashioned look. The apartment door, on the ground floor, was on the latch and I squeezed into a large luxurious room crammed with men.

In my insular way I had never imagined, in well-bred American society, any variation from the norm of the deep-voiced, clean-cut, all-male college product. Here they all were, from sixteen to sixty, weirdly womanized and each dispensing to his opposite the vivacious stare of an over-excited schoolgirl, with an occasional dislocation of the eyes and a tip-up of heels to glimpse more of the landscape.

All anybody got a full view of, however, above a fireplace

which I guessed to be fireless, was an over-framed portrait of the mother of one of the hosts: another Daughter of the American Revolution, looking the whole party squarely and benevolently in the face. I realized that nothing gives away a rich room more than a poor painting.

Between the shrieks and jostles I heard only one pronounce-ment, just behind me: 'Mamma mia, this is the *Mauve* Hole of Calcutta!' In a corner, the incongruous flash of white uniform: two young sailors, American. I thought of Bill.

One of my two rough-tweed hosts spotted me and waved in an ecstasy of surprise, 'Martini?' He elbowed gracefully through and introduced me inaudibly to four young men who inaudibly told me their full names.

Both my fans had discarded their rugged looks as one would a false moustache. The virile voices too had suffered a land-change, such as happens when a wilful finger whirls a gramophone record to a higher pitch. They waved to a new face and were off.

From an inscrutable waiter worming his way between the yielding mass, I took a second martini. Nobody took any interest in me: not that I craved it, I just wanted to go.

And I went. It was just as well I had looked before taking my high dive into adventurous water: the pool was empty. I gulped the fresh air, walked briskly to the Saint Hubert and sat back in the nice little foyer of my nice little hotel.

I felt the two martinis drain steadily down my legs, and into the carpet.

The old trouble. What had I imagined a party like that would do for me? Why had I not asked Guthrie to dinner at Sardi's? I sat like a man who had had his wallet pinched and missed his last train. Then I went into the dining-room—genteel, empty—and in the middle of the most active city in the world, dined alone.

If I was to spend weeks in a Broadway success without enjoy-ing it I would be committing a crime, this must not go on...I hurried up to my room, typed *Spring, 1600, Act Two* and stared at the page for five minutes; then I wrote for twenty, then stared at the page again.

But the car was out of the ditch and the engine running. I went to bed.

❋   ❋   ❋

My life assumed a new pattern, not an exciting one but it warded off melancholy. Forming a habit which went with New York, I wrote late at night.

After the play, I called at the corner drug-store, sat at the counter for eggs and bacon while I read tomorrow's paper for murders and rapes and the gossip of Gotham, went up to my room and got into my dressing-gown. By midnight I was settled at my desk as if in an office, and I typed, on what my father would call a night shift.

The hotel supplied a small radio, and my background was the jazz music and raucous mutterings of the Manhattan night. Somehow it accorded perfectly with what I was working at: the evocation on paper of a vibrant extrovert company of Renaissance players.

Round about four o'clock I would stop, reach to the top of my wardrobe for the bottle of scotch, pour out one nightcap, step out on to my private terrace, breathe in the ice-cold air and survey the sleeping, murmurous glow around me. After that moment of fulfilment I went to bed to the voice of Louis Armstrong, to wake up at eleven with a crystal conscience and new ideas.

A walk round the corner to Central Park and a grim tramp round rock and reservoir; a hamburger in a drug-store, a film, typing from five till seven, another drug-store snack opposite the Belasco, the performance, then back to the most important four hours out of the twenty-four.

I set aside one afternoon session a week for letters home. My feelings for Bill had solidified into abiding affection, which made me able to write more lovingly than when I had been in love: I was relieved to hear that he was to be in *For Services Rendered*, the new Maugham play with Cedric Hardwicke and Flora Robson.

I had one week-end break with the Philadelphia Harts, as enjoyable as ever, the only difference being that I had bought my own ticket. At a Sunday cocktail party the sisters showed me off unashamedly. On the stool, the *Theatre Arts Monthly* happened to lie open at a full-page photo of the Epstein.

Night shift: in the Burbage bedroom, while the great man sleeps away debauchery in the great double bed the players mill round him, bickering and talking scandal. Ned Pope, the ageing leading lady, holds court with news of the next play, *Hamlet*. 'I shall play the leading part, Gertrude the Queen...'

One night as I finished at four, my thoughts were far from the White Way as I raised my one whisky to drink to that moment: morning in 314a, the packing up for the Big Move.

'My dear Son George, There is only one word for our new home, *champion*. There is grass-seeds in the garden, Job is busy cleaning the windows and I just painted the gate. I have to train your Mother not to go out of the back door for the Water. As for the Hoover, at the first she looked at it as if it would blow up but now she is never done rolling it around, now your Mam.

'Dear Goerge, the work is lighter here and the curtains dont get dirty, we had a nice sermon on the wireless in Welsh from Cardiff, the Rev Roger Jones was at it...'

Night shift: and the time came when, at five in the morning, I reached the first performance of *Twelfth Night* and typed the final nine words of *Spring, 1600*.

And a fine line they made: the last in my play, the first in Shakespeare's. I stumbled wearily on to the roof to hear the great city start to wake. A rumbling truck, the rattle of the El.

'If music be the food of love, play on...'

* * *

The Broadway lights seemed to race even quicker than last time, people got more exuberant over success than in London and the excitement was catching.

One night after *Criminal at Large* a radiant gorgeously-gowned young beauty appeared at our stage-door and called up the stairs, 'Bill, he's got a smash hit!'

It was Harrigan's young sister Nedda, who had just come from a first night. 'He' was her husband Walter Connolly and the play *The Late Christopher Bean* by Sidney Howard, a major American playwright (*The Silver Cord, They Knew What They Wanted*). I thought, I've finished a play too, it's at the typist's...

I went to a matinée of the Howard play; it was a true comedy about American countryfolk, and I wished I could have written it.

Two days later, a letter from Gilbert Miller. He was to present *The Late Christopher Bean* in London and was worried that the action took place in New England. The idea was to re-set it in (old) England, John van Druten had suggested making the maid Welsh and that I should do the re-setting.

In my room at midnight I opened the script. THE LATE CHRISTOPHER BEAN, a comedy by SIDNEY HOWARD. Then in small letters, 'adapted from *Prenez Garde à la Peinture* by René Fauchois.'

I had not spotted this in the theatre programme and was astonished. This in French, set in France?

I now read what to me was 'the Howard play'. With the most minor adjustments it would 'transfer' perfectly and the beautiful central character of Abby the maid-of-all-work—whom I re-christened Gwenny—would become a picture of my mother and all the Welsh peasant-women of my childhood.

When I phoned Miller he said, 'That's swell, I'll have the French play sent over ... But you speak fluent French, that's one of the reasons ...'

'I know, but to me the Howard play is such an entity I'd sooner not read the French, and hasn't he adapted it very freely?'

Finally Miller agreed and I set to work that minute, 'Act One, The action takes place in a Cheshire village ...'

It was not even work; even the subtle changes I made were as easy as manipulating gears in a fine car. When I came to Gwenny's great speech, it was my mother speaking if she were articulate. '... *Chris learned me that old chairs can be more than old chairs just fit to throw away, that some can be beautiful ... He learned me that a man can get drunk and not be no different, only just more so ... I have lived over and over again the time that he wass here. Over and over again, since he died ...*'

Within a week I had finished. I would receive two per cent of the weekly gross and a small credit in the programme, 'The play anglicized by ...' For a quick stint it was more than fair.

In the meantime our play had moved from the Belasco to the 48th Street; it was not quite the same thing and by the New Year our audiences began to thin out. The slide was accelerated by our Lady Lebanon falling ill. Out of the cast for good, she was replaced by Florence Reed, famous as the flamboyant Mother Goddam in *The Shanghai Gesture* and still a big Broadway name. She was game enough to promise to be ready in three days, and to save time said she didn't need to rehearse our one short scene together. I would have liked a quick run-through, but thought no more of it.

The evening she opened, I went into her room at the half-hour with flowers and while she made up, her hair under a towel, we quickly ran through the words. She was a fine-looking woman with a presence, a rich voice and the theatre friendliness I was familiar with.

The performance proceeded. I came down the stairs for my scene with my mother, as I had come down many times, heard her voice—'Willie'—faced her, stood still and forgot my part.

Lady Lebanon, as played by Cathleen Nesbitt and—only last week—by an actress as stately as her name, Alexandra Carlisle, had been a cold English aristocrat pale of face and sombre in dress. I was now confronted with what looked at first sight like a Christmas tree.

My mother was in black, certainly, but it was thick velvet cut so low that she was like Queen Gertrude, cleft in twain. Lower still the velvet, drawn tight over the waist and then flared to bolster bursting hips, was encrusted with false jewellery. I saw before me a swollen Gladys Frazin, with plump hands weighed down with rings, and bangles climbing the arms.

On the shoes which peeped from under the velvet, diamond buckles. The hair was ebony-black with a fringe and the face afire with make-up: blue lids, thick mascara, pink cheeks, and a false scarlet upper lip which gave an idea that her Ladyship had been down in the ancestral pantry nosing in a jampot. My blue-blooded mother had turned overnight into a bedizened brothel-keeper in a Far East port.

I had hardly caught Bill Harrigan's eye and adjusted to the shock when she turned to him.

'Inspector,' she purred, 'is there anything . . . you require?'

The châtelaine then placed her hands on her black hips and surveyed him, first up and then down. He blushed.

When she turned to me and said, 'Willie, I want to . . . speak to you . . .' her voice was so packed with innuendo that I thought she was going to look me up and down too, but she must have thought better of it. I was, after all, her son. I could only pretend that my father had once gone ashore at Shanghai, sown his wild

[275]

rice and married a couple of leagues beneath him. It was almost worth a change of mother.

*   *   *

Back to my real mother: '... Your Mam's only worry is that Miss Cooke has asked to come to tea, Watch Out...'

Since they had only met properly once, for ten minutes, I had an idea what Mam felt like.

A week later: 'My dear Son George, Well the great Visit has happened, Miss Cooke's Teachers Meeting in Chester had finished early so she got to us at 5 instead of 6.30 and when your Mother heard the rat-a-tat she did a big jump, she showed Miss Cooke every inch having arranged her cleaning day for this purpose.

'After a big spread for the Guest, Miss Cooke asks for pen and ink to write down her address and over goes the ink on the table-cloth you bought, but she was moppin up in a trice and is sending your Mam a new cloth. Miss Cooke is a Character. After we waved her off your Mother said Well, she should be used enough to ink by now not to spill it. What about that going into one of your plays?'

Then followed the visitor's account. 'I was curious to see what an artist & dreamer had achieved in the way of building & furnishing a house!!! I arrived early & having knocked, heard yr father inside say to yr mother, "It's her, you're caught."

'*He* was caught too, not yet shaved & without his best coat, but unruffled & stayed as he was which was the right thing to do. And unshaved he looked jolly well, he's a good-looking man & lots of men spending hours on their appearance would envy him ... George, Glasdir is worthy of a better pen than mine, I said, "What about the move, aren't they awful days?" Yr mother said, "Oh, no, we had beautiful days." And out came your diagrams you had left with Job; child, if you ever produce a play as smoothly as that house, the cast will rise & call you blessed.

'Yr father & mother are nearer perfect happiness than is allowed many mortals, I walked down the hill nearer tears than I usually am. I think I've got the likeness between yr mother & me—straightforwardness. I couldn't get the right word for yr father, I've got it now—we're both buccaneers...'

*   *   *

Walter wrote favourably of *Spring, 1600*, hoping that a costume play would not be too difficult to place. A couple of days later he sent a cutting about John Gielgud's unprecedented success in a new play about Richard II called *Richard of Bordeaux* and I took heart. Also I had never known Miss Cooke so enthusiastic, 'fresh atmosphere of spring and youth...' *Criminal at Large* closed in early March and on our last night Guthrie asked about my plans; I said I was sailing the day after tomorrow and had finished a new play.

'What are you calling it?'

I told him.

' "Spring 1600", that's a Manhattan phone number, is it a murder mystery?' But he added, 'Come and read it to me, is tomorrow night O.K., ten o'clock?'

For my last night in New York I had planned to see *Gay Divorce* but this was worth it. The fact that my play was so British would make his ruthless reaction invaluable.

I arrived to find him just back from a dinner party, in black tie and glittering form—'Can't wait to hear this'—then he went to the phone. 'No calls till I call.'

Before my ordeal he relaxed me with easy talk, then, 'Right!' he said suddenly, placed between us a decanter of brandy so I could 'wet my whistle', sat in the armchair opposite, lit a cigarette and gave me the penetrating look I knew well. It would be my first verdict.

I began. Ann's sad protest before she abandons marriage and takes flight—will he find it affected? *'The windows are locked, so the bride may catch no cold; the swallows brush against the pane, and fly away...'* I felt him sit back to enjoy. After that, he never stirred.

'The meadow waves after the wind, as if the grass would fly too. For it is the quickening of a new century...' If this could do this to a hard-boiled American...

'Stay at home, or let me go with you...' I read out, *'The curtain falls slowly on Act One'*, heard my voice break, and in the silence felt the gimlet eyes on me. I looked diffidently up at them.

They were closed. It had been a good dinner party, and the great director had turned into a sleeping baby. I looked at the decanter. Like me, it was depleted.

I was tempted to leave a note, 'Please phone me at Spring 1600', but refrained. I shut my script, tiptoed to the door and walked home.

In the morning I sent him a telegram, 'Thank you for enjoyable engagement'. It crossed one from him to the boat, 'Thanks for performance and friendship love Guthrie'.

He never again mentioned the evening to me, nor I to him. It had made a funny last night in the New wide-awake World.

CHAPTER TWENTY-FOUR

REBUILDING FOR SPRING

I had been away six months. At Southampton, looking down from s.s. *Majestic* at the waiting crowd, I was surprised to pick out Bill.

He looked no better, no worse; in the train he had little news. No inquiries from Connies, my film agent; his Maugham play had been a distinguished failure and *Men of Tomorrow* had achieved the West End distinction—unusual for a film—of being hissed off the screen, which seemed to explain 'No inquiries'.

In the flat, Bill had broken four tumblers and singed an arm-chair but Mrs Tilley had patched it and *Richard of Bordeaux* was the talk of London, which reminded him of a letter in his pocket. It was from Walter, telling me that Gielgud had read *Spring, 1600* and wanted to direct it. I could not have hoped for such a golden apple, and here it was in my palm.

Bill was philosophical about having worked three months out of twelve; I asked the personal questions. There had been the odd adventure, and one night he'd met a delightful woman in Old Ben's flat and brought her back; yes, on the rug in front of the gas fire.

When he asked about New York, I realized that apart from the stray peccadillo there had been nothing, unless you count two enjoyable affairs with a typewriter.

'All those weeks?' Bill said. 'What a waste.'

It seemed pointless for him to move out now that I was free of him, and I suggested he stay on 'for the time being'.

'I hoped you'd say that,' he said with a childish smile. He was hopeless.

I was only half-free.

❊   ❊   ❊

Dad's welcome-home letter from Glasdir brought me once more abreast of the international film situation, embedding journalistic titbits in his own idiom.

'We see by our Film Weekly that the whole British caboodle is on its feet with this formidable new Company Gaumont-British under such stalwarts as the Ostrer Brothers and Michael Balcon, they sound a sharp lot and will be after your services in a jiffy for you to put your foot in the World of Celluloid.'

I ought to get him on to the staff at Connies. *Men of Tomorrow* may have been hissed in London but it was hailed at the Hip, Connah's Quay. 'In the course of the film I noticed that while you were going through your Antics your dear Mother was smiling, now this is a credit to you personally.'

I rang Gielgud. 'I love your play, do come round tomorrow eleven-thirty, goodbye.'

He had spoken so quickly I could barely understand him and even I, uneasy on the phone and inclined to curtail any call, was left looking at the receiver. After New York, he had sounded like a melodious machine-gun.

I enjoyed my first red bus past the flowering parks; then a walk past the New, RICHARD OF BORDEAUX JOHN GIELGUD. Along the side and round the corner, the pit-stools for the matinée; at the box-office, a long queue. I studied the large photographs of Richard. With the crown to which he had been born set on the long blond hair, the robes flowing, the etched mouth sensitive and fired with the defiance of spoilt youth, the nobly androgynous figure struck a new note in the theatre. I watched three schoolgirls stare at him, bemused, then turn and join the queue.

In 7 Upper St Martin's Lane I climbed steep, narrow stairs to a top flat. I had never met Gielgud except for the occasional hello, when he seemed affable but a little haughty; though he was little more than two years older than me, I felt in awe of him. Knowing of his fanatical dedication to his work I was prepared for an impeccable room with one good painting, a classical bust and lofty talk about Shakespeare with a couple of reverent acolytes hovering.

The door was opened by Richard Clowes; I was relieved, he would ease my visit. As I followed him up more stairs—he was in his long overcoat, as if he were just leaving—he said without turning round, 'John gave me your play, hope you don't mind, I think it's beautiful.' Once more he made it sound a simple truth and I was cheered.

Music, from a fine gramophone; I guessed Bach. After my dra-

matic records the severe beat of phrase after disciplined phrase
was a little chilling, and prepared me for the impeccable room.

It was nothing of the sort, being unpretentiously small with
good furniture and family pictures and comfortably lived in by
bachelors, with many books and play-scripts. Dick introduced me
to John Perry, who shared the flat: he was my age, tall, gauntly
handsome with thinning hair and a mocking manner which contrived to hide a kind heart. 'Dickie, you're not house-trained, how
many times have I told you?'

He turned to me. 'Spends the morning with his nose in the
theatre column, then leaves the papers all over the floor like dirty
laundry. Dickie, I bet you don't get away with that at The
Laurels.'

Bach beat flawlessly out. The talk, casual and free as thought,
was typical of mornings to come.

'John Perry, that's unkind, my family live in Surbiton but the
house is not called The Laurels.'

'It'll always be The Laurels to me, Richard Clowes, you've got
suburbia written all over you. You must be boiling, why don't
you take that overcoat off, haven't you got anything on underneath?'

Richard Clowes seemed not to have heard. Picking up his newspapers, he asked if John G. was still asleep.

'He's in the bathroom massaging the old temples, I keep telling
him it's no use playing Canute, we'll both be bald by forty.'

The phone rang. John P. answered it and called down the
stairs, 'Get your roller-skates on, it's Basil Dean!' It was like
being in digs on tour.

Gielgud hurried in, bare-legged and with the familiar dragging
stride. The shabby old dressing-gown suggested a toga, the white-
lathered cheeks the beard of a Senator and the shaving-brush a
sliver of papyrus. Yes, the twenty-eight-year-old hair was receding.

'So sorry, Basil, I was shaving . . .' Behind the musical machine-
gun there was a nervous deference. 'Very kind of you but if all
goes well I'll be directing the new Maugham, thank you so much,
goodbye.'

He hung up, strode to the door and turned. 'When I remember
how beastly he was to me when I took over from Nöel in *The
Nymph* Emlyn how nice to see you again'—a quick smile as he

shook hands with me as if we were fully dressed in a restaurant—
'did you love America? Dean called it an understudy performance and you should have heard him just now, it's a mad world,
me masters!'

A giggle of pleasure, unexpected and high-pitched, and he was
gone. Bach tinkled into silence.

John P. prepared coffee, I looked at a book, Dick read the
papers. 'Here's a snap of Garbo, she looks so like an aunt of mine
I can never take her seriously...'

John G. returned from the bedroom, elegant from head to foot
in a light spring suit. He put on the other side of Bach, sat back
in an armchair, closed his eyes with a sigh and looked completely
exhausted. 'Oh dear...'

I thought the conversation might now take a more elevated
turn, and was glad it did not. John P. said, 'We've been touching
on the hair situation.'

'Don't, I'm only happy in a hat or on the stage. Why can't men
lunch out in hats like women? The women *have* their hair, it's
the men who need the hats. I mean look at Dickie here, his
widow's peak's practically in his glasses, it's not fair.'

'That's not hair,' John P. said, 'it's wire-wool.'

'Pray continue,' Dick said, opening another newspaper, 'you
make me sound irresistible. God took one look at me and said,
"Must compensate for all that, we'll take the hair away from the
beautiful ones and give it to this poor old thing."'

John G. gave a quick look at my forehead. 'You're as lucky as
Dick, aren't you?'

John P. caught my eye and gave a delighted laugh. 'Things
that could be better put, you'll get used to it.' In most people there
exists between mind and tongue a brake which swiftly advises
rephrasing or even 'Don't say it at all'. The Gielgud brake was
missing.

'They say thin hair means you're brainy, I wonder if one *could*
get away with putting "To be or not to be" before the scene with
the Players, I'd love to try it. I may be losing my hair but that
was the seventh offer since yesterday morning, isn't it marvellous?'

'Marvellous,' John P. murmured, 'so long as you aren't losing
your head as well.'

Dick turned a newspaper page, 'I wouldn't think there's much

chance of that with you around.' He knew them better than he
had implied.

John G. sighed again. 'Must remember to tell Jimmy to order
three hundred more postcards, after the show I sit signing them
in my costume as people come round. Yes, John, I know it's vulgar
but I can't resist it, I'm a Star!'

After the crow of an excited child, he sat back again and closed
his eyes. Dick turned a page, 'Good notice for last night's play in
Auntie *Times*, didn't you see a run-through?'

When the answer came, the pale fastidious Roman profile was
as perfectly married to the music as it was divorced from the
words. 'Yes, I did. It was piss, oh dear . . .'

He again looked exhausted. I was soon to understand that it
was a physical attitude as habitual as it was deceptive. He was
never tired, had a constitution composed of a million fine tough
wires, and 'oh dear' meant that the mind was wheeling like a
kestrel preparing to pounce, direction unpredictable.

'And so badly acted, do you like Bach or hate it?' The head
jerked up and the young death-mask flashed back into life. 'Dick
don't you think this bit would make a thrilling background for a
very cold-blooded *Duchess of Malfi* murder?'

He talked; out of the machine-gun, interspersed with schoolboy
puns, the names followed one another like grapeshot, I almost
needed footnotes. 'The girls' were the firm of 'Motley', three-
brilliant young designers he had discovered for *Richard of Bordeaux* and 'Bronnie' was his presenter, Bronson Albery. He
addressed himself to me, with a courtesy which made it hardly
noticeable that after each question no breathing-space was
allotted for my answer.

'The girls would do *Malfi* marvellously and so cheaply, have
you seen *Mata Hari*? I wept buckets but then I cry at everything,
John says the tears start when I see the Censor's certificate. D'you
know anything about the new Cagney film when was *Malfi* last
done . . . ?'

Without warning, the eyes fixed me like a searchlight. 'I loved
your play, how d'you feel about the last act? But there's so much
to it, Peggy for the girl d'you think, or Jessica or Celia? What
about Edna? She was beastly to me too in *The Nymph* but she
has quality. Then there's Angela, she wouldn't play it Baddeley
but Edna might be Best'—a shrill cackle, then the director again

—'I'll show it to Bronnie when we've got the last act right, you've done it so well...'

I left to the pulsating strains of César Franck. The passers-by in St Martin's Lane looked dull. There were many more stools round the New, and the box-office queue was even longer.

It was not going to be the plain sailing I had imagined, but I was uplifted.

❄   ❄   ❄

On my first visit to my parents' new home it felt odd to be getting out at Queensferry, two stations before the Quay. I walked up Aston Hill, and as I turned into the semi-circle of new bungalows the western sun was turning them into a serene village.

When I saw GLASDIR on the garden gate, I was glad it wasn't HOLLYWOOD. As I opened the gate the front door opened, Dad had been watching for me. He looked better than for years as he pumped my arm, 'Croeso i Glasdir, welcome to Glasdir!' Mam stood in the hall. 'Well, well...' I pursued the new habit and kissed her.

I hardly needed my swift conducted tour, I might have stayed here many times. It looked like a show house at the Ideal Homes Exhibition. The bathroom I kept to the last. In the living-room, for my benefit Dad settled into his armchair, rocked back and fro to show off the springs, then—to symbolize his retirement —crossed hands over his waistcoat and feigned sleep.

Out of habit, I wriggled behind the table on to the old horse-hair sofa where I had always sat reading. My mother knelt on the divan and parted the lace curtain an inch. 'There's that little Bronwen.'

'In 314a,' Dad said, 'your Mam had nothing but the trains. Here she don't miss a move, she'd do well as a bobby in mufti.'

He went out by the kitchen door and the little girl ran up to him. 'In the mornin's,' Mam said, 'he goes round the estate as he calls it and knows all the children by their names.'

I asked if he missed the Works. 'No, once a week he takes the bus down to that Station Hotel in Shotton to see his old mates. They make a fuss of him and he has his pint and shows his cuttin's and back for his dinner.'

After supper in the living-room, Dad winked and looked at Mam, sitting opposite him plaiting her white hair ready for bed.

She rose and produced a tray with three small glasses, a jug of water, and a half-bottle which looked familiar. White Label Whisky.

Solemnly she poured out three tots, placed a glass before each of us, took hers and sat in her armchair.

'I couldn't put it in a letter,' Dad said, 'but she's took to the drink. With the blood pressure, one is *my* ration.' To see my mother, after the hard years, sitting with a whisky in her hand, was too good to be true.

Miss Cooke had not exaggerated, she was at peace at last. And so was he.

✻   ✻   ✻

Back in 71a I found Bill on the rampage, and on hang-over morning it was amicably settled that he would go back to his little room over the garage.

Which meant that for the first time I was living alone in the flat. Walking in the evening, I looked down into lighted basement sitting-rooms, each with its own domestic tableau, and hated going back.

A morning session with John G. pulled me out of myself; just the two of us, we went through the first act of *Spring, 1600* in detail. He had made a close study and produced suggestion after suggestion, each bringing the script to stage life imaginatively and yet realistically. Many he had noted down, but even more came as he talked. 'I've got it—suppose we start music in the house here instead of there, then we could move the . . .' It was like a vigorous game of tennis.

My living-room suddenly looked shabby: the armchairs showed birthmarks, floorboards had lost their stain, the carpet was thread-bare in the sun. I thought for half a minute, put my cheque-book in my pocket, took the 29 bus to Tottenham Court Road, walked into Maple's, the enormous furniture store, and asked for Mr Fairby.

Duggie had swallowed his Long Bar pride and was now a floor-walker. He had always behaved carefully even when loung-ing, but I hardly recognized the sedate figure which now advanced towards me down a long strip of carpet, in swallow-tail coat, black waistcoat, striped trousers and pearl tie-pin.

His smile broadened when I told him I wanted to spend a hundred pounds. Something told me this was not the way to shop, but I had rejected the idea of bargain-hunting at sales for days on end; my impulse was irresistible. For Duggie it was a windfall, and he showed me round with the quiet ecstasy he would have accorded to Royalty.

Sofa, two armchairs in a warm golden pattern to go with my orange curtains, desk, sideboard and upright chairs in dark wood carved into little arches which gave a mediaeval look. A jar-shaped table-lamp in heavy glass, coloured a rich dark violet. Above all, wall-to-wall carpeting. When I left, Duggie was as happy as I was.

Film bulletin from Dad: 'We see by our F. Weekly that their annual poll for the British actor or actress is under way and readers are invited to vote for Leslie Howard or Herbert Marshall or Edna Best or Emlyn Williams or Ivor Novello, etc. I give you one guess how we are voting. We are sorry to read that the Crawford–Fairbanks marriage is cooling...'

The Late Christopher Bean would go into rehearsal in a week. I had forgotten all about it.

I told Gilbert Miller I would stand by for dialogue queries, but as I had so little to do with the play would prefer to stay away. There was one use for me. Edith Evans was less to do with Wales than her name implied, and Miller asked me to coach her in the accent.

She was playing, in *Once in a Lifetime*, the unlikely part of a wise-cracking American secretary, and had waits in the middle of the play. Every evening for a week I walked up to the Queen's in time for them.

Aged forty-five and at the height of her powers, she had the eager enthusiasm of a young girl. Though she normally talked a great deal and fluently, when she came to discuss the part her vocabulary halted and she made me think of Epstein, feeling his way in an instinctive dark.

'Must be sure first what she *looks* like. Gwenny's simple isn't she, *simple*...And clean. Apron spotless, shoes worn but *polished*, hair brushed and brushed and then parted in the middle perhaps and back to a bun, now read to me...'

I spoke her lines with slow care, like a schoolmaster. When she started, stumblingly, to speak the same lines she reminded me now of Laughton as she shut her eyes and felt her way into

Gwenny's apron: an attempt extraordinary to watch in an actress who sat before me boldly made up, dressed and hair-styled as a smart American woman.

She repeated after me like a child, but behind the lines I could see starting a ferment of creation. Then the call-boy's knock. 'Lawks, I've got to get back into America!' and she was gone.

The schoolmaster had a promising pupil who, with application, should do well.

* * *

I rang Molly—back from staying with Polly in Bordighera—to ask her and Jack for a drink. She arrived without him, tanned and glowing in an Italian dress. 'But the room looks marvellous...'

I asked about Jack, and the confidences came slowly but easily: the reason she had gone was that he had paid her fare, having left her for Phyllis Weaver, a small-part actress playing in *Wild Violets* at Drury Lane. She had caught him out before, which puzzled me; I had never envisaged him even as an importunate husband, never mind a roving one.

'After seven years,' she said, 'what a waste,' and her lip trembled. 'Cheer up,' I said jokingly, 'at least there isn't a little Carus-Wilson toddling around asking where Daddy is.'

'Golly, yes, that would be awful.' I asked her why there wasn't one.

'I don't know really, I don't think there's anything wrong with me. It's just that it never happened properly, somehow...' Her voice trailed into silence.

I decided to shock her out of depression, 'Get him out of your system by having a marvellous affair!'

Her face brightened. 'But I have!'

I looked at her, delighted. 'You have?'

'In Bordighera.'

'Tell me.' Encouraging a girl to describe her lover was a new experience, and an agreeable one; he was Russian, Count Dimitri Something. 'Does that mean you're going to be a Countess?'

No, he hadn't a penny; Polly had told her he was a gigolo but he was a darling and Dima to his friends... Oh, utterly different from Jack, only a year older than her, not very tall, dark, very Russian and a marvellous dancer, they had danced 'La Cucharacha' over and over again, in the Wonder Bar.

'The important thing is,' I said, 'was he a good lover?'

Her face lit up again, like a child's. 'Marvellous, I realize now that I hadn't known what sex could be like, we used to go walking up into the hills.' She had always been fun, but always fun-with-a-husband; this was a new side to me. I saw her and that hot-blooded little Russian devil abandoned on a scented Italian hill-side. The picture pleased me, and made me happy for her.

'Polly didn't approve but I didn't care, I thought it would make me forget about Jack. It hasn't, of course, but it was fun . . .' She asked about me and I told her about Rouen and Montreal and Marseilles.

She was living in a spare room in some girl's mews-flat in Belgravia, and had just started as an assistant in Pellier's, a small dressmaking establishment in Bond Street: two pounds a week 'plus commission'. Madam Pellier was a hard-faced woman who said 'Molly' was a vulgar name and insisted on 'Margaret'. 'The trouble is that when she screams into the basement for Margaret it never crosses my mind it's me she's after.'

She tried to make it funny, but looked suddenly so woebegone that I gave her a second gin-and-tonic. She curled up on the sofa. 'Oh, to sit back in a comfortable room . . .' The raid on Maple's had been worth it.

It had done her good to talk. I got her out an armful of books and walked her to her deserted mews, where I kissed her good-night. Tripping up the dark stairs, she looked small and lonely.

I should have asked her to dinner, and would have if there had been a third person. Which meant that however simple the rela-tionship, I was shy of a tête-à-tête with a woman.

A complex which made for a dull evening.

✳   ✳   ✳

After more stimulating sessions with J.G., in mid-May came the dress rehearsal of *The Late Christopher Bean*. Although there was only a handful of audience, I enjoyed the play as much as I had in New York. So much so that I wanted to enjoy it again in a packed theatre, and for the first night Bill and I stood at the back of the pit.

From the first moment the play was a success, and I was proud to have had a little to do with it; at the end, the audience gave a roar which continued into the National Anthem as Bill and I hurried into King Street. We waited to watch the outpour into the foyer.

It did not happen. Nobody was coming out. We went back; the curtain was still down, the auditorium still fully lit and the audience still applauding. And on its feet. In the British theatre, such an occurrence after the Anthem was unprecedented.

The curtain finally rose on a ragged line of bewildered actors: silence for speeches. We left again; I felt so exhilarated I took Bill to supper at the Troc.

Taking out my programme, I was about to open it when I sat back with a jerk.

The cover read 'GILBERT MILLER presents THE LATE CHRISTOPHER BEAN adapted from René Fauchois' Comedy BY EMLYN WILLIAMS.'

CHAPTER TWENTY-FIVE

UNDER FALSE PRETENCES

As Bill was asking me what the matter was I jumped up and hurried to a phone. From the Savoy, Miller's secretary, Gertrude Butler, was radiant. 'Mr Miller says in all his experience this is unique ...'

'There's a serious mistake in the programme ...'

'Oh dear, have they spelt your name wrong?'

'It's Sidney Howard, he's not in it!'

'Oh that ... Mr Miller felt that three authors might give a handle to the critics, too many cooks, et cetera, and Sidney said he's working on two new plays and quite happy so don't mention him to the Press—congratulations, aren't you thrilled?'

When I went back to Bill he was studying the programme. 'The critics,' I said, 'know I know French and will assume I've adapted it direct ...'

'What of it? I can't imagine it being by anybody but you, you've got the most enormous success on your hands ...'

'It's not on my hands, it's on Sidney Howard's ...' I went to bed with feelings more mixed than any playwright before or since.

Next day: 'gloriously hilarious ...', '... terrific ...'. 'The author watched his brilliant play from the back of the pit ...'

The doorbell rang. It was a girl from the *Sunday Dispatch*, with a photographer for whom I assumed the surprised smile of success. They could not know how surprised I was. 'Mr Williams, I remember your *Murder on the Second Floor*—sorry, that was Vosper—but this is your first *real* success, would you say?'

An evening paper had a headline EMLYN WILLIAMS NEW PLAY GREATEST HIT FOR MONTHS. I thought of *Glamour*, walked to a post-office red in the face, cabled Howard WARMEST CONGRATULATIONS ON MY NOTICES and felt better.

As the weeks went by, I almost believed that without one prompt from either France or America I was the author of *The Late Christopher Bean*. Duggie Fairby stopped me in the street, he had just been to see the Hollywood film of it at the Empire, with Marie Dressler. 'But, my dear, how distressed you must have been by them setting your beautiful play in America of all places, they've ruined it!'

I started to explain but he had just hailed a taxi; it seemed best to stop explaining, to anybody, and settle for my royalties.

They were a windfall, and would remain so: from the London run and subsequent tours and repertory productions—NEXT WEEK THE LATE CHRISTOPHER BEAN BY EMLYN WILLIAMS—my two per cent would ultimately add up to a total which one could assess at seven thousand pounds. For a week's tinkering in New York I was to earn at the rate of a thousand pounds a day.

A week after the opening I went into Clemence Dane's new play about the Brontës, *Wild Decembers*, replacing Brian Aherne as Branwell, at five hectic days' notice. My memory of the first night—a top-notch Cochran one starring Diana Wynyard, but unfortunately yet another 'interesting evening'—is of a moment which was a negative one. Had it been positive, it would have spelled disaster.

At the end, during a cordial reception with the principals in line curtseying or bowing, there came a sudden chorus from the gallery: 'Emlyn ... EMLYN!'

Flushed and happy after my five gruelling days, I was about to step out of line and give a quick diffident bow—my foot was just leaving the ground—when I saw Ralph Richardson look at Beatrix Lehmann, who had given a superb performance as my sister. What the gallery was shouting was, 'Emily ... EMILY!'

I handed her forward. It had been a narrow escape.

*   *   *

The play was to have a short run; during my long wait after dying I studied *Spring, 1600*, line by line. Yes, all would come right when that ship was launched; I would work at it till it was perfect ...

A note from Connies, 'Have a look at *Film Weekly* and ring back.'

I only connected the name with Glasdir. Opening the magazine, I stared. A headline, EMLYN WILLIAMS WINS. 'Leading with 7978 votes, he far outstripped Leslie Howard with 6307, Herbert Marshall with 3756 and Jack Hulbert with 1721 . . .'

My first thought was of Dad: he had been right, of course his son was a Film Star. I rang Connies, they had been rung by Gaumont-British; I could tell that it was as if I were living quietly in Hollywood and being told that M.G.M. had phoned.

The front office had glanced at Dad's favourite reading and noted that all the top candidates were under contract to them, with one exception: the winner. And G.B. wanted to put that right by offering me a three-year contract as actor 'but also as writer, they were very impressed by your *Christopher Bean*'.

First year, a hundred pounds a week, then—if the option were taken up—second year a hundred and fifty, third year two hundred. Big money.

I could hardly refuse and went in with open eyes. As to the parts to be played or the scripts to be written, I might be called upon to do anything. If I were to act on the stage, they would be entitled to half my stage salary. No quarrel with that, and I was also assured that I would have plenty of time off to indulge in my hobby of writing plays, provided they had first refusal of film rights. Fair, and flattering. They had 'nothing specific in mind for me yet' but I would be on the pay-roll from the following week, June the 1st. Between everything I was becoming rich.

But I found that being comfortably off does not stop you finding things on your mind. I had two.

First, *Spring, 1600*. Morning sessions with John G. continued to stimulate and as we worked, the gramophone played Purcell and Byrd himself. Our down-to-earth tidying and improving— 'Why shouldn't *she* have the line instead? Much funnier, no I've got a still better idea'—was illuminated by the background of flute and clavichord.

It began to echo plaintively in my sleep, and in my sleep I smelt the herbs of an Elizabethan garden and the wind of adventure. I could not be satisfied until all that was put together on the stage: the simple gaiety of the country scene, the bawdy tang of the playhouse, the sweet Byrd-song of unrequited love. Patience.

July, the last week of *Wild Decembers*. A special morning with John G. devoted to Act Three. He felt that Lady Coperario was such a colourful character—'whores always are, let's call it "Whores for Tennis" '—that she must carry on into the third act.

'Then Isabel Jeans might consider it, perhaps a scene in her palatial lodgings, with a couple of dabs of paint the Motleys would make them look like gorgeous Tiepolo draperies, a rostrum on wheels perhaps, Burbage drunk on her bed, panic in the theatre...'

He made it sound thrilling. Then home for an interview with Margaret Lane, a very pretty girl who was becoming a prominent journalist, 'the *Mail* want to do a whole page'. Life wasn't so bad.

The second matter on my mind was Bill. Our relationship was now easy, we met every other day for a meal and if sober he often stayed the night. He was proud of my progress, bumpy though it could be. 'Your ears must have been burning, Cedric was in the Club talking about you to Richardson and du Maurier.' When I told him of the film contract, he patted my knee and smiled. 'Little did I think when I saw that quiet kid rehearsing *On the Spot*...'

But still no work. How did he live?

I was nagged by the fact that I could be lending him money. No, not lending—I remembered Miss Cooke—*giving*. But to offer help to an out-of-work actor is to imply that he will never work again; and if I had, it would have gone on 'the chaps at the Club'.

Sometimes, looking at him through my mother's eyes as he sat tranquilly by my fire reading a Maugham short story or chuckling over the young Evelyn Waugh, I was as baffled as a Chinese faced with a Western custom. Without a penny in the bank at the age of forty-six, how could he sleep at night?

I loved him, but could do nothing for him.

❖   ❖   ❖

The Friday after the play closed I rang Molly. Pellier's was no better, but Sonny was back in Thames Ditton—Polly still in Italy —and had suggested her coming down for week-ends for the rest of the summer and keeping house for him, and could I come down? I knew I would be happy there.

On Saturday morning I walked to Number 37 The Island

carrying my typewriter and a bottle of whisky. Sonny was in a deck-chair reading, Molly cooking lunch.

I sank on to the lawn, wound up the gramophone—one of the old records, 'Tip-toe Through The Tulips'—lay back with closed eyes and floated in summer. I loved the tinny jaunty tune, but my heart was with the fluting airs of another century.

I asked Molly about her life. 'Just the same . . . No, not a penny, I don't think he ever will . . . Never mind, it's lovely here, let's put on another record.'

It was an effort to go in and work on my last act. I emerged at lunch-time to find Sonny reading the Margaret Lane interview, 'Look at the headline, VILLAGE BOY WHO MADE GOOD, I say! . . .' A man friend of his arrived for dinner and afterwards he and Molly took turns punting us round the moonlit island; then we sat on the lawn so late that the visitor missed his last train.

He suggested sleeping on the lawn, but it would get coldish later. He could hardly share Sonny's marriage bed, so it was decided after much ribaldry that he would have my cubicle and I would share the big double bed in Molly's room, where she had once or twice stayed with Jack.

'After all,' I said, 'we know each other well enough! Though we might as well put that sword between us, she's still a married woman.'

They saw us to bed: many jokes but nobody was embarrassed. For both of us it had been a long sun-struck day of work and play. We were soon asleep, and when I woke she was already making breakfast. I got into my bathing shorts and went in to help her: 'In the middle of the night I did think of waking you up with a thick Russian accent, then thought that would be cheating.'

'Ah,' she said, 'dear Dima,' and poured out cornflakes.

We travelled up early, I dropped her at Pellier's by taxi, then walked to my bank and drew out thirty pounds in pound-notes— I felt a large amount would be unsuitable—wrote on a piece of paper in block letters A PRESENT FROM VILLAGE BOY WHO MADE GOOD and posted it to MRS CARUS-WILSON.

I was worried about her.

※　　※　　※

I had just finished my last act when the phone rang. 'This is Angus MacPhail, how are you?'

He sounded like a plummy Oxford don. 'Could you bear to make tomorrow your first day at the office?' I thought, wrong number . . .

'I'm so sorry, this is Gaumont-British, the same initials as something far less important, Great Britain. We're to work together, if you could bear it . . .'

I took the bus to Shepherd's Bush and walked to the side street enshrining the Mecca of the British Film Industry: an immense glittering beehive. Following a messenger boy, I felt apprehension; but expecting Hollywood bravado enthroned in Hollywood plush I found neither.

Mr MacPhail, a lean young intellectual with a cynical gleam hovering over his glasses, sat behind his desk in a small plainly furnished room. He seemed straight from Eton, Oxford and the Café Royal and knew Dick Clowes. It was a relief.

We had hardly shaken hands—'Victor's blowing in any minute, he'll be directing this'—when he did indeed blow in: Victor Saville, a bouncing business man who radiated rosy confidence in himself and in others. Birmingham-born, *né* Salberg, after much success directing silent films he had fallen in love with the Talking Pictures. His glasses brimming with enthusiasm, he wreathed us both in smiles and plumped down as if to a toothsome meal.

The meal was *Friday the Thirteenth*, taken from somebody's 'treatment', and I was to furnish the dialogue. A London bus, see, has a handful of passengers when a crane crashes on it and kills some and not others, see? Open with the accident, flash back to the separate lives, who's going to die and who isn't, and lead back to accident at end, all-star cast led by Jessie as a chorus-girl —see what I mean?

'I do see,' Angus said, poker-faced, 'a sort of Bus of San Luis Rey.' Victor roared with delight and slapped his thigh, 'Kid, you've got it! Isn't it a swell idea?'

On a fleeting visit to Hollywood he had picked up, as well as the lingo, one local custom. In full working spate, he sat with a dust-sheet round his neck being serviced, like a Roman senator, by a barber bowed over his head cutting his hair and a blonde crouched at his feet cutting his finger-nails.

Over pencils and wads of paper, between the incongruous

[295]

three of us the suggestions sparked to and fro; names went down, for the film must be crammed with stars and up-and-comings.

I observed one harmless bit of jargon which nevertheless offended me: the Hollywoodese for 'Gary Cooper has accepted the part' was 'I'm using Gary Cooper'. It made actors sound like utensils. 'We'll use Leonora Corbett and Robertson Hare, him trying to get off with her in Hyde Park...'

For me it was a new way to work, an enjoyable game flavoured with power: any suggestion I made could give a fillip to the careers of a dozen players who five years ago had been beyond my reach, 'Had you thought of Frank Lawton?'

'Swell, let's use Frankie... What about your part Emmer-lun?' I suggested a smooth young blackmailer who follows his victim into a hotel lounge. 'I got it, kids, an exact replica of the Regent Palace with back projection, keep it reel...'

So it went on, for several mornings, 'a good yack-yack gets the ball rolling'.

Then we evolved a working schedule: twice a week I read them 'my stuff', we discussed it, I went home, revised it and went ahead. It worked well and trained me to weed luxuriance out of dialogue which had to be streamlined.

And there were diversions. In the Jessie Matthews 'story', her young lover (Ralph Richardson) would be shown buying the chorus-girl flowers. How to get the scene off the ground, huh?

'I got it,' said Victor, his glasses glistening with schoolboy mischief, 'we'll go out on a limb with the guy behind the counter, let's make him a *fairy*! How sophisticated can you get, huh? Oh, we don't *say* so, good God, no, that would be bad taste. No, we'll just have him smelling the flowers and saying, "Sheer heaven!"'

To show how sophisticated he could get, Victor put a hand on one hip, sniffed at imaginary flowers, shut his eyes and said, 'Sheer heaven!' It was terrifying.

I had my foot in the World of Celluloid.

CHAPTER TWENTY-SIX

LONG DAY'S JOURNEY INTO SPRING

By August the script of *Friday the Thirteenth* was buttoned up and the last act of the play back from the typist and in the almighty Albery's hands.

'I have a feeling,' John G. said, 'he'll like it now, the last act's stronger but you never know with him, Bronnie soit qui mal y pense . . .'

Richard of Bordeaux being in its seventh month, its star was given two weeks' holiday, 'to make a break', took a suite in the Royal Crescent, Brighton, littered it with scripts, and asked me and Dick down for a couple of days.

He went for walks between us along the front, the ozone fertilizing his mind with ideas while his eyes spotted theatre faces with the excitement of a Gallery First-Nighter. 'I've got rather a good idea for *A Midsummer Night's Dream*—look, there's Binnie Hale!—to do it nude, or as near as one could go—wouldn't it be superb?'

He made it sound just that, till he added, 'With everybody starkers we could just call it *"Bottom"*,' and shrieked with nursery laughter. Back in the suite, while Dick and I sat on the balcony reading, he would emerge holding his shaving-brush.

'Dickie, we could offer the ham old actor in *Spring* to Frederick Volpé, is he dead?'

'Yes.'

'Oh. Then we couldn't.' Exit.

Another time he would glance imperiously down at a front page, 'I don't like Ramsay MacDonald's face, is he a good Prime Minister?' and was gone.

Dick said, 'The nearest he's ever got to politics is the plot of *Julius Caesar*.'

One rainy afternoon he decided on a night out in London. By now I knew him well enough to guess that he would take us to a theatre, but not well enough to know which one.

After a fine early dinner at the Café Royal, Dick and I found ourselves sitting in the front of a stage box, with the holiday-maker lurking in the shadows. We were at the New Theatre, watching *Richard of Bordeaux*, 'I'm curious to see it from the front.'

As the theatre darkened Dick whispered to me, 'Would you call *this* "making a break"?'

Glen Byam Shaw was playing Richard as a rehearsal for his tour in the part, and playing well. At the end of one emotional scene between the king and his wife, I stole a look behind me: John G. was not just moved, he was weeping. I was in the company of a child playing with double mirrors.

When at the end we hurried through the pass-door, the stage-hands stacking scenery looked through the visitor without recognizing him. They had plainly never seen him in a suit.

Glen was staggered—'Thank God I didn't know'—and delighted by praise generous and sincere. Then John took Dick and me out to supper as if after a first night he had enjoyed.

Dick said, 'John dear, I know the play moved you, but I did once see you lean forward and count the house through your tears.'

'Dickie Clowes, that's a wicked thing to say. Actually it wasn't at all bad, I was surprised...'

*　　*　　*

My holiday from Gaumont-British was broken by my part in *Friday the Thirteenth*: six days' work in a month, during which the money rolled into my bank. But I hated the idleness as much as I had when I was penniless.

Then Bill had good news. He was rehearsing for *The Ace* with Raymond Massey, and I took Molly to the dress rehearsal. A pretty girl who appeared to be wearing several cushions under a smart summer dress squeezed into the front row.

I said, 'Who on earth's that?'

Molly said, 'Isn't it his wife, Adrianne Allen? I read somewhere she's having her first baby.' I wondered if she was thinking of Jack.

But *The Ace* was a failure, and still no pronouncement from the oracle Bronnie.

After aimless evenings with Bill or Dick I would call on John G. in his dressing-room, feeling an intruder because my visit was only in case there might be news. I usually arrived a minute before the last curtain was down and waited in the unnatural silence of his great room, gently smiled on by his great-aunt Ellen Terry in daguerreotype.

Sweeping in, hot and happy, he would give me the same welcome he accorded to all his callers, courteous and absent-minded, sit down in his robes, still painted and bewigged, and sign a couple of dozen postcards as resignedly as if they were death-warrants.

He always talked as he scribbled. 'I gave Ralph Richardson your play and he's very taken with Burbage but on second thoughts he's not right. Burbage needs a combination of his virility and my romantic quality, his is fundamentally a clown's face. I'm afraid I told him so and I do hope it's not the end of a long friendship. Oh dear, Jimmy, this pen needs refilling ...'

Visitors would be announced and Richard the Second would rise to receive them.

One night I arrived later and the one caller still there was spread on the sofa: a stout old lady in a rag-bag of a black evening dress ornamented with what looked like jet. Her hair, an improbable black, was done in old-fashioned loops above a face to which, earlier in the evening, make-up had been applied, hastily and liberally. She looked like a grand theatrical landlady on a night out, who had herself once trod the boards.

'Stella dear, this is Emlyn Williams—Mrs Patrick Campbell.'

'Oh, he won't recognize the name of an old has-been ...'

She would anyway have been identified by a voice imitated in a hundred anecdotes: throaty and over-articulated, sounding anxious to please until you realized that the humble pie was flavoured with arsenic.

It was my first and last meeting with a sacred monster who so perfectly lived up to herself that next day I wrote it down. I waited for the darts, and they came.

John said, 'Emlyn has a great success at the St James's, with Edith and Cedric.' I wondered if the mention of the foremost contemporary actress was the happiest of strokes.

'*Do* tell me more, but you look a *child*, did you write it all by yourself?'

She cannot have known how lethal that dart was. John looked nervous. 'He's adapted it from the French.'

The black eyes fixed on me with horror and there was a weight-lift of beringed fingers, 'Oh, you poor dear, a *translation*?' She made it sound like a dirty book. 'Translations remind me of those short-sighted spinsters slaving over their abominable copies in the Louvre. John, dear, do you remember our *Ghosts*, the pro-gramme should have read "*Mangled* from the Norwegian by William What-was-his-name..." Bowmen? Arrowsmith? *Archer*, that was it...'

She turned to me again, 'Now I've got a *spiffing* idea, why not write a play out of your *very own head*, for a penniless old harri-dan who can still act? Goodbye dear John, such lovely costumes, and goodbye you naughty *cribber*, goodbye...'

❋ ❋ ❋

A phone call from John. 'Dreary news, I'm afraid, Bronnie's turned *Spring* down as too slight for the amount it would cost. Infuriating, of course the last act is still a bit on the thin side...'

He added that he had just accepted to direct the new Maugham play *Sheppey*. Mine was postponed indefinitely. It was a blow.

Summer turned to autumn; I took Molly's advice, got some beech-leaves, dipped the ends in glycerine, pressed them under a rug and arranged them in vases to last the winter, but my heart was not in it.

Dick's faith in *Spring, 1600* was unshakeable, and on one of our gypsy evenings he played with the idea that we should all get the show on between us. His solicitor-father was an intimate of millionairess Lady Ashtead—suppose she put up most of the money, then we might find the rest, John and I might even put up four or five hundred ourselves... No harm in supposing.

But I had another play, the one for which Walter Peacock had prophesied a long amateur life: a life which now took in a very special performance.

'EVENT OF THE YEAR! ASSEMBLY HALL, HOLYWELL. THE OSWESTRY DRAMATIC SOCIETY in EMLYN WILLIAMS'S GREAT PLAY A MURDER HAS BEEN ARRANGED. The Chair will be Taken by Miss S. G. Cooke, M.A., Holywell County School.'

Miss Cooke: 'My speech will begin "When asked to occupy

this Chair, I cld not well refuse." I loathe speeches, hearing 'em, making 'em, anything to do with 'em. Anyway, did you ever hear of anything funnier than a chairman speaking before a drama, in Wales chapel tradition dies hard . . .'

Then Dad, 'We are booking seats to represent the Author's Family, viz his Dad Mam Job, and will take a taxi what ho! . . . Fancy the King and Queen being present in the Royal Box for your Chris Bean, more power to them, I will think of that each time I look at your Coronation Mug when you were 5.'

His verdict: 'We had a good performance of the Murder Business by some top-notchers in the Amateur field, we enjoyed it immensely especially the Taxi part. The only mistake was in the programme where it says By J. Emlyn Williams, Miss Cooke should have taken the stick to the Printers for that. Job said perhaps the J is for Job and he wrote half of the play. Miss Cooke took her part well . . .'

I was glad they were there for that, for she had written 'What I shall tell the audience is—"I wish to pay tribute to E. Wms' home life. Over & over again in my dealings with him I have thought, where has he learnt that, & there was only one answer, his home: that was where he acquired his passion for order & method, his delight in work finished meticulously, in my opinion no boy has ever had more reason to be grateful for home training." I thk you'll approve, anyway I have the urge to say it.'

Just as I was deciding that *Spring, 1600* had turned to frost, an electric boost was provided by, of all agents, Adolf Hitler. For he was the cause of the flight, from the storm, of Germany's most celebrated star: the only stage actress since Bernhardt and Duse to be known by her surname. Bergner. She had arrived in England as mysteriously as a North Sea fog and was hermetically sealed 'in outer London'.

One morning, however, her secret leaked into the Press in the form of headlines. She was 'under secret contract' to Cochran to star in any play she chose, FEY GENIUS NOW OURS . . . THE STAR MARLENE WORSHIPPED FROM THE WINGS! . . . 'The boyish quality which has made her the ideal Saint Joan, Constant Nymph, Viola . . .'

John G., Dick and I read this separately. Each phoned the others and all met at Number 7. John said, 'I feel it in my bones, this is meant to be.'

Dick struck a note of realism, faint but out of tune. 'Die Kleine has never ge-played in englisch, ja? I bet she's got an accent you could cut with a knife. What do we change Ann Byrd to, Anna von Vögel?'

But John was ready. 'Byrd sent his daughter at an early age to relatives in Germany, I'll ring Cocky.'

Dick persisted. 'You mean he'd had a German first wife?'

By now I was on John's side. 'Who's to know, except the *Sunday Times* music critic?'

He did ring Cochran, and after hanging up said, 'She's got fifty offers already, they're pouring in like circulars.'

It was agreed that I should deliver the script myself with a covering letter from John. As I watched him compose it in his meticulous spidery writing, I hoped he was not adding a P.S. to the effect that the last act was thin.

By three o'clock I was hurrying down a prim avenue in Golder's Green, an errand boy with a parcel. I rang the bell at a villa and delivered it: Bergner had her fifty-first offer. At the gate I ran into a messenger boy about to deliver her fifty-second.

*　　*　　*

Luckily I was able to banish Bergner from my mind for several weeks, otherwise the tension would have been grim.

After *Friday the Thirteenth* had opened at the Tivoli as a big money-maker, I stepped back on to the golden treadmill for the zestful assembly of 'another winner'. My assignment was the whole screenplay of *Evergreen*, an ambitious musical film with Rodgers songs and starring 'our Jessie'. Then, at the moment my script was 'in the bag' there came, via the exiled German underground, an unbelievable message. Accidentally, John had met an intimate of Mr and Mrs Czinner (Bergner), an inarticulate refugee who whispered to him that of the hundred scripts Elizabeth had been offered she liked my play the best and was making up her mind this week.

Should John ring Cocky? We decided not. We would tell nobody till all was signed and sealed.

For days I floated on a cloud anchored in reality. What more likely than a little English girl reared in Germany returning with a broken accent? ...

We waited a week. A week and a half.

One afternoon Bill turned up at the flat smiling with good news. He had just signed a contract to play a nice part, forty a week, run guaranteed. I was overjoyed. 'Tell me more!'

'What's so good about it is that it's for Cochran. He's presenting Bergner in her first play here.'

Was he to play Burbage?

'It's called *Escape Me Never* by the author of *The Constant Nymph*, and we open in Manchester on November the 20th and at the Apollo before Christmas, isn't it incredible?'

'Incredible,' I said, sat down, and buried the still-born dream of being associated with Europe's greatest star. In the same grave I deposited William Byrd's German wife and all her relatives.

*　　*　　*

The next day was a bad one. Lunch at a cafeteria, a drift in the rain to a cinema, and halfway through the picture a drift to another. Home by six, demoralized, I lit the fire and turned on the lamps. The dried beech-leaves threw pictorial shadows on the ceiling, the room was cheerful. I was not. I put on a record and looked blankly into the fire. 'Scheherezade.'

The bell. Bill, he was not yet rehearsing and had had a convivial celebration at the Club. I was glad to see him happy about his job. Behind him, a shadowy figure.

' 'Lo, ole boy, I brought a pal, all right? We got acquainted just before lunch, didn't we chum? Emlyn, this is Fess.'

They followed me upstairs.

'Short for Festiniog,' Fess explained. 'You see, Dad was born in Blaenau Ffestiniog in North Wales same as you, Emlyn, and wanted me christened with the whole lot, but Mam wouldn't hear of it so Fess is what I am.'

He laughed, shyly but surely.

We were all three standing up in front of the fire, with the bold music beating behind us. Fess was twenty, half an inch taller than me, dark hair brushed correctly back, grey eyes, short nose and full lips loose enough for you to wonder how they could retain the tag-end of a cigarette.

His accent was Welsh enough to disarm me with a swirl of childhood memories, but free of the over-vivacity which on first acquaintance, before a current has had time to connect, can fuse it. The voice had flat inflections, the few sustained sentences rambling on without punctuation but with a slow incongruous charm. He was a country boy; what made him sexual in his own way was, instead of rosy cheeks and perfect teeth, a transparent pallor which spelt smoky saloon bars, and—when he smiled lazily—a top tooth missing, just far enough from the centre not to be unsightly.

The gap gave an effect of abandon: I'm not bothering about me looks I'm O.K. as I am, what d'you think? He was a rustic with a quiet self-confidence. I suggested a drink.

'I should say so,' said Bill, 'we've been boozing slowly but steadily, eh Fess, ole boy?'

After the grey day, and the weeks of yack-yacking about how to display our Jessie, and—on another level—how to get a costume play on, in two minutes I was comfortable. I closed the curtains against the winter night, the same orange curtains Bill and I had lived with in Marchmont Street.

The fire burnt bright. I poured them a weak whisky each, myself a stronger one to catch up. We sat down in my Maple's three-piece suite, they in the two armchairs, I on the sofa.

Bill said, 'God, this is good . . .' The firelight and his Bergner contract seemed to make him look years younger, flushed and beaming.

Then he leant over to me and said, drunkenly but not too drunkenly, 'My dearest boy, you've had a disappointment which has brought me luck, and I love you very much.'

The tipsy truth of it got home to me, and when he patted Fess on the knee it reminded me of Wellington Mansions: of the night when he and I became friends. I felt relaxed and warmly wishful for pleasure.

Fess grinned, widely enough to display the tooth-gap.

'Scheherezade' crashed to its climax, and in the silence you could see the oriental floor writhing with ecstatic bodies. I got up and turned off the gramophone.

❖   ❖   ❖

When I left them at Victoria I felt closer to Bill than I had for months. 'Bye, bye, old boy . . .'

Fess said, 'As one Welshman to another, pleased to meet ya, ta ta for now . . . ' As he went his way I thought, I was pleased to meet ya too, but as often happens it's ta-ta for ever . . .

Joining Dick at a pub, I decided the day had not turned out too bad after all. Dick, moreover, had good news. His shadowy plan for *Spring, 1600* was acquiring momentum.

And by the end of November, incredibly, the production was set. The posters would read 'John Gielgud and Richard Clowes present', which would be the front for a syndicate with a capital of £2,500, the investors being Lady Ashtead principally, then John G., Dick's father, Victor Saville, Michael Balcon, myself and Bill Linnit, whose office would handle the play.

Casting meant fevered mornings in Number 7, with the Gielgud mind wheeling and pouncing. '*I* know, Ian Hunter would be *splendid* as Burbage . . .' One coup. Now that Lady Coperario was a stronger part, Isabel Jeans accepted.

But Ann Byrd was the crux. 'Jessie Tandy's in the Ackland play, Peggy if you can believe it is going into the Charell musical farrago at the Coliseum. Who does she think she is, Phyllis Dare? Angela's on tour with Glen in *Bordeaux*—with Bronnie's shilly-shallying we've lost them all, oh dear . . .' The king sat back, sick unto death.

Dick weighed in, unexpectedly. 'I've been thinking about Joyce Bland, I think she'd be perfect.'

It was a startling suggestion: she had made a great success, in *Children in Uniform*, as a beautiful and enigmatic schoolmistress in her thirties.

'But Dick . . .'

'She was playing a character part, she's twenty-seven which makes her—if it interests you—six years younger than a little kleine Fräulein who let us down not so long ago. She could look like a special sort of boy, tallish and solemn, away from that Peter Pan image, I'm for Joyce Bland . . .'

But next morning the *Daily Mirror* displayed a picture of Edna Best, back from Hollywood and in Hyde Park wheeling a pram containing her daughter Sarah.

The king revived. 'But she looks sixteen! . . . Marvellous pathos and comedy and I rather enjoy the thought of employing somebody who's been rude to me, where's she staying?'

Dick said, 'She'll never say yes . . .'

[305]

But she did.

'Wonderful,' John said, 'but who's going to tell Isabel?'

When Miss Jeans had accepted a part second to that of a leading lady, not yet cast, who would probably be less high-powered than herself, she had made an understandable concession. But Miss Best was a star too.

Bill Linnit was appointed envoy, and his report of Miss Jean's admirable reaction was exact. 'Edna? What a good idea, she's thirty-three but one hears she's lost weight and with lighting she'll be marvellous, how's the marriage going?'

*   *   *

Being in a position to suggest friends for jobs, I put forward Freddie Mell for ASM, back from Australia with the aureole of fair hair thinner and the rest thicker.

When it got to the large crowd being chosen I had a first-rate idea: Molly was engaged to walk on and speak lines 'as required' for four pounds a week. 'After Madam Pellier it'll be like a dream, so long as nobody calls me Margaret.'

On December the 8th *Escape Me Never* opened at the Apollo. BERGNER TRIUMPHS, WILL RUN A YEAR. I concentrated on my elation for Bill. His wolf, tired of pawing at the door, had retired to the gate.

I spent Christmas at Glasdir, the breather before the race. Over the bedtime whisky my father drank 'i'r Gwanwyn', to Spring.

Mam said, 'It says in the paper this play goes back three hundred years. It's the first old-fashioned one you've done, isn't it?'

I met Job's five-month-old son. David Emlyn. 'He's a nice little boy,' said Dad, 'our first grandchild.' I was again conscious of being three years older than the grandchild's father.

The next afternoon Dad and I made a curious excursion: down the hill to the cemetery. It had occurred to Mam that as they would be spending the rest of their lives in Glasdir, it would be a good idea to choose 'a nice plot'. 'Your Mother,' said Dad as we walked, 'was always one to look ahead.'

After choosing a nice plot we passed a very old lady depositing a posy on an oblong of crushed stones. Dad whispered, 'She's from our part.' As she walked away I looked at the headstone,

venerable and mossy. 'LLEWELYN POWELL 1835–1895, AGED 60.'
Underneath, to match, 'HIS BELOVED WIFE REBECCA 1839–18 ,
AGED , MAY THEY REST IN PEACE.'

I said it was funny the family hadn't filled in Rebecca's particulars when she died.

'She didn't,' Dad said, nodding his head after the old lady, 'that's her. I figure it out that when she had his particulars chipped in the stone she thought she might as well lump the two o' them together and get a discount.'

I watched her walk purposefully out of the cemetery as Dad leant down to study her date, 1839–18 . 'She was due to pull up anchor by 1900 an' here we are close on 1934. Looks like she's outstayed her welcome.'

On our way out he pointed out one grave with pride, 'Harry Prescott, friend of mine.' The late friend was surmounted by a mausoleum topped by an angel shedding two pairs of granite tears.

Back in Glasdir, while Dad was having his nap I said to Mam, 'He was admiring the monument to a Mr Prescott.'

'So he ought, he helped to pay for it. Mr Prescott was his bookmaker.'

* * *

Jan. 2nd 1934, 10.30 a.m. Shaftesbury Theatre, First Reading *Spring, 1600.*

New Year's Eve, I rang Molly; she would be seeing the New Year in with her Uncle Basil. Bill called in for one seasonable drink and left at seven for a snack and a packed house at the Apollo.

As my mind dwelt on the day after tomorrow, 71a became untenable and I took a taxi back to the Gielgud flat. Dick was there, John Perry back from work, John G. eating scrambled eggs before his packed house and the gramophone playing Vivaldi. It was, in a way, like arriving home.

Sitting having a drink was a tall, strikingly handsome boy who looked like an Oxford undergraduate, which is what he had been until lately. He had written a first play to be produced at the Comedy a week before mine and took a throwaway postcard from his pocket. FIRST EPISODE by Terence Rattigan.

John G. left for his theatre. 'Time I tore myself away and down the road into my drag, help yourselves . . .' We did.

Somebody rang to ask Terry to a party. He had planned to go to the Albert Hall. I thought he meant a concert then realized it was the great night of the Chelsea Arts Ball. Why hadn't I thought of it, and hired a costume?

But Terry had his, in John G.'s bedroom, I was welcome to it. I went and changed into a Tyrolean outfit with leather shorts. More drinks, and John G. reappeared.

For a moment I thought he had come home in mid-play, then realized it was over. He looked exactly as he had when he left, but with the fresh glow actors acquire after achievement followed by soap and water.

I stared at him in shame. While I had sat here whittling the evening away, was it possible that he had walked to his theatre, given a memorable performance, and walked back? How could I, flushed and worthless, ever criticize Bill Wilson again?

But he treated us as sober guests—'In one of my waits I wondered again about Ralph for Burbage, a beard can work wonders but I know Ian will be splendid'—and left with John P. for a party.

I got a taxi, called at the Apollo stage-door and left a note—'Happy New Year dear Will'—then on my way to the Albert Hall I recovered my pride and felt hazily presentable as a sturdy visitant from the Welsh Tyrol. Arriving at ten to twelve, I prised my wallet from the leather squeezing my backside, paid a large sum for a ticket and wandered in.

Gone was the immense area of the ground-floor seats, where mature music-lovers normally leant forward in prudent ecstasy to catch John McCormack's high notes, and even further forward for Galli Curci's, higher still.

All was submerged under an immense dance floor extending from shore to shore: the shores being the tiers of boxes soaring to the great invisible roof.

The vast edifice was bursting with light, colour, music and shoals of people. For the whole of this one night, Dead March and Oratorio had been triumphantly ousted by Tin-Pan Alley, and famous floodlit bands with balding leaders like sexy school-masters followed one another in bland succession—names like Ambrose, Harry Roy, Roy Fox, Jack Hylton, take your choice—

crashing out tunes to make the festive adrenalin flow. The Isle of Capri, Who's Afraid of the Big Bad Wolf, Pettin' in the Park, Shuffle Off to Buffalo, We're in the Money . . .

As the spotlights raked the swarming bedecked crowds, the world of getting up and washing up and going to work became a fuzz of fantasy and only this was real: 1934 was going to be something the world had never before known. Gaiety, which in a restaurant would have been a peal of laughter, became here shriek upon hysterical shriek.

The boxes were graduated. While the top tier, the cheapest, was fleetingly occupied by half-naked Chelsea riff-raff clad in cocoa sunburn and shameless bananas, the next down was grander and packed with fauns and nymphs discreetly veiled, wicked cupids and little Mozarts of indeterminate sex.

But the top-drawer boxes were the big ones on the ground floor. Crammed with gorgeously costumed Society in the shape of fashionable painters, couturiers, theatre designers and ballet dancers, they underwent bold examination by a steady stream of drifters at a zoo.

Except that here it was the animals in the gilded cages who paid the piper, sipping champagne and turning one slumming eye on the overheated populace while the other went a-roving. That porcelain Marie Antoinette, chatting as if in Claridge's, could it be Lady Diana Cooper?

A door would lurch open, at the back of a fish-bowl salon as crowded as a basket of fruit, to give a glimpse of a Nero and his minions, 'Darlings!' Then another door, 'That's Freddie Ashton—no, it isn't . . .' 'Look, there's Hermione Gingold!'

Then the great Parade, for the Most Beautiful or the Most Original Costume, a display as solemn as it was silly.

To slow music, men with earrings strutted past in harem trousers, dressed as nearly as women as they could manage without being arrested, while some of the 'original' creations defied the eye. Competitors invisible except for their feet toiled along as alligators complete with snapping jaws, or staggered as aeroplanes with whirring propellors or clanked as boiling kettles in clouds of steam. They seemed to be having a claustrophobic New Year.

That done with, there was a massive roll of drums and from the crowd a jungle roar silenced by a loudspeaker. 'Ladies and

Gentlemen, look up for the arrival of the great little year 1934—
look UP!' This prefaced the most audacious piece of showmanship
I had ever seen.

Like everybody else, I looked up.

A spotlight travelled and settled, a mile above, on a group
which appeared to be hanging from the roof. Then it picked out
two ropes looping down to a handful of men on the dance floor.

A band started to play, very softly, 'Dancing on the Ceiling'.
It was from 'my' film *Evergreen*, and I felt pleasure. Out of the
group an object crept into the light, attached to one of the ropes,
and started its slow progress down. It was a tiny cradle containing
what looked like a nude doll. But as it travelled lower past the
top boxes a murmur swelled out, and down, 'It's not a doll, it's
a real baby!'

Silence. And at what seemed a hundred feet above the crowd,
the cradle swayed.

And stuck.

There was a vast intake of breath. The silence was so complete
that you could hear distant cheering. The first seconds of 1934
were interminable.

The cradle gave a shudder, then another. Very slowly, it moved.
Down... down... down... until it slid into official arms and
the contents were lifted triumphantly into a spotlight.

It was indeed a baby, a boy a few days old, naked but warm
and asleep. To the roar of the crowd it was laid in a shawl carried
by the father and whisked away. Everybody there must have
hoped, as I did, that he was handsomely rewarded.

The dark roof disgorged a fleet of balloons, the bands blared
again; I found myself in the passages. They were lined with
sprawling figures; among broken bottles and puddles, togas were
filthy and wigs on end. Revellers had been sick.

I felt creeping through my bones the depression I knew well,
and walked home through the wintry small hours. Since six
o'clock last evening, I had led a worthless life.

1934 had better improve on this.

*   *   *

For the reading the whole cast had been called, which meant
that the stage was thronged, and crackling with the usual nervous

badinage. I spotted Molly in a corner, in her best suit and keeping to herself, while Dick sat in a distant chair, inscrutable behind his glasses and invisible inside his overcoat.

A flurry of mink arrived under a beautiful face: Isabel Jeans. It was a simple entrance, but as her director advanced to greet her there was a radiance which would have told an Eskimo that here was a star.

Parts were distributed by Freddie, gold of hair but unrecognizable in his best business suit and manner: subdued, efficient. The buzz sank to a murmur. Quick looks at the stage-door. Everybody was waiting for Edna Best.

Suddenly a slight schoolgirlish figure emerged from nowhere and stepped up to John. 'So sorry, I had to leave a message at the box-office.'

She had arrived by the pass-door: following Isabel Jeans, it made a highly artful device. The schoolgirl wore a coat that was more than mink, and on her snub nose an appendage which, fresh from Hollywood in a London January, looked as odd as an ear-trumpet: dark glasses.

I had never before attended a first reading except as an actor. In front of rows of watchful faces, I—as just the author—was like an adolescent having his clothes publicly removed button by button as he remembers that his rash has not cleared up.

At lunch John's enthusiasm was a relief—'Edna'll be wonderful, just right against Isabel'—and even Dick was sanguine.

Miss Best was unable to rehearse that afternoon so I went to the pictures—Empire, Joan Crawford and Clark Gable in *Dancing Lady*—then wished that, like John, I was playing every night. I rang Molly. She said, 'It was wonderful to feel a small part of it, the others felt the same.'

She was much happier where she was living now; Ida had suggested her moving into her other room at 103a Fulham Road, 'You must know Ida?'

I remembered meeting her at Polly and Sonny's and went straight there with a bottle of sherry; Molly was helping with the dinner, in a small cheerful flat. Ida was thirty, thin, smart and fun, with a flair for half-unconscious clowning. She was like a child who says something unintentionally comic and is happy to go further to see if the mirth will continue.

Like Molly, she had a fond mother who had prodded her on

to the stage; compared with Ida's career, however, Molly's had been Lily Elsie's.

'What was I in? ... Oh, yes, *Poppy*, I was understudy to Annie Croft's understudy ... Then I was in a revue at the Fortune, well sort of, at the dress rehearsal I fell over a brace and my leg opened but I never did, it only ran a week anyway ...

'Then I went to Spain with the Elliot Savonas, it was a sextette of girl trumpeters but I was under false colours. You see, the agent had told me to put my lips to the aperture and pretend, the other girls were sweet except the one who sneaked to Madam. Well, in Barcelona she stopped a rehearsal dead and screamed out, "Will the second from the right kindly *blow*?" She packed me off on the next train and I've never been able to look a trumpet in the face since ...'

Next morning at ten-thirty the whole cast seemed more relaxed, and I felt that from now on the sailing might be plain. As I waved to Molly I wondered from where Miss Best would materialize this time—a trap-door?—when the director was handed a letter. Dick and I heard, 'My God ...'

He read it aloud, 'Dear John, I'm sorry to let you down but I suddenly have to go back to the States, Love Edna.'

By this time six people were listening but John was too concerned to care.

'It's Bart, of course ...'—Bart was Herbert Marshall, Miss Best's husband—'I did hear he's being a bit footloose in Hollywood.' It was not the happiest way to describe a glamorous film star who happened to be one-legged, but only Dick and I noticed.

Then the great joined in while the small openly eavesdropped. Miss Jeans said, 'But John, who do we *get*?'

Somebody called out, 'Madeleine Carroll?' 'Oh no,' John said, 'she's like Emlyn, at the beck and call of that ghastly Gaumont-British ...'

By now it was a free-for-all and even the cleaners were listening. I half expected one of them to call out, 'Jean 'Arlow!'

'I know,' John said, 'Adèle Dixon, she was my Ophelia and so good.'

It was then that Freddie, the correct executive, gave a verdict on Miss Dixon which carried across the stage and bounced back: 'Oh, I *agree*, what's more I'm told the men like her!'

In a general silence, he went slowly pale to the roots of his golden hair and studied his script. But the pronouncement had sailed over the director's head, 'No, she's too bulgy for a boy, back to Joyce Bland.'

And Joyce Bland it was. She rehearsed quietly and truly. *'Perhaps it is a fine spring because it is a new century. A new world, so they say ...'* I looked at Dick; she was good.

And got better. The third day, when Ann's solo was reached and the director started to say 'Cut to dialogue', she began to sing. *'Farewell my love, I must needs take my leave ...'* The notes had the poignant purity of a choir-boy's voice, and by the end the denuded stage was filled with Elizabethan beauty. John's face was damp, and even Dick blinked behind his glasses.

Day after day, he and I sat in the stalls and watched the play lurch and grow under the feverish, merciless care of its director. He wanted me there 'in case', and as I was not at the moment 'at the beck and call of that ghastly Gaumont-British' I had no alternative.

These were the first—and last—rehearsals for me to attend as a haunting author. I felt lazy and useless, yet by five p.m. I was exhausted.

Bill I could never see, and the first couple of evenings I spent with Dick. He was the usual good company until his nervous doubts tended to unsettle me.

'Suppose on the first night the monkey on Lady Coperario's shoulder elects to leap down and into the stalls and bite Jimmy Agate on the nose and wake him up?'

'It's on a chain, I've seen it.'

'Then it can still bite Miss Jeans ... Suppose we end up with a flop and Lady Ashtead loses her drawers?' In between I was glad to spend evenings with Molly and Ida.

The first big day came when the director took the play straight through, scene by scene. After a back-breaking five hours, the quick change to a front-of-cloth rabble milling around in panic was followed by an incident which was to amuse Dick for a long time.

John was sitting immediately in front of us, pale as death and strong as steel, holding the megaphone through which—to save his voice for the evening and pacify Bronnie—he would marshal the crowd. Just as the scene got under way there was a noise like thunder, 'Stop!'

They all obliged, and peered over the footlights like a row of dutiful Tudor pupils.

'Sorry everybody,' the director boomed through his artificial aid, 'but you're all being too slow, we must get it tearing along here. Emlyn agrees with me that from now on his last act is thin.'

As the boom died away Dick heard me say, without aid but from the heart, 'John, I agree with you that it's thin but *please* not through a megaphone...'

'Terribly sorry, how stupid of me, how good-tempered you are. Right everybody? Off!' The scene turned into a horse-race, and whether that helped to fatten up my last act I was not in a state to judge.

At the last Sunday all-day lighting rehearsal, when the Motley sets and clothes came slowly and ravishingly to life, quaintly fresh and redolent of a lost spring, I sat alone in the Upper Circle and felt the first pangs of the birth I had awaited so long.

By now too numb to suffer from them, I sat in a trance, coming to life when the dialogue stopped for lights to be adjusted. At those moments, when the players stood still like chess figures, in the silence of the empty theatre they became imbued with the colours of a classical painting—Lady Coperario, lying on her bed still as a statue, for ever serene, beguiling: Ann, her own hair cropped, sitting on a stool in doublet and hose, seemingly in thought like a lovesick schoolboy poet.

If only playwriting could seem so effortlessly beautiful...

At the dress rehearsal on Tuesday afternoon I sat in the same eyrie. Hurrying round for notes I ran into Bill, who shook my hand warmly and said he was proud of me. I was glad and yet, unaccountably, as I watched his back recede I felt distress. Other matters were so much absorbing me that from the exchange we had just made we might have been strangers.

I edged him out of my mind, and the play took over.

* * *

Wednesday, January the 31st. It was on me at last.

John phoned, 'Glad I've got a matinée, take my mind off...' Then a bombardment. 'I'm happy to have done it whatever hap-

pens, you've been so patient it's a lovely play.' Later Dick's doleful drawl, 'I'm proud to be with it even if Lady Ashtead does
lose her drawers.'

I was glad to have my mind deflected by duty. For the first time
Miss Cooke was playing truant from school; I met her and her
old school-friend May Swallow at Euston and drove them to the
Court Hotel, Sloane Square. At dinner before the play—I had
never seen Miss Cooke in a long dress before—I turned the conversation to Holywell. It was what I needed.

'Oh, George, something last week...' She talked of the headmaster, R. T. Davies, an eccentric bachelor of Welsh-Noncon-
formist integrity, but with a vague innocence which relied heavily
upon the Senior Mistress.

'George, there are times when I could spank him... Nine p.m.,
a rat-tat-tat and there he was with his brief-case, brought out a
whole batch of statistics, couldn't read his own writing and
wanted me to decipher it, then just as he settled next to me on
the sofa, hey presto a power failure and every light in the house
went out.

'No candles, so we chatted solemnly in the dark till bang, on
came the lights and R.T. went on with his sentence. When I
started to laugh, he just stared and I hadn't the heart to tell him
it had just struck me what the Honours Form would make of the
fact that the Headmaster and Miss Cooke had spent twenty
minutes on her sofa alone and in the pitch dark—poor old R.T.
he's a good sort really.'

It was indeed what I needed. I walked them round to the
theatre, 'We want to sit and watch the people come in.' There
was already a sizeable crowd on the pavement waiting for
celebrities to arrive; I arranged to meet them for lunch tomorrow.

What was I to do? I was so near this first night that I could
neither submit to making myself part of the audience nor duck
the whole performance, as I had in the case of *A Murder Has
Been Arranged*.

I compromised, hopelessly, by running up the back-stage stairs
to the top floor and opening a door which I knew led to the flies, a
dark dusty desert of ropes and pulleys.

From the stage far below, chinks of light. I sat on a stool.
Again far below, like waves lapping at the mile-away shore, the
murmur of the audience. Dick, at this moment, would be follow-

ing the redoubtable Lady Ashtead into her box. Miserably I pictured her carrying a programme and white gloves in one hand and holding on to her drawers with the other.

I got up, and in the nine square yards of space around me began to walk to and fro, in a self-imposed dungeon in the sky. Then I stopped to listen to the tinkle of the orchestra.

Suddenly, in mid-music, there was a flurry and something loomed up, swishing near me to a standstill. Loud applause, but the music continued.

The curtain had gone up, too soon, in mid-overture! I ground nails into wet palms. Then I remembered that the Motleys had designed an inner curtain, an exquisite Elizabethan map, including Ongar and the Globe Theatre, wreathed in spring flowers. It had just been unveiled... The overture done, this curtain came softly up towards me.

The play.

There was a mutter of voices, why aren't they speaking up ... ?

They were, I was too far up to make out words I knew by heart. A stage-hand sauntered past, as unconcerned as a porter in a railway station. I sat on and on, through the first interval as I would through the second: the idea of emerging into the top corridor and risk running into actors was out of the question. When Ann's song came, floating up faint and pure and true— *'Farewell my love, I must needs take my leave'*—I wept as copiously as John ever could and felt better for it.

My bladder began to trouble me, till I was forced to cross to a disused wash-sink near me, with a tap that ran a silent trickle of water.

As I stood at it, looking down at the lines of light I could even see the faint veering of shadows, the shadows of my shadows. When I reported this later to Dick and John, John said, 'You must be the first playwright who's peed over his own play.'

By the end I was numb, and at the same time sore. As the curtain descended slowly from sight, I raced out of the dark into the blinding corridor and down the stairs to the stage-door, meeting nobody and then hurrying into back streets where I wandered till it was time to go to the Gielgud flat.

No first-night party has ever been easy, but usually the conversation can be kept general, 'what witty scenery', 'I adore music in a play ...'. But at this party there was one person who did not mince his questions: the host. 'Did the last scene hold? Did the monkey behave? Did anyone overhear any of the critics?'

I was too tired to lose myself in the champagne poured by John, morning-fresh after two shows.

And I had done nothing. I went home.

*　　*　　*

Sitting on my bed opening the papers, I reminded myself that the running expenses of the play were high enough to require startlingly good notices.

They were not startling either way. 'The first act is a master-piece but...' 'The first act is mild'... 'It may not satisfy every-body'... 'Full of good things'...

Then a headline, GIELGUD AS MANAGER, UNFORTUNATE CHOICE OF PLAY. 'It needs a good deal of cutting...'

The old *Port Said* trouble: too long.

John telephoned. 'Not bad are they but I do feel a few judicious cuts. It's my fault, at the dress rehearsal Frank and Martita both said too long but I didn't want to upset the cast. I'm having them called at five, can you have some cuts ready?'

I was determined to. It was a strain to take Miss Cooke and May out to lunch, but I had invited Molly. Her tact and Miss Cooke's practical enthusiasm made it easy.

After seeing them off, I sat in a Lyons and worked grimly on at the judicious cuts. Choice lines came under the axe, but an execu-tioner cannot afford to blub. It blurs his aim. On the Shaftesbury stage, at 5 p.m., the cast behaved well. John rapped out, 'I'm told you were all so good last night. Please remember the critics are in tonight too, those dreaded weeklies, so please give the same splendid show.' He was not a Terry for nothing. The actors left mouthing the cuts like sour wine, but mollified.

Dick and I walked to a Lyons tea-shop in St Martin's Lane, it seemed the day for Lyons tea-shops. Over a pot-for-two-please we heaved a sigh and looked at the table. I remembered that, since this bird's habitat was Fleet Street, he was adept at gleaning hard facts. And I knew the bird's heart was broken. I said, 'Is it too late?'

He sighed again, 'The one thing we needed was *Christopher Bean* notices.'

I had hoped for comfort. It is one thing to face the truth, another to be faced by it, and I was devastated. I felt tears steaming up and beat them back. My instinct was that Dick was so disappointed that it would have given him a kind of self-lacerating pleasure to see me break down, 'I'm afraid, dear John, our little author was somewhat larmoyant...'

I spared him the larmes. 'I should have cut before.'

'Yes.'

Two of the backers of a big West End show sat each munching a bun.

He continued, truthful and ruthless. 'Joyce Bland is as good as I said she would be but won't bring a penny in, neither will Hunter or even Isabel Jeans once she's not carrying the play.'

He was even more upset than I was. At least he kept Lady Ashtead's drawers out of it.

* * *

That evening I could not face the second performance; I walked to the other end of Shaftesbury Avenue and dropped into the Long Bar. Was I turning into Bill, who at that moment was in a dressing-room in the Apollo across the road, dead sober and preparing to play to a sold-out house?

For a moment I thought, I must go to see Bill's play tonight, of *course*, then thought, no, I can't...

'Hello, Emlyn, how's tricks, seen Bill lately?'

A flat voice, an easy smile, a fag-end dangling. Fess. 'Ta, Emlyn, bitter please, how's things?'

He knew nothing of the play. I was glad, and picked up the easy clichés. 'Not too bad, Fess, can't complain, how's tricks wi' you?'

'Oh bearin' up, hopin' to get a job as a shawfer'—he sounded like my father—'landlord's been gettin' a bit shirty sort o' thing, well, more a land*lady* if you follow me which was a bit o' luck at the start, meant you could keep him sweet for weeks on a couple o' quick gropes, strickly rationed mind you an' he's not sweet any more, but I just wrote me Dad, dear Dad seein' you work in the Post Office wi' them postal orders right under your nose what about sparin' one for your lovin' son, that'll make him smile and he'll send one by return I know my Dad.'

He grinned, showing the tooth-gap. He was a relief. I said,
'Try a short one.'

He did. 'Cheers.'

On impulse I said, 'Until something turns up, why not stay with
me?'

'Oh . . .' His expression of vague amiability did not change.

I reminded him that he knew the flat. A smile and a wink,
'Nice place from what I remember, thanks Emlyn, that'd be nice.'

I took him to the Palladium and left him standing there laughing silently at Nervo and Knox. I had promised to call in at John's
dressing-room.

Dick was sitting in a corner in the long overcoat, sipping a
whisky as if it were medicine. John was removing his make-up in
between ticking off a list with an eyebrow pencil.

'Oh dear, I am sad for you, we don't seem to have quite got
away with it, all that work and love and then it just evaporates
but Freddie just rang from the stage-door and your cuts worked,
tightened it up no end, forty-five minutes saved, can you believe
it? I do apologize for not having gone into it before . . . Sorry to
be doing this, it's the list for the party.'

'Party?'

'Tomorrow night, for the anniversary of *Bordeaux*, you'll come
of course? Dick, can you believe it's run a whole year?'

Without looking at Dick I said, 'I'd like to have come but I'm
going out to supper.'

Fabia Drake arrived, an old friend of John's. When she saw me
her face lit up. 'I've come straight from your lovely play, what a
success!'

This was better. 'I'm so glad . . .'

'Aren't Edith and Cedric marvellous?'

It had been a hard day.

* * *

Next evening, after hours in 71a trying to read, I rang Fess and
met him at the Fitzroy, where we ran into Dick.

For him he was quite cheerful about the Shaftesbury. 'I saw
the first half-hour, not bad for a third night and I hear Leslie and
Glad Henson loved it, we must tell J.G.'

Fess looked puzzled. 'J.G.?'

We explained. 'Ay, I have heard the name, proper jaw-breaker I call it. Pity he doesn't call hisself G.G. and then you could back him for the Derby.' At that stage of the evening it seemed delightfully funny.

We took a taxi and called at Fess's boarding-house for his few things. And that night Fess, amiably and with the cigarette-end glued to his lower lip, moved into 71a.

I lit the gas-fire in my bedroom and was just going up to do the same for him in the spare room when he stood in the doorway. 'That's a mighty big bed for one chap to kip in on a cold winter's night!' He grinned.

It was good not to be alone. In the morning I woke at ten and sat in bed reading the paper, Fess still asleep by my side. The door opened. It was Bill. I looked at him in surprise, he was never out before twelve. I said, 'Hello.'

'Who's that in the bed?'

The sharp question, a quotation from any French farce, woke Fess up. He turned a tousled head and blinked.

''Lo, Bill, how's tricks?' He was still half asleep, with the dependable friendly smile. Bill went red in the face and looked unexpectedly bewildered. Unhappy.

'I see,' he said slowly, 'I certainly did start something...' Then he turned smartly and went. I heard the heavy footsteps recede down the stairs.

'Mornin', Emlyn,' Fess said with a yawn and a stretch, 'what's the matter wi' poor old Bill?'

*   *   *

Next morning, Sunday, Agate's headline made my heart leap. LOVE'S LABOUR GAINED.

'This unusual and charming play... The best of it is its wit...' Dick arrived, beaming, 'What's more, last night's house was a corker!' The three of us lunched at the Windsor Castle, came back and played records.

Dick asked Fess about his early life in Gloucester, to which his parents had moved when he was ten. 'Some o' the girls are hot stuff up there, by the time I was fifteen I was well away, lovely cathedral too...' He went up to make tea.

'He's nice and restful,' Dick said, 'I like that slow talk, none of that up-and-down drama-school stuff.'

Fess came back with a tray, whistling. 'And it's got a good choir, I made some toast.'

Dick was right, he was like a slow-moving dog that does not bark. At the end of a tolerable day, Dick reverted—as he always did—to *Spring, 1600*. 'I've a feeling the patient has turned the corner.'

The next morning, the fog. A London fog is the tourist's dream, transforming the Albert Memorial into a faery castle haunted by the Hound of the Baskervilles. To the London theatre it is death.

As the air thickened into daytime twilight, my despair toughened into a new sense of loyalty to the Shaftesbury: not so much to my play as to its players, battling their way to work. I reminded myself that I had not been near *Spring, 1600* since I had spent the first night above it.

Knowing that tonight the theatre would be three-quarters empty, I who had always shrunk from watching any play of mine even with a full house now found myself stumbling to Victoria Tube Station. I re-stumbled from Leicester Square and was sitting in the dress circle in good time, behind the people who had turned up. I felt like thanking them individually. It would not have taken long.

The curtain rose on the glorious Motley curtain, which then rose on the Byrd garden. I was seeing my play as part of an audience, and it became dear to me—again not so much the play as the performance of it.

How well they acted! And through the haze of fog the sets and costumes looked more softly beautiful than they ever had, while my technical side noted that the many cuts I had made were imperceptible even to me.

I went round, saw them all and said I had enjoyed the show so much I was coming again. I think many of them realized I was not being a smug author. Molly certainly did.

I did come again, the next night and the next, and the next. Each audience was that bit smaller than the last. 'Even the nurses,' Dick said, 'don't fancy a free seat with fog.'

It was a penance poignant and valuable. At each performance I learnt something new.

I noted that the audience, however scattered, never varied in

its response to a scene, or even to a line in a scene. If anything
was below par there came an almost audible slackening of attention, while as soon as anything good was said or done, that
attention would tighten. I grew to wait for it.

Ann's song never failed to enchant. And while the ageing
female impersonator's best lines, perfectly delivered by Frank
Pettingell, drew no gusts of laughter—I recalled Bill, 'You cannot
blame a quiet audience for the empty seats next to them'—the
quiet audience chuckled with delight. I learnt.

But in the middle of the next week, crawling home after my
eighth vigil, I broke. Next morning I rang Gaumont-British. No,
I wouldn't be needed on the assembly line for at least a month.

I had an idea. 'Fess, you drive, don't you?'

'Since I was fourteen.'

With his guidance I bought a second-hand Morris-Oxford,
paying the forty pounds by cheque, which impressed him. We
would take the car by ferry to France, and then drive ... anywhere. He went off for road-maps.

Passports ... I had mine, but Fess? I was surprised he had one.
'Coupla years back a feller on the Stock Exchange asked me over
to Boulogne for a long week-end sort o' thing.'

After my farewell attendance at *Spring, 1600* I did not go
backstage; there was no talk of the show finishing and it would
look as if I were parting from it. Play on, if music be the food ...

Should I walk down to the Apollo and say goodbye to Bill?
No, the curtain would be down and so would the first couple of
whiskies ...

The next day Dick waved us off to a drive in the rain down to
Southampton. It was my first long journey by car, Fess could not
believe it.

He spoke little, asking me at intervals to put a cigarette to his
lips and light it. Sometimes he would whistle or sing a jaunty
snatch. 'If you were the Only Girl in the World ... I used to be
in the choir, oh Rose Marie I l-l-ove you ...' In a ridiculous way
it was soothing.

Southampton. In the middle of a monosyllabic dinner, I looked
at my watch. It was eight o'clock. Should I ring the Apollo stage
door to say goodbye?

No, a trunk call's a bore and he won't have a phone in his

room and would have to pant down to the stage-door and then he'll ask who's driving me . . .

Next morning the car swung out of Le Havre, and it was good to feel the straight roads and the straight poplars flit endlessly by without even having to look.

My mind wandered uselessly. Fess is a born driver . . . I've not packed a single book, just the one Spanish phrase-book, *gasolina para el coche*, I've forgotten it all . . .

Am I in worse shape than in Ceylon? Yes, for then I had the excuse of being alone, homesick and three years younger . . . When was I last in these parts? It was ten years ago, cycling from Oxford, a year younger than Fess is now. Why am I obsessed by time . . .?

It's good to be with a companion so utterly undemanding. Is he stupid? Ye-es, yet no, Dick was right, he's as much himself as John G. Speaks as he thinks, and if what comes out isn't too bright, too bad, it doesn't worry him . . .

After twenty kilometres of silence—except for 'Emlyn, mind slippin' a cig in my mouth an' lightin' it for me?'—there would come the thought for the day. 'Emlyn, did you know Bulmer's Cider in Hereford is the best in the world, known to all an' sundry, way down upon . . . the Swanee River . . .'

In the winter twilight we sighted Rouen. Memory was at work again. I told him about the Breton sailor who had helped me to pick up a woman. 'I was shy, being nineteen and never had one . . .' The cigarette nearly dropped from the shawfer's mouth. 'A feller who's never had a woman, at *nineteen*?'

'No. He waited on the mat while I had her, then the other way round, Box an' Cox sort o' thing.' I had aped his speech and his mind to minimize a memory which had stayed both exciting and tender.

'Box and Cox, I get you. Dependin' how you spell Cox.' I laughed. He could surprise you.

After dinner we found the Rue des Cordeliers, with the same prim old ladies sitting on the stools at each door. The girls naked to the waist had been replaced and so they looked the same too. I aired my French, but Fess made no comment. He had been much more impressed by the fact that a feller could be a virgin at nineteen.

A girl came up, 'coucher avec?' He winked at me and followed her upstairs. I was glad, it made an agreeable first night for his working holiday. For me brothels had lost their thrill, and I sat with a beer, feeling much more than eight years older than him. Yet his common sense made him seem more mature than I was.

The straight roads went on and on. In Bordeaux, in the restaurant I picked up a week-old *Times* and turned to the theatre list.

Shaftesbury, yes, there it was ... His Majesty's, YVONNE PRINTEMPS NOËL COWARD IN CONVERSATION PIECE *BY NOËL COWARD*, opens Feb. 16th 8 p.m.; I looked at my watch, five to, I drank a silent toast.

As the straight roads became Spanish ones, my mind tired of its vacancy. An idea for a play? I could no more have found one than solved an advanced problem in algebra.

Dear short-nosed, generous-lipped Fess was not much help. 'Emlyn, what's this play Spring-what-d'ye-call-it about...? A girl dressed as a boy? Sounds like a panto ... there's a long long trail awindin'...'

I stole an occasional look at him: the profile of a plebeian Greek god, and in expression as changeless as any head unearthed at Delphi.

I began to indulge, listlessly, in conjecture about the people I was near to, feeling at the same time wilfully pleased that not a soul had any idea where I was. I thought of Glasdir which always cheered me, of Miss Cooke, of Molly. Her four pounds a week from my play could not be for ever, would she go back to Jack which would only make her unhappy...?

But thank God Bill was good for a year's run and off my hands at last. On my return I would go to his play ...

Then as we drove south into the sun, first overcoats were crushed into the boot and later jackets discarded. Even if the mind stayed stale, the body began to warm.

With Gibraltar coming up, Fess turned on his wide grin— honest-sly, sly-honest, it was hard to separate the two—'I was in the Navy for five minutes, ever heard o' the Alameda Gardens?' I had.

* * *

In the jostling main street we entered a café which could have been in Portsmouth on a rowdy Saturday. Teams of homesick

British sailors were getting drunk. Fess wandered away alone. Again I thought, thank God he's easy, his life's his own . . . Soon after eleven, I approached the Gardens.

By day, with expanses of flower beds and avenues under shady trees, they were the godsend of British nannies and strolling officials and wives. But by moonlight, and still warm from the sun, they became a place of shadows, half of which were some of the same sailors who had their own idea of a stroll. The other half I was soon to know about.

As I wandered along a spectral avenue I was both nervous and exhilarated. Within the trees there were gliding movements. On a bench, a solitary sailor. As I passed he said softly, 'Evenin' señor, buenas noches, got a light for cigaretta?'

'Sorry, I don't smoke.' I sat beside him.

'Never mind, I got a match, I was just doin' me stooff.'

I said, 'Liverpool?'

'New Brighton.' I told him my father's sister was married to a policeman there, 'Jack Hesketh his name is.'

'Good God, I know Jack Hesketh, he arrested me when I was thirteen for pinchin' rotten apples off a barrow, I got off with a caution, decent bloke.' In the middle of Gibraltar, it was funny.

Not so funny though, when in the bushes behind us I heard a long hiss. I thought it was a snake. Then tittering.

'Don't mind them, they're the local Spanish queens an' they 'eard you talk English, they reckon the Gardens is their beat you see. What d'you say to a turn round the deck an' they'll calm down . . .'

I thought no more of the hissing till I was walking—towards my hotel—still in the Gardens and down a long avenue which in the day was a dull procession of bouncing prams and now stretched under the moon, deserted and sinister. My footsteps echoed as if they were somebody else's.

After two minutes, I would have given anything to run into a bouncing pram. From the impenetrable trees which flanked me, the chattering of twenty castrated Rock moneys, shrill gibberings of rage. Came the stones.

In the moonlight I was a target. They were not big, and all the more lethal for it: sharp as Toledo steel. The first landed a yard behind me, sparking smartly off the gravel. Then I heard a shrill giggle as another whistled past my ear.

I thought, if I am to die suddenly this is not the way to do it. St Stephen may have been canonized for having been stoned to death but his conscience was clearer than mine.

I was determined, however, not to lose face by running, and with an immense effort I maintained a measured pace, taking as much pride in keeping my head as a Governor-General. As the barrage kept doggedly abreast of me, I knew that each burst of falsetto invective would be followed by a missile which might find its mark. The last hundred yards, with at the end a great gate and the lamps of the main road, were very long ones.

Entering the Rock Hotel I decided not to tell Fess or anybody. On second thoughts, when I got home I would describe every detail to Bill, it would make him laugh.

Passing the British citizens drinking nightcaps in the lounge I felt unique in my fashion. To be hounded out of the town gardens by every male prostitute known to the town's police is one way to high-light a holiday in a great outpost of Empire.

*　*　*

The next morning I bought last Friday's *Telegraph* and turned to the theatre list. 'THE LATE CHRISTOPHER BEAN by Emlyn Williams, 350 perfs.' Two lines underneath, 'SPRING 1600 by Emlyn Williams, last 3 perfs.'

I sat down and crushed the paper over my knee.

Last Sunday those rare sets had been huddled against a warehouse wall as if to be shot. Worse, the superb clothes would go as crumpled bargains to Nathan's the costumiers, to be clumsily sported for years in amateur productions of *Merrie England*. Lady Ashtead had lost those drawers after all.

I had forgotten I had told Gaumont-British that by now I would have reached the Rock Hotel, and there was a phone call. Would I return immediately, to write additional dialogue for Hitchcock's *The Man Who Knew Too Much*.

I was thankful. The car was shipped home, a couple of hours later we were in a train and stayed in trains for two days. Never was a journey so tedious. I was glad of Fess's imperturbable silences. The wittiest talk would have been unbearable.

When we arrived at Victoria at half-past ten at night, I was aching from head to foot with boredom and like Fess, ravenously hungry. I bought sandwiches, then at a flower stall I saw a last bunch of daffodils. They would brighten the flat.

The sitting-room had that look of cold reproach which greets every traveller returning to an empty home. I closed the orange curtains while Fess lit the fire, whistling contentedly. Then I rang Angus—I wasn't wanted for a week after all—poured us a drink each and sat with a sigh of relief.

An accumulation of letters. I only opened the one from Glasdir: 'To welcome you home whenever it is, we hope you will not stay out of Circulation too long...' There was one phone message, 'Sir, Mr Lamb rang.' Then my eye caught red print on an envelope. I picked it up, and Fess asked what was amusing me.

'It's for Bill, a final income tax demand, they've caught up with him at last... No, what's funny is that it's so long since they heard from him they've given him up—wait for his face when he sees "To the Executors of the Late W. Cronin-Wilson!"'

I looked again at the phone message, and walked to the desk. 'Ben? You phoned, I'm just back from Spain—'

'Emlyn, we did everything to find out where you were, nobody knew. I'm awfully sorry old chap, but Bill died two weeks ago.'

PART THREE

Into the Clear
1934–1935

CHAPTER TWENTY-SEVEN

OUT OF CIRCULATION

I heard everything he said, answered rationally and hung up. It was my first bereavement and I was unable to take it in.

The day Fess and I had left, Bill had caught a cold which the fog had seized on. He had insisted on playing that night, which meant pneumonia, and next day he had collapsed and been rushed to Charing Cross Hospital. That evening he had died.

Ben and I would meet in the morning, so sorry, old chap.

I stared at Fess, then at the daffodils I had bought at Victoria. Funeral flowers, two weeks too late. He just looked at me, and again I was reminded of a friendly dog.

'Fess,' I said weakly, as if I had known him all my life, 'what's the matter with me, why aren't I crying?'

'Take it easy, I'm here.'

He sat on the arm of my chair, put an arm clumsily round me and patted my back. 'Take it easy, here ...' He put the glass to my mouth.

I looked again at the envelope. 'The Late W. Cronin-Wilson'. It's the name of a play, like 'The Late Christopher Bean'. An ugly word 'Executors', sounds like the Tower of London. W. stands for William, I haven't called him Will for a long time ...

Had the phone call really happened?

In two months he would have been forty-seven. There was no trace of him in the flat—not a snapshot, not a worn tie, not a scrap of writing. He had left the world as he came into it, with nothing: with not even, at his bedside, the hand of the only human being who loved him.

No, not with nothing. Searching for comfort I remembered the twin sons he had once carelessly fathered. They were somewhere on the face of the earth just as he was under it, both moving beautifully in his image. Though I was never to see them, the thought of them did help me.

'Fess, d'you remember when I said the fog was killing the theatre?'

'You mustn't think like that. They're bad sort o' thoughts those kind are, have another whisky.' I couldn't, neither could I eat.

Then I was hit, by the pile-up of the journey and the news, and just managed the stairs. Fess lit the gas-fire, made up the bed and helped me undress.

Before I got into the double divan bed, I stared at it. It had travelled from Wellington Mansions to Marchmont Street to here.

I looked at the doorway. That was the last time I had seen him, the morning he had looked unhappy and turned his back on us. On me.

Fess went up to eat his sandwiches while I lay awake. Then he came down and undressed. Before turning to sleep he pressed his cheek against mine, both stubbly after the journey. He had never before made a gesture implying affection.

I went on flogging myself feebly with what he had called bad thoughts. I thought of Southampton, when it had crossed my mind to ring up. A trunk call; had I been too mean to make it?

I heard rain pattering against the window, and remembered that when I was a child, lying awake at night, the sound had never failed to bring the tears as I imagined the people I loved lying friendless and alone in the wet earth. But the tears had never lasted long, and I had soon fallen asleep.

Now I could neither weep nor sleep. The body I had known had begun to rot.

Fess grunted and moved. His back was to me; not only could I feel the warmth of it, I could breathe in—since he had not been out of his clothes for two days—the healthy smell of his living flesh. My arms jerked forward and I held on to him as if I were drowning.

He woke with a start, 'I'm here, you'll feel better in the morning.' He sounded like a drowsy elder brother. With my hand still on his arm he was quickly off again, and I must then have slept fitfully.

We got up early and I mechanically shaved, bathed and had breakfast. Fess talked little, as always, and normally. There was nothing urgent to occupy me, which was hard.

As I walked at noon to Victoria to meet Old Ben at the

Windsor Castle, the passers-by looked callously cheerful; I thought of the little room over the garage, three minutes away, no emptier now than when he had occupied it.

I could have asked him to stay at 71a again while I was abroad. Mrs Tilley would have looked after him and lit fires, it might have made the difference ...

Then I warned myself that I must not get emotional in front of Old Ben. Or—come to think of it—in front of anybody. Dick and John P., with all their concern, would be embarrassed; as for John G., he was like many people who shed tears when artistically moved—an outburst would freeze him into helpless distress. And though Fess would not be ill at ease if I let myself go, he could not be expected to voice comfort.

No. While Old Ben had taken it for granted that I was the nearest to being next-of-kin, I was—unlike the bereaved husband, wife, parent or child—denied the expression of grief.

He was at the bar, Old Ben, the well-preserved lady-killer—he must be sixty-something by now—holding a beer and watching the swing-doors with a suitably serious face.

They had been pals for so long. As we shook hands—'Ben, I can't thank you enough'—I remembered that he had known Bill five times as long as I had.

Over beer, I asked the questions. 'February the 16th, eight p.m.' I was in Bordeaux, having just drunk to *Conversation Piece*.

'They all liked him at the Apollo but didn't know a thing about him ... No, just a couple of pounds in his wallet. Bergner and Cochran were jolly decent but I couldn't very well tell them he was—well, destitute, though Cochran must have sensed something as he sent a cheque. A great relief as I'm not very flush at the moment and there were expenses here and there as well as the hospital, you'd be surprised ...

'No, just one second cousin who didn't seem to have a bean and took away the effects ... Brookwood Cemetery, the big one in Surrey, I'd have gone down for it of course but I had one day on a film. The Apollo cast sent a big wreath but you couldn't expect any of them to go all that way ...'

'How much did the funeral cost?'

He looked down into his beer, 'Hardly anything really, you see there was no money ...'

'Was it what they call a ... pauper's funeral?'

He did not look up. 'Well, you could call it that. You see . . .'

I thought of the fat pile of investment slips in my desk, felt something rise in my throat and thought I was going to be sick. And the last place to be sick in is a crowded bar.

The something was an instinct I had inherited from my mother's long fight against the shameful shadow of the workhouse; I felt as she would have done if this had happened to my father. The overheard phrase echoed from the past. 'He should have had a decent burial.'

There was irony here too: growing up, I had felt harden in me a conviction that the dead body is unimportant and that there should be a civilized minimum of ostentation in the act of disposal. But my mother prevailed.

'Ben, can you work out roughly how much you had to spend?'

'Thank you, old chap, roughly thirty.'

I went to the lavatory, took a cheque from my wallet, filled it in for fifty pounds, returned, slipped it into his pocket and reminded him to forward bills. I was not being generous, it was conscience money.

I asked him if the nurses had told him any details. 'Was he distressed or anything like that?'

'Oh, no, he got semi-conscious almost at once and it seems he rambled on about his duty to Cochran et cetera, then got meaningless and kept asking for Ralph Lynn. "Where's Ralph Lynn?" which I'm afraid made them giggle . . .'

It did seem an odd quirk of the subconscious that in delirium he should have picked on the most famous *farceur* of the twenties and thirties. But thank God he had slipped mindlessly away.

I thanked Old Ben again and walked home. Turning into Ebury Street, I stopped short.

Ralph Lynn. It hadn't been 'Where's Ralph Lynn?' at all, and he had known what he was saying. What he had said was, 'Where's Emlyn, where's Emlyn?'

While I had been bowling aimlessly along foreign roads, he had called for me. I walked on through the noises of the street, and still my eyes were dry.

❋   ❋   ❋

Mrs Tilly had been in and had left a message. 'Sir, welcome

home we have been so worried with the bad news about Mr C. Wilson, Mrs C. Wilson rang she has been ringin' reglar.'

For a disorganized moment I thought Bill had been secretly married and now the truth was out: then realized it was Molly, Mrs Carus-Wilson. I laughed out loud, and knew she would too. I rang her at Ida's and asked her round at six.

As she arrived Fess was just leaving—'off to see a couple o' fellers'—and they met on the stairs, 'This is my cousin, Fess Griffith, Mrs Carus-Wilson.' Hadn't my father's mother been a Griffith?

He shook hands politely and left. I preceded Molly into the living-room, poured her a sherry and sat opposite her on the sofa.

The conversation was easy, I was in complete control. She spoke of *Spring, 1600*. 'We were all so sad . . .' Then she hesitated, 'I was worried, not knowing how to get on to you . . .'

Without warning, the dam broke and I burst into sobs which racked me from head to foot. In a second she was beside me with her arms round me: that is, as far round as they would go, she was that much smaller. My head was on her breast and my tears were scalding her dress. Faintly I smelt perfume and was glad of it.

'It's all right,' she said, 'it's all right . . .'

Words wrenched themselves out of me, words I had not uttered even in front of Fess: the choked blurting of affliction, self-accusing and yet self-pitying. 'I let him die, he had nobody except me and I wasn't there . . . A pauper's grave . . . I can never forgive myself, never, never . . .'

In between she said quietly, as if soothing a child who has fallen over and hurt himself badly, 'It's all right, darling, it's all right . . .' I was suddenly reminded of Annie the little maid who when I was six had been the one to comfort me.

She went on, 'You're not a fortune-teller, how could you have known such a thing would happen? He's at peace, he really is, it's all right . . .'

I subsided. 'Come round to Ida's, she always makes you laugh. We'll pick up some sherry, there's a fire and some scrambled eggs, we'll have a nice evening.'

Ida was perfect—'I hear you had horrid news'—and we settled to the nice evening. I drew her out about her early life.

'Oh, by the time I was sixteen the boys were flocking round, they used to call me Ida-Sweet-As-Apple-Cider ... Oh, no, just what we used to call kissie-wissies. I wasn't terribly interested, I can't think why, but darling Mother was so proud of her girls and one day, I can't tell you how embarrassed I was, she said in front of two young men I hardly knew, "Oh, Ida's got lots of boys mad about her and she just tosses them off!" She said it so sweetly, but the two went bright red and so did I, which I shouldn't have done. Oh, it *was* embarrassing ...'

Returning to 71a anaesthetized by friendship, I was glad to look up and see the lights on. As I did so, one curtain was pulled, then the other. A shadow moved away.

I thought, it's Bill come over from his room over the garage: by a trick of light, Fess's outline had loomed bulky enough to be his. It was then that I knew, fully and for good, that he was gone.

Fess told me his evening had been 'not bad, it's a rum pub that Fitzroy ...' Lying next to him I slept.

In the morning, my mother's questionable spirit prompted me again, this time to go down to Brookwood Cemetery. Knowing that Molly shared my aversion, I hesitated before asking her to come with me; but she agreed at once, and we travelled in a hired car on a chill March afternoon.

As we entered the grim gates she took my hand and held it. We walked to an office, then she accompanied me to the edge of a Sahara of pious memorials merging greyly into the weather, where she waited while I picked my way to a far corner.

To a mound of soggy soil, the same soil which covers the earth from end to end, on land and under the sea. A long mound, for he had been tall.

It was nothing to do with him, nothing to do with me. Why was I here?

I walked quickly back to Molly, who had herself turned the other way. She was looking steadily over a wall at a pebble-splashed villa. It had live people in it.

*　　*　　*

'My dear Son George ... Your Mother says that with an un-married gentleman like him, how do we know who would be there

to take care of him in his old age? So perhaps it is for the best.
Poor old Cronnin, I think she may have hit the nail on the
head . . .'

In the context the expression may not have been entirely suitable, but my mother was right. If he had lived, it would have
been tragic. *If he had lived* . . . After a week of incredulity I was
getting used to it.

Next morning at Gaumont-British, Angus told me it was a
question of giving the dialogue for *The Man Who Knew Too
Much* 'some zing'. The picture was an important one—Frank
Vosper, Leslie Banks, Nova Pilbeam, Edna Best. (Hello, Miss
Best, fancy *you* here again . . . But I never met her or Hitchcock.)

I took the script home and sat obediently down to cook up
Additional Dialogue with intermittent zing to it. I spent the
evenings with Fess or Dick or both, or with Molly and Ida,
taking them at least twice a week to Odone's, a restaurant near
Victoria with music and a cabaret.

Inactivity was making Molly low again. Jack had drifted off,
she was no nearer her divorce and was, like me, out of circulation. A couple of times Fess joined us. He contributed nothing to
the conversation and I was sure they were as relieved as I was.
Ida said, 'He's what I call restful, and so attentive when he pours
you a drinkie.'

One afternoon when I rang Molly she was so depressed that
she sounded quite unlike herself; she had been to her solicitor
and Jack was 'back with that Weaver again'. I asked her and Ida
to the flat at six.

Fess poured out drinks. I put the gramophone on 'to cheer us
all up', though Ida and Fess, in their different ways, needed no
help. Molly said, 'I'm sorry I was so dreary on the phone,' and
sat on the sofa, the other end from Ida.

We talked, and I put on a new record, the Yvonne Printemps
song from *Conversation Piece*: 'I'll Follow My Secret Heart'. Till
I find love . . . I thought of the first night, of the overture playing
this as Bill was dying. The thought moved me without making
me miserable, the music was too tender for that. I looked across
at Molly. Perhaps the record was a mistake, her warm smile had
gone and she was looking dispiritedly into the fire. I could not
bear to see her sad, and called out, 'Cheer up . . .'

She moved her head quickly, tried to smile and Ida patted her

[337]

arm, 'You get that divorce, dear, and then you'll be free to marry again.'

'Oh,' Molly said, 'I don't think anybody would want to marry me even if I was free . . .' And she did what I had done, on the same sofa: she burst into tears. The glorious voice sang on. 'My whole life through, till I find love . . .'

Then happened the most decisive ten seconds since the moment, eleven years ago, when I stood in Tom Gate, Christ Church, in front of the notice board which announced that I had won a scholarship. Except that this decision was of my making, instant and instinctive.

Look before you leap? I leapt. Putting down my unfinished glass—my first—I crossed to her as swiftly as she had once crossed to me, knelt on the rug, took her hands from her face and said, 'Molly, if you do get free, will you marry me?'

CHAPTER TWENTY-EIGHT

A LOOK AT THE LEAP

'Will you marry me?' It sounded like the title of a song.

I heard Ida say, 'Oh!'

Molly looked at me, 'Of course I will,' and burst into tears again. Ida said 'Oh!' again and burst into tears herself, 'I've felt it in my bones but this is so *sudden!*'

I sat between them on the sofa, took Molly in my arms and kissed her. She was still crying. 'How can I be so stupid...'

'All we've got to do now,' I said, 'is to move heaven and earth for you to divorce him. Apart from that you've nothing to worry about, nothing.'

I felt passionately protective, and knew the meaning of the phrase 'All I have is yours'. It was a happy evening, and over dinner at Odone's, with Ida and Fess looking on and the champagne opened, we discussed plans.

The divorce would be endangered if during the proceedings wily Jack got wind of what Ida called 'any hanky-panky' and the King's Proctor intervened, so it was essential I should keep in the background.

We would have 'a platonic engagement, like the Victorians' until the danger was past, and I would lease a country place where Molly could spend the summer, entertaining friends among whom I would be numbered.

She said, 'I can't get used to it.' She looked happy if dazed, while Ida was as radiant.

The band played 'I'll Follow My Secret Heart', glasses clinked and three pairs of eyes out of four were moist: I doubted if Fess had cried as a baby and he was certainly not going to start now. He looked friendly without encroachment.

It was a fine brisk March night and we all walked. Fess and I dropped the girls, I kissed Molly on the lips—'Don't forget you're engaged'—and we continued on to 71a.

'Well,' Fess said, stepping out with his measured stride, slightly bandy, 'this is good news.'

'It is, isn't it?' Tonight I had turned a corner in a long tunnel and stepped out on to a new sun-swept landscape. Stirred though I was, I had my best night's rest since Spain.

But when the winter dawn closed its chill fingers round my head, I woke.

* * *

With Fess unconscious by my side, in the noiseless half-dark I had my thoughts to myself. Or rather, they had me.

Had I fallen into a muddle? Worse, had I—in making a gesture as sincere as it was spontaneous, towards the person of whom I was fondest in the world—had I pulled her into the muddle with me? Having leapt, I looked.

Reviewing the few women I had been to bed with, I recalled with dismay that not only had each woman been a stranger to me, I had never been to bed with any of them more than once. I now faced the bridge between temporary pleasure and married life with a girl who, while being physically attractive, had been for seven years a married woman whom—for two of those years—I had loved as a friend. I recalled with a qualm that we had cheerfully shared a bed.

Then I wondered about *her*. The marriage had gone wrong . . . Then I remembered Dima, the Russian faun who had 'made all the difference'—no, the fault had not been hers.

Without waking Fess I got up. The almost-spring sun was out, and I walked to Hyde Park. Skirting the Serpentine, I put myself in Dima's place, on that hillside. As I progressed inside overcoat and suit, the unaccustomed spring warmth had its effect. Mind and body gave themselves to imagination. I was reassured.

And reassured, I faced the final hurdle, the high one I had been skirting: my attitude towards my own sex.

It was one which had never fulfilled me either physically or emotionally. Indeed, remaining obstinately adolescent, it had caused me active pain.

But it was there. And though I had never been a slave to pursuit, however undemanding my sudden sallies I had always been free to indulge in them. The idea that I should be cut off from that freedom was alarming. I heard Dicky's dry voice. 'You want to have your cake and eat it.'

Last night, had I been dishonest? Like Odysseus besieging Troy, I had come bearing gifts. Inside the gift-horse, were there nameless foot-soldiers?

I walked home, had breakfast with Fess and booked a table at the Ivy. There I looked at her in a new way: as my future wife. I knew nothing about women's clothes and less about adornment, but I could tell that in an inexpensive outfit, with one piece of jewellery gleaned from Jack, she looked right.

More important, she looked happy and we had a happy time together as we had always done. Towards coffee she said, 'Don't you think we should wait and see how we go?'

'How d'you mean?'

'Well, there's this tricky business of my divorce, and . . . well, Ida can hear the wedding bells but it's not as simple as that, is it?'

I looked at her, with two blue eyes trying to be honest while facing two brown ones which were.

I said, 'Do you want to get out of it?'

'No, but please don't feel committed. I'd hate that.'

My feelings were mixed. I didn't want to be committed, but I didn't like her being the one to tell me.

'Whatever you say,' I said grudgingly, 'but we have a date at a quarter to three.'

The date was the Midland Bank in Shaftesbury Avenue. In the midst of deep-seated doubt, I wanted to indulge in the most male gesture a man can make to a woman. After seven years of financial insecurity, she was now to have weekly 'house-keeping money' for the first time and I wanted to show her the resources which would be hers when she wanted them. I asked for a complete picture of my 'position'. It was deferentially brought. I showed my fiancée Gilt-Edged, Woolworth's, Shell, Marks and Spencer's: the man who had asked her to marry him was rich. Her eyes filled with tears—it had been an emotional night and day—and she said, 'I'll be all right if you're all right.'

It was so much the thing to say that I had no answer.

* * *

Fess picked up the car at Tilbury and we went house-hunting. Molly had once stayed with friends on the river near Staines, and we drove there. 'Well, sir,' the house-agent said, 'there's one funny unfurnished place, old-fashioned though and might be lonely . . .'

A couple of miles out, on the way to Wraysbury, we turned left through a gateway and bumped down a long, straight path between fields. At the end, a wild wood tangled with nettles.

We left the car in a shed in a clearing and picked our way to a narrow backwater spanned by a foot bridge. Beyond, the back door of a solitary one-storied house; beyond again, the main river with a towpath along the far bank.

The house stood on a tiny island, the front a many-windowed little sun-room in the shape of a ship's prow. In front of this, the lawn narrowed to a point, again like a ship, where the backwater joined the Thames.

And the Thames and the towpath freed the house from loneliness; with the summer the river would be as lively as round the Island, Thames Ditton. The water came from a hand-pump next to the kitchen sink; no electricity, so back to the Aladdins.

Molly signed the lease, for three years at fifty pounds a year. On the days I was working at Gaumont-British, Fess would drop me there and drive Molly and Ida down to 'the bung', as it would always be known. On my free days I drove down with them.

We had a hundred tasks: scouring floors, painting woodwork, washing windows. Fess, part of the household, was invaluable; with my help he set about distempering the walls white, right through, then made cupboards and book-shelves. The rest of the preparations reminded me of Glasdir. While Molly shopped for everything from beds to dust-pan, I bought portable gramophone, deck-chairs, lilos . . .

We were as absorbed as children furnishing a tree-house. She made sure that, while clean and orderly, it stayed the gypsy river-retreat it was meant to be. The only help would be a Mrs Mayhew, arriving on a bicycle one morning a week to 'do the place'.

Sitting in the spring sun on the shaggy lawn—'we must put a mower on the list'—watching a punt slide by with beyond it the chug of a leisurely barge on its way to the lock, and listening to the chatter of birds from the greenery beyond the backwater, I was content as I had never been.

✿   ✿   ✿

My stagnant professional life now took a new turn. John's brother Val Gielgud invited me to play, on the wireless, Clemence Dane's *Will Shakespeare* on the birthday, April the 23rd. A prime presentation.

In spite of the talkies, British radio was still a momentous force. 'You will be playing,' actors were warned, 'to an audience of three million.' Since radio drama was then invariably presented 'live', actors found this reminder a paralysing one: at the instant when they spoke a line in Broadcasting House, London, it resounded, piping hot, all over the United Kingdom. This made newcomers so nervous that many was the time, in a million homes, when there also resounded the counterpoint of foolscap crackling between palsied fingers.

The first day, Gielgud led us into a vast, windowless, padded studio—it was impossible to believe that outside was a summer's day—and introduced us to the microphones as if they were human. 'The sooner you get acquainted the better.'

Each was a robot with three splayed feet of grey metal, a long unbending metal-grey body and a square pin-head with one dead eye. They seemed to have little to do with the art of acting.

The only player who refused to be intimidated by her microphone was Haidée Wright, a redoubtable little old lady who, in the stage production, had made a success as Queen Elizabeth. After insisting on the robot being lowered to her lack of inches, she had it stunted still further so that she could play her scene in an imposing chair, where she sat glaring at it as if for tuppence she would box its ears and would do it again on the night: a couple of slaps reverberating round the million puzzled homes.

The first rehearsals were a battle between her and the mutterings of her script. The script lost. It was taken from her, laid on a music-stand at eye-level to be later silently and fastidiously removed, sheet by sheet like soiled linen, by a cultured young employee of the Corporation.

I worked, but the play, of immense interest by a gifted woman, was mostly poetry splashed on to the page from an over-rich palette, in exciting colours which tended to run. The author had swallowed an overdose of blank verse, hook, line and Stephen Phillips.

The broadcast was like a first night. At 7.30 I was directed to an enormous cushioned reception room next to the studio, adorned with enormous flowers and enormous vases which—B.B.C. or no B.B.C.—were only just the right side of ostentation.

The cast was received by Val Gielgud, several high-ups and Miss Dane, for whom the room and the rest seemed to have been custom-built. She was an outsize author with a handsome generous face topped by hair as overflowing as her talent. It had been scooped hastily back into a bun and seemed about to come tumbling down and be sat on.

In a cascade of black to the floor, with a corsage of big happy flowers which accentuated her size, she looked as if, were the world not larger than she was, she would cradle it in her lap. A photographer advanced to arrange the cast round her chair, just as she was handed a vast bouquet which she embraced with a beautiful smile. She was a mother at a prize-giving where all her children have ended up First.

The performance was an experience tremendously unreal. In our dungeon we stood fearfully at the ready, eyes tick-ticking between the microphone and the cultured studio clock as its long hand glided impeccably round towards zero hour. No last voice to whisper, 'You'll be marvellous!'

Icy airless silence. Then, along the regiment of robots, each dead eye turned bright red and stared at its victims. 'For the next ninety minutes we can make you or break you, and that goes for you too Good Queen Bess'. In a far corner, the flick of a single, big red light; then a beat while the world waited . . .

'"Will Shakespeare", a play by Clemence Dane.' The words emerged immensely from a deserted corner of the studio: a disembodied voice so cultivated that it could have been God's.

And God spake. 'The cast is as follows, Will Shakespeare Emlyn Williams . . .' Staring at my script, I saw Dad nodding in quick recognition, his hand cupped over his weak ear and his eyes fixed beatifically on 'the machine' as if I were crouched inside it. Then Molly, Miss Cooke . . .

I tried hard to hit the note of quiet inner pain, and to turn my pages as if they were spun glass.

The moment came when Will kissed a lady love passionately on the lips. Since our microphones stood six feet apart our positions were not ideal. If the photographer had lingered to register the highlight for the *Radio Times* he would, during the kiss, have snapped the lady peering through spectacles at the page she was gingerly turning, then me clasping my script while I pressed my mouth to the knuckles of my other hand and rained hungry kisses on them. The radio actor's lot is not a happy one.

At last it was over: the spiteful red eyes blinked off and the universal hush was lifted. We could tear up the script, cough, bellow, spit or hiccup or even shout, 'Balls to the B.B.C.!' without being beheaded outside Broadcasting House.

I was glad I had done it. But I had not enjoyed it and never would.

*　*　*

Once more I had many free days, and the river weather stayed perfect. At week-ends, visitors came and went: Freddie Mell, Moira and Warren Chetham-Strode, and Polly and Sonny came over from Sutton Courtenay: their lives had changed again. Sonny had bought the Asquith house, the Wharf.

We decided to tell the five of them and nobody else. I loved the pleasure with which Molly showed them round.

It was on one of these visits that Ida most markedly displayed her flair for memorable small-talk. One Sunday morning, we were all on the lawn browsing through the papers, relaxed and not talking. Ida turned the front page of the *Express*—'Storm at Sea, Pictures Overleaf'—studied photographs and broke the silence with a sigh. 'I always think there's something rather sad about a ship going down ...'

A message from the studio: conference tomorrow, would I bring my additional dialogue.

I had not finished the job, but it was a big day at the bung, more furniture to be painted. I decided to stay for that, drive up at five with Fess, sit up late at the flat and—contrary to habit—polish off my work at the last minute.

After a busy, happy day I was reluctant to leave. Fess and I got to London about six and he dropped me at 71a before putting the car away, 'See you in a minute.'

I poured two drinks, balanced the typewriter on the edge of

my armchair and started work. As on many occasions before in this room, I was glad of a restful companion.

I looked at my watch. Twenty minutes had passed. There must be some little thing wrong with the car. I turned on the wireless, and music kept me company.

Half an hour. The phone rang.

I jumped to it. It was the studio, fixing the exact time tomorrow morning. There was a talk on the radio and I switched it off.

The flat was very quiet. I stared at the typewriter. I had written ten lines.

I looked at the sofa opposite. The same sofa at which I had made a proposal of marriage. On which I had sat when Bill had brought Fess to meet me.

It was the first time for me to be properly alone since the news of his death. Desolation clutched at me as if I had heard it on the phone a minute ago.

A car passed. Then another . . .

Where had I experienced this before?

With a sharp breath I remembered. Nearly four years ago, Marchmont Street: when I lay ill and waited for a step on the stairs. I put on another record, sat back and looked at the ceiling: with me, a sign of turmoil.

Staring, I saw through to the bedroom above. In the doorway, a big, middle-aged man looking at me as I sat in bed reading, a boy of twenty asleep by my side. I heard his voice speak again the last words he was ever to say to me. 'I certainly did start something . . .'

The night the news had been broken to me, when I reflected that he had left not a single memento of himself in the flat, I was wrong. He had left Fess.

And the deceased cannot alter their wills; what they have left to the living is irrevocable. This silent boy, with the lithe, smooth body and the amiable smile, was my bond with a dead man.

CHAPTER TWENTY-NINE

THE LOVED AND THE FEARED

Molly and Fess.

I looked at the door. If it opened, which of the two would I hope to see?

But it was not as simple as that. I was waiting for him in a torment I had not expected and if he entered now, I would feel tormented relief. If she appeared, I would be delighted by the sight of the person I loved.

But the door did not open. A dog, was he? The dog had strayed.

It was getting dark. I turned on the lights and sat down to grim work. For three hours I injected zing into dialogue. It was like sawing logs.

I went up to the kitchen, boiled myself a couple of eggs, and went to bed. Was it midnight? I did not look.

I was half-asleep when the light clicked on and I turned, half expecting a burly, middle-aged man. Instead, a boy with a few drinks aboard but glowing with health, 'Hello . . .'

'Car O.K.?'

'Fine, I just thought wi' you workin' I'd take the night off sort o' thing.'

'That's all right, I'm sleepy, goodnight . . .'

But it was the warm body next to me that slept. Thought I'd take the night off . . . Well, why not, when you're on duty night and day, shawfer, handyman? . . .

Had he taken the car? If he had, could I blame him?

I was in a bad way. And I had not even the advantage that the two sides of my problem were separate: one in Fulham Road and the bung, the other in a furtive bed-sitter in King's Cross. They were daily and inextricably mixed.

Whom could I talk to? Dick? I shrank from his realism. 'Well, now you've made your two beds you'd better lie between them.'

I took the weak course. I would do nothing, and see how things went.

*   *   *

Next day I delivered my Hitchcock homework to the factory, where it was checked and passed, like laundry.

The film was to be a great success. It is possible that my additional dialogue, in the amplified mouths of Edna Best, Frank Vosper et al., sprang to life in Odeons all over Britain, in the Paramount, New York, and in flea-pits throughout the globe. Maybe it made the inscrutable Japanese sit up and twitter 'What is name of hon'lable gent who put zing in jokes, pass please ploglamme?' I was never to know.

My Welsh cousin seemed so much taken for granted that he was hardly ever mentioned. I was glad, for I was getting no ounce of pleasure from a presence which was essential to me. The characteristics which had amused me as those of an acquiescent young body—the animal stillness, the cigarette-end, the slow smile exposing the gap, the strong hands on the wheel—were now disturbing.

One morning Molly and Ida and I were sitting in the sun when he came strolling round the house, shirtless and in his old working flannels; he had been cleaning the car. He stopped in front of us and removed his shoes and socks.

'Oh, look,' Ida called gaily, 'the boy's gone mad, he's taking his trousers off!'

We looked. He had unfastened his belt and was slowly undoing his fly-buttons. When he had finished, he dropped the trousers over his ankles and stepped smiling out of them as Ida gave a shriek of mock relief. He was in bathing-shorts, new, white, tight.

He stood poised on the edge of the lawn, then dived with sudden grace. Disappearing for long enough to be awaited, he emerged some distance off. His hair was in his eyes, and he shook it briskly free.

'He's got a nice figure,' Ida said as she stitched, 'and not a hair on his chest, a Greek statue. I don't *mind* hair on a man but I don't miss it either ...'

I wished I had no hair on my chest. And I couldn't dive like that, or stay under as long. I wanted to compete.

Out of affection? No, because he was younger. As he vaulted

[348]

out and hopped up and down to get dry, I watched him coldly. I had no affection for him because I knew he had none for me or for anybody else; the news of Bill had brought no flicker of grief to the young face.

When he returned from changing, I watched him lope across the grass, settle serenely in a deck-chair and take out a packet of cigarettes. For a moment he seemed about to pick up the newspaper next to him and to open it, but he did not. I had never seen him read anything.

His eyes narrowed lazily as he looked past a curl of smoke at the far bank. A strong face? No. Weak? No. Just a face. What was he thinking of? Nothing.

From the river, a thin thread of music: Al Bowlly singing 'The Very Thought of You', I must get the record. In the trees, the birds sang and I was beginning to hate that. The repeated twitters seemed to be forming refrains, jingles to taunt me. Watch out, watch out, watch out . . .

Molly looked up and smiled. 'Won't it be lovely if the weather's like this all summer? . . .', then went back to her work, as intent as a child while her delicate fingers worked over a bowl of peas and pods. 'It's so boring I'm quite enjoying it.'

I loved her and wanted to tell her so. It would have pleased her, delighted Ida, and Fess would not have heard. But that sort of thing did not trip lightly off my tongue.

'Molly,' I said instead, 'what would you feel about Fess giving you driving lessons so I can give you a little car as a housewarming present for the bung?' The lessons started next day.

Then, for me, a distraction in the shape of an acting stint at the studio: a juvenile 'supporting' Jan Kiepura in *A Song For You*, a musical film which was not one of the G.B. epics. Needless to say I did not sing, but in between speaking interrupted sentences, while half-hidden from the camera, I played the piano, triumphantly front-face.

Or rather I did not play the piano: my fingers darted up and down dummy keys in reasonable agreement with a pianist who had obliged several weeks back and was at the moment, in absentia, well in evidence on a sound-track pouring out of a loudspeaker.

The end of my solo was so wildly applauded off-screen by a

night-clubful of sneering extras that I was required, in my only close shot, to rise and take a bashful bow.

Miss Cooke, after I wrote of my day's work, described it as 'money for bad jam'.

❋   ❋   ❋

The Saturday after I finished, Molly was to attend a wedding in Ascot. 'They're nice and they'll expect me. I wonder what the trains are like . . .'

'Fess'll take you,' I said, 'won't you, Fess?'

'Wi' pleasure.'

When they got there, was she to introduce him and leave him to small-talk over champagne with puzzled gentlefolk?

I said quickly, 'He'll wait for you in the village. You'll be much happier there, won't you, Fess?'

'Oh, yes, I'm happy anywhere.'

That Saturday brought our first bad weather. Our river, empty and rain-pocked, looked as if it had taken umbrage.

Molly appeared in the wedding essentials of high heels and a hat. She disliked hats. This one was a simple pink halo which enhanced her, but she knew it made her look social and unlike the person who belonged to me.

Fess got into his raincoat, I took her arm and held an umbrella over her. We stumbled after him as he strode bandily on through the bedraggled wood. He opened the car door for her and clambered in behind the wheel. In front of the wedding hat, on his glistening brown head he wore nothing.

Yet he did. An invisible peaked cap. The car receded into the damaged day.

I had never been alone in the bung, and no longer lulled by the fine weather I felt growing alarm. Ida and Freddie arrived, we lit a fire in the unfamiliar big room and at six Molly and Fess arrived back. She looked depressed. 'Isn't it nice to see a fire? I'll just take off this beastly hat . . .'

The reception had been indoors of course, everybody asking about Jack: how's old Carus, where are you living now? . . .

'Silly of me to go, Fess was the lucky one.' Fess laughed appreciatively. Seeing her miserable made me miserable too.

Ida put on 'I'll Follow My Secret Heart' and the drinks flowed faster than usual. But the sherry made us both more depressed. Our eyes met, hers filled with tears; I jerked away my head and stared dejectedly into the fire.

I heard her say, 'Will you all think me dreary if I go to bed? I don't feel too grand, it's been a bit of a day. Thank you, Fess, for driving me ...'

I wanted to follow her into her darkened little bedroom before she looked out at the rain-soaked wood, and put my arms round her. But a corner of me would not move.

Was I afraid?

Next morning the summer was back and she had cheered up. I kissed her, 'Better?'

'Yes of course, the weather makes all the difference.' In the night I had done a lot of thinking: I took her hand, 'Let's go to the end and talk.' We sat next to each other.

I said, 'I'm sorry about the wedding.' And added quickly, 'yesterday.'

She said, 'Darling, do you want to get out of it?'

I looked at her, taken aback. She had said it once before. 'Get out? ... Oh, no ...'

'Because if you do, you must. Why not look for a little bungalow a few miles off? Fess can look after you.'

Suddenly the idea of living alone with him was intolerable; I realized that now he not only obsessed me, he bored me. I held her hand tight and forged ahead. 'At the wedding, did you feel in a false position?'

She hesitated. 'I didn't like being there on my own.'

'Shall we risk it? I mean, forget the King's Proctor, let Jack divorce you and cite me as co-respondent, then we can get married and have a child. Shall we go up to town this afternoon and spend the night together, do you approve?'

She looked at me. 'Yes, if you do.'

'I do.'

In the kitchen I said to Fess, 'We plan to go up for the evening. Would you like to go off on your own?' He grinned. 'Suit me fine.'

Over dinner at Odone's I smiled at Molly and turned to Ida. 'Can I come back for the night?'

She looked at us in delighted surprise. 'But I've been waiting for this!'

She was as tickled as Juliet's Nurse, 'Now not too much wine, you know the proverb; and, Molly, that narrow bed of yours just isn't right, we'll put the mattress on the sitting-room floor with a lot of cushions. I'm told the floor can be scrumptious!'

Back in 103a I lugged the mattress in, Ida said, 'Bless you, my children' and went to bed. We were alone.

I put my arms round her. 'We've both done this before but we're both nervous, and for obvious reasons that's more worrying for me. You know I love you very much, which in a way isn't to do with this so you'll make allowances, won't you?'

'I'm nervous too. The only thing . . . It sounds planny . . .'

'You mean precautions? Let's worry later. Anyway, the way I feel, we'll be lucky if we have to worry.'

She laughed, and we kissed again. Then I said, 'You won't expect Dima, will you?'

'I'd forgotten Dima . . . He was nervous the first time and it was an awful failure.'

If true, it was a generous admission; if false, a most tactful invention.

But even with its help I could not forget the importance of the moment. We were as clumsily and aimlessly loving as two adolescents, and like two adolescents we went to sleep in each other's arms.

The sleep was serene and dreamless, because we knew that from now on, whenever our bodies met, there would be both stimulation and rest.

*   *   *

Out of the house—before the charwoman arrived—and walking down Draycott Avenue, I savoured the secrecy of my position: a young man of the world striding away from his mistress's lodging. I was released.

I told Mrs Tilley that Mrs Carus-Wilson and I had married quietly the day before—'Oh, I am pleased, she's a nice lady'—and that next day she would be moving into 71a. Then I told Fess, adding that he would be moving one flight higher, to the little room.

Never has a demoted favourite taken the news with such serenity. 'O.K. I'll move me stuff up.'

After lunch I bought flowers, called for Molly and her belongings—not in the car, with Fess at the wheel, but in a taxi—and
Ida saw us off as if to a honeymoon in the West Indies.

Momentous changes can be marked by the most trivial signs.
Mid-morning, from the wardrobe facing the double bed, two
suits, a pair of flannel trousers and two square-faced pairs of shoes
had made their stolid way upstairs. Mid-afternoon, they were
replaced by three or four short skirts, an evening gown, a fur
jacket and a handful of tiny high heels.

Mrs Tilley had stayed on specially, 'Welcome home, Mrs
Williams.' The only Mrs Williams I knew was my mother, it was
hard to get used to.

And on my next visit to the studios, I had to get used to saying
casually, 'Oh, my wife's calling for me.' It made me feel older, but
it was worth it. It was good to tell friends, and to ask them to
memorize, 'Is Mrs Williams in?', though I knew there would be
times when Mrs Tilley would hear the name of Mrs Carus-er-
Williams.

Molly took me to dinner with her old friends Jo and Alan
Bott. I could not remember the last formal dinner-party I had
been to; to be at one with her was like being already married
and I enjoyed the novelty of it, completely.

I thought, now I know what it means in books when a man
thinks, I will do anything to make her happy, anything . . . I asked
Ida what I should buy. She said, 'Molly's always wanted a
Persian lamb coat,' and I took the hint.

Then one morning on the lawn I opened my typewriter to start
a letter, 'Where do I write to Jack, to where he works?'

She hesitated. 'I think we should clear one thing up.'

I looked at her. What was coming?

She said, 'I don't know any reason why I can't have a baby but
if I couldn't, would you want to marry me?'

I thought. 'No, there'd be no point in not going on as we are
now. What do you say we wait till you start a baby, then I'll
write to Jack, make a clean breast of the whole unspeakable
business and ask him to divorce you? Then we can beg the discretion of the court due to your disgraceful condition and get
married at once. What about it?'

'I was hoping you'd suggest that.'

Next day she said, 'There's a furniture sale ... I've seen an old tallboy, is it all right?'

I didn't know what an old tallboy was, all I could think of was a retired policeman. A beautiful antique chest-of-drawers arrived at 71a, the first of her bargains and our first piece of furniture.

Two days later we were walking along Oxford Street when I caught a glitter of metal on the pavement. We stopped and I picked up a ring. A gold wedding-ring. I examined it. On the inside a name was engraved. I said 'They've spelt it wrong, they've missed out the S'. The name was 'William'. Before we entered Selfridge's I made Molly try the ring on. It fitted, and went on fitting. The coincidences of real life are unusable in fiction.

Everything about her interested me. In an old box she found a cutting from the *Sporting and Dramatic News* of ten years ago: a full-page colour photograph of A CABARET SOUBRETTE MISS MOLLY O'SHANN ONE OF THE ATHOS BEAUTIES AT PRINCE'S.

Above the legend, the head of a pretty girl of nineteen who had been told to look as like the sultry vamp Theda Bara as she could manage. A long straight dark bob was cut in a fringe, the chin rested fatefully on intertwined hands, mascara-ringed eyes probed deep into the camera. But the sultriness had gone astray. Instead of smouldering, a schoolgirl was giving a solemn stare as she tried to obey instructions.

I said 'D'you mean that when I was at Oxford I could have dropped into a London night-club and seen you sing and dance?' 'Of course.'

Since by day and by night she and I travelled closer, I took it for granted that my devil was exorcised. But it was not so.

While the protective love grew more secure, the other darkened and exulted. I felt inside me a rumbling as unmistakable as the inner disorders of the body: the sound of the battle between good and bad. To my alarm the bad, in the shape of a harmless young Welsh cousin about the house, was becoming more insistent than before.

There was a reason. The weather stayed so unusually constant and my attendance at the studio was once more so nil, that we hardly ever drove to London. When we did, he would drop us at

71a and disappear. 'I might pop up an' stay the night wi' me Auntie in Hendon...' Was there one?

The lack of privacy meant that any time we found ourselves alone for a minute, usually on the lawn, I looked at him, he would wink lazily through cigarette-smoke, and a fog of conspiracy wafted across the sunny day to spoil it.

It was at such a moment that he said, 'I heard from me Dad this mornin', me cousin Glyn called on his new motor-bike, sounds a beauty, I like motor-bikes.'

I remembered that in a few weeks Festiniog Griffith would be officially grown-up. I heard myself say—I who had no affection for him—'Would you like one for your twenty-first birthday?'

He blinked and smiled. 'Ta very much, I wouldn't mind one at all.'

But he had gone red with pleasure. The sane side of me noted what a foolish gesture I was making. Since during any absence of his I wondered where he was, how would I feel every time he roared off into liberty?

Next day he came back from Staines and showed me an ad in *The Motor Cycle*, BE THE KING OF THE HIGHWAY, GET THAT BIKE! I suggested he went up in a couple of weeks and had a look round.

When I told Molly it was 'because he'd been such a help getting us in,' she said, 'What a marvellous present, he must be thrilled.' I was glad her little car was on its way.

*　　*　　*

We agreed that I should phone Dick, tell him our news and ask him down. 'Emlyn, I'm very happy for you. No, no, I'll find my own way. I've only the old toothbrush and pyjamas, you know my simple tastes...'

And one hot noon he crossed our hot bridge. No flannels or open neck for this staid bespectacled solicitor with newspapers under an arm and a shabby attaché case which looked as if it contained a writ. His only concession: no overcoat.

He sank into a deck-chair, straightened his tie and was handed a cup of coffee by Ida. Sitting opposite him in bathing shorts, I felt undressed. Fess gave him a cigarette. 'Comin' for a dip,

Dick?' Dick doing a high dive was a spectacle less probable than Dick floating above the trees.

He looked round with a sigh. 'I'll never get over *Spring, 1600*, people still go on about it. When I'm up at John G's and hear that music my poor old glasses mist right up and I reach for a hankie . . .'

Left alone with me he said, into his paper, 'Well, dear Emlyn, I think you and your little woman are going to be very happy, you're lucky. How's Fess?'

Watch out, this is a wise old owl . . . 'He's fine. He's my Welsh cousin, did you know?'

'No, but I'll remember.'

'He's teaching Molly to drive.'

Then a question, through his *Telegraph*, like an arrow. 'I imagine when that's over he'll go back to Gloucester?'

'I expect so.' I was relieved to see Ida come out with a tray.

'John's doing *The Maitlands*, the new Mackenzie piece.' Mack, the Wallace ASM . . . He went on, 'It's modern of course, John says if his public don't see him soon in a pair of trousers they'll think he hasn't got any.'

The new Mackenzie piece . . . I shut my eyes against the sun, which hardens the flesh and softens the mind. I must write a play . . .

Two days later Ida teased Fess, 'I saw you nattering with that blonde in Woolworth's. Did I hear her say, "See you Tuesday night?"'

He grinned amiably. On Tuesday evening, after dinner, 'I gotta date, see you all in the mornin',' and he smiled at Ida.

'All right,' Ida twinkled, '*I* know . . .' When he had gone she said, 'He's rather sweet, must find it a bit dull being with all of us so much.'

On the lawn, by the light of the moon and of an Aladdin lamp, Molly was doing tapestry, Ida reading a magazine and I running up extra dialogue urgently requested for—of all things—*Chu Chin Chow*, which Gaumont-British had decided to disinter for the veteran comedian George Robey. 'Just give it a touch of that class from *Spring, 1600*. See what I mean, Emmer-lun?'

I settled down to tapping out pseudo-Khayyam, a copy of a copy. 'Thine eyes beloved have the bloom of the fresh fruits of Paradise . . .' I thought of Miss Cooke, this was even worse jam.

Where was he?

I said I would work on for an hour. Molly and Ida went to bed. I carried the Aladdin into the sun-room and worked there. 'O gift of Allah, I have strange misgivings...'

I stared at the keys and my thoughts wandered into a fantasy more Oriental than *Chu Chin Chow* could ever be. I was a mediaeval emperor who has engaged a bodyguard to report on any sexual misdemeanour on the part of his servant: when they do, he is stretched and held down on a rack while I grasp the screws, stand looking down into the calm, expressionless eyes and whisper...

'Never has that face been disturbed by tenderness, never have those full lips been pressed hard together in momentary ecstasy. Well my boy, let us find out what can be done by bodily pain, let us see the beads of sweat roll down that serene brow, let us watch the lips twist into a snarl of supplication. Come on, show...' The creak of the screws.

The house was silent. My pulse had quickened, I was afraid of my own bad fancies. I need not have been, I was the one on the rack.

I blew out the lamp and went into the kitchen to pump water for tomorrow. On the bridge, a soft step. A shadow crossed the window. I opened the door, 'Sh, everybody's in bed.' A distant owl.

He was standing with his back to the moon, hands in pockets and the face masked, framing the glow of the cigarette. But I knew he was smiling. The obscurity and the lowness of our voices troubled me. They made us intimate without friendship.

'Sorry,' he whispered, 'I'm a bit late for down here.'

'That's all right,' I whispered back, 'does you good to get away. How d'you get on, chum?' I was roughing up my accent, to suit his. 'D'you take her to a pub?'

'No fear, I don't believe in the palaver, took her off into a field.'

'What was it like?'

He gave me back the two words I might have known would fall out like a packet of cigs out of a slot-machine. 'Not bad.' He stood, hands still in pockets, rocking slightly. Then a hand came up to flick the cigarette, and in the second's glow the mouth was scarlet.

I whispered again. 'Did you take her clo's off?'

'No, just the essential.'

Then, in a moonlight which has inspired the poets he added, 'Got a couple o' thistles round me balls, but O.K. I got her address, what d'you say to a threesome?'

In this place it offended me.

And what right had I to be offended? 'I'm getting cold,' I said, and went to bed for a sleepless night.

*   *   *

The silky river weather spun miraculously on. One morning Fess drove us up to London to a garage in the Fulham Road, where Molly acquired a Baby Austin. As she drove it for the first time to the bung, I could tell she was a born driver, also that it immensely strengthened the independent status she had missed for so long.

Another stint for me, this time for the theatre: Korda was to present a successful German comedy, *Josephine*, and wanted me to adapt. For three weeks, the click of the typewriter soothed the unquiet breast.

Then another studio call. To play in *Evensong*, a big semi-musical film based on Beverley Nichols' play and starring Evelyn Laye. Starting out as her adolescent lover, while she sang 'The Rose of Tralee', I further enlarged my musical versatility by accompanying her, out of focus, on the organ. The rest of the film I spent, like Miss Laye, growing old. Our big scene was in a mental home which she visited as a graceful lady in the misty sixties—she was a luscious thirty-four—to find me in a wheel-chair, shaking very slightly with my hair powdered grey and a grey moustache.

All of which made me look like my father, out of his mind and heavily disguised as a young man impersonating an old one. As I shook away I thought, when my mother sees this in the Alhambra Shotton it won't be her favourite bit. ('I liked when you played the organ . . .')

One evening, the hottest yet, I had to be in Henley to dine with a German from the Korda office who would help me over language queries in *Josephine*.

Fess drove me, and as I came out of the Angel Hotel he was

waiting. 'Oh yes, had quite a nice time at the pub ...' The river bobbed with coloured lights, there was a line of cars out for a summer jaunt. Frivolity was in the air. Laxity.

He was merry, though I knew it could never affect his driving. 'A coupla beers, then a chap at the bar treated me to a coupla wee whiskies ... Blimey it's as hot as Spain, remember Spain?' He winked at me.

It was the first time we had been alone in the car since then, but if I had said so it would have sounded sentimental. I did not feel sentimental.

The car coursed between high-lighted hedges, while the grey eyes were fixed on the obedient road.

'Pass a cig will you, Emlyn, an' light it for us?'

In the dark, the glow of the mouth. He hummed a snatch of song.

'You're right,' I said, 'it is like Spain.'

I undid my top shirt-button and loosened my tie. The car turned into our long drive. Blackness.

'It's on 'ot nights like this,' drawled the voice, 'that people forget theirselves an' forget the old motto, if you can't be good be careful.' I smelt a whiff of whisky, was reminded of Bill and hung on every valueless word.

He went on. 'It stands to reason, doesn't it? It's bloody old Nature, God bless 'er.'

A careful bumpy progress, then the car slowed down. And down. I stared at the hedges, still and emerald in the lights. Then I looked at him, just as he negotiated a bad rut and accelerated.

'Did you think I was stoppin'?'

'Looked like it for a minute.'

'An' then turn the lights off? No, mother's boy wouldn' do a thing like that.'

The others were in bed, lights out except for one Aladdin for us, turned low in the kitchen. The house was still hot from the day. Fess tiptoed softly into the big room where he had his folding bed and switched a torch on.

I turned to go to my room. His door was open.

I went in. 'Sorry, I just want to check a speech in the German copy of the play.'

'Carry on, don't mind me.'

I picked it up from the bookshelf he had made and pretended to look something up. There was the rustle of shirt and trousers, then the elastic snap of shorts being pulled down and the scratch of a match. He sat on the edge of his bed and lit a cig, while the torch on the table made strange shadows. I replaced the book, crossed to the door, closed it softly and walked back to him.

On a hot night—cold, cold. Since during the rest of the time there was pain, and no pleasure now, what meaning was there?

He yawned and took a puff at his cigarette. 'Sleepy, must be the heat.'

'I'm sleepy too, goodnight.'

I had said it so abruptly that anybody else would have said, 'What's the matter?'

He had not noticed. I tiptoed out.

Getting into bed I changed my mind, went out into the passage and opened another door. I did this many nights, so though awakened from sleep she was not startled.

I whispered as usual, comfortably, 'Can I get into bed?', slid beside her and put my arms round her. I was home, and warm with relief of body and of mind.

Later I said, 'Can I sleep here?' The bed was so narrow that I didn't usually. I lay a moment with my arms round her, at rest. Then, hearing regular breathing, I worked my lower arm from under and turned to go to sleep myself.

I could not. I swivelled gently, stared up at the black of the ceiling, and thought in circles. The night silence was deep. She stirred and said, 'You're in love with him, aren't you?'

I did not move. Had I dreamt it? The silence was deeper. Whatever words would be spoken from now on, I would remember for ever.

'Yes.' I was still staring upwards. Then I added, 'You guessed?'

'If you love somebody yourself you sense things without being told.'

Words started to tumble out of me. 'Except that I'm not, not really—I did love Bill . . .'

'I know.'

I remembered the day I had laid my head on her breast and, for the first time, had wept for him. I turned round and again laid my head. But I did not weep. I had no cause to.

She said, 'Oh, I'm glad we're talking, it's seemed so long . . .'

Then I muttered into her warm flesh, 'It's not the same as Bill, I don't even like him, it's a horrible feeling . . .'

'It's been making you unhappy and that's what worries me.'

'I'll get over it, I promise I will. You don't mind?'

'I don't even like you asking me that.'

In the summer dark of our first home we pressed close together, and all was well.

We talked till dawn. I told her my dossier. Night conversation, in a shared bed in the dark, has a timeless ease unknown to the day. Over and over again it curls inconsequently into a shared pause, to glide easily out the other side.

At the end I said, 'I have to ask it again—you don't mind?'

'No.'

'I've heard of sweethearts and wives going mad and rushing white-lipped to their lawyers.'

'Then there must be something wrong with me. After what I went through for seven years, those awful girls, the petty decep- tions, Weaver laughing in my face in the street—oh no, there's all the difference in the world.'

'We've talked about Dima—do you wish in your heart I was as straightforward?'

'But you are straightforward, if you weren't you wouldn't have told me all that.'

'You know what I mean. Do you wish I was as . . . uncompli- cated?'

'I'm not sure Dima was as simple as all that. He talked a lot about his life-long friend Vladimir, I think Dima'd been around.'

It occurred to me more and more that what I had my arm round was not only the interpreter of Kiki, Riki-Tiki, The Cocky- olly Bird and Nicolette, but a small woman of the world.

The birds were singing, without guile, to a happy summer dawn after a happy sleepless night.

CHAPTER THIRTY

A BRUSH AGAINST THE DARK

Now as near to each other as two people can get, we had break-fast on the lawn before anybody else was up. I was telling her more about Bill when Fess came out in his bathing shorts—'Mornin' all'—and dived into the river.

I watched her watching, and said, 'What are you thinking?'

She looked at me and smiled. 'I'm wondering what you see in him.'

'I've wondered too. Do you like him?'

She hesitated. 'I've never liked him.' Splash, splash ...

'You've been tactful. What don't you like in him?'

'Well, he's stupid, and lazy—oh, he's been useful around the house, but he never does anything on his own initiative. Also, I don't trust him.'

This took me aback. 'You don't?'

'I've nothing to go on, I just don't.'

He was climbing out of the water. 'Wakes you up a treat.' I watched him as he walked slowly into the house.

No longer a secret, he was a dull country boy, stupid and lazy. I smiled at Molly and took her hand. 'Shall I suggest him going home now?'

'Oh, no, that would make a situation. Don't you think he'll get restless and move on of his own account?' That made sense. Fess took the others up in my car; he was going to town anyway, to shop for his motor-bike. We had a perfect day together. I lay on the lawn, as if recuperating.

Fess was back by six, pleased with his visit. 'Just eighty-one pounds including tax and registration. It's a lot but it's a Rudge, one of the new ones, you don't mind? I'm to pick her up to-morrow.' He handed me the typed bill.

'Fine, I'll make out a cheque.'

He looked embarrassed, 'They said I could only take it away if I paid cash.'

I saw their point, dealing with a boy of twenty, and made the cheque out to 'Cash'. Next morning he walked to Staines and took the train up. 'All right if I stay with me Auntie in Hendon?'

The morning after that, from the bridge, the carefree whistle of the young racing driver. He handed me my receipt. 'Would you both like to come over and see her?'

We followed him. Outside the shed, with the shabby old Morris in the background, 'she' stood lucent with spank-newness, an all-powered pet whose power was at the beck and call of her master. 'I'll just give her a breath o' the local air, anybody want a go on the pillion?'

As he bestrode her, I guessed he wanted to show her off in Staines. For the first time, he loved. He showed us what he called the ignition key, turned it, the pet gave a savage roar and they were off, nearly knocking the postman off the path.

He brought two household bills and a letter which I opened on the lawn: 'To F. Griffith Esq.' I had not looked at the envelope.

The typed note had a pound-note clipped to it. 'Dear Sir, We note that when you just paid us in cash the sum due, namely £51.3.9., you miscalculated in our favour by handing us £1 too much, viz. £52.3.9. We have pleasure in enclosing £1 refund, Yrs faithfully . . .' £51.3.9? A slip of the typewriter? It should be £81.3.9.

I looked again. A second mistake; instead of £52.3.9. it should be £82.3.9.

Would a business firm do that?

I went to the desk and took out the typed bill and the receipt Fess had just handed to me. Both said, clearly, £81.3.9.

Then I noticed something, remembered a Christmas present and took it from the desk: a magnifying-glass. I trained it on the bill, then on the receipt. On both, the 8 was not quite symmetrical. It had been carefully treated, with a razor-blade and a fine pen, to change from a 5 to an 8.

Feeling like Scotland Yard, I opened my typewriter, typed 555555, took a razor-blade and a pen and worked on each digit. It took several tries for me to compete with the two items of evidence.

I looked at them again. Neat, very.

I felt queasy, and searched in my memory. Yes, this was the

first time for me to encounter this. Forgery. On a petty scale, but forgery.

I tried to understand, but it was beyond the boundary of my mind. I looked at my sunlit surroundings: at the grass, the river, the loved and simple house which for me held happiness.

Branches which had swayed with slow grace were now stealthy, with every leaf watching, and the birds had new notes. Not taunting but warning: careful, careful, this is only the beginning. On a summer morning outside an English bungalow, the world had tarnished.

Molly came out of the sun-room with coffee. 'What's the matter?' I explained and handed her the magnifying-glass. She examined the evidence and stared back at me.

A dinghy passed. A young girl, a young man rowing and laughing. Were they like us? Or had they something to hide . . . ?

I tried to be sensible. 'It's only thirty pounds . . .'

'Only? You once sent me exactly that and it was a fortune. What are you going to do?'

'Spring it on him unawares, and I want you to be there.'

In the middle of a landscape we were speaking low like conspirators. Then we heard something: a distant hum growing to a confident roar, and I knew what it must feel like to recognize the approach of the invader.

I lifted a cushion and slipped the evidence under it. Silence. The day had come to a standstill. Then a whistle, and on the bridge the jaunty step of the speed-merchant.

As he disappeared into the house I got up and walked over the bridge and up the path—yes, there was the key still in its lock. I pocketed it, walked back and sat again just as we heard the stolid tread on the sun-room step. He was holding a fresh cigarette.

I said, 'Did you have a good run?'

'Not bad.'

He sat in the deck-chair between us with a sigh of satisfaction and lit the cigarette. As I looked across him at Molly I became conscious of something as physical as a smell, or the radiation of heat or cold. The feeling that between us sat a foreign creature disguised, in broad daylight, as a human being.

He spoke. 'I thought I'd tootle up to Gloucester on the bike for a couple o' days sort o' thing——'

'I'm afraid you can't.'

He looked at me inquiringly. 'Beg pardon?'

I removed the cushion and handed him the letter, the pound-note dangling from it. As he read he took his time, moving his lips slightly. Then looked up at me, with no expression. 'But this is addressed to me.'

'It was with two letters for me, I opened the envelope without looking at it.'

'You *opened* it?' He looked from me to Molly and back, with wide, scandalized eyes.

I felt myself flushing. 'I get more letters than you do and I took it for granted it was another one for me.'

This wasn't going right, why was I doing the explaining?

'Expect me to believe that?' The tone was incredulous enough to be just short of impertinence.

'Do you mean,' Molly said coldly, 'that Emlyn's lying?'

'I never said anythink about lies. Funny, all week I been expectin' a letter from a girl-friend. I wondered where it had got to.'

There was no answer to that. But the process of his mind confirmed that Molly and I, speaking with the intonations of everyday talk, were sharing an open-air morning with a potential criminal.

I took the letter from him, unclipped the pound-note, folded it into my wallet and handed the letter back. The incorrigible watching corner of me thought, a nice piece of stage business . . . 'I could ask for the other twenty-nine back, but I'm not going to.'

'I'm glad, I can be doing with it.'

'You know perfectly well that if you had said you needed money I'd have given it you.'

'But that would ha' been beggin', wouldn't it?'

I thought, my next question is going to start the scene I'm trying to avoid but I've got to ask it. 'Would you say begging was more of a come-down than forgery?'

But the scene did not happen. Instead, a quick smile behind the cigarette and a shrug. 'Forgery, this isn't forgery, it's a fiddle. What's wrong with a fiddle?'

Again the feeling of an alien body. I said, 'Could I have the keys of here and 71a, and then will you go and pack?'

'Right.' He rose smartly, took the keys from a pocket, tossed them to me. 'O.K., I'll push off now.'

Turning to go, he hesitated. Not from doubt. He had a practical problem.

'I don't think I can get my case on to the back o' the bike.'

'You're not taking the bike.'

A pause. The answer came. Flat, not even antagonistic. Factual. 'Oh, yes I am; it's my bike.'

'Not now it isn't, it's mine. I've got the key.'

He stared from me to Molly, and back. His loved one had been taken from him, and for the first and last time his face expressed something. It drained of colour, the eyes blazed and the lips twisted into rage. It was a look as primitive as I had ever seen on a human being.

He turned on his heel and walked quickly into the house.

We looked at each other, too taut to speak. Then we sat back in the sun, closed our eyes and tried to relax.

On the bridge, his footstep. Then more footsteps, receding, the slow confident walk. I imagined the shabby suitcase.

He would pass his gleaming toy without a look, a love that was already passing. Then the steps would proceed up the drive in the heat of the day. The tread of a boy of twenty-one who was no different now from what he would be at fifty: empty of affection, of conscience, of humanity.

We were both happy for the rest of the day. Acting as my own doctor I had diagnosed a clean bill of health. A mysterious fever had abated.

But the doctor was wrong.

*   *   *

For when I woke next morning, as certainly as if a thermometer had confirmed it, the fever was back. Its return demoralized me as much as a physical relapse would have done.

As if to cool it, I got up early, put on bathing shorts, ran out and dived into the river. As I came up, I realized that I had tried to dive as well as he had, and that I was now giving my head the same quick jerk. But this was absurd . . .

I sat in my deck-chair, Molly in hers. We did not mention him, but I knew how relieved she was by his absence. Between us was the deck-chair in which he sat yesterday. In which he would never sit again.

Molly said, 'You're very quiet.'

'I'm enjoying us being alone together.'

I was too. Is everyone two people, constantly? In the midday heat I wandered over to the shed and looked down at the inanimate beloved, studying it for the first time. And the last: I sold the machine back to the puzzled firm for thirty pounds, and was lucky at that.

Then one morning I walked out to the shed, got into the old Morris—my car—and sat in it: at the wheel. For five minutes I indulged my mind. Then I walked into Staines and engaged a garage attendant to teach me to drive.

Up and down the straight roads, I was a good pupil if a singing one is good who attacks the notes in the right order but out of tune. Once at a garage, I turned the car correctly but instead of the brake I pressed the accelerator—they seemed dangerously close to each other—and nearly hurtled my helpless instructor into a petrol pump.

I would never have passed a test, but I learnt. Just. And felt I was accomplishing something which baffled analysis.

What was he doing? Was he sitting at home in Gloucester, extracting postal orders from his father's brief-case and meticulously doctoring them? Or in a haystack, the body warm but the heart cold, foraging?

*　　*　　*

With August, a small part in a big film. Gaumont-British presents . . . GEORGE ARLISS !

He was an enormously successful Hollywood star at the height of his career, and a great catch for G.B. Which makes him sound like the Valentino of 1934, slant-eyed. sinuous. But there was nothing of the tango about Mr Arliss—he was never known as anything else—who was sixty-six, two years older than my father.

Having made his debut in the mists of the English provinces and graduated to the West End as a respected character actor, he had proved the exception to a strict rule. A small man with a big, hooked nose and thin lips was, inexplicably, a Film Name.

Hollywood, in one culture-part after another, had deified him: the nose and the lips, surrounded by false hair of varying shapes and sizes, have on celluloid honoured the physiognomy of Disraeli, Voltaire, Alexander Hamilton, Rothschild and Cardinal Richelieu, each demanding a four-hour make-up session and each ending up, in crowded cinemas all over the world, as Mr Arliss.

In private life he was a quiet-mannered, quietly dressed dry little Englishman of a school so old that it must have been pulled down years ago. His wife, who made discreet appearances in his films, was a lady of the same school, and as quiet. Two money-making mice.

Mr Arliss was to play the Duke of Wellington. No one at Gaumont-British could discover who had suggested that he should be invited to impersonate an immensely tall, handsome soldier-lover whose advances in the alcove were known to be as intrepid and as penetrating as in the field. Everybody protested, 'It wasn't *my* idea!'

Mr Arliss had the makings of the Wellington nose but it would seem that from there down the resemblance dwindled.

There would be two weeks' rehearsal—unheard of then—in a school across from the Studios and empty for the holidays. In a spacious classroom, on the first morning, every important G.B. executive seemed to turn up to join the large cast; the chatter died, everybody not standing rose and the star entered.

After presentations he stood against a background of blackboard and delivered a lecture on *The Iron Duke*. Quietly, whimsically; there were titters, the class was on his side. I would have liked to raise my hand, please, sir, may I leave the room; please sir, why are you Wellington when you're shorter than Napoleon?

Instead I made my mind wander as I used to in chapel when the sermon was on. And my mind knew where to go. To a motorbike gleaming in the sun.

I saw again the massive seat, shiny and black-leathered, moulded so as to be tightly hugged and warmed by its master's inner thighs, with in between the upward thrust of the prow which had confidently supported the delicate burden of the conqueror.

The courtly voice purred on. 'In this film, gentlemen, we must not be afraid to be daring in our ideas ...'

It turned out to be Mr Arliss's first failure.

❖   ❖   ❖

One week-end I was pumping in the kitchen when my eyes followed a ray of sunlight to a corner. It was picking up a pair of men's shoes, dark brown, scuffed, their laces trailing. He had left them behind and they must be thrown away.

I took them, walked to the thick vegetation beyond the back door and looked down at them, held between finger and thumb.

They stared up at me like two blind, unblinking moles; then they turned into shoes again. The ridges of their backs were worn thin and blackish where heels had worked up and down in the steady purposeless stroll through life.

I turned round, and saw nobody. A bird alighted on a twig, looked at me, then soared into the sky as if not to disturb my privacy. I held up the shoes and sniffed at them. They had been long enough in the sun to smell of warm old leather, as they would have smelt if they had that moment been pulled off by the owner. I lowered them from my face, looked at them again and thought of the motor-bike. It was the first and—with luck— the last time in my life for me to glimpse the meaning of an aberration which had puzzled me. Fetishism.

I took off my sneakers and, with the excitement of a secret act, inserted my own feet into the abandoned shoes. They were big on me. I walked a couple of steps, tried to imitate the bandy walk, came to my senses and kicked them off.

But I did not throw them away. I went back in, opened the bottom drawer of my desk and stuffed them into the back of it.

I had made up my mind not to burden Molly with my relapse, but once more she surprised me. I had been sitting in silence for some time.

'You must try and get him out of your system.'

I said I *had* tried, hard: adding that I had even concentrated on visualizing him at fifty, 'when he'll be a fat clod, but it doesn't work.'

'Anyway,' Molly said thoughtfully, 'by the time he's fifty we'll be fifty-eight. It hardly seems worth waiting for.'

I told her that I didn't like the fact that finding him out had made it worse—'knowing there's a side to him that's incomprehensible to me.'

'Yes.' She looked worried. Visitors arrived and we were glad.

Next morning as I helped her to wash up she said, 'Why don't you go up to Gloucester?'

I nearly dropped a plate. 'What?'

Now that he's no longer here, he's turned into something elusive. If you saw him——'

'If I saw him I might be mad enough to bring him back to 71a.'

'Why not? I think you ought to see enough of him to get sick of him.'

'Suppose I don't?'

'We have to risk that.'

✳   ✳   ✳

After two or three drives alone as far as Windsor, I was ready for Gloucester. As Molly saw me off, I could tell she was far more worried about my journey than about its end.

But I had no fears. Sitting at the wheel with my legs splayed a fraction more than they need be—to give the bandy feeling—sailing down a long, straight road at fifty miles an hour and humming in a cheerful monotone, I felt in charge at last.

In the main street of one large town my confidence as a racing driver was bruised by a contretemps. Driving carefully, I heard a long scraping noise, then an outraged shout, 'I say, you, what the hell d'ye mean by bawgein' into my caw? Who d'ye learn your drivin' from, your blawsted grandmothah?'

I had had the bad luck to misjudge the distance between me and a car with at its wheel a species which I thought extinct: the retired Indian civil servant, complete with tomato face, white eyebrows and a moustache of a bushiness which, at a dress rehearsal, would have been laughed off the stage. I remembered I was in Cheltenham and that an English spa is a zoo.

We exchanged addresses, a ritual which sounds prompted by love at first sight, and I was glad to return to the open road. Soon after noon I arrived at 29 Julian Road, Gloucester, dusty but unscathed after seventy miles. It was a bow-fronted house in a respectable street. Mrs Griffith answered the door, a shy housewife, just as respectable. 'Oh, it's not Mr Williams? You've been so good to our Fess, I'll get him . . .'

As I stared at the empty doorway, suddenly and silently he

was standing there, in shirt-sleeves and with no collar. The hairs on his forearm glinted in the sun.

'Hello,' I said casually, 'I was just passing through from Wales on my way to London, thought I'd pop in and say hello. Like to come out and have a bite?'

'Don't mind if I do. Who's drivin' you?'

'I am.'

For him he was startled. 'Well, wonders never cease.' As we walked into the centre of town, he broke the silence. 'Like to see our Cathedral?'

It surprised me. 'All right.' Conditioned though I was against religious show, the vast twilit hush humbled me; we walked round saying nothing until he pointed with a knowing smile—'That's where I used to sit when I was in the choir. How's that for a laugh?'—and went on.

I stopped and looked from him up to the winging arches. An organ was playing, merrily, beautifully. It could have been Byrd-music from *Spring, 1600.*

It was impossible to believe he had set foot here before, or even that he was here now; the presence of a wild animal would have been no more alien. Except that the animal would not have known where he was. This creature did know, and sneered.

He stopped, waited, pointed to a dark little corner which wound itself under the circular staircase leading up to the pulpit, and smiled again. 'In between the 'ymns we used to 'ave fun an' games in there. Got to watch out though, wi' them surplices.'

The organ played on. From most young men the words would have sounded no more than mischievous, but he had brought me into this place to hear him make fun of it, and I was offended.

Mortified too, for I was—more than ever—drawn. There was no retreat. We crossed to the best hotel for drinks and lunch. 'How's tricks,' he said, 'down at the bung...?'

'I want you to come back and stay in your old top room in 71a.'

He looked at me with no expression. 'O.K., suits me for the time bein'.' I laid his keys on the table and we walked back.

As he packed upstairs his mother made tea. 'We're sorry to lose our Fess but glad it's another job with you, Mr Williams.'

His father arrived home from the post-office, and surprised me by being an articulately intelligent man who could have been a

Welsh schoolmaster. He had sent his only son to a grammar school, but the son was one of those boys born to slide down the scale. Facing me, a framed snap of a child of six sprawling on its mother's lap in a cornfield: our Fess. Once more I was struck by the juxtaposition of conventional daily life and the fringe of the underworld.

As the parents stood in the doorway to wave us off, he started to climb into the driver's seat. I said, 'I'll drive.'

He looked at me, and for the second time I saw him angry. He flushed red, walked round the car and got in. In front of his parents, it was a double emasculation.

I got in and slowly did the right things, making a mental note to go on separating the accelerator from the brake. Once out of the town my hands closed on the wheel as purposefully as I could manage. It was important for my morale that I should not land my passenger in a ditch. I concentrated.

At seven in the evening I drew up at 71a without a scratch, and when he got out and went in while I garaged the car it was the reverse of the night he had gone off and come home at two.

Fess poured whiskies, 'Cheers.' There was no conversation but no strain either, and no mention of anybody; it was rather like Spain. We took a taxi to the West End and had a quick one at the Long Bar. I looked at him. Catapulted from his mother's kitchen to this, he was not turning a hair.

Duggie Fairby waved to me, and I told Fess about him and the murderer Sidney Fox; he was mildly interested and turned to look. Duggie felt the scrutiny and returned it, but with no more than a flick. Fess turned back to his whisky, whistled soundlessly and poured soda into it, with the hand which had carefully completed the forgery.

I took him to dinner at De Hem's, where Bill and I had eaten so often. The wine made him talk of his Gloucester pals and girls, slowly, seriously. In the taxi home I sat like an absent-minded detective handcuffed to a prisoner, handcuffs decorously out of sight between buttocks.

As we went upstairs I did not open the door of the bedroom near the bathroom, but continued up to the top floor. To his little room. He followed.

Waking next morning downstairs, alone in the expanse of the marriage bed, I realized I had slept well and was glad. It was

Friday. I said, 'I'm driving down to the bung. Would you like to stay up tonight, and come down by train tomorrow morning? Ida'll be on it, I'll meet you with the car.'

I gave him a five-pound note. 'Ta.'

Driving down the Great West Road, I looked forward immensely to being with Molly. Again I found her more concerned about my driving than about my emotional problems, but Cheltenham made her laugh.

And when I said I had found Fess a dull dinner companion she said, 'I knew it was a good idea.' Then she told me news I had been longing for, though out of superstition we had not discussed it. She was late.

Next morning I drove to Staines Station to fetch him, as he had sometimes fetched me. Ida came out and got in by my side. He was not on the train.

From the bung I phoned 71a, every two hours, for the rest of the day. Molly said, 'But I thought you told him he could come and go as he liked?'

'He's taking it literally.'

During Sunday, I rang up only twice. On Monday morning there was a step on the bridge: the same postman. Opening the letter I realized I had never seen his writing before.

'Dear Emlyn, I have decided against London and am hitch-hiking home, all the best, Fess.'

Clipped to the letter was the five-pound note.

* * *

'You have to admit,' Molly said, 'it's not a bad exit.'

Then she added, 'Five pounds off a debt of twenty-nine is twenty-four, perhaps there'll be another windfall next week.' I could not tell which was uppermost in me: anger, humiliation or grief. No, grief was too noble.

But before I could brood, somebody phoned from the Westminster Theatre, would I consider the part of Piers Gaveston in *Rose and Glove* for two weeks?

It was a plodder of a play about Gaveston and Edward II, but at this juncture I would have jumped at a revival of *Glamour*.

The costumes were no more inspiring than the play. I had imagined tights, but at the dress parade I found myself in a pleated skirt descending well below my knees. I looked ridiculous, but the designer maintained that any abbreviation would 'clash with his concept'.

That evening I behaved extremely unprofessionally by taking the dress home—it was hardly a costume—and by midnight Molly was snipping and hemming.

In the middle of the operation she said, 'I'll be back in a minute'. When she returned she was pale and woebegone. 'I'm afraid it was a false alarm'. I must have been the first expectant father to see his hopes dashed while having his skirt shortened by his bride-to-be.

The play opened on a very hot night, and during my only wait I went out on to the fire-escape. It was a moment of beautiful sunset and ten feet from me, in the light, was the kitchen of a council flat; two young boys of twelve and ten were having their supper, their mother pouring out cocoa.

The boys glanced out, looked me over in my mediaeval clobber and my paint and powder, and went back to food. They were real, what was I?

In the middle of London, I was a cardboard figure. Stifling a powerful urge to run down the fire-escape and get on a bus, I hurried back in and on for my duel. Clumsily brandishing a great sword, I was appalling.

Rose and Glove was kept on for its two weeks. It was not important enough to be disaster.

Disaster was to come.

*   *   *

It had given me a fillip to read in *The Times* of the impending *Josephine*, 'adapted by Emlyn Williams'. It was to be the most ambitious presentation of the autumn season, not only sealed with the name of Korda, but headed by Mary Ellis and Frank Vosper as Napoleon, both at a peak of success.

On the last Saturday of *Rose and Glove*, with the play opening the following Wednesday, a message from them both. They were unhappy about the boy playing Josephine's young son, would I do it for the first two weeks?

It would be another task to occupy me and I was uplifted by the thought of being in the theatre again; I did not count *Rose and Glove.* While the costume was being altered to fit me I slipped into the stalls for a run-through of the first act, in the set. Seeing the curtain down and the footlights on, I felt the old stir.

Looking round, I did remember that when His Majesty's had been announced I had wondered if it was on the big side for a wry, satirical-sentimental little comedy more suited to the Criterion. I remembered too, that the designer was Vincent Korda, the brother who had been brilliantly responsible for many a lavish film décor.

When the curtain rose I thought of *Glamour*: while at Aldershot I had been appalled by the star's apparent poverty, in the West End I was now taken aback by her wealth. The Paris retreat of a Creole divorcée on her uppers was not large, it was vast. Korda had carefully created yet another film set, with real panelling, statues, bronze doors, priceless paintings. After her present floodlit mansion it was difficult to picture Josephine's imperial future, pigging it in the Tuileries.

I learnt too, during the run-through, that the little comedy had been overloaded not only with scenery, but with players. Smallish parts were filled, to bursting point, by such names as Sam Livesey, Lyn Harding and Lady Tree, while George Grossmith, the popular musical comedy star—*No, No, Nanette!*—was making a spectacular return in a straight part.

I dressed with three actors playing no more than bits. One, 'An Orderly', was already a recognized name, Donald Wolfit, and now I was to add my measure. A theatre column had described His Majesty's as 'glowing with reputations'. It was more than glowing, it was on fire.

From the dress rehearsal one thing emerged. Vosper had discovered, late, that he had the same problem as Mr Arliss in *The Iron Duke*, but in reverse. Six-foot-one next to his diminutive Josephine, he had sought to remedy his handicap by having his tight breeches cut in a way which would make his legs look shorter—that is, by cunningly placing the crutch four inches lower than where it belonged. It was an ingenious idea but all it accomplished was to make the great Napoleon look like a tall man whose trousers were coming down. Like the sets, he was too big for the show.

The Korda equerries had worked hard over the first night, and it was less a West End opening than a Film Première. With every tick of the clock, beautiful celebrities poured into Tree's beautiful theatre in jostling anticipation of a beautiful experience. The curtain rose, and in our room four actors peering in mirrors cocked ears to the applause greeting Mary Ellis.

Wolfit pronounced on it. I had not taken to him at the dress rehearsal when he had said, in the rich—nay, opulent—voice which was wasted in a shared dressing-room, 'Oh, Williams, I once filled in with a tour of your *Murder Has Been Arranged*, nice little play . . .' and doubted if I would be won over now. 'Well, chaps, the whistle's gone, sounds as if we're off to a spankin' start.' He made it sound as if I had adapted, from the German, a Cup Final.

Twenty minutes later, waiting for my call, I was jumpy enough to pace up and down the corridor just inside the stage-door. Through glass I saw the stage-doorkeeper stroking his cat, a black one. It would bring luck.

The backstage hush was suddenly broken, from the street, by an irruption as startling as a drunk at a funeral service. Through the glass door, two viragoes glared at me.

One shrieked, 'Will you go now an' tell Miss Ellis an' Mr Vosper that the Gallery First Nighters can't 'ear a bloody word up there an' if they don't speak up there'll be trouble!' They vanished like the witches in *Macbeth*.

Did they expect me to go onstage and say, 'Maman, the neighbours are at their windows and find it difficult to catch what you are saying?'

I tried to blot out the incident, rushed on to cue, and yelled the place down.

During the interval Wolfit again pronounced. 'They're starting to cough, chaps, I don't care for that . . .'

After twenty-five minutes the curtain rose on the ruined palace, as big as the Forum, and I sauntered on for my bright three minutes with Mary Ellis, who still looked beautiful but was shrill with fright.

We started our badinage, when there came a murmur from the stalls. Then, from the gallery, a roar. Looking down past Miss Ellis, I saw a shape move towards us with confident grace. The lucky black cat.

With the desperate bravery of crisis I cried out, 'Maman,

Napoleon's mascot has caught up with us!' As I knelt to pick up the little favourite it sprang away, turned back and hissed at me as if I were a stray dog.

The audience laughed as uncontrollably as at an Aldwych farce. The cat strolled off. I said, 'Maman...'. From the gallery a voice. 'Bring back the cat! We want Pussy!'

Hysteria broke out. I battled on, made my exit—my last—ran up to the dressing-room and took to drink.

At the beginning of the last act our elderly dresser shambled in with a soda-syphon. When the first curtain had risen to exciting applause he had been depressed; he now looked fresh from a wake.

'Looks very bad,' he said, 'but never mind, Mr Grossmith ain't on yet. Wait till 'e makes 'is entrance for 'is one turn, 'e'll bring the 'ouse down an' we'll run a year...'

Ten minutes later he was back. 'Just afore 'e went on he 'eld his thumb up to me in the wings an' blew me a kiss God bless 'im an' strode on the stage like a king an' got booed.' He was near tears. 'Forty years afore the public an' then to get the bird, it ain't right...'

When the curtain fell we all scuttled onstage like puppets, to bow and be hissed. With one exception: Vosper had ordered a taxi to be ready at the stage-door and at the moment we were all face to face with the enemy, he was climbing into it in costume and with the sweat pouring down his make-up. Napoleon's retreat from the Haymarket.

Then the party. On the stage. More than a party, a film gala reception. A dance band filled the orchestra pit and as I entered, bleary by now, it was playing something like 'Happy Days Are Here Again'.

It was like the funeral of a variety star.

I happened to stand next to a tall, pale man, wearily distinguished in tails, with a small elegant moustache and a tumbler in his hand. 'He saw the show,' beamed Vincent Korda, and walked on to do more mischief.

A silence, which the band filled up with 'Little Man You've Had a Busy Day'.

'Nice tune,' my neighbour murmured, bowed and moved on. It was my first and last encounter with John Barrymore.

In the morning there was no need to open a paper. On a front page I was faced with something the like of which I had never seen: a photograph of Napoleon and his love in gay embrace with underneath 'Mary Ellis and Frank Vosper in *Josephine*, last night's first night. It is a flop, see Page Four.'

'BOOS AND LAUGHTER . . . Adapted by Emlyn Williams . . .' 'Childishly stupid, pretentiously heavy . . .'

On the second night, on my place in the dressing-room lay a sheaf of notices. Wolfit's rich voice rang out, cheery and unimpaired. 'Thought you'd like to see them, old chap, must be the worst since the turn of the century.'

They were, and we closed on Saturday.

* * *

By October the eternal summer was behind us, and we had closed the bung against the winter floods. One scowling London day I felt the stab of restlessness.

Molly said, 'Darling, you've been so little in London, why don't you get on to Dick or somebody and have a night out?'

I hadn't thought of it. 'Are you sure you'll be all right?'

'Of course, I'll ring Moira and Warren.'

'You sound as if you want to get rid of me.'

'Well, I do, people should get away from each other sometimes.'

Obediently I left, as free as air. In a raincoat. And the air was not only free, it was cold.

For years I had been assured that one should visit, on a solitary crawl, the pubs east of St Paul's Cathedral, affording a tang of Limehouse Blues, of Boxing and even of Crime, and each rumbustious with broadminded fun.

I took the Tube from Victoria to the heart of Dockland, past names out of Dickens: Blackfriars, Cornhill, Ludgate . . .

The explorer stepped out into a maze of dank deserted sidestreets and alleys slippery with rain and creeping with fog. The first bar housed a couple of elderly cloth-capped dockers bowed over a beer, a pimply youth with a club foot and a moody man in a bowler who looked like a burglar off duty.

It was as bad as Ceylon, if not so far. Was it a gift of mine, to turn every fair prospect into a non-Arabian Night?

I hurried to the next den of dullness. In the third I asked my way to the nearest station, to crawl from there to Charing Cross.

I took a taxi to 71a, back to the fire and eggs and bacon and the knowledge of love.

What was the matter with me, that I could not bask in the simplicity of that? Will you—I asked myself bleakly—will you drive again to Gloucester, are you capable of *any* foolishness?

On top of that, *Rose and Glove* and *Josephine*. In little more than a year I would be thirty. And what was the point of becoming a success later than thirty?

Something had to happen. If I had been asked to guess what form it would take, in a hundred tries I would not have hit on it.

CHAPTER THIRTY-ONE

SHORT DAY'S JOURNEY INTO NIGHT

Tuesday October the 9th was an aimless London day. In the afternoon we went to the pictures.

At six, sitting opposite Molly before the fire, I opened the evening paper and my eye caught a small headline. 'Mancini Trial Fixed, Birkett To Defend'.

On the evening of July the 15th, the jolly seaside heliopolis of Brighton had been shaken from Hove to Black Rock. The police, combing back-streets for criminals, had found something in a boarding-house attic which they had not bargained for: a smell, and it was not ozone. It came from a trunk. From the naked torso of a woman.

I well remembered reading the next morning's papers on the riverside lawn and thinking, where was the murderer now? Was he scanning the same *Telegraph* as I was, in the same sunlight, holding it in the same hands which had . . .

What was he like? 'Extensive inquiries are being made, as far afield as Birmingham.'

At that moment my obsession had been strong enough for me to wonder . . . Gloucester? Then I had read that the police were anxious to interview a Mr Mancini who 'might help them with their inquiries'.

'Trial fixed, Birkett to Defend.' As I now looked at the item, sitting before our hearth, I felt start inside me a chain of small fireworks, one splutter igniting the next as the print went slowly out of focus.

On that same riverside lawn, the blank self-righteous face of a thief. One can't write about a boy who has turned a 5 into an 8 . . . A boy pointing in a cathedral, with a derision beyond atheism. Long Bar, Sidney Fox. Hanover. The butcher of Hanover.

Then, like a face flashed on to a screen, I saw the charming smile of Patrick Mahon, the tall, blond adventurer who in 1924 killed a girl and left the body in a trunk. In a bungalow.

He melted before me into a younger type, more boy than man. Welsh. With a mother.

A play. And I would play him. What had my absurd aping been but an unconscious preparation?

Don't rush, I thought, you have rushed before.

*　　*　　*

'If you notice me just sitting,' I said, 'it doesn't mean I'm depressed.'

'I've noticed.'

I made my notes. In the play, he must be more colourful than the other was. This boy is more Welsh, just as outwardly pedestrian but more amusingly so, more beguiling until suddenly, with the murderer's compulsive desire to show off, the mask slips...

The murderer suffers no more remorse than the petty forger, but he has unexpected panics which he confides to... whom? To a girl. Who distrusts him and is at the same time drawn against her will. When she guesses the truth, to her horror she finds herself more drawn than before. His mother: a common, mean, old harridan, amusing but hateful enough not to elicit pity when she meets her fate. In her own bungalow, it must be a bungalow...

The idea simmered for days in bus, underground, taxi. And when on radio at home or at a film I heard a burst of ominous music, it boiled with an urgency which made me think once more, don't rush... I only prayed that Gaumont-British would go on forgetting me.

Mother hypochondriac, in wheelchair, hence bungalow, no stairs... Relief would be needed, I must just try not to make it too comic...

Then I scribbled three words which came instinctively, NOT HIS MOTHER. In real life certain things happen which, if a straight play is not to degenerate into a rag-bag of shockery, are unacceptable on the stage. I knew in my bones that even if one included in the programme a factual account of the Fox case, no audience would believe for a moment that the mother they were watching could be murdered by her own son.

I made rapid notes. Boy arrives as stranger—page-boy in road-house—has already committed one murder—must have money to get away—has heard the old woman has money and arranges to charm himself into the house.

Music . . . My instinct was strong to use it. Whenever the boy is reminded of his crime, or is dwelling on it, or is preparing for the next, I heard as a background to his mind weird haunting themes which would seem to swirl round his head, in between—and even during—perfectly normal dialogue. It sounded exciting.

The title? It must indicate the one thing which had urged me towards the whole project: the sinister behind the ordinary. The sunny morning will go, during the play the shadows will lengthen as the lonely house is encompassed by other shadows, invisible and inevitable.

'The Inevitable Dark'. Clumsy, bookish. I fell back on the self-question which is in every conscientious writer's gospel. 'Is there a simpler way of putting it?'

What is a simpler way of say 'inevitable'? It's got to happen. It's got to get dark. It's got to be night. It must get dark. Night must fall.

I typed it, carefully, in capitals. And still Gaumont-British had not called.

*　　*　　*

In between we had good times. Dinners on trays at 71a, with Ida and others, out to dinner with Moira and Warren or the Alan Botts. Film, theatres, Priestley's *Eden End* at the Duchess, a fine play. Then one day Dick said John G. would like me to bring Molly to lunch at the flat. He could not, of course, remember Molly from *Spring, 1600*. 'I remember *him* though,' she said, and was apprehensive.

Dick had explained that we were 'Mr and Mrs Williams'—'but you never know what he might come out with'. The other guest was one of the Motley girls. John always blossomed in the company of attractive women who did not flaunt their attraction, and all was well.

The only personal note: 'I'm so glad for Emlyn, you'll be so good for him. People keep telling me I ought to marry Peggy but much as we love each other I don't think she'd have me, Gwen's such a darling she might at a pinch, oh dear . . .'

The conversation was liable at any moment to be toppled by one of the schoolboy puns, mostly indiscreet, when Dick would protest, 'Please remember, dear John, that you are a pillar of the theatre.' The lunch was a success.

November the 26th, my twenty-ninth birthday. We gave our first party, nine onwards, fifteen to twenty people. Polly and Sonny came up, there were flowers and on my Maple's sideboard a buffet seemingly from nowhere.

And the next morning I made a start. '*The church bells die away . . .*' Mrs Bramson, in her wheel-chair: '*My heart's going like anything. Give me a chocolate . . .*'

Once embarked, I fell back into my New York routine. Sitting up in the divan bed in the back part of the living-room, my typewriter on my knees, I worked from midnight till four, then the whisky nightcap.

One night at two I reached my first hurdle: the boy Dan's first entrance, cigarette-stub in mouth, pill-box hat over one eye, 'Good mornin' all.' The dialogue, remembered and heightened, came easily. 'I must apologize to all an' sundry for this fancy dress, but it's me workin' togs . . .'

As the scene proceeded, looking up from my bed in the stillest of small hours, I was alone with him. Beyond my table-lamp, he stood in the shadows facing me. Looking at me. Returning the look, I remembered with an effort sitting in a car forging a sterile trail through Spain when, slumped next to the driver, I had thought—*what* can I write about?

Facing me now was a third person, a human being confidently two-dimensional, as opposed to the fuzzy shape presumably existing in Gloucester, or even the fuzzy shape manipulating a typewriter.

But as I approached the middle of the play—the span of a bridge where there will be either progress towards the far bank or a hurtle into the depths—something shook the venture to its half-foundations.

✿   ✿   ✿

One night we were at Frank Vosper's house in St John's Wood. I liked him more and more, for his generous character and for the sensitive talent under the buffoonery. He mentioned that he was in the middle of a new play. I mentioned that I was too and he asked how mine was getting on.

'Slowly, you know how it is.' I didn't want to sound too cocky and asked after his.

'On the way. We sound like two expectant mothers,' and he roared with laughter. 'What's yours about or aren't you telling?'

'Oh, it's another murder play . . .'

He looked at me. 'Really? So's mine.'

'Oh, really?'

'Based on an Agatha Christie short story.' That sounded safe. 'A detective play, like *Alibi?*'

'Oh, no, not a mystery. I've turned it round so I could base it on the Patrick Mahon case.'

I stared at him. He went on, 'D'you remember it? He cut the woman up and nobody would believe it, he was such a charmer.'

I had to say something. 'Mine's about a charmer too, who cuts up a woman.'

It was his turn to stare. 'Is there a girl who falls for him?'

'Yes.'

'What are you calling yours?'

I told him.

'Good title. Mine's *Love from a Stranger.*'

That was a good title too. They were interchangeable. Then he said, 'Are you by any chance writing the part for yourself?'

'Yes.'

'So am I. Who d'you have in mind for the girl's part?'

'A star if possible,' I said, 'emotional but with restraint. Edna Best, for instance.'

'I've just written asking her if she'll read my play when it's finished.'

Another silence. Then he beamed and added, 'Just as well we like each other, we need a drink.'

In the taxi I was so quiet that Molly asked why. I told her, adding, 'Apart from the exact similarity, there's something ridiculous about two actors each writing the part of a charmer for himself.'

'I don't think so. You're entirely different personalities and that's bound to make the plays quite separate from the start.' She did her best, and it was a good best.

I looked at my typewriter: at the half-filled sheet headed ACT TWO, p. 38. I had broken off in the middle of a sentence: a question from Dan. 'Why d'you lie awake ...?'

Nobody would ever know why, now. Should I light the fire and put the whole lot on it?

In the morning I sat about. Molly looked worried and said once, 'You are going on with it, aren't you? Please ...'

But I was like a spoilt boxer defeated after the first round. Walking round the Serpentine I thought, is this Fess Griffith's revenge on me? Back in the flat—Molly out shopping—I sat and stared at the typewriter. I had reached the heart of a crucial scene, when the murderer half-consciously reveals himself to the girl. At the top of the unfinished sheet:

DAN (*cigarette-stub in mouth*): Yes, I should ha' been a preacher. I remember, when I was a kid, sittin' in Sunday school, catchin' me mother's eye where she was sittin' by the door, wi' the sea behind her; an' she pointed to the pulpit, an' then to me, as if to say, that's the place for you. (*Far away, pensive.*) I never forgot that.

OLIVIA: I don't believe a word of it.

DAN: Neether do I, but it sounds wonderful.

I read it again, this time aloud. It was he speaking: flesh-and-blood Dan, the murderer, piercing my eyes with his, defying annihilation. 'To hell with Agatha Christie chum', he was saying, 'to hell wi' Frank Vosper, I'm me and on me own, you get on wi *me*...' I looked at the half-finished sentence, poised my two fingers and finished it. 'Why d'you lie awake all night?'

OLIVIA: How d'you know I lie awake? Shall I tell you why— because you're awake yourself—*you can't sleep!* There's one thing that keeps you awake, isn't there? Something ...

The bridge, having suffered a lurch from an earth tremor, stood firm.

*   *   *

One afternoon as I was typing, Molly came in and sat down, 'Darling, I've just been to the doctor and I'm having a baby.'

I crossed to her as I had once before and said, 'So we're all set.'

I wrote to Jack. Would he connive or not?

Molly said, 'He's so unpredictable I wouldn't know.' He was. He wrote suggesting that he and I should meet for a drink, which might mean anything.

I rang him, and through some inner mischievousness suggested the Long Bar at six.

I met him outside, we greeted each other affably—we had been good friends—went in and sat at a table for two where I ordered him a lemon squash. Would the barmaids assume we had picked each other up in the Avenue?

Chit-chat, how's little Mole, how's the theatre? I said, 'Jack, you will do this for us, won't you?'

'On one condition.' I thought, here we go . . .

The condition was certainly unpredictable. 'I want little Mole to meet me tomorrow outside Holborn Tube Station, six p.m., with thirty pounds in pound notes.' We parted just as affably.

When I told Molly she said, 'Well, I knew our romance was over but I did think his little Mole was worth more than that.' We wondered, was he so overdrawn that it was his only way to get to Crockford's tomorrow evening?

Next morning, when at my bank I drew out thirty pounds in notes, the clerk said, 'Another gift, sir?' I was puzzled, then remembered my present to Molly last year.

Her assignation was at six. What to wear . . . ? Scarlet woman's weeds? A mixture of blue and pink, the expectant colours? She settled for her best dress. I noted that while I had been to the bank she had been to have her hair done.

'Are you still in love with him?'

'No, but I'm nervous, after seven years. And he'll be so flippant. And outside the Tube . . . When you think I've never seen him *inside*.'

My only condition was that after handing over the ransom money she should hail a taxi in front of him.

When she got back she said, 'It was easier than I'd expected.'

'Did you kiss?'

'No, shook hands.'

'Did you put out the hand with the thirty pounds in it?'

'No, they were still in my bag. I just took them out and gave them to him, then I said good luck and he said good luck and I hailed a taxi.'

'What did you feel as you walked away?'

'I thought, lordy how pale he is, and isn't he tall . . .'
I laughed, but not before drawing myself up to my full height.
We were free.

❋   ❋   ❋

Our situation was a curious one, but so factual that it would be
hard to sentimentalize about it. While she was slowly forming a
child for both of us, I—nervously, calmly, for better or for worse
—was shaping another. I was caring for her and she was caring
for me.

We had a quiet Christmas and New Year—Molly intermittently
prostrate with sickness—before a 1935 which had to be, for us,
of paramount importance.

Through January the typewriter battered on, until it snapped
out THE CURTAIN FALLS. A breather followed: a weekend at Polly
and Sonny's with Moira, Warren, Ida and Freddie.

I drove Freddie in my old Morris, Molly the others. In a lane
a couple of miles from the Wharf, I was following her at a sensible
twenty miles an hour when a bicycle approached her. She braked
abruptly, and I followed suit.

At least I thought I had. Again mistaking the accelerator for
the other, I shot into the back of her car and pitched it into the
ditch. The car was dented and Molly cut her lip. We arrived
shaken. The next week I sold the Morris and never drove again.

And had no desire to. Fess Griffith was exorcised, for good.

Anyway, I had not really finished the play. A month of revision
followed, more intensive than I had ever done—cutting, rephrasing, switching, clarifying.

One major excision I made after much thought: the idea of
music behind Dan's mind was not feasible. In 1935 panatropes
were only beginning to be used for off-stage musical or noise
effects and there were not yet the technical devices to cope with
what I had in mind. It also occurred to me that I would be
tackling an immensely difficult stage innovation on which, for
years, the films had relied shamelessly: background music. The
words must do their own work.

The deadline I had made was a Monday morning when the
script, scarred and blotched and patched, would go to the typist.
The day before, I decided to work all night, cutting. I had not for-

gotten the first night of *Spring, 1600* with its forty-five minutes of overweight. That must never happen again.

So at eight in the evening I set out on my last crawling journey through the script, with a police searchlight dwelling for a microscopic second on every consecutive line.

Freddie had called, and when Molly went early to bed he suggested sitting up to keep me company. He sat contentedly reading through old *Play Pictorials*—'Oh, there's me standing just behind Phyllis Dare wi' one eye in one of her ospreys. I should ha' moved in time, *fool!*'—and putting on an occasional record. Whatever the music, it made the words leap from the battered page and sharpened my rethinking. This night-shift was the most enjoyable stretch of work I had ever experienced.

The marathon of nip-and-tuck was broken in the small hours by an operation which was, by comparison, a momentous one. Soon after the beginning of the last act, just as the room is slowly darkening, Mrs Bramson wheels herself from her bedroom.

MRS BRAMSON: I woke up all of a cold shiver. Had a terrible dream.

DAN: What about?

MRS BRAMSON: Horrors . . . There were funny tunes playing all the time, and I was standing on the top of a steep roof with my arm round a chimney pot and a lot of people trying to pull me down, and just as I felt meself slipping somebody kicked them all off and put his arms round me and I woke and Danny it was you . . . Get me my shawl, will you, dear?

It was a speech much longer than that, the longest in the play, and I was pleased with it as a grisly counter-allegory of the truth. Working up as it did to a climax of fright for the performer, it would be a *tour de force*. But I had eight years behind me and addressed myself in judgment. 'When you started this act, isn't it true that you thought it might run short—"a little thin", which it isn't—and so subconsciously let the monologue run on?'

Should I wait and see how it goes at rehearsal?

No. I knew that the most easy-going actress, faced with losing this speech, would fight for it—'but you can't do *this* to me!'— took up my pencil and performed a swift appendectomy by excising the speech from top to bottom. Twenty-four lines. The scene now ran, for good:

MRS BRAMSON: I woke up all of a cold shiver. Had a terrible dream.

DAN: What about?

MRS BRAMSON: Horrors . . . Get me my shawl, will you, dear?

At eight in the morning, with Freddie asleep on the sofa opposite, I had done. Mrs Tilley, after breakfast, left by taxi for Charing Cross Road—'I haven't been up West since Armistice Day'—clutching a brown-paper parcel, and I fell into the bed Molly had not long left.

Sinking into exhaustion, I did wonder if Mrs Tilley, on the typist's stairs, had passed another Mrs Tilley on her way down who had just deposited the finished script of *Love from a Stranger*.

The day after Walter read the play he said he would like to pass it on to J. P. Mitchelhill, a new manager who was presenting Priestley. Four days later I met Mr Mitchelhill and signed the contract. He was an eccentric, old Cockney financier with the manner of a kindly conceited uncle. 'Well, me boy, yer play's very 'orrible but it grips yer all right an' I'm one o' those funny blokes not influenced by the public, people ought to see things like that.'

They asked if I wanted to direct the play. I said my part was too important for that and Walter suggested Miles Malleson, a distinguished and sensitive actor–author–director. We set about casting.

For the cook—yes, I might as well face it, the comic cook—he favoured an actress who had caught the critics' eye in a series of tiny maid parts: Kathleen Harrison. Would she be too comic, and seriously over-balance the play . . . ? Olivia would be—great luck —Angela Baddeley. Which would mean a reunion with Glen.

But there was a problem. The old girl. The audience must detest her and yet be amused; she must convey reality and yet be able to sustain, in the last act, her big solo scene of hysteria. It called for a star of the past, and the one name loomed up, legendary and doom-laden. Mrs Patrick Campbell.

She would be, without a doubt, superb: hateful, funny and in the big scene transcendent. But as I surveyed my prospects as an actor, my spirits squelched into my boots. I could see her sweeping her wheel-chair round so that she could punctuate one of Dan's speeches with audible hisses calculated to terrify any mass murderer out of his wits. Have you *seen* the woman in the front row fast asleep, shall *I* prod her or will *you* . . . ?

Heaven forbid. Then I heard she was in America and could not come home because of Moonbeam. Her Peke. Heaven might not forbid, but Quarantine would.

The field was not a wide one; both Edith Evans and Sybil Thorndike were busy. Then the name came up of an elderly actress whom I was ignorant enough to think of as an amateur, a plump genial soul who had been indefatigable on so many committees that she had been created Dame May Whitty.

In her spare time, it seemed to me, she had graced small, well-bred parts just behind Gerald and Gladys. I said to Miles, 'Can she sustain a part this long? Isn't she too sweet for the audience to dislike her?' Miles wanted her, I respected him and she was engaged.

She accepted the part with even less enthusiasm than I had shown at the mention of her name. 'Well,' she wrote to her daughter Margaret Webster, 'it's just a thriller and it won't run and she's an old beast in a wheel-chair, but I suppose I'd better do it . . .'

The *Stage* announced that 'Emlyn Williams' new thriller *Night Must Fall* will open on April the 29th at the King's, Edinburgh. On the same evening Frank Vosper's new thriller *Love from a Stranger* will open at the King's, Glasgow.'

For one bemused moment I thought the two plays were opening not only on the same night, but in the same theatre.

*   *   *

On April the 1st, the first reading was to me one more trance. Concentrating on my own part, I heard the other voices through a wall of fog, speaking words vaguely familiar. It was only afterwards I realized they had all spoken them exactly as I had imagined.

It was clear at once that Kathleen Harrison would be perfect: indignantly real and funny. About May Whitty I was even more wrong. In herself she was indeed plump and genial, but when she spoke her first lines it was clear that she was an actress of immense experience. Moreover, though she had played with such stars of the old school as Forbes-Robertson and even the Kendals, there was no residue of the grand manner. She spoke with the malicious bite of real life, and without attempting an accent made the vile old creature as common-minded as she was meant to be.

She also had a dry humour, and in between her spells at a corner table scribbling a stream of letters with at her elbow a fat address book—she was known and respected by everybody in the London theatre—she was sharply intelligent about her part and the scenes she was in.

Rehearsals were negatively smooth. In the middle of the day, at one of those plodding moments when the play—any play—seems much ado about nothing, I would be bounced up by the thought that Molly, house-hunting in Chelsea, had settled on a small, three-storey house in a quiet street off King's Road—5 Lincoln Street, tenancy to start May the 15th, £150 a year for seven years—and that every day from now on, with a marked catalogue and a careful eye, she would be at the sales.

A message from Walter: Mitchelhill confirmed a three-week try-out tour starting on April the 29th, followed by 'a London theatre . . .'

At rehearsal, an occasional cut, and I was always glad when it was in my part. Every time I asked Mrs Bramson what her dream had been about and she answered, 'Horrors, get me my shawl,' I remembered her vanished speech of twenty-something lines and imagined suggesting dropping it *now* . . . No, the play was exactly the right length, I had learnt my lesson.

On my one free week-end in mid-rehearsal we went down to the bung to re-open it for the fine weather; by now it was so wrapped up with the play that I was startled. I went into the big room and opened a drawer. When I drew out an old pair of shoes it seemed the most natural thing in the world that I should wear them on the stage.

During the third week, Walter phoned that the new Priestley play at the Duchess—*Cornelius*—was not a success and that since Mitchelhill ran the theatre there was every chance of our getting it.

From Gaumont-British, an official letter. 'To remind you that your contract with the Company is now under consideration for renewal for a third year at an increased salary. As these matters depend on so many shifting plans, you will understand our not giving a decision for a couple of weeks.' In plain English, 'We want to see if your play's good enough for us to take you on for another year for the film rights.' I couldn't blame them.

Saturday, April the 27th, we would travel to Edinburgh.

The previous evening, at the Court Theatre—I tried to forget *Glamour*—we had our first dress rehearsal with a handful of audience: Mitchelhill, Walter and their group, further back Molly, Ida and Freddie. With Miles in front with pencil poised, I found it easy to forget I had written the play and to concentrate on practical adjustments—where to leave the cigarette-butt, how to peel overalls off in the time. That evening, the person up against something was 'the Dame'.

At the age of seventy she had the most difficult technical problem a player can face, and—since the set was up for the first time—at the last moment: how to steer a chair round a fully furnished room, timing lines to the speed of the vehicle and spinning it with such expertise as to prove that she had not only spent years on wheels, but on wheels in this room.

On top of this, during the rough afternoon's rehearsal on the stage, dreadnought May had discovered a second snag. The stage, as in many theatres, sloped down towards the audience; in the first scene, the moment she turned the wheel-chair to face forward she found herself rolling steadily into the footlights. Another second and she would have been tipped into the orchestra pit.

The chair had immediately to be fitted with a hand-brake which she would have to remember to clamp on at each danger point.

That done, for an hour before the night rehearsal, like a foot-baller practising goal-kicks, she had felt her way around, from one move to the next. Every time she barged into something she looked down and muttered imprecations at the chair as if it were a donkey she was training. 'Idiot, blithering dolt, what did I tell you . . . ?'

Stage-hands watched in delight—'a great old geyser'—and she enjoyed being watched. She sounded like her part, and knew she did. Just before the curtain went up, at the oppressive moment when a joke helps, she settled squarely on top of her enemy and said, 'I've been chairman on more committees than I can remember, but this is a chair I wasn't counting on.'

The lights dazzled and our voices echoed through the empty

theatre, but Miles reported that it had been a good rehearsal. Molly: 'It'll be all right, I know it will . . .'

As we left she said, 'Just a couple of tiny things . . .', then came out with constructive suggestions which were indeed tiny but stemmed from acute observation and identification with the kind of audience I wished to satisfy. 'Isn't it a bit obvious when . . . ?' 'It doesn't really matter, but wouldn't it be better without . . . ?' I learnt to glean.

I piloted her slowly across to the Queen's Restaurant—she was wonderfully well by now, but we were taking no chances—for a quiet dinner.

It turned out to be quieter than I had bargained for.

We settled into a corner. Sitting back in relief, I saw Mitchelhill facing me three tables away, with opposite him a fleshy back-of-the-neck and a thread of pipe-smoke. The two men were in earnest conversation.

Molly was able to have a small glass of wine, and I was savouring a whisky when Mitchelhill came over.

'Good evenin' Mrs Williams—Emlyn, J. B. would like to meet you.' It was Priestley. I was glad I had not known he was in the huddled group in front.

He was sitting relighting his pipe, a tubby, baldish man of forty who looked older, and as plain as he had been described. But standing before him I was only conscious of admiration for *Eden End*, and of the fact he had found time to come to the rehearsal.

He finished lighting up, then as Mitchelhill sat again he extended his hand with a nod, 'I was in froont this evenin'.' He had been a Cambridge undergraduate and the Yorkshire accent surprised me.

I said, 'I appreciate your coming very much.' Should I add something about his play? No, too gushing . . .

'Not at all'—puff, puff—'ye're a very good actor.'

'Oh. Thank you.' I was still standing.

Puff, puff. 'One thing you might look into, that scene where they all go through his luggage is clumsily contrived. I mean, it's pretty obvious they'd go to the lad's room to do it and not bring the stoof onstage, see what I mean?'

I had indeed examined what was, at that time, one of many boring problems for a naturalistic playwright, and thought I had covered it by making the scene a four-handed one: four intruders

[393]

could hardly crowd into Dan's tiny bedroom, so the luggage had to be brought into the main room, only a few feet off.

Should I hint that I knew a little more about my craft than I was being given credit for?

'Oh,' I said, 'yes, of course . . .'

I realized my situation. Mitchelhill was my headmaster, Mr Priestley the visiting Minister of Education, and I a schoolboy candidate for the West End Playwrights' Academy. And I had been turned down.

I also guessed that Mitchelhill—not a model of tact—had mentioned that when *Cornelius* expired at the Duchess, my play was a possible successor.

'Well,' I said with a deferential bow, 'I must thank you again for coming.'

'Not at all; good luck.' Had he really written *Eden End*?

I said goodnight to them both and went back to my table. It felt like a desk.

❋ ❋ ❋

Next morning though, Saturday, there was good news: 'Dear Sir, This is to notify that the divorce suit brought by . . .'

It was to be heard the following week. Neither of us need appear, but a witness had to materialize to swear that he or she had seen a certain George Williams in the same bed as a certain Mary Marjorie Carus-Wilson *née* Shann, and eating breakfast off the same tray.

For us that meant a delicate two minutes with poor Mrs Tilley which gave her a double shock. Not only were we living in sin, she was being asked to say so in public. It was like suggesting it to my mother. She clasped her hands, 'Oh dear, all me life I was never in front of a judge, never . . .'

But she liked us well enough to say yes. Molly would drive her there and back.

A phone call from Walter. Mitchelhill would wait till Saturday to see the play at Edinburgh, 'to let it settle down'. I was glad. 'Oh, and I'm afraid business has perked up at the Duchess and it doesn't look as if we'll get it but we're having a good look round. Wyndham's would be the ticket, wouldn't it?'

Yes, it would. But we only had three more weeks out, and I asked if we shouldn't extend the tour.

'We're going into that too, don't worry, you've got enough on your mind...' I didn't like the sound of that.

At King's Cross, however, the sight of NIGHT MUST FALL scribbled on several carriages was heartening and the name Edinburgh had a hundred romantic echoes. Angela Baddeley was very well known and after *Friday the Thirteenth, Evensong* and *The Iron Duke* I was a film name touring 'in person' for the first time.

On the platform I presented 'my wife' to Dame May, who immediately remembered the elocution lessons thirteen years ago.

In the train, I dreamt of *Film Weekly*, EMLYN WILLIAMS WINS ... As it slowed down, the outlook was as rosy as Edinburgh itself in the spring evening light, rising boldly on every side. The pride of it was admirable—Mary Queen of Scots, her baby lowered in a basket from that very window up there, Knox, Walter Scott, Burns...

From the taxi in which I took Molly to old digs of Freddie's, we saw Princes Street thronged with week-end crowds and passed an enormous poster, EMLYN WILLIAMS in his own play NIGHT MUST FALL with ANGELA BADDELEY and MAY WHITTY WORLD PREMIERE!!! I thought of the same crowds being imminently drawn to the King's Theatre.

We sat down to a Scottish high tea in a room like Glasdir. *Tovarich*, also London-bound, was tonight finishing its week at the King's, and the landlady informed us that 'a gude show the report was, and not an empty seat the whole week!' Molly was feeling better every day, we had a relaxed evening and forgot about the play.

All over Sunday lay the preternatural hush of the Scottish Sabbath; after mid-day dinner I set off on a long walk through the city. On my way I caught a glimpse of a spry, middle-aged woman swinging into a side-street and tripping up steep steps to doors marked CHRISTIAN SCIENCE READING ROOM. It was seventy-year-old May.

I remembered hearing she was an ardent believer. She was certainly a prize advertisement, and would be for me a bastion. I concentrated on walking as briskly myself.

At five I arrived at the stage-door for the dress rehearsal, consulted the dressing-room list—One Mr Williams, Two Miss Baddeley, Three Dame May Whitty—and descended to my quarters.

In many theatres the star room is hardly to be distinguished from others on the same floor; at the King's it was on its own, right on to the stage—the others upstairs—and of a size and opulence which would have mollified Mistinguett.

I was setting out my few bits of make-up when the stage manager appeared. 'Sorry, spot of bad news.'

CHAPTER THIRTY-TWO

DAYLIGHT

Could it be Molly? 'A phone call from my digs?'

'It's Dame May. She's got her heart again.'

'Oh, I am sorry . . .' I was puzzled as well. A couple of hours ago, hadn't she been striding along?

'She said she'd like to see you.'

I hurried upstairs, passed a door marked MISS BADDELEY and knocked on the next one.

'Come in . . .' The voice was unrecognizably tremulous.

Dame May was lying on a sofa under a rug. After an intake of breath her hand went to her side.

'May,' I said, 'I'm sorry to hear . . .'

'It's the stairs. They defeat me.'

A defeated Christian Scientist? Standing before the reclining figure, I was put ludicrously in mind of the frail and frightened Elizabeth of Wimpole Street.

But this invalid was neither frail nor frightened. It would seem an impossibility to be at the same moment prone and on the war-path, but the Dame was both. She had fought, selflessly for years, in order that fellow-actors should be protected by Actors' Equity; now, for five concentrated minutes, she was applying every nerve to a cause named May.

'I tell you what,' I said, 'we can fit up a little corner on the side of the stage where you can write your letters in your waits . . .'

'That would be putting people out.'

She sighed and closed her eyes. I was faced with an actress who, after fifty years of dressing upstairs, wanted to dress on stage level. I had been dressing upstairs for eight, and she was four years older than my mother.

I had to make a decision quickly, one immensely trivial and trivially immense. Once she got my room here, she would have it in every theatre. I imagined her in London, say at Wyndham's, enthroned in Charles's old room, with at the door a stream of admirers out of her address book. 'Do go up and see Emlyn...'

The admiring author would be the first to approve, but the aspiring actor favoured the idea that actors should dress where their contract indicated.

Without opening her eyes she played her trump card. 'I had the same problem last month with the stairs at the Shaftesbury in *The Ringmaster*, when Larry Olivier was a darling and let me have his room.'

Over to me.

In that second my decision was made, and it was the unattractive one. I sat opposite her.

'May, Larry's position was very different, he was an established star offering his room to a small-part player, much older and presumably ill.'

'Presumably' had slipped in unconsciously. Was I the Christian Scientist of the two?

I replunged, 'May, I have written the play with all the integrity I'm capable of, but also with the firm intention of playing the star part. But your part is important enough for the actress playing it to claim the star dressing-room, if she were a star like —say—Mrs Pat.'

The invalid's eyes flickered open, and there was a glimmer of grey steel. She now reminded me of another Victorian figure. How superbly she would play Florence Nightingale, older and desentimentalized, with her feet doggedly up for life, the Lady who discarded the Lamp for the Bedpan! We looked at each other, and I knew that while she was admitting defeat by an unchivalrous careerist, her honesty respected me. She sensed that I, in turn, respected her and that the respect might, with time, turn into affection.

'A great old geyser.' The stage-hands were right.

I felt justified but mean, and did make a point of seeing she had her little canvas retreat in the wings, for her letter-writing.

✸   ✸   ✸

At the dress rehearsal a different problem soon took over. Unused to touring, I was not prepared for enormous auditoriums. From the back of the wilderness of stalls, the bungalow was a toy theatre lost between acres of black curtain. 'Heavens,' May muttered, 'let's call ourselves *Murder in the Cathedral* and have done with it . . .'

Amplification was not yet in use and over-emphasis seemed inevitable: at the end the director had many notes but seemed pleased. Also Glen, on tour in the Gielgud *Hamlet*, had arrived in time for the rehearsal and I was cheered by his enthusiasm. We all went home, to hotel or digs, after a long evening in a vacuum.

Monday evening, World Première.

I felt dwarfed by the dressing-room. Serve me right perhaps. Sitting at my table I listened for the panatrope to play the music I had chosen for the opening and for between scenes: the first phrase of Holst's 'Perfect Fool'.

Suddenly it came: the long note of a trumpet, swelling in accusation and menace and speaking exultingly for the whole play. I felt the hoped-for tingle at the back of the neck, took heart, and walked into the wings in time to hear a line which I had secretly hoped would 'be a big laugh'.

The belligerent old woman had just been told by the little snivelling maid that she had been seduced by Dan. I heard May's vibrant scolding voice: 'So you're expecting a baby? When?'

'Last August Bank 'Oliday . . .'

I heard a titter, then its echo, and went whizzing back seven years to the World Première of *Glamour* in Aldershot. O to be a Christian Scientist . . .

I made my first entrance to scattered applause. Speak up and yet be natural, be natural and yet speak up . . .

The laughs were scattered too, but the audience seemed attentive, *toujours la politesse*. At the end, each of the five calls was more gracious than the last. It was like playing at Balmoral.

Molly was the first to come round. No, not very full, and a tough audience not knowing what to expect. She had overheard people saying that Edinburgh audiences were cautious about a new play and you had to wait for the word of mouth.

Without having sat an exam, she was already qualified for the post of actor-author's wife on a sticky wicket.

Angela brought in two fans of her sister Hermione's. The wife

said, 'We're more used to musical shows, it was most *unusual* ...'
He said, 'Where's your ferrst-night parrty, at the Caledonian?'

When I told them there wasn't one, they were amazed. After
a World Première?

Our landlady was welcoming. 'And did ye have a lovely fule
house like *Tovarich*?'

Molly said, 'It looked very good to me.'

Sitting by the fire, I meditated over one proven point: none of
my films had ever visited this historic city. If they had, my face and
name had been erased from public memory.

*   *   *

Next morning brought the sinister rustle of newspapers. 'The
Scotsman's the one to watch for ...'

Opening it, I was about to see the first pronouncement ever,
in print, on a play the fate of which would govern my professional future, and my hands were shaking. I found a markedly
long article, nearly a whole column, which squeezed to the bottom
the new presentation at the repertory theatre. I was at that
moment too flustered to notice what it was: Lyceum, *Dangerous
Corner* by J. B. Priestley.

The review of my play was as careful as it was long; my eyes
darted up and down past the account of plot and pounced on
essentials. The first sentence was 'This may be described as a
play of abnormal character.'

I sat up. It was somehow unexpected.

More plot, then: 'We are invited to suppose on the part of the
murderer a power to mesmerize the girl. This is the unusual
carried to the edge of credibility ... It is not to be inferred that
Night Must Fall fails as an entertainment ...'

Cautious. Promising. But I was worried that 'we' had baulked
at the character of Olivia. 'We are invited to suppose a power
to mesmerize ...' Not invited at all: she was a bored, repressed
girl disturbed at finding herself physically and emotionally at-
tracted by a murderer ... But the word 'entertainment' was valuable currency.

A column away, LOVE FROM A STRANGER, King's, Glasgow. I had
forgotten. 'Strong flavour of humour, though it ends in grim
tragedy ... Miss Edna Best as the distracted prey of a cold-

blooded murderer...' I only just noticed that the author was not
in it after all, the part being played by Basil Sydney. No matter,
whichever play got to London first would kill the other, and
nothing to be done about it.

My first evening notice—out in the early afternoon—brought
the headline, CAN A WOMAN LOVE A MURDERER, PROBLEM OF NEW
PLAY. I had not meant to pose any PROBLEM, I had written a
NEW PLAY.

'Whatever the fate of *Night Must Fall* it will cause endless
controversy... When the murderer, who has the head of his last
victim in a hatbox in his room, kisses the heroine without being
repulsed, some women in the audience said, "Absurd!"'

But from my second paper, a positive reaction. 'You must not
miss this play... It enthralled me from start to finish...' In
Princes Street, threading my way through affluent chattering
shoppers who had obviously read this, I was reassured by the
realization that two out of three must be reporting that 'you
must not miss this play'. Was I not in the Athens of the North?

In the evening we realized that last night's sparse audience had
been well sprinkled with complimentary tickets. Tonight we had
paying customers only and the house was as good as empty. It
was Aldershot all over again, only bigger. It would seem that not
one shopper had drawn any other shopper's attention to the
King's Theatre.

Sitting during an interval in my gigantic room, I thought of
May and felt my face get hot. What was I achieving to deserve
a star room, why the hell hadn't I let her have it?

On the Wednesday Molly returned to London and the sales, 'I
know it's going to be all right...' She knew that Angela and the
Dame would be of great moral support; May, having realized she
had the part of her life, believed unshakeably in the future.

The Wednesday matinée was really empty. In an interval she
said it would help her performance if she worked herself into a
temper, and she did.

'This city's always been a citadel of snobbery. Last week they
had Sir Cedric and Leontovich as Russian aristocracy masquerading as servants and in the end she put a tiara on and they flocked
—yes, I know I'm a Dame, but where's the tiara? Can't you hear
the matinée matrons over their muffins—a head in a hatbox no
thanks, now if it had a *hat* in it which Marie Tempest was

going to take out and try on, that'd be verra different—blithering idiots! Wait for Newcastle—these are *sheep!*'

That night we were all invited to a party by pen-friends of May's and thought it would cheer us up.

'What a puir house ye had! Of course it is a verra *unusual* play. Tell me, Mr Wulliams, have ye always had this morrbid streak . . . ?'

'D'ye know what the wife and I thought was the most remarkable thing about your show? The way that auld lady got around in that chair, it was werrth the price of admission!'

Nobody else there had been to the play. 'Actually,' said one kilted wag, 'it's not a bad idea to kick off here, we're harrd to please and a show Edinburgh likes today, London will like to-morrow.' How can you like a show you have no intention of seeing?

'If *Tovarich* ran two weeks in London,' I asked him, 'and then came straight back here, would the people who were turned away last week rush to the box office?'

'Naturally.'

It was untrue, but if I had said so I would have been battering my head against Edinburgh Rock.

The next night, a woman came round who worried me because she seemed intelligent. 'A fascinating play but I found the girl puzzling. I mean, you'd *never* find a sensitive woman shielding a murderer . . .' She was in her forties, Miss Something, had a nervous repressed manner, and I could imagine her doing just that.

But the following night another woman came round with the same comment, and on top of the newspaper reaction it began to prey on my mind that, as actor, I did not project a sexual image powerful enough to make the situation convincing. I was not to know that ten years later, in play, novel and film, the same sex relationship would be accepted by the most conventional spinster from Edinburgh to Exeter, and that in twenty years it would be a cliché.

By Friday afternoon I had transformed the pride that was Caledonia, as reflected in the Princes Street crowds, into unqualified smugness. I also hated Robert Burns, Walter Scott, Mary Queen of Scots and Mary Queen of Scots's baby.

At the Saturday matinée the listless few were joined by Walter

Peacock and Mitchelhill. Walter rang me from the hotel to say that the latter was 'pleased with the performance'. I pressed no further.

That night I opened my weekly return from the box-office. I knew that last week *Tovarich* had played to £2,600. Our figure was £437.

Farewell, Athens of the North.

* * *

Rough-and-ready Newcastle was raucous with bunting and Union Jacks for this week's Royal Jubilee, and the beautiful Theatre Royal, much smaller than last week's, made the set and the play feel different. I cheered up.

A polite sparse audience, polite sparse applause.

Chronicle, TRIUMPH OF NEW PLAY. '*Night Must Fall* cannot fail . . .'

It might just as well have been written in invisible ink. In wonderful weather, the Jubilation seemed kept sternly in check till the evenings, when every sort of outdoor jollity broke loose: bands, Morris dancing, balloons and bonfires on vast Town Moor outside the city.

Playgoing? Not this week. On Wednesday night after the show, Angela and I took a tram out to the Moor, to find crowds eddying round the flames, gratis, and enough of them to fill the Theatre Royal for six weeks. God bless the King and Queen and boil the Northumbrians in the same cauldron as the Athenians.

From Gaumont-British, a second communiqué. 'The Company regrets that owing to change of plans, etc., it finds itself unable to renew its option on . . .' They had sent their spies.

'My dear Son George, Your criticks are good. Since we have not yet had the privilege to see you in a Drama of yours, we may—D.V. as the godly put it—one day travel to London D.V.'

By now I had such a presentiment that Mitchelhill would drop the play a week from this Saturday in Glasgow that I wrote to Glasdir enclosing their fares.

That night we were at supper when the phone rang among the ferns in the hall. It was Malleson, from London. 'How's it going?'

'All right.'

'A shame about the business.'

'Yes, I'm told we've been hit by the Jubilee.' As I said it, it sounded like a mammoth railway accident.

'I've been talking to Mitchelhill.'

Oh, had he? The Duchess Theatre, yes or no?

It was neither. 'He's scared of the Vosper thing, he's a cagey old bird and, Emlyn, there's a feeling the title is wrong—that it suggests a highbrow play and puts people off. Would you subscribe to that?'

I was ready to subscribe to a wreath in my own memory. 'You mean something more straightforward?'

'Yes, like *Bungalow Murder*, something like that. Think about it.'

I did. *Bungalow Murder...The Head in the Hatbox. The Boy Who Was Bluebeard. Two Murders Have Been Arranged...*

Angela, ringing Glen the next morning, told him the suggestion. When she came back, 'I've never known him so angry, couldn't you *hear* him? He said if you alter one letter of that title he's going to divorce me. What are you going to do about that, dear?' I retained the title and she her husband.

At the Royal the weekly capacity figure could be £2,100; we had played to £321. On the Sunday there was a gritting of teeth as we entrained again for Scotland; in Glasgow posters shouted IMMEDIATELY PRIOR TO LONDON ! ! !

Next morning, in the *Telegraph*, DUCHESS CORNELIUS LAST WEEK. So business had not perked up that much. What was going there, *Love from a Stranger*?

That night we faced yet another polite audience which emitted polite applause. O for a good Scottish boo and a clump of thistles flung from the gallery in protest against a shockin' show!

'Any news?' called May the invincible, still taming her wheel-chair as if in training for a year on the racecourse. 'Any news from those fools?'

She was dashing off more letters than ever. Angela said the performance had to come when she would career on to the stage propelled by a stage-hand and licking a stamp.

Saturday night was the deadline.

* * *

More friends of friends came round, 'Tryin' it on the dog, eh?'

'What Glasgae thinks today...' 'My mother and I couldn't understand why the wee gerrl didna go straight to the police...'

On Tuesday I decided there was nothing more I could do and sat about in a stupor, reading the landlady's film magazines as if they were literature, HAS MONTGOMERY THE GLAMOUR OF GABLE? 'The report that on the M.G.M. lot Joan Crawford actually conversed with Garbo is exaggerated...'

Wednesday. The gallery may not have booed on the first night, but one gentleman in the stalls would have liked to.

'Dear Sir, As a theatregoer of long standing and a personal friend of C. Aubrey Smith I have seldom been so offended by a portrayal of a type now rife in our society and nowadays to be found in my own club, i.e. a pageboy who thinks he is better than his betters. Your performance is disgusting, Yours faithfully...'

I was glad to have my mind taken off by meeting my parents. 'Oh yes, the play is going to the West End but we're not sure when...'

They were dressed exactly as they had been on their arrival in London three years ago—the elder statesman and his timid spouse—except that my mother wore the fur I had given her. It looked glad to be in the open, as if the interim had been spent in a safe.

They were happy to find that the digs were 'homey'. Tonight they would rest, tomorrow night the play.

But one date I had to arrange for them. On Monday a letter had awaited me. 'Dear Cousin George, You will be surprised but I am the daughter of your mother's first cousin and would be glad if you could come to tea. As you see from the above I have fallen on my feet and Scotland certainly agrees with me, Yours sincerely, Dilys Protheroe.'

The 'above' was her embossed address. 'Lomond Hall, Kelvinside.'

I answered at once, saying I would like to bring my parents on Thursday. I now showed the letter to Mam. She studied it through her glasses with a frown, holding it gingerly away from her. We asked the landlady about Kelvinside. 'Merrcy, it's the smarrtest parrt...'

'Dilys...,' my mother said, 'she's Aneurin's second.' She handed the letter to Dad.

'What's the matter, Poll?'

'It's the address. She's married money.'

'Well,' Dad said, 'you can't put her in jail for that. If we treat her civil she might leave us a bit of it. P'r'aps their place looks like George's did on the film when he was Lord Lebanon, remember?'

He was in his element. 'Congraddulations, Poll, we never had anything like this in our lot. The nearest was an auntie in St Helen's who landed a vicar, but he wasn't as high up as this. In the eyes of God he was, of course, but not regular. Thank the good Lord you brought your fur.'

On Thursday afternoon, we set off by taxi. Kelvinside, beyond doubt, was the smarrtest parrt of anywhere. Great mansions were lost in their own gardens and strangled by ancestral ivy.

The taxi turned into an avenue marked 'Private No Hawkers' and stopped at a pillared porch; I asked the driver to come back in an hour and rang the bell. My mother stood between us, her hand firmly on Dad's arm. Footsteps. I felt her tighten.

The door was opened by my mother's cousin's daughter herself, and her eyes lit up. 'Auntie Mary!'

I saw my mother's face soften into relief. Her cousin's daughter was a pretty girl, younger than me, in neat cap and apron. She was the maid.

She preceded us excitedly into the basement, getting more Welsh with every word. 'Mrs McLarnan is that kind to me. They came to the play Monday and have bought a seat for me Saturday and set their hearts on me asking George to tea, I mean Emlyn.'

We had an hour of Welsh talk with her. Then she preceded us upstairs, knocked on the drawing-room door, announced, 'My relations, Mum,' and slipped out again behind us.

If Mrs McLarnan had had two heads I would have taken to her; she had been to the play and that was enough for me. But she was very pleasant, as were the three ladies invited to tea. My father held court. 'Our second son is in the same line as I was, steel ...'

A knock at the door. 'The taxi, Mum.' They all waved us off, my mother's cousin's daughter in the centre, in her cap and apron.

'Well,' Dad said, 'that was very nice.'

*　　*　　*

After that night's performance, as the cast took the calls the audience was small enough for me to pick out my father clapping loudly. Mam was too timid to applaud. What would a first night be like with the auditorium filled with her?

I took them to meet my two leading ladies. As I introduced them to May, I remembered I had not briefed Dad as to what to call her. But he was ahead of me, 'My dear Dame, may I congraddulate you . . .'

Not correct, but it sounded unassailable. Next door he was again inexact but again sounded good: 'Miss An*geela* Budd*eely*? Did your better half not appear in my son's first venture?'

About the play, each was true to form.

Mam: 'I didn't like it at the end when that policeman took you off in them handcuffs to be hanged.'

Dad, when I saw them off: 'It seems to me, George, with the sort of play you have put together here, a small crowd can get more of a grip on it, they feel nobody is watchin' but theirselves and that they are bein' favoured.'

Through the last long three weeks, he should have been my publicity agent. Richard a'i Fab: Richard and Son.

Saturday morning, twelve hours to go. I phoned, 'Walter, are we coming to London or not?'

After a pause, 'I'll give Mitchelhill another ring.' Which meant that Mitchelhill had made up his mind and that Walter was going to have a shot at changing it. The same Mitchelhill who had said, 'My boy, I'm one o' those funny blokes not influenced by the public . . .'

After the last matinée, I was on my way out when it came to me that after tonight's performance the curtain would come down and night would indeed fall, on this play, for ever.

I opened the little attaché case in which I carried my script for last-minute study, sat in a chair with the case on my knee and stared at it. My eyes travelled to the shoes I wore in the play, had they brought me irremediable bad luck?

I was distracted for a moment by Jevan Brandon-Thomas, a big name in Scotland who ran his own repertory, calling with a prominent young member of the company, Simon Lack. Their enthusiasm, after seeing a play with a non-audience, was unmistakable. Lack, an undemonstrative Scot, blurted out, 'If I had money I'd put it into this, now.' But my pleasure wore off.

Half an hour, please. Fifteen minutes, please. May said, 'Mr Mitchelhill's being cruel.'

Five minutes before the play I was called to the phone. It was Walter. Next Friday week *Night Must Fall* would open in London at the Duchess. 'By the way, *Love from a Stranger* is closing on tour. Vosper wants to rewrite and recast with himself playing the murderer and do it later.'

May said, 'What did I tell you?' and Angela put her arms round me.

In the first interval I rang Molly, who also had good news. The divorce had gone through and we had been granted the great Discretion, which meant she was free to marry immediately. We decided to make it Friday, at a register office in Slough.

At the station early next morning, Sunday, we were a small school steaming home for the hols. I would be in 5 Lincoln Street by tea-time.

In the taxi from King's Cross, I realized I was arriving to live for the first time in our first London house; moreover, I had only seen it once, in a hurry when it was empty. As Molly opened the door holding my key, in the sun, I could tell that she was as nervously eager for me to like the house as I had been for her to approve of the play.

Stepping inside and seeing the bowl of flowers on the little hall table, I felt something steal over me like the faintest of narcotics. A feeling of familiarity with a place never before visited. A sense of security. We went through every room, she preceding me up the stairs with my index finger pressed against the small of her back: a magic psychological boost to a climber in need of help.

She had worked so hard that the whole house—from basement kitchen through nursery up to top bedroom—looked as if it had been lived in for months. By me. By the time I got down again to the drawing-room, I felt tears.

Through them, the first thing I registered, simple and ample, were the pelmets. The second, the lined curtains.

The tallboy looked magnificent. Knowing as little about antiques as about all-in wrestling, I looked twice at my mock-mediaeval windfall from Maple's, and after tea—Spode, a sales bargain—I said, 'What shall we do with my stuff?'

'Oh ... Don't you want it here?'

'It doesn't go, does it?'

She tried to hide her relief, 'I tell you what, in a country cottage it would look lovely in the nursery, stripped.'

She sounded almost as if she had just thought of it. I said, 'You mean the bung?'

'Oh, no, we'd have to give it up.'

I was puzzled. 'Why?'

'All that lawn straight on to the water, terribly dangerous.'

I was lost. 'Dangerous?'

'For a baby starting to walk.' It was a sobering thought.

She showed me a notebook in which she was listing her purchases. 'Linen Bedspreads £1.6.0, Silver Candlesticks £1.5.0, Settee £4.5.0, Persian Rug £3.15.0, 6 French Chairs £7.7.0, Regency Sofa Table £12.18.0 . . .' She had spent less on the whole house than I had at Maple's on one room.

A doubt as to whether a picture was at the right height developed into an argument—don't let's make an issue of it, but who's making an issue, it certainly isn't me . . . A quarrel which evaporates after half an hour—or even after twenty-four—and leaves a residue of love, is not important.

In the drawing-room stood my big splash, a radiogram which played six records running.

I said, 'What's wrong with a bit of sentiment?' and put on 'I'll Follow My Secret Heart'. Ida arrived, and cried. I was home.

❋   ❋   ❋

Monday, Tuesday and Wednesday I spent at the Duchess.

The set was up, and the bungalow just fitted the tiny stage; it, too, looked as if it had been there for months. During the lighting rehearsal, watching lamps fade in and out over the bungalow, I again felt something creep over me. A sense of belonging.

High above the stage in the actors' quarters everything fitted too, for there was no star dressing-room. The first nearest the lift was imperceptibly bigger than the others and I was happy to see May settle into it like a mother hen; she also had her little writing-room in the wings.

On Monday, while I was at the theatre, Molly had driven down to Slough Town Hall to apply for us to be married. It was plucky of her: she had to walk along a corridor past a row of girl typists, and as she progressed slowly and heavily she heard sniggers.

I invented a dentist appointment for Friday morning, and at ten Molly drove Ida and Freddie and me down; they would be our witnesses. Just in time I remembered the wedding ring, and it took a moment to prise it off Molly's finger and into my pocket.

In a bare government office, a wooden official who might have been selling us postage stamps made a short severe speech about marriage, and we filled up a couple of documents. Giving my father's occupation, I described him as he had described himself on my birth certificate, 'Labourer'. The official, on reading it, ceased to be wooden and gave me a puzzled look, which I took as a compliment.

I replaced the ring. With no more ceremony than had attended the lease of the bung, Mary Marjorie Carus-Wilson had become Mrs George E. Williams.

Next morning I wrote the two letters which had been hanging over me. The one to Miss Cooke was the easier. 'Dear Dad and Mam ... So in the end we decided to live as man and wife and to plan for a baby, which will arrive towards the end of August, please answer by return.'

Next day, Sunday, I took a dive into a dreaded Sabbath repository of scandal, large and small: the *News of the World*. And no news was too small, it doggedly dredged up the week's every peccadillo and so blighted many an obscure life. Page Seven, Theatre Notes: Mr Emlyn Williams's new Play will open on ... at the ...

On to Page Nine, Divorce Notes. It was like looking for exam results, Watkins, Wilkins ... Carus-Wilson, M. M., by C. C., citing George Williams. I thanked Dad for having christened me after his Prince of Wales, now his Gracious Majesty.

The dress rehearsal—nobody there—was as smooth as a pond. Friday, May the 31st. My opening night was overlapping the day when my contract with Gaumont-British, with no bad feelings on either side, lapsed. Was it a bad omen, or a good one?

The audience, Walter had told me, would be the right sort, intelligent lovers of the theatre. And Molly would be safely tucked into one of the small boxes at the back.

I followed my old opening-day routine. Lunch at home, then a film, alone: Jean Harlow in *Reckless*. Home for scrambled eggs,

bath—must be extra clean—and goodbye to Molly until tonight.
'It's silly to keep saying it,' she said, 'but I know it's going to be
all right...'

Should I tell her I loved her? I was shy of it, I would say it
tomorrow. One should always say it at the time. Sooner or later,
there will not be a tomorrow.

Then my walk to my working destination.

I had ample time, and for this first night I took a roundabout
route, quiet and steady: round the corner into Sloane Square—
Court, *Glamour*—down Pimlico Road, past 71a Ebury Street.
Down Victoria Street, past Vincent Square. Number 34, my first
London room.

Across past the Westminster Theatre, *Rose and Glove*. Across
Green Park and past the St James's, *A Murder Has Been Arranged*,
Etienne, *The Late Christopher Bean*. Across St James's Square to
the Haymarket, His Majesty's, *Josephine*, up to Shaftesbury
Avenue, past the Long Bar and the Apollo, *The Silver Tassie*,
The Man I Killed, *Wild Decembers*.

Two doors on, the Queen's, *Mafro, Darling!* and *The Mock
Emperor*. Further up, the Shaftesbury, *Spring, 1600*.

Round the back of it into the Charing Cross Road. Wyndham's,
On the Spot, *The Case of the Frightened Lady*, *Port Said*, then
down the street to where I had led my parents to see my name
in lights over the Garrick in *Man Overboard*.

A look up St Martin's Lane; I could almost see the Gielgud
flat, and Wellington Mansions. I thought of Bill, with sadness
but through a haze, and without poignancy. The other way,
Trafalgar Square. I walked down to the Keith Prowse window
where, long ago, walking late at night back to Vincent Square,
I had hungrily scanned the playbills. There it was, NIGHT MUST
FALL.

Back up again and along Maiden Lane, past the Vaudeville
stage-door—*French Leave*—and down the side passage to the
Strand and the Savoy Theatre: *And So To Bed*, eight years ago,
'first professional appearance'. Finally the Duchess Theatre,
Tunnel Trench.

I had certainly been around.

I crossed the front of the theatre, deserted as yet—'Tonight
at 8, subsequently 8.30, Mats W.S.' How long was 'subsequently'?

I was tranquil enough not to dwell on it, streaked up the side alley to the tiny stage-door—many telegrams and flowers—and walked slowly up the long flight of stairs.

I had plenty of time, hesitated over opening two letters and decided to risk them.

Miss Cooke: 'George yr predecessor must be a darned fool, fancy disposing of a val'ble property for £30! Gd to know you are now a family man, it will enrich yr life, was it Montaigne who said "A man without a wife, leads only half a life" or have I made it up, dunno . . .

'I am v. flattered you shd both invite me to be g'dmother in the company of J. Gielgud as g'dfather, I hope I won't prove too intimidating. I'm re-reading "War & Peace", isn't it masterly . . .?

'P.S. Dear Molly, I am so happy for you & happier for G., he needs a wife & I'll bet my bottom dollar you will be *it*, Yrs affectionately S. G. Cooke.'

From Glasdir, not the letter I expected at all. After a message in block letters YR YDYM YN DYMUNO AMSER DEDWYDD AR NOSON GYNTAF Y NOS A DDAW—We wish you a blessed time on the first night of the Night which Falls—it read like a communiqué from Queen Victoria to her eldest son which had later been tampered with by somebody below stairs.

'My dear Son George and Molly, It is with the greatest of pleasure that we write these few lines on behalf of your Mother and myself to congraddulate you both on your Marriage and that the future holds in store a Happy Event. We will know that there is someone that will take care of you, your Mother was always anxious about your Laundry etc. We shall be delighted to receive Molly as one of our own, now your Mam.'

'Dear Goerge, Your father has told you all there is to say, it is not her fault but the fault of that fellow with the long-winded name, she will find Williams more comfortable, good riddence i say, she is a nice respectable girl and i hope you will be worthy of her your lovin Mam.'

I had misjudged her, and looked forward to showing the letters to a nice respectable girl.

Long afterwards Job told me that Dad was so elated by the news of the Happy Event that on his morning visit for his pint with his mates in Shotton—he must have felt frustrated not to be able to disseminate the news, preferably via a cutting—he had bought a miniature bottle of whisky, no larger than a man's hand.

And in the secrecy of the bedroom, where he should have been taking his afternoon nap, he had drunk to the future, opened a window and tossed the empty phial into grass. There it had been found by his horrified wife. 'A nice way to bring luck to a poor child, I've a good mind to tell on you...'

But a toast is a toast.

*　　*　　*

In our tiny community in the sky, all quiet. Half an hour, please.

I settled at my dressing-table. On it stood four framed photographs: my father, my mother, Miss Cooke, Molly.

Fifteen minutes, please. By now she would be in the hired car, half-way down the Mall, heavy of body but—I knew—lighter of heart than I could ever have expected.

I drew my pageboy trousers on, buttoned them and reached for my shoes. But they were not mine, nor Fess Griffith's. As I slid my feet into them, they were Dan's.

To pass the time I opened telegrams—one was from the Philadelphia Harts—propped up the three I had been looking for and opened a package. Cuff-links, 'with my love always'.

A knock at the door. Molly. Yes, she had come up in the lift as I had asked her, and not used the stairs. She was wearing a white stole, her wedding-first-night present, and looked shiningly serene.

'Five minutes, please...' She told me that as she got out of the car she had nearly bumped into John G., in dinner-jacket with Gwen Ffrangcon-Davies on his arm.

'He looked much more nervous than I could be, I could tell because he giggled and said, "Oh, Molly dear, do be careful, I'm delighted to be godfather but this is hardly the moment for me to be midwife as well!"'

She had seen the others in the foyer—Ida, Dick, Freddie, Glen, all coming back to the house afterwards. As we held each other— not too tight, by the arms only—she said, 'I can only say again, I know it'll be all right...' and was gone.

Beginners please. The whirr of the lift. I went to see the others off as if to a journey, then in my own time wandered down the deserted stairs to the stage. At that moment, did I know that this play would be my first solid success? If I did, I had enough theatre superstition in me not even to formulate the thought in my mind.

From beyond the curtain came the excited chatter. The sound of London. On stage, the half-light and half-life which precedes the burst of action.

I stood waiting. Behind the crackle of sound, Molly was safely alone. No, not alone. And behind her, 5 Lincoln Street.

But for tonight, marriage must make way for murder. I heard a whisper, 'Take your house-lights out,' and the excitement beyond simmered into silence. The stage lights went to nothing. Out of the profound silence and out of the dark, the trumpet soared in triumph.

As it slowly faded, still in the dark, above my head there came the sound I had first heard before that Easter Monday matinée eight years ago. A rustle and a sweep, like a strong calm wind.

The curtain was up.

THE END

INDEX

(The six main characters in this book—Emlyn, 'Dad', 'Mam', Miss Cooke, 'Bill' and 'Molly'—are mentioned so frequently that it is felt that to enumerate all references to them in the Index would be impracticable.)

INDEX